A Course in Language Teaching

CAMBRIDGE TEACHER TRAINING AND DEVELOPMENT

Series Editors: Marion Williams and Tony Wright

This series is designed for all those involved in language teacher training and development: teachers in training, trainers, directors of studies, advisers, teachers of in-service courses and seminars. Its aim is to provide a comprehensive, organized and authoritative resource for language teacher training and development.

Teach English – A training course for teachers
by Adrian Doff

Trainer's Handbook
Teacher's Workbook

Models and Metaphors in Language Teacher Training –
Loop input and other strategies
by Tessa Woodward

Training Foreign Language Teachers – A reflective approach
by Michael J. Wallace

Literature and Language Teaching – A guide for teachers and trainers
by Gillian Lazar

Classroom Observation Tasks – A resource book for language teachers and trainers
by Ruth Wajnryb

Tasks for Language Teachers – A resource book for training and development
by Martin Parrott

English for the Teacher – A language development course
by Mary Spratt

Teaching Children English – A training course for teachers of English to children
by David Vale with Anne Feunteun

A Course in Language Teaching – Practice and theory
by Penny Ur

A Course in Language Teaching

Practice and Theory

Penny Ur

CAMBRIDGE
UNIVERSITY PRESS

PUBLISHED BY THE PRESS SYNDICATE OF THE UNIVERSITY OF CAMBRIDGE
The Pitt Building, Trumpington Street, Cambridge CB2 1RP, United Kingdom

CAMBRIDGE UNIVERSITY PRESS
The Edinburgh Building, Cambridge CB2 2RU, United Kingdom
40 West 20th Street, New York, NY 10011–4211, USA
10 Stamford Road, Oakleigh, Melbourne 3166, Australia

First published 1996
Reprinted 1997

Printed in the United Kingdom at the University Press, Cambridge

Typeset in Sabon

A catalogue record for this book is available from the British Library

Library of Congress Cataloguing in Publication data
Ur, Penny.
A course in language teaching: practice and theory / Penny Ur.
    p.   cm.
Includes bibliographical references.
ISBN 0 521 56798 X hardback
ISBN 0 521 44994 4 paperback
1. Language and language – Study and teaching. I. Title.
P51.U7 1995
418′.007 – dc20   94-35027
                                                   CIP

ISBN 0 521 56798 X hardback
ISBN 0 521 44994 4 paperback

Contents

Module 5: Teaching vocabulary

Module 6: Teaching grammar

Module 7: Topics, situations, notions, functions

Part III   *Teaching the language (2): The 'how'*   103

Module 8: Teaching listening

Module 9: Teaching speaking

Module 10: Teaching reading

Contents

Acknowledgements

I should like to thank all those who have contributed in different ways to this book:

- To editor Marion Williams, who criticised, suggested and generally supported me throughout the writing process;
- To Cambridge University Press editors Elizabeth Serocold and Alison Sharpe, who kept in touch and often contributed helpful criticism;
- To Catherine Walter, who read the typescript at a late stage and made practical and very useful suggestions for change;
- To my teachers at Oranim, with whom I have over the years developed the teacher-training methodology on which this book is based;
- And last but not least to my students, the teacher-trainees, in past and present pre-service and in-service courses, to whom much of this material must be familiar. To you, above anyone else, this book is dedicated; with the heartfelt wish that you may find the fulfilment and excitement in teaching that I have; that you may succeed in your chosen careers, and may continue teaching and learning all your lives.

The authors and publishers are grateful to the authors, publishers and others who have given their permission for the use of copyright information identified in the text. While every endeavour has been made, it has not been possible to identify the sources of all material used and in such cases the publishers would welcome information from copyright sources.

p7 diagram from *Experiential Learning: Experience as the Source of Learning and Development* by David Kolb, published by Prentice Hall, 1984 © David Kolb; *p15* from 'Exploiting textbook dialogues dynamically' by Zoltan Dörnyei, *Practical English Teaching*, 1986, 6/4: 15–16, and from 'Excuses, excuses' by Alison Coulavin, *Practical English Teaching*, 1983, 4/2:31 © Mary Glasgow Magazines Ltd, London; *p15* from *English Teachers' Journal*, 1986, 33; *pp49–50* from *Pronunciation Tasks* by Martin Hewings, Cambridge University Press, 1993; *pp80–81* (extract 1) from 'How not to interfere with language learning' by L. Newmark and (extract 2) from 'Directions in the teaching of discourse' by H. G. Widdowson in *The Communicative Approach to Language Learning* by C. J. Brumfit and K. Johnson (eds.), Oxford University Press, 1979, by permission of Oxford University Press; *p81* (extract 4) from *Awareness of Language: An Introduction* by Eric Hawkins, Cambridge University Press, 1984; *p122* adapted from *Teaching Listening Comprehension* by Penny Ur, Cambridge University Press, 1984; *pp135–6* from *The Language Teaching Matrix* by Jack C. Richards, Cambridge University Press, 1990; *p135* (extract 2) from *Teaching the Spoken Language* by Gillian Brown and George Yule, Cambridge University Press, 1983; *p135* (extract 3) from *Discussions that Work* by Penny Ur, Cambridge University Press, 1981; *p139* from *Role Play* by G. Porter-Ladousse, Oxford University Press, 1987, by permission of Oxford University Press, *p159* from *Task Reading* by Evelyne Davies, Norman Whitney, Meredith Pike-Blakey and Laurie Bass, Cambridge University Press, 1990, *p160* from *Points of Departure* by Amos Paran, Eric Cohen Books, 1993; *p162* from *Effective Reading: Skills for Advanced Students* by Simon Greenall and Michael Swan, Cambridge University Press, 1986; *Beat the Burglar*, Metrolpolitan Police; *p166* (set 3) from 'A few short hops to Paradise' by James Henderson, *The Independent on*

Sunday, 11.12.94, by permission of The Independent; *pp168–9* from Teaching Written English by Ronald V. White, Heinemann Educational Books, 1980, by permission of R. White; *p218* 'Teevee' from *Catch a little Rhyme* by Eve Merriam © 1966 Eve Merriam. © renewed 1994 Dee Michel and Guy Michel. Reprinted by permission of Marian Reiner; *p263* from *English Grammar in Use* by Raymond Murphy, Cambridge University Press, 1985; *pp281–2* (episode 1 and 3) from *Class Management and Control* by E. C. Wragg, Macmillan, 1981, (episode 2 and 5) adapted from research by Sarah Reinhorn-Lurie; *p281* (episode 4) and p305 from *Classroom Teaching Skills* by E. C. Wragg, Croom Helm, 1984; *p337* based on *Classroom Observation Tasks* by Ruth Wajnryb, Cambridge University Press, 1992.

Drawings by Tony Dover. Artwork by Peter Ducker.

Read this first

▶ ## To the (trainee) teacher

This book is a course in foreign language teaching, addressed mainly to the trainee or novice teacher, but some of its material may also be found interesting by experienced practitioners.

If it is your coursebook in a trainer-led programme of study, then your trainer will tell you how to use it. If, however, you are using it on your own for independent study, I suggest you glance through the following guidelines before starting to read.

How to use the book

1. Skim through, get to know the 'shape' of the book
Before starting any systematic study, have a look at the topics as laid out in the Contents, leaf through the book looking at headings, read one or two of the tasks or boxes.

The chapters are called 'modules' because each can be used independently; you do not have to have done an earlier one in order to approach a later. On the whole, however, they are ordered systematically, with the more basic topics first.

2. Do not try to read it all!
This book is rather long, treating many topics fairly fully and densely. It is not intended to be read cover-to-cover. Some of the units in each module are 'core' units, marked with a black arrowhead in the margin next to the heading; you should find that these give you adequate basic coverage of the topic, and you can skip the rest. However, glance at the 'optional' units, and if you find anything that interests you, use it.

3. Using the tasks
The tasks are headed *Task*, *Question*, *Inquiry*, etc., and are printed in bold. They often refer you to material provided within a rectangular frame labelled *Box*: for example in Module 1, Unit One there is a task in which you are asked to consider a series of classroom scenarios in Box 1.1, and discuss how the teacher presents new material in each.

The objective of the tasks is to help you understand the material and study it thoughtfully and critically – but they are rather time-consuming. Those that are clearly meant to be done by a group of teachers working together are obviously impractical if you are working alone, but others you may find quite feasible and rewarding to do on your own. Some you may prefer simply to read through without trying them yourself. In any case, possible solutions or comments usually follow immediately after the task itself, or are provided in the Notes section at the end of each module.

If you are interested in more detailed information about the material in this book and the theory behind it, go on to read the Introduction on pages 1–9.

To the trainer

This book presents a systematic programme of study intended primarily for pre-service or novice teachers of foreign languages.

Structure

It is composed of 22 chapters which I have called 'modules', since they are intended to be free-standing. Each module is divided into units of study; a unit usually takes between one and two hours to do.

A foundation course is provided by the core units (labelled with black arrowheads in the margin where they occur in the book, and in the Contents); such a course would take about 60–80 hours of class time if you do not supplement it in any way. Some of the optional units may be substituted for core units where you feel it appropriate for your own context, or simply added for further enrichment. An even shorter course may be based on the core units of only the first eleven modules.

Individual modules may be used as bases for short in-service courses; a single module, studied in its entirety, should take about one study day (about six hours) to get through.

Content

The material in the modules includes information, tasks and study based on practice teaching and observation.

The information sections can furnish either a basis for your own input sessions or reading for trainees. There are often brief tasks (questions, checks on understanding) interspersed within these sections, which may be used for short discussions or home writing assignments.

Tasks are usually based on responses to material laid out in the boxes: for example a box may display a short scenario of classroom interaction, and the reader asked to criticize the way the teacher is eliciting student responses. Where appropriate, possible solutions or my own ideas on the issues are given immediately below the task. This close juxtaposition of questions and answers is intended to save the reader from leafing back and forth looking for the answers elsewhere, but the disadvantage is that trainees may be tempted to look on to the answers without engaging properly with the task themselves first. The most practical solution to this problem is probably to make copies of the relevant box (which should be marked © Cambridge University Press) and hand them out separately, giving any necessary instructions yourself, so that trainees do not need to open the book at all in order to do the task; they may later be referred to the possible solutions in the book for comparison or further discussion.

How much you use the tasks involving teaching practice and observation depends, of course, on whether your trainees are actually teaching or have easy access to active language-learning classes. Peer-teaching and the viewing of video recordings of lessons (for example, *Looking at Language Classrooms* (1996) Cambridge University Press) may be substituted if necessary.

The Trainer's notes at the end of the book add some suggestions for variations on the presentation of the different units, and occasionally comment on the background, objectives and possible results of certain tasks. They also include estimates of the timing of the units, based on my experience when doing them with my own trainees; however, this is, of course, only a very rough approximation, and varies a great deal, mainly depending on the need felt by you and the trainees to develop or cut down on discussions.

The following Introduction provides more details on the content and layout of the book and its underlying theory and educational approach.

Introduction

Content

The main part of this book is divided into 22 modules, each devoted to an aspect of language teaching (for example 'grammar', or 'the syllabus'). At the end of most modules is a set of Notes, giving further information or comments on the tasks. Also attached to each module is a section entitled *Further reading*, which is a selected and annotated bibliography of books and articles relevant to the topic.

The modules are grouped into seven parts, each focussing on a central aspect or theme of foreign language teaching: Part I, for example, is called *The teaching process*, and its modules deal with the topics of presentation, practice and testing. Each part has a short introduction defining its theme and clarifying the underlying concepts.

Each module is composed of several separate units: these again are free-standing, and may be used independently of one another. Their content includes:

1. *Input:* background information, both practical and theoretical. Such input is intended to be treated not as some kind of objective 'truth' to be accepted and learned as it stands, but as a summary of ideas that professionals, scholars and researchers have produced and which teachers therefore may benefit from studying and discussing. These sections may simply be read by teachers independently, or mediated by trainers through lecture sessions. Input sections are usually preceded or followed by questions or tasks that allow readers to reflect on and interact with the ideas, check understanding or discuss critically; in a trainer-led session they can serve as the basis for brief group discussions or written assignments. The point of this is to ensure that trainees process the input and make their own sense of it rather than simply accepting a body of transmitted information.
2. *Experiential work:* tasks based on teaching/learning experience, which may be one or more of the following:
   a) Lesson observation: focussing on the point under study.
   b) Classroom teaching: where the teacher tries out different procedures with classes of foreign language learners.
   c) Micro-teaching: the teacher teaches small groups of learners or an individual learner for a short period in order to focus on a particular teaching point.
   d) Peer-teaching: one of a group of teachers tries out a procedure by 'teaching' the rest of the group.

e) Experiment: teachers try out a technique or process of learning or teaching, document results and draw conclusions.

f) Inquiry: a limited aspect of classroom teaching is studied through observation, practice, or limited survey; the results of the study may be written up and made available to others.

Most experiential work is followed by critical reflection, usually in the form of discussion and/or writing. Its aim is to allow teachers to process new ideas thoughtfully, and to form or test theories.

For teachers who are not in a position to try out experiential procedures themselves, some possible results and conclusions are given within the unit itself or in the Notes at the end of the module.

3. *Tasks:* learning tasks done by teachers in groups or individually, with or without a trainer, through discussion or writing. These may involve such processes as critical analysis of teaching materials, comparison of different techniques, problem-solving or free debate on controversial issues; their aim is to provoke careful thinking about the issues and the formulation of personal theories. Brief tasks may be labelled *Question*, *Application* or *To check understanding*, and usually follow or precede informational sections. As with the experiential tasks, suggested solutions, results or comments are supplied where appropriate: immediately following the task if they are seen as useful input in themselves; or in the Notes at the end of the module if they are seen rather as optional, perhaps interesting, additions (my own personal experiences, for example, or further illustration).

Different components are often combined within a unit: a task may be based on a reading text, or on teaching experience; an idea resulting from input may be tried out in class. This integration of different learning modes provides an expression in practice of the theory of professional learning on which this book is based, and which is discussed in the Rationale below.

Note that although this course is meant for teachers of any foreign language, examples of texts and tasks are given throughout in English (except when another language is needed for contrast). The main reason for this is that the book itself is in English, and I felt it was important as a courtesy to the reader to ensure that all illustrative material be readily comprehensible. Also, of course, English itself is probably the most widely taught language in the world today; but if you are concerned with the teaching of another language, you may need to translate or otherwise adapt texts and tasks.

The collection of topics on which the modules are based is necessarily selective: it is based on those that furnish the basis for my own (pre-service) teacher-training programme, and which seem to me the most important and useful. The last module of the book includes recommendations for further study, with suggested reading.

Rationale

Defining concepts

'Training' and 'education'

The terms 'teacher training' and 'teacher education' are often used apparently interchangeably in the literature to refer to the same thing: the professional preparation of teachers. Many prefer 'teacher education', since 'training' can imply unthinking habit formation and an over-emphasis on skills and techniques, while the professional teacher needs to develop theories, awareness of options, and decision-making abilities – a process which seems better defined by the word 'education' (see, for example, Richards and Nunan, 1990). Others have made a different distinction: that 'education' is a process of learning that develops moral, cultural, social and intellectual aspects of the whole person as an individual and member of society, whereas 'training' (though it may entail some 'educational' components) has a specific goal: it prepares for a particular function or profession (Peters, 1966: Ch.1). Thus we normally refer to 'an educated person', but 'a trained scientist/engineer/nurse'.

The second of the two distinctions described above seems to me the more useful: this book therefore uses the term 'training' throughout to describe the process of preparation for professional teaching, including all aspects of teacher development, and reserves 'education' for the more varied and general learning that leads to the development of all aspects of the individual as a member of society.

Practice and theory

Teachers commonly complain about their training: 'My course was too theoretical, it didn't help me learn to teach at all'; or praise a trainer: 'She is so practical!' Or they say: 'It's fine in theory, but doesn't work in practice.' It sounds as if they are saying that theory is useless and practice is what they want. And indeed this is what many teachers feel. But they are understanding the two words in a very specific way: 'theory' as abstract generalization that has no obvious connection with teaching reality; 'practice' as tips about classroom procedure. The two concepts are understood rather differently in this book.

Practice is defined here as (a description of) a real-time localized event or set of such events: particular professional experiences. Theory is a hypothesis or concept that generalizes; it may cover a set of practices ('heterogeneous classes learn better from open-ended tasks than from closed-ended ones'); or it can describe phenomena in general terms ('language is used for communication'); or it can express a personal belief ('language learning is of intrinsic value'). (For a more detailed discussion of different types of theory, see Stern, 1983: 23–32.) Experiencing or hearing about practice is of limited use to the teacher if it is not made more widely applicable by being incorporated into some sort of theoretical framework constructed and 'owned' by the individual. For example, you might learn about a brainstorming activity ('How many things can you think of that ... ?') which can be used at certain levels for practising certain language; but if that is all you learn, then you will only ever be able to use it in the particular context where you learnt it. However, if you then think out why the activity is useful, or define its basic features and purposes in general terms, or relate it to the kind of learning it produces – in other words, construct theories to explain it – you are enabled to criticize and design other ideas and will know when and why to use them. Good theories generate practice; hence Kurt Lewin's famous dictum: 'There is nothing so practical as a good theory.' A teacher who has formed a clear conception of the principles underlying a particular teaching procedure can then use those principles to inform and create further practice; otherwise the original procedure may remain merely an isolated, inert technique which can only be used in one specific context. In other words, practice on its own, paradoxically, is not very practical: it is a dead end.

Theory on its own is even more useless. A statement like 'Language is communication', for example, is meaningful only if we can envisage its implementation in practice. If you really believe in the theoretical concept called 'communicative language teaching', and have made it your own, this will express itself in the kinds of practical communicative techniques you use. If you in fact use mostly mechanical drills in class, your practice is inconsistent with the theory, and clearly you do not genuinely believe in the latter: you have not made it your own, but have merely, in Argyris and Schön's (1974) terms, 'espoused' it. 'Espoused' theories that are claimed by an individual to be true but have no clear expression in practice – or are even contradicted by it – are the foundation of the kind of meaningless theory that trainees complain about.

Predictive hypotheses produced by researchers or theorists are similarly dependent on classroom practice for their validation and usefulness. For example, according to audio-lingualism, people will learn languages best through mimicry and repetition. Does this accord with your own classroom experience? If not, then the theory as it stands is useless to you; but if you can process it and reformulate it for yourself as something that is true in the light of your own experience ('Mimicry and repetition help students X to learn Y under conditions Z') then it becomes meaningful and helpful.

This book attempts to maintain a consistent link between practice and theory: theoretical ideas are tested through and illustrated by practical examples, while samples of practice are discussed and analysed in order to study their wider theoretical implications.

The integration of practice and theory within the process of professional learning is described in more detail in the section *'Enriched reflection'* below.

Foreign language teaching

Finally, two brief comments on the term 'foreign language teaching', as it is understood in this book.

Learning may take place without conscious teaching; but teaching, as I understand it, is intended to result in personal learning for students, and is worthless if it does not do so. In other words, the concept of teaching is understood here as a process that is intrinsically and inseparably bound up with learning. You will find, therefore, no separate discussion of language learning in this book; instead, both content and process of the various modules consistently require the reader to study learners' problems, needs and strategies as a necessary basis for the formulation of effective teaching practice and theory.

Second, it is necessary to distinguish between 'teaching' and 'methodology'. Foreign language teaching methodology can be defined as 'the activities, tasks and learning experiences used by the teacher within the [language] teaching and learning process' (Richards, 1990: 35). Any particular methodology usually has a theoretical underpinning that should cause coherence and consistency in the choice of teaching procedures. 'Foreign language teaching', on the other hand, though it naturally includes methodology, has further important components such as lesson planning, classroom discipline, the provision of interest – topics which are relevant and important to teachers of all subjects. Such topics, therefore, are included in this book as well as the more conventional methodology-based ones such as 'teaching reading'.

Models of teacher learning

Various models of teacher learning have been suggested; the three main ones, as described in Wallace (1993), are as follows:

1. The craft model
The trainee learns from the example of a 'master teacher', whom he/she observes and imitates. Professional action is seen as a craft, rather like shoemaking or carpentry, to be learned most effectively through an apprenticeship system and accumulated experience. This is a traditional method, still used as a substitute for postgraduate teaching courses in some countries.

2. The applied science model
The trainee studies theoretical courses in applied linguistics and other allied subjects, which are then, through the construction of an appropriate methodology, applied to classroom practice. Many university- and college-based teacher-training courses are based, explicitly or implicitly, on this idea of teacher learning.

3. The reflective model
The trainee teaches or observes lessons, or recalls past experience; then reflects, alone or in discussion with others, in order to work out theories about teaching; then tries these out again in practice. Such a cycle aims for continuous improvement and the development of personal theories of action (Schön, 1983). This model is used by teacher development groups and in some recently designed training courses.

Which is likely to be most effective? Or, perhaps a better question: how do teachers learn most effectively, and how can this learning be integrated into a formal course of study?

I have several times asked groups of teachers in different countries from what, or whom, they feel they learned their present teaching expertise and knowledge. Various possible sources were suggested, such as colleagues and 'master teachers', the literature, pre- or in-service courses, their own experience as teachers, their students, their own experience as learners; and teachers were asked to rate each of these in importance for professional learning. Every time the majority replied that personal teaching experience was by far the most important. (Try this yourself with teachers you know!)

This answer makes sense on an intuitive, personal level as well. I myself have done my best to read, study, discuss with colleagues, attend courses and conferences in order to improve my professional knowledge. Nevertheless, if asked, I would make the same reply as the teachers in my survey: I have learnt most through (thinking about) my own teaching experience. This does not mean that other sources of knowledge and learning processes do not contribute; but it does mean that they are probably less important.

Thus, I have chosen to base this course primarily on the 'reflective model' as defined at the beginning of this section.

My only reservation is that this model can tend to **over**-emphasize experience. Courses based on it have sometimes used the (student-) teachers themselves as almost the sole source of knowledge, with a relative neglect of external input – lectures, reading, and so on – which help to make sense of the experiences and can make a very real contribution to understanding. As I see it, the function of teacher reflection is to ensure the processing of any input, regardless of where it comes from, by the individual teacher, so that the knowledge becomes personally significant to him or her. Thus a fully effective reflective model should make room for external as well as personal input.

Perhaps we might call this model 'enriched reflection'! It is described below.

'Enriched reflection'

Kolb's (1984) theory of experiential learning elaborates the idea of 'experience + reflection'. He defines four modes of learning: concrete experience, reflective observation, abstract conceptualization and active experimentation. In order for optimal learning to take place, the knowledge acquired in any one mode needs to be followed by further processing in the next; and so on, in a recursive cycle. Thus, concrete experience ('something happened to me in the classroom'), which involves intuitive or 'gut' feeling, should be followed by reflective observation ('let me step back and look at what took place'), which involves watching and perception; this in its turn is followed by abstract conceptualization ('what principle, or concept, can I formulate which will account for this event?'), involving intellectual thought; then comes active experimentation ('let me try to implement this idea in practice'), involving real-time action which will entail further concrete experience … and so on (see Box 0.1).

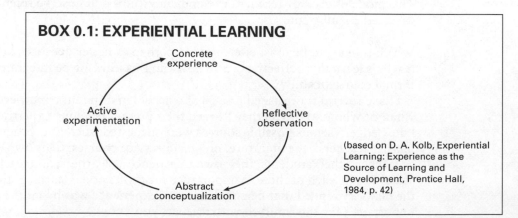

BOX 0.1: EXPERIENTIAL LEARNING

Concrete experience

Reflective observation

Abstract conceptualization

Active experimentation

(based on D. A. Kolb, Experiential Learning: Experience as the Source of Learning and Development, Prentice Hall, 1984, p. 42)

This model, however, needs to be enriched by external sources of input. It is unrealistic and a waste of time to expect trainees to 'reinvent the wheel': this is like expecting physics students to discover known laws of physics through their own experiments. There is a lot to be learnt from experienced teachers (as in the craft model), from experts, from research and from reading (as in the applied science model) – provided all this can be integrated into one's own reflection-based theories. So at each stage of Kolb's circle let us add the external sources: experience can be vicarious (i.e. second-hand, such as observation, anecdote, video, transcripts); descriptions of other people's observations can add to our own; theoretical concepts can come from foreign language researchers and thinkers; ideas for or descriptions of experiments from writers or other professionals. And the initial stimulus for a learning cycle of this kind can occur, of course, at any of the eight points, not just at the point of experience (see Box 0.2).

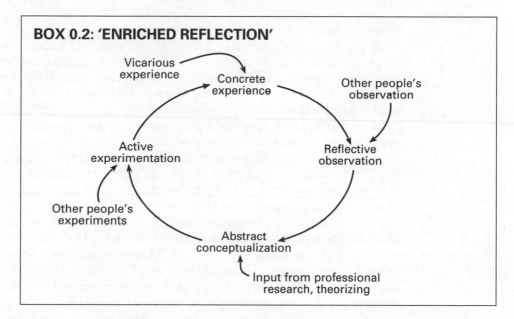

BOX 0.2: 'ENRICHED REFLECTION'

Thus, sources of knowledge may be either personal experience and thought or input from outside; but in either case this knowledge should, in principle, be integrated into the trainees' own reflective cycle in order that effective learning may take place.

To summarize: the most important basis for learning is personal professional practice; knowledge is most useful when it either derives directly from such practice, or, while deriving originally from other sources, is tested and validated through it. Hence the subtitle of this book: *Practice and Theory*, rather than the more conventional *Theory and Practice*.

The role of the trainer

Such a model of professional learning has, of course, implications for the role of the trainer. In the 'craft model', the trainer is the master teacher, providing an example to be followed. The 'applied science' model also gives the trainer an authoritative role, as the source of theory which the teacher is to interpret in practice. The conventional 'reflective model', in contrast, casts the trainer in the role of 'facilitator' or 'developer', giving little or no information, but encouraging trainees to develop their own body of knowledge.

According to the model suggested here, the function of the trainer is neither just to 'tell' the trainees what they should be doing, nor – just as bad – to refuse to tell them anything in order for them to develop all their knowledge on their own. The functions of the trainer, I believe, are:

- to encourage trainees to articulate what they know and put forward new ideas of their own;
- to provide input him- or herself and to make available further sources of relevant information;
- and, above all, to get trainees to acquire the habit of processing input from either source through using their own experience and critical faculty, so that they eventually feel personal 'ownership' of the resulting knowledge.

What the trainee should get from the course

Teachers, as mentioned above, generally agree that they learned most from their own experience and reflection while in professional practice. Some even claim that they learned everything from experience and nothing from their pre-service course at all – this is especially true of those who took courses that were predominantly theoretical.

Pre-service courses, however good, cannot normally produce fully competent practitioners who can immediately vie with their experienced colleagues in expertise. This is probably true of training courses in all the professions. On the other hand, without an effective course incoming teachers will merely perpetuate the way they were taught or the way colleagues teach, with little opportunity to encounter new ideas, to benefit from progress made in the field by other professionals, researchers and thinkers, or to develop personal theories of action through systematic study and experiment. The primary aim, then, of such a course is to bring trainees to the point at which they can begin to function competently and thoughtfully, as a basis for further development and improvement in the course of their own professional practice. Occasionally course graduates are already well on their way to excellence, but most of us start(ed) our teaching careers at a fairly modest level of competence.

Thus, a second, important aim of the course is to lay the seeds of further development. The course should be seen as the beginning of a process, not a complete process in itself: participants should be encouraged to develop habits of learning that will carry through into later practice and continue for their entire professional lives (See Module 22: *And beyond*).

Finally, there is a more long-term aim: to promote a view of teachers as autonomous and creative professionals, with responsibility for the wider development of professional theory and practice. This is in clear opposition to the 'applied science' model of teacher learning, which carries with it the implication that there is a hierarchy of prestige and authority. In such a hierarchy, the research experts and academics take the highest place, and the classroom teachers the lowest (Schön, 1983; Bolitho, 1988). The job of the classroom teachers is merely to interpret and implement theory which is handed down to them from the universities. They (the teachers) are allowed to take decisions, but only those which affect their own classroom practice. In contrast, this book supports a view that teachers can and should develop theories and practices that are useful both within and beyond the limits of their own classrooms (see Stenhouse's writings in Rudduck and Hopkins, 1985); and that such a message should be conveyed through pre- and in-service training. Courses should lead trainees to rely on their own judgement and to be confident enough to discuss and criticize ideas put forward by others, whether local colleagues, trainers, lecturers, or university researchers. They should also promote individual research and innovation, in both practical and theoretical topics, and encourage the writing up and publication of original ideas for sharing with other professionals.

References

Argyris, C. and Schön, D. A. (1974) *Theory in Practice: Increasing Professional Effectiveness*, San Francisco: Jossey Bass.

Bolitho, R. (1988) 'Teaching, teacher training and applied linguistics', *The Teacher Trainer*, **2**, 3, 4–7.

Kolb, D. A. (1984) *Experiential Learning: Experience as the Source of Learning and Development*, Englewood Cliffs, New Jersey: Prentice Hall.

Peters, R. S. (1966) *Ethics and Education*, London: George Allen and Unwin.

Richards, J. (1990) *The Language Teaching Matrix*, Cambridge: Cambridge University Press.

Richards, J. and Nunan, D. (1990) *Second Language Teacher Education*, Cambridge: Cambridge University Press.

Rudduck, J. and Hopkins, D. (1985) *Research as a Basis for Teaching: Readings from the work of Lawrence Stenhouse*, London: Heinemann Educational Books.

Schön, D. A. (1983) *The Reflective Practitioner: How Professionals Think in Action*, New York: Basic Books.

Stern, H. H. (1983) *Fundamental Concepts of Language Teaching*, Oxford: Oxford University Press.

Wallace, M. (1993) *Training Foreign Language Teachers: A Reflective Approach*, Cambridge: Cambridge University Press.

The process of teaching a foreign language is a complex one: as with many other subjects, it has necessarily to be broken down into components for purposes of study. Part I presents three such components: the teaching acts of (1) presenting and explaining new material; (2) providing practice; and (3) testing. Note that the first two concepts are understood here rather differently from the way they are usually used within the conventional 'presentation–practice–production' paradigm.

In principle, the teaching processes of presenting, practising and testing correspond to strategies used by many good learners trying to acquire a foreign language on their own. They make sure they **perceive and understand** new language (by paying attention, by constructing meanings, by formulating rules or hypotheses that account for it, and so on); they make conscious efforts to **learn it thoroughly** (by mental rehearsal of items, for example, or by finding opportunities to practise); and they **check themselves** (get feedback on performance, ask to be corrected). (For a thorough discussion of the cognitive processes and strategies of language learners, see O'Malley and Chamot, 1990.)

In the classroom, it is the teacher's job to promote these three learning processes by the use of appropriate teaching acts. Thus, he or she: presents and explains new material in order to make it clear, comprehensible and available for learning; gives practice to consolidate knowledge; and tests, in order to check what has been mastered and what still needs to be learned or reviewed. These acts may not occur in this order, and may sometimes be combined within one activity; nevertheless good teachers are usually aware which is their main objective at any point in a lesson.

This is not, of course, the only way people learn a language in the classroom. They may absorb new material unconsciously, or semi-consciously, through exposure to comprehensible and personally meaningful speech or writing, and through their own engagement with it, without any purposeful teacher mediation as proposed here. Through such mediation, however, the teacher can provide a framework for organized, conscious learning, while simultaneously being aware of – and providing opportunities for – further, more intuitive acquisition.

Thus, the three topics of presentation, practice and testing are presented in the following units not as the exclusive source of student learning, nor as representing a rigid linear classroom routine, but rather as simplified but comprehensive categories that enable useful study of basic teaching acts.

Reference

O'Malley, J. M. and Chamot, A. U. (1990) *Learning Strategies in Second Language Acquisition*, Cambridge: Cambridge University Press.

Module 1: Presentations and explanations

▶ ## Unit One: Effective presentation

The necessity for presentation

It would seem fairly obvious that in order for our students to learn something new (a text, a new word, how to perform a task) they need to be first able to perceive and understand it. One of the teacher's jobs is to mediate such new material so that it appears in a form that is most accessible for initial learning.

This kind of mediation may be called 'presentation'; the term is applied here not only to the kind of limited and controlled modelling of a target item that we do when we introduce a new word or grammatical structure, but also to the initial encounter with comprehensible input in the form of spoken or written texts, as well as various kinds of explanations, instructions and discussion of new language items or tasks.

People may, it is true, perceive and even acquire new language without conscious presentation on the part of a teacher. We learn our first language mostly like this, and there are some who would argue for teaching a foreign language in the same way – by exposing learners to the language phenomena without instructional intervention and letting them absorb it intuitively.

However, raw, unmediated new input is often incomprehensible to learners; it does not function as 'intake', and therefore does not result in learning. In an immersion situation this does not matter: learners have plenty of time for repeated and different exposures to such input and will eventually absorb it. But given the limited time and resources of conventional foreign language courses, as much as possible of this input has to become also 'intake' at first encounter. Hence the necessity for presenting it in such a way that it can be perceived and understood.

Another contribution of effective teacher presentations of new material in formal courses is that they can help to activate and harness learners' attention, effort, intelligence and conscious ('metacognitive') learning strategies in order to enhance learning – again, something that does not necessarily happen in an immersion situation. For instance, you might point out how a new item is linked to something they already know, or contrast a new bit of grammar with a parallel structure in their own language.

This does not necessarily mean that every single new bit of language – every sound, word, structure, text, and so on – needs to be consciously introduced; or that every new unit in the syllabus has to start with a clearly directed presentation. Moreover, presentations may often not occur at the first stage of learning: they may be given after learners have already engaged with the language in question, as when we clarify the meaning of a word during a discussion, or read aloud a text learners have previously read to themselves.

The ability to mediate new material or instruct effectively is an essential teaching skill; it enables the teacher to facilitate learners' entry into and understanding of new material, and thus promotes further learning.

Question   **If you have learned a foreign language in a course, can you recall a particular teacher presentation or explanation that facilitated your grasp of some aspect of this language? How did it help?**

What happens in an effective presentation?

Attention
The learners are alert, focussing their attention on the teacher and/or the material to be learnt, and aware that something is coming that they need to take in. You need to make sure that learners are in fact attending; it helps if the target material is perceived as interesting in itself.

Perception
The learners see or hear the target material clearly. This means not only making sure that the material is clearly visible and/or audible in the first place; it also usually means repeating it in order to give added opportunities for, or reinforce, perception. Finally, it helps to get some kind of response from the learners in order to check that they have in fact perceived the material accurately: repetition, for example, or writing.

Understanding
The learners understand the meaning of the material being introduced, and its connection with other things they already know (how it fits into their existing perceptions of reality, or 'schemata'). So you may need to illustrate, make links with previously learnt material, explain (for further discussion of what is involved in **explaining**, see Unit Three). A response from the learners, again, can give you valuable feedback on how well they have understood: a restatement of concepts in their own words, for example.

Short-term memory
The learners need to take the material into short-term memory: to remember it, that is, until later in the lesson, when you and they have an opportunity to do further work to consolidate learning (see Module 2: *Practice activities*). So the more 'impact' the original presentation has – for example, if it is colourful, dramatic, unusual in any way – the better. Note that some learners remember better if the material is seen, others if it is heard, yet others if it is associated with physical movement (visual, aural and kinaesthetic input): these should ideally all be utilized within a good presentation. If a lengthy explanation has taken place, it helps also to finish with a brief restatement of the main point.

Group task **Peer-teaching**

One participant chooses a topic or item of information (not necessarily anything to do with language teaching) on which they are well informed and in which they are interested, but which others are likely to be relatively ignorant about. They prepare a presentation of not more than five minutes, and then give it.

As many participants as possible give such presentations.

For each presentation, pick out and discuss what was effective about it, using where relevant the criteria suggested under *What happens in an effective presentation?* above.

▷ Unit Two: Examples of presentation procedures

In Box 1.1 are four accounts, three written by teachers and one by a student, of four quite different types of presentations. The first describes how a teacher of young children in a primary school in New Zealand teaches them to read and write their first words; the second is a recommendation of how to introduce a short foreign language dialogue in primary or secondary school; the third is an unusual improvised presentation of a particular language function with a class of adults; and the fourth is the first presentation to a middle-school class of a soliloquy from a Shakespeare play.

The task below may help you study the texts; my own comments follow.

Task **Criticizing presentations**

For each of the descriptions in Box 1.1, consider and/or discuss:

1. What was the aim of the presentation?
2. How successful do you think this presentation was, or would be, in getting students to attend to, perceive, understand and remember the target material? You may find it helpful to refer back to the criteria described in Unit One.
3. How appropriate and effective would a similar procedure be for you, in your teaching situation (or in a teaching situation you are familiar with)?

Comments

This is obviously only a small sample of the many presentation techniques available to language teachers.

1. Reading words

The teacher has based this presentation on the students' own choice of vocabulary, derived from their own 'inner worlds'. She is thus tapping not only intellectual but also personal emotional associations with the vocabulary; such associations, it has been shown by research, have a clear positive effect on retention, as well as on immediate attention, general motivation, and – her main objective – ability to read the material.

BOX 1.1: DIFFERENT PRESENTATIONS

Presentation 1: Reading words

… But if the vocabulary of a child is still inaccessible, one can always begin him on the general Key Vocabulary, common to any child in any race, a set of words bound up with security that experiments, and later on their creative writing, show to be organically associated with the inner world: 'Mummy', 'Daddy', 'kiss', 'frightened', 'ghost'.

'Mohi,' I ask a new five, an undisciplined Maori, 'what word do you want?'
'Jet!'
I smile and write it on a strong little card and give it to him.
'What is it again?'
'Jet!'
'You can bring it back in the morning. What do you want, Gay?'
Gay is the classic overdisciplined, bullied victim of the respectable mother.
'House,' she whispers. So I write that, too, and give it into her eager hand.

(from Sylvia Ashton-Warner, *Teacher*, Virago, 1980, pp. 35-6)

Presentation 2: Learning a dialogue

The main objective at the beginning is to achieve a good working knowledge of the dialogue in the textbook, so that it can be altered or elaborated afterwards …

1. Read out the dialogue, utterance by utterance, and ask the students to repeat it in different formations, acting out the roles in the following ways:
   a) together in chorus;
   b) half of the class take one role and the other half take the other role;
   c) one student to another student;
   d) one student to the rest of the class …

(from Zoltan Dörnyei, 'Exploiting textbook dialogues dynamically', *Practical English Teaching* 1986, **6**, 4, 15–16)

Presentation 3: Accusations

It can happen to anyone who commutes – a traffic jam, a last minute phone call, a car that won't start – and you realise you are going to be late for a lesson … However, attack being the best form of defence, I recently found a way to turn my lateness to good account. A full ten minutes after the start of the lesson, I strode into the classroom and wrote on the board in huge letters

YOU'RE LATE!

Then I invited the students to yell at me with all the venom they could muster and we all laughed. So I wrote:

You're late **again**!

and:

You're **always** late!

So we practised these forms. They seemed to get a real kick out of putting the stress in the right place … When we had savoured the pleasure of righteous indignation, I proposed that everyone should write down the accusations most commonly levelled at him (or her). A rich and varied selection poured out such as:

You **always** eat my sweets!
You've lost the keys!
You haven't lost the keys **again**!

(from Alison Coulavin, 'Excuses, excuses', *Practical English Teaching*, 1983, **4**, 2, 31)

Presentation 4: Dramatic soliloquy

… I shall never forget Miss Nancy McCall, and the day she whipped a ruler off my desk, and pointing it towards her ample bosom, declaimed, 'Is this a dagger which I see before me?' And there we sat, eyes a goggle, hearts a-thumping, in electrified silence.

(a letter from Anna Sotto in *The English Teachers' Journal* (Israel) 1986, 33)

© *Cambridge University Press 1996*

Certainly the use of items suggested by the learners themselves can contribute to the effectiveness of any kind of presentation; however, this idea may be more difficult to implement in large classes, or where classroom relationships are more formal.

2. Learning a dialogue

The aim of this presentation is to get students to learn the dialogue by heart for further practice.

The writer describes a systematic procedure involving initial clear presentation of the target text by the teacher, followed by varied and numerous repetitions. The resulting preliminary rote learning of the words of the dialogue would probably be satisfactory.

But nothing is done to make sure the dialogue is meaningful and interesting to the students. As it stands, the method of teaching does not provide for cognitive or affective 'depth': it fails to engage the students' intellectual or emotional faculties in any way. It is important to emphasize learners' understanding of the meaning of the dialogue from the beginning, not just their learning by heart of the words, and to find ways of stimulating their interest in it, through the content of the text itself, the teacher's presentation of it, visual illustration, or various other means.

3. Accusations

The first two examples were accounts of systematic presentations of planned material. This, in contrast, describes an activity improvised by a resourceful teacher with a sense of humour and a friendly relationship with the class, who exploits a specific real-time event to teach a language function (accusation, reproach), with its typical grammar and intonation patterns.

The presentation seems likely to produce good perception and initial learning: not because of any carefully planned process, but because of the heightened attention and motivation caused by the humour (rooted in the temporary legitimizing of normally 'taboo' verbal aggression) and by the fact that many of the actual texts are personally relevant to the learners (compare with Presentation 1 above).

4. Dramatic soliloquy

This classroom event is recalled from the point of view of the student, and it was obviously successful in attracting the students' attention, getting them to perceive the material and imprinting it very quickly on their short-term (indeed, long-term!) memory – all these, probably, being part of the teacher's objectives. As to understanding: if the class was native English-speaking then one would assume that the teacher's acting and use of props was probably sufficient to cover this aspect also; foreign language learners would presumably need a little more clarification.

Not everyone, it must be said, has the dramatic ability of the teacher described; the applicability of this example for many of us may be limited! However, if you can act, or have video material available, dramatic presentations can be very effective.

Unit Three: Explanations and instructions

When introducing new material we often need also to give explicit descriptions or definitions of concepts or processes, and whether we can or cannot explain such new ideas clearly to our students may make a crucial difference to the success or failure of a lesson. There is, moreover, some indication in research that learners see the ability to explain things well as one of the most important qualities of a good teacher (see, for example, Wragg and Wood, 1984). (The problem of how to explain new language well is perhaps most obvious in the field of grammar; for a detailed consideration of grammar explanation, see Unit Four of Module 6, *Teaching grammar*.)

One particular kind of explanation that is very important in teaching is **instruction**: the directions that are given to introduce a learning task which entails some measure of independent student activity. The task below is based on the experience of giving instructions, and the following Guidelines on effective explaining may be studied in the light of this experience. Alternatively, the Guidelines may be studied on their own and tried out in your own teaching.

Task ## Giving instructions

Stage 1: Experience

If you are currently teaching, notice carefully how you yourself give instructions for a group- or pair-work activity in class, and note down immediately afterwards what you did, while the event is still fresh in your memory. Better, but not always feasible: ask a colleague to observe you and take notes.

Alternatively, within a group of colleagues: each participant chooses an activity and prepares instructions on how to do it. The activity may be: a game which you know how to play but others do not; a process (how to prepare a certain dish, how to mend or build something); or a classroom procedure. Two or three volunteer participants then actually give the instructions, and (if practical) the group goes on to start performing the activity.

Stage 2: Discussion

Read the guidelines on giving effective explanations laid out below. Think about or discuss them with colleagues, relating them to the actual instructions given in Stage 1. In what ways did these instructions accord with or differ from the guidelines? Can you now think of ways in which these instructions could have been made more effective?

Guidelines on giving effective explanations and instructions

1. Prepare

You may feel perfectly clear in your own mind about what needs clarifying, and therefore think that you can improvise a clear explanation. But experience shows that teachers' explanations are often not as clear to their students as they are to themselves! It is worth preparing: thinking for a while about the words you will use, the illustrations you will provide, and so on; possibly even writing these out.

2. Make sure you have the class's full attention

In ongoing language practice learners' attention may sometimes stray; they can usually make up what they have lost later. But if you are explaining something essential, they must attend. This may be the only chance they have to get some vital information; if they miss bits, they may find themselves in difficulties later. One of the implications of this when giving instructions for a group-work task is that it is advisable to give the instructions **before** you divide the class into groups or give out materials, not after! Once they are in groups, learners' attention will be naturally directed to each other rather than to you; and if they have written or pictorial material in their hands, the temptation will be to look at it, which may also distract.

3. Present the information more than once

A repetition or paraphrase of the necessary information may make all the difference: learners' attention wanders occasionally, and it is important to give them more than one chance to understand what they have to do. Also, it helps to re-present the information in a different mode: for example, say it and also write it up on the board.

4. Be brief

Learners – in fact, all of us – have only a limited attention span; they cannot listen to you for very long at maximum concentration. Make your explanation as brief as you can, compatible with clarity. This means thinking fairly carefully about what you can, or should, **omit**, as much as about what you should include! In some situations it may also mean using the learners' mother tongue, as a more accessible and cost-effective alternative to the sometimes lengthy and difficult target-language explanation.

5. Illustrate with examples

Very often a careful theoretical explanation only 'comes together' for an audience when made real through an example, or preferably several. You may explain, for instance, the meaning of a word, illustrating your explanation with examples of its use in various contexts, relating these as far as possible to the learners' own lives and experiences. Similarly, when giving instructions for an activity, it often helps to do a 'dry run': an actual demonstration of the activity yourself with the full class or with a volunteer student before inviting learners to tackle the task on their own.

6. Get feedback

When you have finished explaining, check with your class that they have understood. It is not enough just to ask 'Do you understand?'; learners will sometimes say they did even if they in fact did not, out of politeness or unwillingness to lose face, or because they think they know what they have to do, but have in fact completely misunderstood! It is better to ask them to do something that will show their understanding: to paraphrase in their own words, or provide further illustrations of their own.

Further reading

Brown, G. A. and Armstrong, S. (1984) 'Explanations and explaining' in Wragg, E. C. (ed.) *Classroom Teaching Skills*, London and Sydney: Croom Helm.
(A practical analysis of the skill of explaining in the classroom, in various subjects)
Schmidt, R. W. (1990) 'The role of consciousness in second language learning', *Applied Linguistics*, **11**, 2, 129–58.
(A discussion of the importance of conscious attention to input in language learning)

Reference

Wragg, E. C. and Wood, E. K. (1984) 'Pupil appraisals of teaching' in Wragg, E. C. (ed.), *Classroom Teaching Skills*, London and Sydney: Croom Helm (Ch. 4).

Module 2: Practice activities

▶ ## Unit One: The function of practice

Practice can be roughly defined as the rehearsal of certain behaviours with the objective of consolidating learning and improving performance. Language learners can benefit from being told, and understanding, facts about the language only up to a point: ultimately, they have to acquire an intuitive, automatized knowledge which will enable ready and fluent comprehension and self-expression. And such knowledge is normally brought about through consolidation of learning through practice. This is true of first language acquisition as well as of second language learning in either 'immersion' or formal classroom situations. Language learning has much in common with the learning of other skills, and it may be helpful at this point to think about what learning a skill entails.

Learning a skill

The process of learning a skill by means of a course of instruction has been defined as a three-stage process: verbalization, automatization and autonomy.

At the first stage the bit of the skill to be learned may be focussed on and defined in words – '**verbalized**' – as well as demonstrated. Thus in swimming the instructor will probably both describe and show correct arm and leg movements; in language, the teacher may explain the meaning of a word or the rules about a grammatical structure as well as using them in context. Note that the verbalization may be elicited from learners rather than done by the teacher, and it may follow trial attempts at performance which serve to pinpoint aspects of the skill that need learning. It roughly corresponds to 'presentation', as discussed in the previous module.

The teacher then gets the learners to demonstrate the target behaviour, while monitoring their performance. At first they may do things wrong and need correcting in the form of further telling and/or demonstration; later they may do it right as long as they are thinking about it. At this point they start practising: performing the skilful behaviour again and again, usually in exercises suggested by the teacher, until they can get it right without thinking. At this point they may be said to have '**automatized**' the behaviour, and are likely to forget how it was described verbally in the first place.

Finally they take the set of behaviours they have mastered and begin to improve on their own, through further practice activity. They start to speed up performance, to perceive or create new combinations, to 'do their own thing': they are '**autonomous**'. Some people have called this stage 'production', but this I think is a misnomer for it involves reception as much as production, and is in fact simply a more advanced form of practice, as defined at the beginning of this unit. Learners now have little need of a teacher except perhaps as a supportive or challenging colleague and are ready, or nearly ready, to perform as masters of the skill – or as teachers themselves.

This model of skill learning is briefly summarized in Box 2.1. For further information on skill theory in general, see Anderson, 1985; and on skill theory applied to language learning Johnson (1995).

BOX 2.1: SKILL LEARNING

VERBALIZATION   →   AUTOMATIZATION   →   AUTONOMY

Teacher describes and demonstrates the skilled behaviour to be learned; learners perceive and understand.	Teacher suggests exercises; learners practise skill in order to acquire facility, automatize; teacher monitors.	Learners continue to use skill on their own, becoming more proficient and creative.

Question Can you think of a skill – other than swimming or language – that you successfully learned through being taught it in some kind of course? (If you cannot, some possibilities are suggested in the Notes, (1).) And can you identify the stages described above in the process of that learning as you recall it?

Much language practice falls within the skill-development model described above. But some of it does not: even where information has not been consciously verbalized or presented, learners may absorb and acquire language skills and content through direct interaction with texts or communicative tasks. In other words, their learning starts at the automatization and autonomy stages, in unstructured fluency practice. But this is still practice, and essential for successful learning.

Summary

Practice, then, is the activity through which language skills and knowledge are consolidated and thoroughly mastered. As such, it is arguably the most important of all the stages of learning; hence the most important classroom activity of the teacher is to initiate and manage activities that provide students with opportunities for effective practice.

Question Do you agree with the last statement (which expresses my own belief) or would you prefer to qualify it?

► Unit Two: Characteristics of a good practice activity

Whether or not you think that organizing language practice is the most important thing the teacher does in the classroom, you will, I hope, agree that it does contribute significantly to successful language learning, and therefore that it is worth devoting some thought to what factors contribute to the effectiveness of classroom practice.

Practice is usually carried out through procedures called 'exercises' or 'activities'. The latter term usually implies rather more learner activity and initiative than the former, but there is a large area of overlap: many procedures could be defined by either. Exercises and activities may, of course, relate to any aspect of language: their goal may be the consolidation of the learning of a grammatical structure, for example, or the improvement of listening, speaking, reading or writing fluency, or the memorization of vocabulary.

Try doing the task below before reading on.

Task **Defining effective language practice activities**

Stage 1: Selecting samples

Think of one or more examples of language practice of any kind which you have experienced either as teacher or as learner, and which you consider were effective in helping the learners to remember, 'automatize', or increase their ease of use. Write down brief descriptions of them. (If you cannot think of any, use the example given in the Notes, (2).)

Stage 2: Analysis

Consider: what were the factors, or characteristics, that in your opinion made these activities effective? Note down, either on your own or in collaboration with colleagues, at least two such characteristics – more if you can.

Stage 3: Discussion

Now compare what you have with my list below. Probably at least some of your ideas will be similar to mine, though you may have expressed them differently. If I have suggested ideas that are new to you, do you agree with them? What would you include that I have not?

Characteristics of effective language practice

Validity

The activity should activate learners primarily in the skill or material it purports to practise. This is an obvious principle that is surprisingly often violated. Many 'speaking' activities, for example, have learners listening to the teacher more than talking themselves.

Note that 'validity' does not necessarily imply that the language should be used for some kind of replication of real-life communication. Pronunciation drills and vocabulary practice, for example, may also be valid if they in fact serve primarily to rehearse and improve the items to be practised.

Pre-learning

The learners should have a good preliminary grasp of the language they are required to practise, though they may only be able to produce or understand it slowly and after thought. If they are required to do a practice activity based on something they have not yet begun to learn, they will either not be able to do it at all, or will produce unsuccessful responses. In either case the activity will have been fairly useless in providing practice: its main function, in fact, will have been as a diagnostic test, enabling the teacher to identify and (re-)teach language the learners do not know. If, however, they can – however hesitantly – produce successful responses, they have a firm basis for further effective practice of the target language material.

Volume

Roughly speaking, the more language the learners actually engage with during the activity, the more practice in it they will get. If the lesson time available for the activity is seen as a container, then this should be filled with as much 'volume' of language as possible. Time during which learners are not engaging with the language being practised for whatever reason (because nothing is being demanded of them at that moment, or because they are using their mother tongue, or because they are occupied with classroom management or organizational processes, or because of some distraction or digression) is time wasted as far as the practice activity is concerned.

Success-orientation

On the whole, we consolidate learning by doing things right. Continued inaccurate or unacceptable performance results only in 'fossilization' of mistakes and general discouragement. It is therefore important to select, design and administer practice activities in such a way that learners are likely to succeed in doing the task. Repeated successful performance is likely to result in effective automatization of whatever is being performed, as well as reinforcing the learners' self-image as successful language learners and encouraging them to take up further challenges.

Success, incidentally, does not necessarily mean perfection! A class may engage successfully with language practice in groups, where mistakes do occasionally occur, but most of the utterances are acceptable and a large 'volume' of practice is achieved. This is often preferable to teacher-monitored full-class practice, which may produce fully accurate responses – but at the expense of 'volume' and opportunities for active participation by most of the class.

Heterogeneity

A good practice activity provides opportunities for useful practice to all, or most, of the different levels within a class. If you give an activity whose items invite response at only one level of knowledge, then a large proportion of your class will not benefit.

Consider the following item in an activity on *can/can't*:

> *Jenny is a baby. Jenny (can/can't) ride a bicycle.*

Learners who are not confident that they understand how to use *can* may not do the item at all. Those who are more advanced, and could make far more complex and interesting statements with the same item have no opportunity to do so, and get no useful practice at a level appropriate to them.

However, suppose you redesign the text and task as follows:

> *Jenny is a baby. Jenny can hold a toy and can smile, but she can't ride a bicycle. What else can, or can't, Jenny do?*

then the activity becomes heterogeneous. You have provided weaker learners with support in the form of sample responses, and you have given everyone the opportunity to answer at a level appropriate to him or her, from the simple ('Jenny can drink milk', for example) to the relatively complex and original ('Jenny can't open a bank account'). Thus a much larger proportion of the class is able to participate and benefit.

Teacher assistance

The main function of the teacher, having proposed the activity and given clear instructions, is to help the learners do it successfully. If you give an activity, and then sit back while the learners 'flounder' – make random uninformed guesses or are uncomfortably hesitant – you are not helping; even assessments and corrections made later, which give useful feedback to learners on their mistakes, do not in themselves give practice, in the sense of contributing to automatization. If, however, you assist them, you thereby increase their chances of success and the effectiveness of the practice activity as a whole. Such assistance may take the form of allowing plenty of time to think, of making the answers easier through giving hints and guiding questions, of confirming beginnings of responses in order to encourage continuations, or, in group work, of moving around the classroom making yourself available to answer questions. Through such activity you also, incidentally, convey a clear message about the function and attitude of the teacher: I want you to succeed in learning and am doing my best to see you do so.

Interest

If there is little challenge in the language work itself because of its 'success-orientation' and if there is a lot of repetition of target forms ('volume'), then there is certainly a danger that the practice might be boring. And boredom is not only an unpleasant feeling in itself; it also leads to learner inattention, low motivation and ultimately less learning.

However, if interest is not derived from the challenge of getting-the-answers-right, it has to be rooted in other aspects of the activity: an interesting topic, the need to convey meaningful information, a game-like 'fun' task, attention-catching materials, appeal to learners' feelings or a challenge to their intellect. A simple example: an activity whose aim is to get learners to practise asking 'yes-no' questions may simply demand that learners build such questions from short cues (by transforming statements into questions, for example); but such an activity will get far more attentive and interested participation if participants produce their questions as contributions to some kind of purposeful transfer of information (such as guessing what the teacher has in a bag or what someone's profession is).

▶ Unit Three: Practice techniques

In Box 2.2 is a series of descriptions of classroom scenarios, which are fictional representations of types of procedures that I have witnessed or administered myself. They are all intended to practise some aspect of language; and they are all, in my opinion, less than optimally effective in doing so. This may be because of the design of the activity, its text(s), the way the teacher is behaving – or all of these. I suggest you study these through doing the task below before reading on to my comments.

Task **Assessing practice activities**

For each scenario, ask yourself:

1. What is the apparent goal of the practice activity?
2. How far is this goal achieved?
3. What are the factors that make it effective or ineffective?
4. If you could redesign the material or offer advice to the teacher, what would you suggest?

If you have studied the previous unit you may find it helpful to apply some of the criteria suggested there.

Comments on the Scenarios in Box 2.2

Scenario 1: Spelling

The procedure as described here is apparently meant to practise the spelling of the word *journal*. But out of (say) a minute spent by the students on the total guessing process, they engage with the actual spelling of the target word for not more than a few seconds at the end: the rest of the time is spent on more or less random calling out of letters, or on mistaken guesses. In other words, we have an activity at least nine-tenths of which contributes little or nothing to practice of the target language form: it lacks validity and 'volume'.

This is an interesting example of an activity which is superficially attractive – motivating and fun for both learners and teacher, as well as demanding little preparation – but which when carefully examined proves to have very little learning value. Its usefulness is pretty well limited, in my opinion, to its function as a 'fun' time-filler.

If we wish to practise the spelling of a set of words, then it is better to display the words from the beginning, and think of a procedure that will induce learners to engage with their spelling, as in the example given in the Notes, (2).

Scenario 2: Listening comprehension

The aim of this exercise is apparently listening practice, but it lacks validity. For

BOX 2.2: PRACTICE SCENARIOS

Scenario 1: Spelling

(This is based on the game 'Hangman'. If you are not familiar with it, a full description can be found in the Notes, (3).)

The teacher writes seven dashes on the board, and invites the students to guess what letters they represent. They start guessing letters:

Student 1:   E.
Teacher: No. (Writes E on the board, and a base-line indicating the foot of a gallows)
Student 2:   A.
Teacher: Right. (Fills in A on the second-to-last dash)
Student 3:   S.
Teacher: No. (Writes up S, draws in a vertical line in the gallows-drawing)

… And so on. After a minute or so of guessing, the class arrives at the word 'JOURNAL', which is written up in full on the board. It is then erased, and the teacher, or a student, thinks of another word, marks up the corresponding number of dashes, and the guessing process is repeated.

Scenario 2: Listening comprehension

The class listen to the following recorded text:

Ozone is a gas composed of molecules possessing three oxygen atoms each (as distinct from oxygen, which has two atoms per molecule). It exists in large quantities in one of the upper layers of the atmosphere, known as the stratosphere, between 20 and 50 kilometres above the surface of the earth.

The ozone layer filters out a large proportion of the sun's ultra-violet rays and thus protects us from the harmful effects of excessive exposure to such radiation.

The teacher then tells the students to open their books and answer the multiple-choice questions on a certain page. The multiple-choice questions are:

1. The passage is discussing the topic of
   a) radiation.   b) oxygen.   c) ozone.   d) molecules.

2. Ozone molecules are different from oxygen molecules in that they
   a) have three atoms of oxygen.
   b) exist in large quantities.
   c) may have one or two atoms.
   d) have one atom of oxygen.

3. The stratosphere is
   a) above the atmosphere.
   b) below the atmosphere.
   c) more than 20 kilometres above the surface of the earth.
   d) more than 50 kilometres above the surface of the earth.

4. The ozone layer
   a) prevents some harmful radiation from reaching the earth.
   b) stops all ultra-violet rays from reaching the earth.
   c) protects us from the light of the sun.
   d) involves excessive exposure to ultra-violet rays.

When the students have finished, the teacher asks volunteers for their answers, accepting or correcting as appropriate.

≫→

Scenario 3: Grammar exercise

The teacher writes on the board a sentence that describes a present situation:

> Tom is looking in all his pockets, but he cannot find his keys. (lose)

She asks the students to suggest a sentence in the present perfect that describes what has happened to produce this situation, using the verb in brackets at the end. A student volunteers:

> Tom has lost his keys.

The teacher approves this answer and writes up a second, similar sentence:

> The Browns live in that house on the corner, but they are not there at the moment. (go away)

Another student volunteers the answer; this time it is wrong, and the teacher asks someone else, who produces a correct answer.

The teacher continues the same process with another four similar sentences.

Scenario 4: Vocabulary

Teacher: Who knows the meaning of the word disappointment? (Puzzled looks; a student hesitantly puts up his hand) Yes?
Student 1:   Write a point?
Teacher: No … anyone else? (silence) Come on, think everybody, try again!
Student 2:   Lose a point?
Teacher: No, it has nothing to do with points. Try again. It has something to do with feelings.

(After another few guesses, the last of which, after broad hints from the teacher, comes fairly near, the teacher finally gives the correct definition.)

© Cambridge University Press 1996

one thing, there is more reading than listening: the reading text (the questions) is longer than the listening, and more time is spent dealing with it during the procedure as a whole. For another, it relies heavily on memory rather than on ongoing comprehension: learners need to recall accurately a set of facts presented very densely and quickly, which may be extremely difficult for those who did not know them before, since this is a specialist area of knowledge which may be unfamiliar to them. If, on the other hand, they did know them, then they will probably be able to answer the questions without listening at all. The activity also scores low on 'volume' (the listening text is very short) and on 'heterogeneity' (there are no opportunities for giving responses at different levels).

A better task might be to ask the learners to take notes on the text as they hear it, and then compare with each other or with a replay of the original text. Alternatively, brief questions might be given in advance, so that learners can listen out for the answers and note them down as they hear them. And the text itself of course would be improved if it presented the information in the form of an explanation improvised from notes.

For a more detailed discussion of effective classroom listening practice see Module 8: *Teaching listening*.

Scenario 3: Grammar

This exercise practises the present perfect tense and aspect.

Again, the target language is not very efficiently practised. For one thing, more than half the time and energy of teacher and class is spent on writing and reading sentences which do not use the present perfect at all, but only the present (in other words, it lacks validity). For another, the whole exercise produces only six instances of the target structure: not very much (lack of 'volume'). Moreover, the exercise is not very interesting, and lacks 'heterogeneity': the questions are closed-ended, allowing for little or no variety of response.

'Cue' items in grammar exercises of this kind, particularly if they consist of entire sentences, are best presented to the class either orally or through prepared texts (overhead transparencies, worksheets, textbooks): writing them out on the board is very time-consuming. But it is in general best to keep such cue items fairly short and have the learners use most of their time in responses that involve the structure. For the present perfect, for example, you might suggest a series of exclamations (*Oh!*, *Thank you!*, *Congratulations!*, etc.) and invite the class to suggest what *has happened* to provoke them. Or present pictures of situations and ask what *has*, or *has not happened*. Such exercises are also more interesting than the closed-ended example given here, since they invite learners to use their imagination and originality in thinking of answers, as well as allowing for both simpler and more advanced use of language.

Even the original items can be made more productive, interesting and heterogeneous simply by omitting the verb in brackets at the end of the cue sentence, and inviting learners to base their responses on their own ideas.

Scenario 4: Vocabulary

This may look like a caricature of vocabulary teaching; but I have seen it happen. The students do not know the target word – a fact which should have been obvious to the teacher immediately – and his or her response should have been to present its meaning as quickly and clearly as possible, and then use the remaining time for further illustration and practice. Instead, the students have been allowed 'flounder' unsuccessfully for a wasted minute or two, adding nothing to their knowledge of the word, and contributing only to their feelings of frustration, failure and inferiority. The activity is 'failure-oriented' and fails to give much real practice in the target item, mainly because of the lack of assistance – indeed, of teaching itself, as I understand the term – provided by the teacher.

If learners do not know (or remember) the words to be practised, these should be (re-)taught, and then practised through contextualization in sentences or situations which induce repeated use of the words. For example, the class is given a cue which is the start of a sentence such as 'I felt very disappointed when …' and suggest different completed versions.

▷ ## Unit Four: Sequence and progression in practice

The individual practice procedure should ideally be integrated into a series of activities that help the learner progress from strongly teacher-supported controlled practice at the beginning to later automatic and eventually autonomous reception and production of the language. This unit deals with the design of such a series, and is based on a task as described below.

The sample activities shown in Box 2.3 deal with cardinal numbers, from one to twenty. These are items that have to be mastered fairly early on in the learning of any language, and are at once a set, with an obvious progressive order, and separate meaningful items. The most important problem I have found in the teaching of numbers is rooted in this last feature: learners seem to learn the series (*one*, *two*, *three*, *four* …) by heart quite easily, but then have considerable difficulty identifying, say, *eight* as corresponding immediately to the particular numerical value it represents. Often they have to count up through all the lower numbers, using their fingers, until they reach it and can identify it by its mother-tongue equivalent.

The activities shown in Box 2.3 are designed for learners who have previously been taught the numbers and can recite them from memory, though they may still hesitate and make occasional mistakes.

Task   **Thinking about the sequencing of practice activities**

Stage 1: Ordering

Rearrange the activities in Box 2.3 in the order in which you would do them in a lesson or series of lessons.

Stage 2: Improving

Suggest any alterations or additions you might make to any of the activities in the list to improve their effectiveness. You may, of course, decide that there is one (or more) that you would not use at all.

Next, note any aspects of the language topic that you think are inadequately covered or not covered at all during the practice series. Create or select from textbooks some further activities which would cover the inadequacies you have noted and/or enhance learning of the target language in any way. Decide at what stage you would insert them.

My solution, with comments, follows.

Possible solution to the task

The order in which I would do these activities is: 3, 4, 1, 2.

Activity 3 demands nothing from most of the students beyond the memorization of their own number; other numbers they do not need to respond to. The 'caller' needs to know some other numbers, but not all. Essentially, the numbers are used here only as names, participants do not need to relate to their meaning.

In Activity 4 they need to be able to recognize the correspondence between numerical value (as expressed in the figures) and foreign language number-names; in Activity 1 they actually need to produce the same names themselves. Finally, in Activity 2 they need to both recognize and produce a whole series of numbers at once.

BOX 2.3: SEQUENCING PRACTICE ACTIVITIES

Activity 1
The teacher has written on the board a selection of random numbers, in figures. He or she points to a number, the students call out its name.

Activity 2
The teacher has prepared a duplicated list of telephone numbers; the list has at least as many numbers as there are students in the class. On each paper a different number has been marked with a cross; this indicates to the student who gets the paper which is 'his/her' number.
A student 'dials' a number by calling it out, and the student whose number has been 'dialled' answers, repeats the number and identifies him- or herself. Other students can then fill in the name opposite the appropriate number on their lists. The identified student then 'dials' someone else, and so on.

Activity 3
Pairs of students are allotted numbers from one to twenty, so that any one number is shared by two students. They then mix, and sit in a circle. One student in the centre of the circle calls out a number, and the two students who own that number try to change places. As soon as one of them gets up, the student in the centre tries to sit in the vacated place before it can be filled. If successful, he or she takes over the number of the displaced player who then becomes the caller.

Activity 4
The students write down, as figures, a series of random numbers dictated by the teacher. The answers are then checked.

© Cambridge University Press 1996

Comments

If I were to omit one, it would be Activity 3. It is a lively game, but contributes only to the learners' familiarity with the sounds of the words, not to their knowledge of their meaning. Note also that it is not very appropriate for older learners.

Activities 1 and 4 are as simple to do as they are easy to describe, and provide very useful practice. Activity 2 is rather more elaborate and lengthy, and might get tedious with a big class; perhaps one would need to have relatively short telephone numbers, or activate only some of the learners.

An overall criticism is that there is no activity which involves actual counting. I would therefore add one which includes it – even something as simple as a count of how many doors/windows/lights/chairs/tables/students there are in the room – as one of the earliest number-practice tasks they do.

Other useful contexts for getting learners to engage with numbers are: simulated buying and selling of priced commodities (or pictures of them); doing simple sums aloud; surveys, such as working out the average ages or heights of relatives or number of siblings of the students; estimating quantities or weights of displayed foods and then checking; discussion of sports results, or athletic achievements; planning an itinerary with estimated distances and times. Also, of course, learners should be encouraged to use the foreign language in lessons when summing up results of other activities. For example: how many items did you find in a brainstorming task? How many questions in this exercise did you get right?

The most advanced activity is that where learners are quickly and automatically producing the foreign language number in order to represent the appropriate numerical value, and can also manipulate the numbers easily in simple arithmetic. This is, of course, within a situation where a learner is communicating with others: it is unrealistic and, in my opinion, pointless to expect learners to stop counting to themselves or doing mental arithmetic in their mother tongue!

The practice activities shown in this and the previous unit are only a tiny sample of the wide variety of techniques available to the language teacher. For more, see language textbooks, or teacher's handbooks (some suggestions are given under *Further reading* below).

Notes

(1) Skills

Some skills that people commonly learn through instruction are: driving a car, dancing, cooking, using a computer, playing a musical instrument, working a piece of electrical equipment or machinery.

(2) An example of an effective practice activity

Spelling

The teacher wrote up a set of ten words with problematic spelling, scattered over the board. The students were given a minute or so to look at them and review their spellings. The teacher then announced that she was going to erase one of them, and the students would have to write down its spelling from memory. A brief 'wander' over the board with the eraser ended with due elimination of one of the words, and the students wrote it down. (One student said he could not remember what it was; the teacher repeated it orally.) The process was repeated until the board was empty. Students then compared their results with each other, helping each other to correct wherever necessary. At the end of the activity the teacher rewrote the original words on the board for a final check.

The students remarked afterwards that the activity had helped to fix the spellings in their minds; and the teacher noticed that this was borne out by their subsequent performance in free writing.

(Variations on this activity: the teacher erases all the words and asks students in pairs or small groups to try to recall as many of them as they can; or they are asked to find similarities between the spelling of two or more words in the group – for example, that these two words end with the same letter, or those two have a double consonant in the middle.)

(3) 'Hangman'

The game is played as follows. One player thinks of a word and writes down a series of dashes, which represent the series of letters that make up the word. The other players then guess what the letters are. If they guess a letter right, the first player has to fill it in on the relevant dash(es). If they guess wrong, he or she may draw one (more) component of a drawing of a man hanging on a gallows. The guesses continue until either the whole word has been guessed, or the hangman drawing has been finished. The completed drawing looks something like this:

If the first player completes the drawing before the others have guessed the word, he or she wins, and may choose another word to be guessed. If the word is guessed first, then the player to fill in the last letter(s) of the word may choose the next.

Further reading

BACKGROUND

Anderson, J. R. (1985) *Cognitive Psychology and its Implications*, New York: Freeman, Chapter 8, pp. 222–54.
(The process of learning a cognitive skill clearly presented, with evidence from research)
Gatbonton, E. and Segalowitz, N. (1988) 'Creative automatization: principles for promoting fluency within a communicative framework', *TESOL Quarterly*, **22**, 3, 473–92.
(Interesting article on effective practice and automatization in spoken language, with practical suggestions)
Johnson, K. (1995) *Language Teaching and Skill Learning*, Oxford: Basil Blackwell.
(A more detailed discussion of the model of language learning suggested in Unit One)

TEACHER'S HANDBOOKS

Gairns, R. and Redman, S. (1986) *Working with Words*, Cambridge: Cambridge University Press.
Ur, P. (1988) *Grammar Practice Activities*, Cambridge: Cambridge University Press.
(Two books with a wide range of practice activities in vocabulary and grammar respectively. They are based on English; but most of the techniques are easily transferable to other languages)

These are only samples of a wide range of handbooks available; see also books in the following series:

Cambridge Handbooks for Language Teachers, edited by Michael Swan: Cambridge University Press.

In Action series: Prentice Hall International.

Resource Books for Teachers, edited by Alan Maley: Oxford University Press.

Module 3: Tests

Note: This module covers issues of purpose, design and administration of tests in language teaching in general. Tests of some specific topics are discussed in other modules: see particularly Unit Five of Module 5: *Teaching vocabulary* and Unit Six of Module 9: *Teaching speaking*.

▶ Unit One: What are tests for?

Some preliminary definitions

A test may be defined as an activity whose main purpose is to convey (usually to the tester) how well the testee knows or can do something. This is in contrast to practice, whose main purpose is sheer learning. Learning may, of course, result from a test, just as feedback on knowledge may be one of the spin-offs of a practice activity: the distinction is in the main goal.

It is often conventionally assumed that tests are mostly used for assessment: the test gives a score which is assumed to define the level of knowledge of the testee. This may be in order to decide whether he or she is suitable for a certain job or admission to an institution, has passed a course, can enter a certain class. But in fact testing and assessment overlap only partially: there are other ways of assessing students (an overview of assignments over a long period, for example, or the teacher's opinion, or self-evaluation) and there are certainly other reasons for testing (see below, Box 3.1). This unit concentrates on testing as a teaching act; some discussion of aspects of **assessment** can be found in Unit Two of Module 17: *Giving feedback*, or for more thorough coverage see Brindley (1989).

Inquiry **Reasons for testing**

Stage 1: Inquiry

Think about and write down the main reasons why you (would) test in the language classroom. Ask one or two experienced teachers what their main reasons are; and then ask some learners if they think being tested is helpful or important, and if so why. Note down the answers.

Stage 2: Critical reflection

Look at the list given in Box 3.1. These are the main reasons why I test in the classroom – not necessarily in order of importance. Consider, or discuss, the following questions about them.

1. How do the ideas in Box 3.1 compare with the results of your own inquiry and/or your own ideas?
2. Are there any ideas suggested by your respondents or yourself that are not mentioned here?
3. Are there any ideas here that you did not find or think of before?
4. Would you reject any of them as not significant, or irrelevant to your situation?

Stage 3: Reservations

As a by-product of your investigation and thinking up to now, you have probably come across some convincing reasons for *not* testing: the tension and negative feelings tests cause learners, for example, or the fact that they are very time-consuming. Note down all such reasons you can think of before moving on to the summary suggested in the next stage.

BOX 3.1: REASONS FOR TESTING

Tests may be used as a means to:

1. give the teacher information about where the students are at the moment, to help decide what to teach next;
2. give the students information about what they know, so that they also have an awareness of what they need to learn or review;
3. assess for some purpose external to current teaching (a final grade for the course, selection);
4. motivate students to learn or review specific material;
5. get a noisy class to keep quiet and concentrate;
6. provide a clear indication that the class has reached a 'station' in learning, such as the end of a unit, thus contributing to a sense of structure in the course as a whole;
7. get students to make an effort (in doing the test itself), which is likely to lead to better results and a feeling of satisfaction;
8. give students tasks which themselves may actually provide useful review or practice, as well as testing;
9. provide students with a sense of achievement and progress in their learning.

© Cambridge University Press 1996

Stage 4: Summary

Which of your list of reasons for testing are, or would be, the most important for you personally? And how far are these offset by the disadvantages of testing you have just listed?

Summarize for yourself the answers to these questions, perhaps in discussion with colleagues. If you do discuss, note that it may not be appropriate here to try to reach a group consensus, even if you all share a similar teaching situation, as your reasons may depend to some extent on your own beliefs and teaching style, and may vary according to different situations or stages in the course. But try to come to some general conclusions as to when, or if, you yourself would in principle give tests, and why.

▶ **Unit Two: Basic concepts; the test experience**

This unit reviews some basic concepts to do with test design through asking you to prepare and do a test yourself, and then goes on to discuss the test experience as such.

Experiment   **Taking a test**

The test presented here is of the conventional type in which you answer a paper of given questions in writing within a limited time, in silence, in the classroom. The material you will be tested on consists of concepts associated with testing itself.

Stage 1: Preparation

Prepare for the test by learning the material you will be tested on. This consists of the following.

1. The theoretical concepts: validity, reliability, backwash (or washback).
2. The distinction between the following pairs of concepts:
   – achievement v. proficiency tests
   – diagnostic v. prognostic tests
   – discrete-point v. integrative tests
   – subjective v. objective tests.
3. The form of the following types of test items:
   – multiple-choice (including the concepts of 'stem', 'options', 'distractors')
   – cloze.

The necessary information can be found laid out as short sample answers in the Notes, or more fully in Heaton (1990), and in other sources listed in *Further reading*.

Stage 2: Doing the test

When you are ready, try doing the test in Box 3.2. You have twenty minutes. Your results will be expressed as a percentage; each of Questions 1–10 is worth ten marks. Question 11 is optional.

Stage 3: Checking

Check your answers against those given in your sources in the literature, or using the brief sample answers in the Notes. Give yourself a mark out of 100.

Stage 4: Reflection and discussion

Reflecting on the test experience you have just had, and perhaps on other test experiences, think about and/or discuss the following questions.

1. (If you did optional Question 11, look at your answer.) How did you feel about being tested? You may have felt: irritated, unpleasantly stressed, acceptably or even pleasantly tense, indifferent. Any other reactions or comments?

BOX 3.2: TEST ON TESTING

1. What is a 'valid' test?
2. What is a 'reliable' test?
3. What is 'backwash'?
4. What is the difference between an 'achievement' test and a 'proficiency' test?
5. What is the difference between a 'diagnostic' test and a 'prognostic' test?
6. Can you give an example of a 'discrete-point' test?
7. Can you give an example of an 'integrative' test?
8. Are Questions 1–7 above examples of 'objective' or 'subjective' test items? Why?
9. Give examples of:
   a) a multiple-choice item
   b) an extract from a cloze test.
10. Within the multiple-choice item you have given, can you identify:
    a) the stem?
    b) the options?
    c) the distractors?
11. (Optional) How have you felt about doing this test?

© Cambridge University Press 1996

---

2. Did the fact that you knew you were going to be tested make any difference to how well you learned the material in advance?
3. Would you have preferred not to sum up your overall result (so much out of 100)? Or do you feel it important to get some kind of (numerical?) assessment after a test?
4. Would you have preferred someone else to check your answers?

Stage 5: Implications for teaching

You have just experienced a test from the point of view of a testee, and discussed that experience. Returning now to the role of teacher, go through your answers to each of the questions above and think about how they might affect the way you would, or should, test in the classroom.

Some comments of my own follow.

Comments on the questions

1. People vary very widely in their reactions to tests. Some like the sense of challenge; others find it unpleasant. Some perform at their best under test conditions, others perform badly.

   Thus, it would be a mistake to come out with sweeping statements like: 'People get very stressed when they are tested', or 'Tests are unpopular'. The amount of unpleasant stress associated with a test depends on various factors, at least some of which may be under the control of the teacher: how well the learners are prepared for it and how confident they feel of success; what rewards and penalties are associated with success or failure (how important the results are perceived to be); how clear the test items are; how easy the test is as a whole; how often such tests are given; and so on. (Some ideas on what the teacher can do to reduce test anxiety may be found in Unit Five.)

2. Here one can generalize: for most people the foreknowledge that there is going to be a test produces more conscientious learning of the material. Whether this is a morally or educationally desirable way of getting people to learn is another question. My own opinion is that testing is one acceptable way of raising short-term motivation to learn specific material, but that if it is used as such very often, and as the main source of pressure to learn, then there may be long-term negative results. Both teacher and learners may cease to seek and find enjoyment or satisfaction in the learning itself, or to see the goal of knowing the language as intrinsically valuable: the whole teaching–learning process is in danger of being devalued, of being seen merely as a means to get good grades.

3. Most learners like to know how well they did on a test, and the assessment is perhaps most conveniently expressed as a number. Even people who do not like being tested may feel cheated and disappointed if they are not told their score. They often do not, however, wish other people to know: so it may not be a good idea to publish results by name.

4. People's responses to this question depend to a very large extent on what they are used to in their own learning experience. Perhaps most tend to prefer their work to be checked by someone they perceive as authoritative; but even more important is their reliance on that person's fair and unbiased evaluation.

▶ Unit Three: Types of test elicitation techniques

Formal and informal testing

Tests in the classroom may be of the conventional type exemplified in the previous unit, where the testees are told in advance what they need to know, what the criteria are for success, and so on. But they may also be informal: a homework assignment may in fact function as a test if the teacher's main aim in giving it is to find out whether the learners have learned some language point or not; questions asked during the routine give-and-take of classroom interaction may serve the same purpose, as may some textbook exercises.

Analysing elicitation techniques

Tests, whether formal or informal, utilize one or more of a large number of elicitation techniques. Some of the more common of these are listed in Box 3.3; more comprehensive taxonomies can be found in, for example, Hughes, 1989.

Which you will choose to use for a certain testing purpose will probably depend mainly on the following considerations:

1. What will it tell me about the testee's knowledge? In other words, for what type of knowledge might it be a valid test?
2. How easy is it to compose?
3. How easy is it to administer?
4. How easy is it to mark?

BOX 3.3: ELICITATION TECHNIQUES

1. **Questions and answers.** Simple questions, very often following reading, or as part of an interview; may require short or long answers:

   What is the (family) relationship between David Copperfield and Mr Murdstone?

2. **True/false.** A statement is given which is to be marked true or false. This may also be given as a question, in which case the answer is yes or no.

   Addis Ababa is the capital of Egypt.
   Is Addis Ababa the capital of Egypt?

3. **Multiple-choice.** The question consists of a stem and a number of options (usually four), from which the testee has to select the right one.

   A person who writes books is called
   a) a booker.   b) an editor.   c) an author.   d) a publisher.

4. **Gap-filling and completion.** The testee has to complete a sentence by filling a gap or adding something. A gap may or may not be signalled by a blank or dash; the word to be inserted may or may not be given or hinted at.

   They (go) to Australia in 1980.
   Or
   They _____ to Australia in 1980. (go)
   Or
   A _____ is someone who writes books.
   Or
   I've seen that film. (never)

5. **Matching.** The testee is faced with two groups of words, phrases or sentences; each item in the first group has to be linked to a different item in the second.

   large   small
   unhappy   many
   a lot   big
   little   sad

6. **Dictation.** The tester dictates a passage or set of words; the testee writes them down.

7. **Cloze.** Words are omitted from a passage at regular intervals (for example, every seventh word). Usually the first two or three lines are given with no gaps.

   The family are all fine, though Leo had a bad bout of flu last week. He spent most of it lying on the sofa watching _____ when he wasn't sleeping!

   His exams _____ in two weeks, so he is _____ about missing school, but has managed to _____ quite a lot in spite _____ feeling ill.

8. **Transformation.** A sentence is given; the testee has to change it according to some given instruction.

   Put into the past tense:
   I go to school by bus.

9. **Rewriting.** A sentence is given; the testee rewrites it, incorporating a given change of expression, but preserving the basic meaning.

   He came to the meeting in spite of his illness.
   Although ….

10. **Translation.** The testee is asked to translate expressions, sentences or entire passages to or from the target language.

---

11. **Essay.** The testee is given a topic, such as 'Childhood memories', and asked to write an essay of a specific length.

12. **Monologue.** The testee is given a topic or question and asked to speak about it for a minute or two.

© Cambridge University Press 1996

Task　**Critical study of elicitation techniques**

Try applying the above considerations to the set of elicitation techniques shown in Box 3.3.

My own comments follow.

Comments

1. Questions and answers

These can be used to test almost anything. The more 'closed' the question is (that is, the fewer the possible options for correct answers), the easier the item will be to mark. It is fairly easy to compose and grade closed-ended questions; more open, thought-provoking ones are more difficult, but may actually test better.

2. True/false

This does not directly test writing or speaking abilities: only listening or reading. It may be used to test aspects of language such as vocabulary, grammar, content of a reading or listening passage. It is fairly easy to design; it is also easy to administer, whether orally or in writing, and to mark.

3. Multiple-choice

This may be used for the same testing purposes as true/false items; it does test rather more thoroughly since it offers more optional answers and is obviously very easy to mark. It is administered more conveniently through writing; but note that since the reading of the question-and-options is fairly time-consuming, the process of comprehension of the actual question items may take more time and effort than the point ostensibly tested, which raises problems of validity. Another important problem is that good multiple-choice questions are surprisingly difficult to design: they often come out ambiguous, or with no clear right answer, or with their solutions over-obvious. They are to be approached with caution!

4. Gap-filling and completion

This usually tests grammar or vocabulary, as in the examples. It is tedious to compose, though not so difficult as multiple-choice; it is more easily administered in writing than in speech; the marking is usually simple. You may need to be aware that there is more than one possible right answer.

5. Matching

This usually tests vocabulary, and is rather awkward to administer orally: thus it is best presented written on the board or on paper, though responses may be either oral or in writing. Items can be time-consuming and difficult to compose, and again, there may be alternative 'right' answers to any particular item. Answers are fairly easily checked.

6. Dictation

This mainly tests spelling, perhaps punctuation, and, perhaps surprisingly on the face of it, listening comprehension: people can only usually write words down accurately from dictation if they understand them. It does not, however, test other writing skills or speech, and involves very little reading. It may supply some information on testees' passive knowledge of pronunciation, grammar and vocabulary. It is very easy to prepare and administer; it is relatively easy to mark, though there may be a problem deciding how much weight to attribute to different mistakes.

7. Cloze

This tests (intensive) reading, spelling, and to some extent knowledge of vocabulary and grammar. It can be adapted to 'target' specific language items, by, for example, omitting all the verbs (in which case it is not, strictly speaking, 'cloze', but rather 'gap-filling'). It is fairly easy to prepare and administer. Marking can be tricky: you may find it difficult sometimes to decide if a specific item is 'acceptable' or not.

8. Transformation

This item is relatively easy to design, administer and mark, but its validity may be suspect. It tests the ability of the testee to transform grammatical structures, which is not the same as testing grammar: a testee may perform well on transformation items without knowing the meaning of the target structure or how to use it in context. Marking is fairly straightforward.

9. Rewriting

This tests the same sort of thing as transformation, but is likely to reflect more thorough knowledge of the target items, since it involves paraphrasing the entire meaning of a sentence rather than transforming a particular item. It is, however, more difficult to compose, and the marking may be more subjective. It is, as its name suggests, usually done in writing.

10. Translation

A technique which, at the time of writing, is for various reasons rather unpopular, but in my opinion undeservedly so. In a monolingual class whose teacher also speaks the learners' mother tongue, the translation of a 'bit' of language to or from the target language can give very quick and reliable information on what the testee does or does not know, particularly when it involves entire units of meaning (phrases, sentences) within a known context. Translation items are also relatively easy to compose – even improvise, in an informal test – and administer, in either speech or writing. Marking may sometimes be more difficult, but not prohibitively so.

11. Essay

This is a good test of general writing abilities. It is relatively easy to provide a topic and tell the class to write an essay about it but marking is extremely difficult and time-consuming. It must be clear in advance, both to you and to the students, how much emphasis you are going to lay on language forms, such as spelling, grammar, punctuation, and how much on aspects of content, such as interest and originality of ideas, effectiveness of expression, organization (see Module 11: *Teaching writing*).

12. Monologue

This tests oral fluency in 'long turns' – something not everyone can do in their mother tongue! It also tests overall knowledge of pronunciation, grammar and vocabulary. To choose a topic and allot it is not so difficult; to assess is very difficult indeed, demanding concentration and a very clear set of criteria and weighting system (see the Unit Six of Module 9: *Teaching speaking*).

▷ # Unit Four: Designing a test

In this unit you are asked to design your own test. This should be for a learner population you know: a class you teach or have taught, or the kind of class you have in the past been a member of yourself. Ideally, of course, the test should be one that can be integrated into your own teaching programme with your own class, and that you will have a chance to administer in practice.

The material to be tested should, similarly, be part of a syllabus and teaching programme you are familiar with: perhaps a section of a coursebook, or certain elements of a set curriculum.

Task **Designing a test**

Stage 1: Preparation

Prepare your test. It is a good idea to list in writing all the material that you want your test to cover: you can then refer back to the list during and after the test-writing to see if you have included all you intended.

You may find it helpful at this stage to refer to the guidelines listed in Box 3.4.

Stage 2: Performance

If possible, administer your test to a class of learners; if not, ask colleagues to try doing it themselves.

Stage 3: Feedback

Look at how your test was done, and ask the testees how they felt about it. You might find it helpful to base your questions on the criteria in the guidelines in Box 3.4.

BOX 3.4: GUIDELINES FOR TEST PREPARATION

Validity. Check that your items really do test what they are meant to!

Clarity. Make sure the instructions for each item are clear. They should usually include a sample item and solution.

'Do-ability'. The test should be quite do-able: not too difficult, with no trick questions. Ask a colleague to read through it and answer the questions before finalizing.

Marking. Decide exactly how you will assess each section of the test, and how much weighting (percentage of the total grade) you will give it. Make the marking system as simple as you can, and inform the testees what it is: write in the number of points allotted after the instructions for each question.

Interest. Try to go for interesting content and tasks, in order to make the test more motivating for the learners.

Heterogeneity. The test should be such that lower-level students can feel that they are able to do a substantial part of the test, while the higher-level ones have a chance to show what they know. So include both easy and difficult items, and make one or more of the difficult ones optional. (See Module 21: *Large heterogeneous classes* for more discussion of materials for heterogeneous classes.)

© Cambridge University Press 1996

▷ # Unit Five: Test administration

The actual design of a test, whether oral or written, formal or informal is, of course, important, but it is not the end of the story. How the test is actually administered and returned can make a huge difference to motivation and performance; in particular, sensitive presentation of a test can significantly reduce learner anxiety.

Task ## Thinking about test administration

Let us assume that you are going to administer and mark a formal written test (whether or not you have written it yourself) in the course of your teaching programme. How will you prepare for, present and give feedback on it? Have in mind a teaching situation you are familiar with – your own class, if you are teaching, or the kind of class you expect to be teaching in due course – and a particular kind of test (preferably a specific one you have administered or taken yourself).

You may find it convenient to use the questions in Box 3.5 as a basis for thinking or discussion. Some suggested answers follow, based on my own teaching experience.

Some possible answers to the questions in Box 3.5

In answering these questions I have in mind the periodic (once-a-month or so)

BOX 3.5: QUESTIONS ON TEST ADMINISTRATION

Before the test
- How far in advance do you announce the test?
- How much do you tell the class about what is going to be in it, and about the criteria for marking?
- How much information do you need to give them about the time, place, any limitations or rules?
- Do you give them any 'tips' about how best to cope with the test format?
- Do you expect them to prepare at home, or do you give them some class time for preparation?

Giving the test
- How important is it for you yourself to administer the test?
- Assuming that you do, what do you say before giving out the test papers?
- Do you add anything when the papers have been distributed but students have not yet started work?
- During the test, are you absolutely passive or are you interacting with the students in any way?

After the test
- How long does it take you to mark and return the papers?
- Do you then go through them in class?
- Do you demand any follow-up work on the part of the students?

© Cambridge University Press 1996

---

tests I give to summarize the end of a teaching unit. My class is composed of adolescents learning English as a foreign language in a state secondary school.

Before the test

I use the period leading up to the test in order to do all I can to ensure that my students will succeed in it. Thus the tests are announced at least a week in advance in order to give them plenty of time to prepare and details are given of when, where and how long the test will be. The class is also told as precisely as possible what material is to be tested, what sort of items will be used, and how answers will be assessed. I sometimes give them 'test-tips' – for example, how best to allot time, or what to do first – particularly if they are coming near to the state school-leaving exam, for which my course is to some extent a preparation. I usually allow at least some class time for revision, in order to encourage and help with pre-test learning.

Giving the test

It is quite important for me to administer the test myself, and more pleasant for my students. Thus, I will be able, if I wish, to remind them about the test content, format and marking system before giving out the papers; and sometimes run through the instructions with them after doing so in order to make sure that everything is clear – as well as wishing them good luck!

During the test, I may help students who still have difficulty with instructions; I do not normally help with the content itself.

After the test

The tests are marked and returned as quickly as possible (within a week) so that we can discuss specific points while the test is still fresh in the students' minds. Usually I will go through the answers in class, but fairly briskly; points that seem to produce special problems I note for more leisurely re-presentation and further practice in the future. I do not usually ask students to copy out corrected answers: this is, I think, more tedious than helpful for them. It is better and more interesting to provide the practice in the same language points in other activities, using new content and tasks.

Notes

Test on testing: Preparation, or sample answers

1. A 'valid' test is one which actually tests what it is designed or intended to.
2. A 'reliable' test is one that produces consistent results when administered on different occasions.
3. 'Backwash' is the effect, positive or negative, that a test has on the teaching and learning that precede it.
4. An 'achievement' test measures how much of the material taught in a given course, or part of one, has in fact been learned; a 'proficiency' test measures the overall language proficiency of testees, without reference to a particular course.
5. A 'diagnostic' test reveals the strong and weak points of a learner's knowledge; a 'prognostic' test predicts how well he or she is likely to do in a language course.
6. 'Discrete-point' tests consist of separate items. For example, the following set of items testing vocabulary:

    Another word for 'sea' is _____ .
    The opposite of 'proud' is _____ .
    Apples, pears and bananas are _____ .

7. An 'integrative' test involves whole pieces of discourse and tests a relatively broad command of the language: writing an essay for example, or doing a cloze test.
8. Questions 1–7 above are, strictly speaking, 'subjective' test items: the exact way you express your answers may vary, and therefore there is an element of subjective judgement in the way the tester will assess their correctness.
9. (a) An example of a multiple-choice item:

    Many people these days _____ have enough to eat.

    (1) doesn't   (2) isn't   (3) don't   (4) aren't

    (b) An extract from a cloze test:

    A cold front is approaching from _____ west and we can
    therefore expect lower _____ tomorrow throughout the

country. There is _____ to be some rain in the morning,
_____ it will become brighter later in the _____ .

10. Within the multiple-choice item above, the stem is 'Many people these days
     have enough to eat'; the options are 'doesn't', 'isn't', 'don't' and 'aren't';
     the distractors (incorrect options) are 'doesn't', 'isn't', 'aren't'.

Further reading

Alderson, C., Clapham, C. and Wall, D. (1995) *Language Test Construction
   and Evaluation*, Cambridge: Cambridge University Press.
   (Detailed and thorough guidance for people involved in composing foreign-
   language tests for assessment)
Brindley, G. (1989) *Assessing Achievement in the Learner-Centred Curriculum*,
   Macquarie University, Sydney: National Centre for English Language
   Teaching and Research.
   (A comprehensive and readable overview of ways of assessment in language
   learning)
Heaton, J. B. (1990) *Classroom Testing*, London: Longman.
   (A simple, readable guide for the language teacher on test design and
   assessment)
Hughes, A. (1989) *Testing for Language Teachers*, Cambridge: Cambridge
   University Press.
   (Longer and more detailed guidelines for teachers on testing; types of
   techniques for assessing different skills; criteria for assessment)
Underhill, N. (1987) *Testing Spoken Language*, Cambridge: Cambridge
   University Press.
   (Readable, interesting; particularly good on elicitation techniques)
Weir, C. (1990) *Communicative Language Testing*, Hemel Hempstead: Prentice
   Hall International.
   (Overview of research and theories, followed by critical analysis of test-types
   (Ch. 4); examples of various standard tests quoted in full)
Weir, C. (1993) *Understanding and Developing Language Tests*, Hemel
   Hempstead: Prentice Hall International.
   (A practical handbook: regular illustrative exercises with following comments
   promote reader understanding and interest)

Just as teaching activities need to be broken down into components for convenient study, so does language itself. In a natural 'immersion' situation learners may be exposed to stretches of naturally-occurring unsimplified language data, and gradually learn the language this way. But in such a situation they may be able to use most of their waking hours engaging with the language, and the ratio of 'teachers' to learners is often one-to-one – luxuries which students on foreign-language courses usually do not have. In any case, even in 'immersion' situations there is some evidence that people speaking to foreigners slow down their speech, simplify and explain more, so that perhaps even here there is a rudimentary selection and grading of language items to be taught and learnt.

In the classroom it is simply more efficient to select and grade the language to be learnt so that learners waste a minimum of time on frustrating incomprehension and have plenty of opportunities to practise what they know and use it as a jump-off point for the learning of new language. But such selection and grading demand first some kind of segmenting of language into 'bits' to be organized into a systematic syllabus (see Module 12: *The syllabus*).

Conventionally, linguists have broken language down into three main components: the phonology, or sound system of the language; the lexis, or the words or phrases which express concepts; the structure, or the way words or bits of words are strung together to make acceptable sentences or phrases. Language teachers define these more conveniently as **pronunciation**, **vocabulary** and **grammar**, and it is the teaching of these three that forms the subject of the first three modules of Part II.

The fourth module describes a different type of language 'segment', but one which is also important and complements the first three. This type of segment may be called 'holistic': language used in a certain context to communicate meanings. Such segments may include the language used to express a certain **topic**, or within a certain **situation**; or that used to express a concept (**notion**) or perform a communicative act (**function**).

A language course may be based on pronunciation, vocabulary and grammar, or on the more 'communicative' categories of topic, situation, notion and function. Probably, however, the most effective teaching and learning result from a combination of them all, in a systematic but flexible programme in which, for example, topics and situations provide a context for the teaching of new words, and structures are learned in order to express notions or functions.

Module 4: Teaching pronunciation

▶ ## Unit One: What does teaching pronunciation involve?

(Much of the content of this unit is specific to English; teachers of other languages may find the general guidelines useful, but should refer to books on their target languages for specific information on their pronunciation.)

The concept of 'pronunciation' may be said to include:

– the sounds of the language, or phonology
– stress and rhythm
– intonation.

The first of these is perhaps the most obvious and clearly defined of the three. However, this does not mean that the other aspects should be neglected: a learner may enunciate the sounds perfectly and still sound foreign because of unacceptable stress and intonation; in Oriental 'tone' languages intonation often makes a difference to meaning.

Sounds

It is useful to be able to list and define the sounds, or phonemes, of the language by writing them down using phonetic[1] representations. Different books vary as to exactly which, and how many, symbols are used; for teachers of (British) English, the simplified, phonemic alphabet shown in Box 4.1 may be helpful. According to this, the sounds of, for example, the sentence 'Peter, come here!' would be represented by /piːtə kʌm hiə/.

To check under-standing Take a dictionary that includes phonetic transcriptions, and check through its phonetic alphabet, some of whose symbols may be different from those suggested in Box 4.1. Look at a few words and their corresponding phonetic representations: make sure you can follow and understand the transcriptions. Now choose ten words at random out of a book, and try transcribing them into phonetic script. If you have used your dictionary's phonetic alphabet, look up the word in the dictionary to check. If you have used the alphabet suggested above, then compare your version with that of a colleague's.

1 The term 'phonetic' is used to refer to transcriptions of the sounds of all human languages which make distinctions between sounds that may not be distinguished in a given language system. 'Phonemic' is used to refer to transcriptions of a particular sound system.

BOX 4.1: THE PHONEMIC ALPHABET

Vowels		Consonants	
Symbol	Examples	Symbol	Examples
/ɑː/	_ar_m _par_t	/b/	_b_ed a_b_out
/æ/	_a_pple bl_a_ck	/d/	_d_o si_d_e
/aɪ/	_eye_s dr_i_ve	/f/	_f_ill sa_f_e
/aʊ/	_ou_t n_ow_	/g/	_g_ood bi_g_
/e/	_e_nd p_e_n	/h/	_h_at be_h_ind
/eɪ/	_eigh_t d_ay_	/j/	_y_es _y_ou
/eə/	_air_ w_ear_	/k/	_c_at wee_k_
/ɪ/	_i_t s_i_t	/l/	_l_ose a_ll_ow
/iː/	_ea_t s_ee_	/m/	_m_e la_m_p
/ɪə/	_ear_ n_ear_	/n/	_n_o a_n_y
/ɒ/	_o_pposite st_o_p	/p/	_p_ut sto_p_
/əʊ/	_o_pen ph_o_ne	/r/	_r_un a_r_ound
/ɔː/	_a_lways m_ore_	/s/	_s_oon u_s_
/ɔɪ/	b_oy_ j_oi_n	/t/	_t_alk las_t_
/ʊ/	w_ou_ld st_oo_d	/v/	_v_ery li_v_e
/uː/	_you_ ch_oo_se	/w/	_w_in s_w_im
/ʊə/	_su_re t_ou_rist	/z/	_z_oo love_s_
/ɜː/	_ear_ly b_ir_d	/ʃ/	_sh_ip pu_sh_
/ʌ/	_u_p l_u_ck	/ʒ/	mea_s_ure u_s_ual
/ə/	_a_go doct_or_	/ŋ/	si_ng_ hopi_ng_
		/tʃ/	_ch_eap cat_ch_
		/θ/	_th_in ba_th_
		/ð/	_th_en o_th_er
		/dʒ/	_J_une a_g_e

(based on Martin Hewings, _Pronunciation Tasks_, Cambridge University Press, 1993, p. vi)

Note that this is quite difficult to do the first time – it takes a good deal of practice and learning to be able to transcribe quickly and accurately.

Rhythm and stress

English speech rhythm is characterized by tone-units: a word or group of words which carries one central stressed syllable (other syllables, if there are any, are lightened). The sentence: 'Peter, come here, please!', for example, would divide into two tone-units: 'Peter' and 'come here, please', with the two main stresses on the first syllable of 'Peter', and the word 'here'.

Stress can also be indicated in writing: probably the simplest way to do so is to write the stressed syllable in capital letters: for example, 'PEter, come HERE, please!'. (Another convention, normally used in phonemic transcriptions, is to put a short vertical line above and before the stressed syllable: /ˈpiːtə kʌm ˈhiə/.)

To check under-standing In pairs: one participant dictates a short sentence, both participants write it down, capitalizing the stressed syllables. Then again, with the other participant dictating. And again, two or three times. Compare your results.

Intonation

Intonation, the rises and falls in tone that make the 'tune' of an utterance, is an important aspect of the pronunciation of English, often making a difference to meaning or implication. Stress, for example, is most commonly indicated not by increased volume but by a slight rise in intonation (Brazil, Coulthard and Johns, 1980). A native speaker usually has little difficulty in hearing intonation changes in his or her own language; others, however, may not find it so easy.

The different kinds of intonation are most simply shown by the symbols ╲ ╱ over the relevant syllable or word in order to show falling and rising intonations; and the symbols ╲╱ ╱╲ to show fall-rise and rise-fall. An appropriate stress and intonation representation for a rather bossy expression of our previous sentence example might be: PEter, come HERE, please.

The rhythm of English is, then, mainly a function of its stress patterns; these may also affect such aspects as speed of delivery, volume and the use of pause.

To check under-standing Listen to a brief recording – one lasting not more than a minute or so – of a speaker of the language you teach (from a listening-comprehension cassette, for example). Write down a sentence from the recording, using conventional spelling, and put in indications of rising and falling intonation and stress. If you are working in a group, compare results with each other.

Flow of speech

It is important also to be aware of the way different sounds, stresses and intonations may affect one another within the flow of speech. For example:

- The way a sound is articulated is influenced by what other sounds are next to it: the *ed* suffix of the past tense in English, for example, may be pronounced /d/, /t/ or /ɪd/ depending on what came immediately before.
- Intonation affects how we hear stress. In fact, stress is not, as mentioned above, usually expressed by saying the stressed syllable louder: it is more often a matter of a raised or lowered tone level, with a slight slowing-down.
- A change in the stress pattern of a word will change its sounds as well: the word *subject*, for example, has the stress on the first syllable when it is a noun, on the second when it is a verb: and this makes a noticeable difference to the sound of the vowels: /ˈsʌbdʒɪkt/, as compared to /səbˈdʒekt/.

Thus, it is useful to be aware of the way sounds, stresses and intonations interact within entire utterances to produce easily comprehensible pronunciation. Having said this, however, it is true that many, perhaps most, words have a 'stable' sound, stress and intonation pattern that can be confidently taught in isolation.

Question Can you think of examples in other languages you know of sounds affecting one another in the stream of speech, or of stress and intonation actually changing the way sounds are articulated?

▷ # Unit Two: Listening to accents

The purpose of this exercise is to find out the specific pronunciation problems of learners by actually listening to examples and having to analyse and define them, and to think about how these problems might be explained to the learners and corrected.

Inquiry ## Identifying elements of foreign pronunciation

Stage 1: Preparing materials

Using audio cassettes, prepare recordings, two to three minutes in length, of foreign accents; this can be done individually or in pairs or groups. The recordings should consist of short interviews with speakers who are not very proficient in the target language. In a country where the target language is not locally spoken, it makes sense to use as interviewees natives of this country, but other accents may be used in addition.

It is, of course, much easier just to ask people to read aloud in order to make the recording, but resist the temptation! There are various reasons for this: someone reading aloud has time to think consciously about how they are speaking, and we are looking for 'intuitive' pronunciation; the reading passage may include words the interviewee does not know; and perception of spelling affects pronunciation. Improvised speech produces much better samples, which may later, incidentally, be used to examine lexical and grammatical errors. If you find it difficult to think of questions for an interview, the interviewee can be asked to describe a picture, or retell a well-known story.

If you have not made such recordings before, make a brief trial recording of a few seconds and play it back in order to check that you have the distance, volume, microphone and so on properly adjusted. Begin the actual interview only when you are sure you are getting a clear recording.

Stage 2: Analysis

Listen to the recordings and try to analyse what it is about the accents which makes them 'foreign'. This is quite difficult; you will find you need to listen to the recording more than once. It is easier if you note the words and phrases which sound generally foreign while listening the first time, and then during later listenings try to define what precisely is wrong with them. If you know the phonetic alphabet and symbols of intonation and stress, this can help, but a rough description of what is wrong in 'lay' language can be quite adequate. You may find it helpful to use the worksheet shown in Box 4.2.

Stage 3: Pooling and comparing

If several such recordings have been made by a group of teachers studying together, then the next stage is to share findings. In small groups, each recording is listened to, and participants try to identify the errors and how and why they think these occur.

BOX 4.2: WORKSHEET: RECORDINGS OF FOREIGN PRONUNCIATION

Speaker's mother tongue: _____

Words/phrases mispronounced	*Define or describe the mistake*

© Cambridge University Press 1996

Stage 4: Drawing conclusions

Discuss your findings, and draw conclusions. Questions that can usefully be investigated here are the following (some possible answers regarding English appear in the Notes).

1. (If only one type of accent was recorded) What seem to be the most common errors?
2. (If there were different accents) Were there foreign-sounding pronunciations that were common to most or all of the speakers, and can you make some generalizations about the kinds of errors?
3. Which errors do you think are the most important to try to correct?
4. Are there any you would not bother to try to correct? Why not?
5. With regard to the errors you want to correct: how would you explain these to the learner?
6. What further ideas do you have for getting learners to improve their pronunciation of the items you have found? (Some suggestions may be found in Box 4.3 below.)

Unit Three: Improving learners' pronunciation

The objective

It needs to be said at the outset that the aim of pronunciation improvement is not to achieve a perfect imitation of a native accent, but simply to get the learner to pronounce accurately enough to be easily and comfortably comprehensible to other (competent) speakers. 'Perfect' accents are difficult if not impossible for most of us to achieve in a foreign language anyway, and may not even be desirable. Many people – even if often subconsciously – feel they wish to maintain a slight mother-tongue accent as an assertion of personal or ethnic identity. This feeling should, surely, be respected.

Inquiry   **Ask a group of learners whether they want to achieve a 'perfect' native accent or not. If they say no, find out whether this is only because they think it is impossible, or because they genuinely do not see it as a desirable objective.**

Why do learners make pronunciation errors?

Learners' errors of pronunciation derive from various sources:

1. A particular sound may not exist in the mother tongue, so that the learner is not used to forming it and therefore tends to substitute the nearest equivalent he or she knows (the substitution of /d/ or /z/ for the English *th* /ð/ as in *that* is a typical example).
2. A sound does exist in the mother tongue, but not as a separate phoneme: that is to say, the learner does not perceive it as a distinct sound that makes a difference to meaning. In Hebrew, for example, both the /ɪ/ and /iː/ (*ship/sheep*) sounds occur, but which is used depends only on where the sound comes in the word or phrase, not what the word means; and if one is substituted for the other, no difference in meaning results. These are called 'allophonic variations' of a phoneme, or 'allophones'. The result is that the Hebrew-speaking learner is not naturally aware of the difference in English, and may not even hear it.

    (On the whole, the second of the two problems is the more difficult. A totally new sound is often easily perceived as alien, and once you can hear a sound you are well on the way to being able to pronounce it. But if you cannot hear it then you cannot even attempt to pronounce it, and the problem of perception needs to be overcome before any progress can be made.)

Question   **Consider some foreign language learners with whom you are familiar – preferably your own students – whose mother tongue you also know. Can you identify instances of mistakes in sound formation and why they make them (for example, the sound does not exist in their own language, or exists only as an allophone)?**

3. The learners have the actual sounds right, but have not learnt the stress patterns of the word or group of words, or they are using an intonation from

their mother tongue which is inappropriate to the target language. The result is a foreign-sounding accent, and possibly misunderstanding.

Question Listen to some not-very-advanced learners speaking the foreign language – or if you did the previous unit, listen again to a recording. Can you identify three or four instances of inappropriate stress or intonation?

Getting learners to perceive

The first thing that needs to be done is to check that the learner can hear and identify the sounds you want to teach. The same goes for intonation, rhythm and stress: can the learner hear the difference between how a competent, or native, speaker of the language says a word, phrase or sentence and how a foreign learner says it?

This can be done by requesting imitation; or seeing if learners can distinguish between minimal pairs (such as *ship/sheep, man/men, thick/tick*; see Gimson, 1978); or by contrasting acceptable with unacceptable pronunciation through recordings or live demonstration.

Note that you can check perception of sounds using single words or even syllables, but work on stress and intonation nearly always needs to be based on longer units.

Question Choose an error that seems to you particularly widespread and persistent. How might you test learners to find out if they really perceive the difference between their version and the correct one?

Telling learners what to do

The next stage for some learners may be some kind of explicit exhortation: this is what it ought to be, this is what you are doing wrong. For sound formation it may help actually to use a sketch of the mouth (see Box 4.3), and to describe the pronunciation of a sound in terms of lips, tongue, teeth, etc. But for other aspects of pronunciation a brief explanation is sufficient, followed by demonstration and an invitation to imitate and practise.

BOX 4.3: PARTS OF THE MOUTH

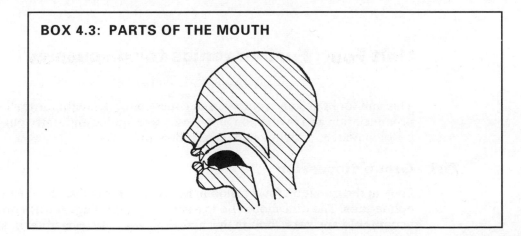

Question Again, choose a typical learner error you are familiar with. How would you explain to the learner what he or she is doing wrong and how to put it right?

BOX 4.4: IDEAS FOR IMPROVING LEARNERS' PRONUNCIATION

- imitation of teacher or recorded model of sounds, words and sentences
- recording of learner speech, contrasted with native model
- systematic explanation and instruction (including details of the structure and movement of parts of the mouth)
- imitation drills: repetition of sounds, words and sentences
- choral repetition of drills
- varied repetition of drills (varied speed, volume, mood)
- learning and performing dialogues (as with drills, using choral work, and varied speed, volume, mood)
- learning by heart of sentences, rhymes, jingles
- jazz chants (see Graham, 1978)
- tongue twisters
- self-correction through listening to recordings of own speech

© *Cambridge University Press 1995*

Practising correct pronunciation

Finally – when we are satisfied that the pronunciation point has been satisfactorily perceived and learners can, if they take care, produce an acceptable version – we come on to the stage of practice: consolidating and establishing the habits of acceptable pronunciation through exercises that provide repetition and reinforcement.

Follow-up task Design some activities of your own in your target language that you feel might give useful practice, perhaps using some of the ideas shown in Box 4.4 as a basis. If you find it difficult to think up ideas on your own, you might find some practical suggestions in the books listed under *Further reading*. Then pool ideas with colleagues; together you should be able to amass a useful 'battery' of activities.

If you have time, try some of them out with students.

▷ Unit Four: Further topics for discussion

This unit looks at some controversial issues connected with the teaching of pronunciation and invites you in the tasks to examine and state your own position on them. My own opinions follow the tasks.

Task **Group discussion**

Look at the questions suggested in Box 4.5, and discuss them with colleagues. The aim should be to arrive at general agreement on acceptable answers, though this may not always be possible. In any case, it is important to clarify exactly what the issues are, and, if there is disagreement, to understand the arguments of all sides.

BOX 4.5: QUESTIONS FOR DISCUSSION ON THE TEACHING OF PRONUNCIATION

1. Does pronunciation need to be deliberately taught? Won't it just be 'picked up'? If it does need to be deliberately taught, then should this be in the shape of specific pronunciation exercises, or casually, in the course of other oral activities?
2. What accent of the target language should serve as a model? (For English, for example, should you use British? American? Other? Local accent?) Is it permissible to present mixed accents (e.g. a teacher who has a 'mid-Atlantic' i.e. a mixed British and American accent)?
3. Can/Should the non-native teacher serve as a model for target language pronunciation?
4. What difference does the learner's age make in learning pronunciation?
5. How important is it to teach intonation, rhythm and stress?

© Cambridge University Press 1996

Before beginning to work on the questions, decide:

– Are there any you wish to omit?
– Are there any others you wish to add?
– Do you wish to change the order?

Decide on and perhaps note down your answers before looking at my own answers as expressed below.

Some possible answers to the questions in Box 4.5

1. The experience of many learners is that pronunciation can be, and often is, acquired adequately by intuitive imitation. Many teachers never teach pronunciation, and their students' command of it seems nevertheless quite satisfactory. However, there is also evidence that deliberate correction and training does improve pronunciation and if this is so it seems a pity to neglect it.

   Probably the deliberate teaching of pronunciation is less essential than, say, the teaching of grammar or vocabulary, but this does not mean it should not be done at all. I would recommend occasional short sessions directing learners' attention to and giving practice in aspects of pronunciation that are clearly problematic for them, as well as casual correction in the course of other activities.
2. In general, it does not matter very much, provided that the model chosen is a standard accent that is easily understood by other speakers of the language. In parts of the world where learners are more likely to have to deal with one particular accent it makes sense to use it, so that for teaching English in Europe the British accent may be preferred, in Japan the American. But even this distinction is becoming less important as time goes on. In any case, even assuming that you are teaching one 'standard' variety as a model, it is a good idea to give learners at least some exposure to others, through the use of 'live' speakers or recordings, in order to raise awareness of other possible accents – and, of course, for listening practice.

3. This question is arguably academic: in many situations the non-native teacher has to be the model whether he or she likes it or not! However, I would say that in any case such a teacher is a perfectly adequate model, provided he or she is, of course, a competent speaker of the language – which one would hope a teacher is anyway! A target language spoken with a slight foreign accent can serve as a model from which learners may acquire perfectly acceptable pronunciation. In any case, it is desirable for learners to be exposed to a number of native and other acceptable accents through the use of recordings, and this is true whatever the mother tongue of the teacher.

4. Children seem to pick up accents very quickly; and the ability to do so seems to diminish with age; though this may be for psychological reasons (a need to preserve one's identity as expressed in the way one speaks) rather than physical or physiological capability. However, this diminished ability is compensated for to some extent by adults' increased ability to understand difficult explanations, discipline themselves and apply instructions. One conclusion might be that conscious pronunciation training is likely to be more helpful with classes of older learners.

5. Intonation in Oriental 'tone' languages has to be taught because it directly affects the meaning of words. In other languages it may affect the implications conveyed by speech, but is very difficult to teach because of the sheer variety and subtlety of the possible patterns. The teacher can, I think, do little more in practice than draw learners' attention to the existence of these patterns, teach a very few common ones, and then rely on exposure and experience to provide the basis for further learning (but see Brazil, Coulthard and Johns, 1980).

We can, to some extent, teach stress and rhythm patterns when teaching vocabulary and grammar; beyond this, what has been said above about intonation applies here also.

▶ Unit Five: Pronunciation and spelling

In most languages there is a fairly clear correspondence between sounds and symbols: certain letters or combinations of letters are pronounced in certain ways, and if there are variations, these are governed by consistent rules: when, for example the letter *c* in English is pronounced /k/ or /s/; when the letter *lam* of the definite article in Arabic is not pronounced. There are, of course, languages where there are many exceptions to such rules, many words whose pronunciation could not be logically predicted from their spelling, and vice versa – English being an example.

The alphabet[1]

The basic sound–symbol correspondence is learned at the stage of learning the alphabet. If the alphabet is a totally new one, then there is a lot to learn, but it is

[1] I am using the term *alphabet* here rather loosely to include the written symbols of language like Chinese, which are not strictly speaking letters but ideograms.

clear that every new symbol needs to be taught with its pronunciation. If, however, the learner is actually using more or less the same alphabet but the letters represent slightly – or very – different sounds (as in the case of English-speaking learners of Spanish, for example) you may have a more subtle teaching problem.

Question (Both questions below apply only if all your students have the same mother tongue.) Either:

1. If your target language uses the same alphabet as the mother tongue of your students, which are the letters which will be pronounced very differently from their native versions? Which will be pronounced only slightly differently? Are there any which are exactly the same? Or:
2. If your target language uses a different alphabet, can you divide it into letters whose sounds have close parallel symbols in the learners' mother tongue (for example, Greek *delta* and English *d*) and those which do not?

Rules of pronunciation–spelling correspondence

Once learners have mastered the basic sound–symbol correspondence they may in some languages be immediately able to decode and pronounce correctly any written text – or, conversely, write down a spoken one. In others, it may not be so simple. They may need a whole set of extra sound–symbol rules: for example, that *-tion* at the end of a word in English is usually pronounced /ʃən/, or that the letter *s* in German is pronounced /ʃ/ when it occurs before /t/ or /p/. Some of these – the more common and urgent for successful reading and writing – you will need to teach consciously and early; others the learners may pick up 'by the way' later on.

Words or sets of words with unusual pronunciation or spelling you may need to teach and practise on their own – some ideas follow at the end of the unit.

Question Can you suggest four or five rules about letter-combinations and their pronunciation in the language you teach that you think it would be important for learners to master in the early stages of learning to speak and read?

Pronunciation and spelling activities

Some ideas that practise pronunciation–spelling correspondences may be found in pronunciation books, such as those listed under *Further reading*; books on spelling usually just give rules, lists of words and then suggest practising through dictation and spelling tests. Dictation is of course one excellent technique (see Davis and Rinvolucri, 1988, for some imaginative variations); and spelling tests can help, but there are many more possibilities. A number of ideas are listed in Box 4.6; note that some of these may not be appropriate if your students do not share a common mother tongue.

Task **Planning and using activities**

Choose three activities for teaching, raising awareness or practising pronunciation–spelling correspondence in the target language: these can be from Box 4.6, or from other sources, or original ideas of your own. Plan actual texts (words, sentences, passages) which you might use in these activities.

If feasible, try using them with a learner in a one-to-one lesson.

BOX 4.6: PRONUNCIATION–SPELLING CORRESPONDENCE: SOME TEACHING IDEAS

– **Dictation:** of random lists of words, of words that have similar spelling problems, of complete sentences, of half-sentences to be completed.
– **Reading aloud:** of syllables, words, phrases, sentences.
– **Discrimination (1):** prepare a set of 'minimal pairs' – pairs of words which differ from each other in one sound–letter combination (such as *dip-deep* in English). Either ask learners to read them aloud, taking care to discriminate, or read them aloud yourself, and ask students to write them down.
– **Discrimination (2):** provide a list of words that are spelt the same in the learners' mother tongue and in the target language: read aloud, or ask learners to, and discuss the differences in pronunciation (and meaning!).
– **Prediction (1):** provide a set of letter combinations, which are parts of words the learners know. How would the learners expect them to be pronounced? Then reveal the full word.
– **Prediction (2):** dictate a set of words in the target language which the learners do not know yet, but whose spelling accords with rules. Can they spell them? (Then reveal meanings.)

© Cambridge University Press 1996

Notes

Pronunciation errors and their correction

Some pronunciation errors common to the speech of many speakers of English as a foreign language are:

– difficulty in pronouncing the *th* sounds /θ/ and /ð/;
– difficulty in pronouncing the neutral 'schwa' vowel (the first syllable of *away*, for example);
– a tendency to give uniform stress to syllables that should be lighter or heavier;
– a tendency to shorten diphthongs and make them into monothongs: for example the sound /ei/ as in *way* tends to be pronounced more like a French é.

You may well find more, or others, that are produced by your learners.

The errors which are most important to correct are those which may easily lead to lack of comprehension, or which make the speech 'uncomfortable' to listen to; by the same principle, errors which produce no comprehension problems but simply make the speech slightly foreign-sounding may not need correcting.

Further reading

BACKGROUND

Brazil, D., Coulthard, M. and Johns, C. (1980) *Discourse Intonation and Language Teaching*, London: Longman.
(Comprehensive discussion of various aspects of intonation and how to teach it)
Roach, P. (1991) *English Phonetics and Phonology: A Practical Course* (2nd edn.) Cambridge: Cambridge University Press.
(Discussion of theoretical background for teacher and learner, some suggestions for exercises)
Swan, M. and Smith, B. (1987) *Learner English*, Cambridge: Cambridge University Press.
(A set of articles on common interference mistakes produced in English by speakers of different languages)

TEACHER'S HANDBOOKS

Bowen, T. and Marks, J. (1992) *The Pronunciation Book*, London: Pilgrims-Longman.
(A collection of imaginative awareness-raising and pronunciation training activities; based on British English but most ideas easily adaptable for use in other languages)
Davis, P. and Rinvolucri, M. (1988) *Dictation: New Methods, New Possibilities*, Cambridge: Cambridge University Press.
(A resource book of varied and imaginative activities based on dictation)
Gimson, A.C. (1978) *A Practical Course of English Pronunciation*, London: Edward Arnold.
(A slim volume: systematic pronunciation training through drills)
Graham, C. (1978) *Jazz Chants*, New York: Oxford University Press.
(Practice in stress and intonation patterns through reciting dialogues in rhythm)
Haycraft, B. (1971) *The Teaching of Pronunciation: A Classroom Guide*, London: Longman.
(Advice on how to teach pronunciation: a readable summary of the issues and practical ideas)
Hewings, M. (1993) *Pronunciation Tasks*, Cambridge: Cambridge University Press.
(Actually a course in English pronunciation; but also an excellent collection of varied and interesting pronunciation tasks that can be adapted for use with other languages)
Kenworthy, J. (1987) *Teaching English Pronunciation*, London: Longman.
(Very readable guidance for teachers: background, ideas for raising learners' awareness, different types of exercises)

Module 5: Teaching vocabulary

▶ ## Unit One: What is vocabulary and what needs to be taught?

What is vocabulary?

Vocabulary can be defined, roughly, as the words we teach in the foreign language. However, a new item of vocabulary may be more than a single word: for example, *post office* and *mother-in-law*, which are made up of two or three words but express a single idea. There are also multi-word idioms such as *call it a day*, where the meaning of the phrase cannot be deduced from an analysis of the component words. A useful convention is to cover all such cases by talking about vocabulary 'items' rather than 'words'.

Question   Can you think of five or six further examples of vocabulary items, in any language you know, that consist of more than one word?

What needs to be taught?

1. Form: pronunciation and spelling
The learner has to know what a word sounds like (its pronunciation) and what it looks like (its spelling). These are fairly obvious characteristics, and one or the other will be perceived by the learner when encountering the item for the first time. In teaching, we need to make sure that both these aspects are accurately presented and learned.

2. Grammar
The grammar of a new item will need to be taught if this is not obviously covered by general grammatical rules. An item may have an unpredictable change of form in certain grammatical contexts or may have some idiosyncratic way of connecting with other words in sentences; it is important to provide learners with this information at the same time as we teach the base form. When teaching a new verb, for example, we might give also its past form, if this is irregular (*think, thought*), and we might note if it is transitive or intransitive. Similarly, when teaching a noun, we may wish to present its plural form, if irregular (*mouse, mice*), or draw learners' attention to the fact that it has no plural at all (*advice, information*). We may present verbs such as *want* and *enjoy* together with the verb form that follows them (*want to, enjoy -ing*), or adjectives or verbs together with their following prepositions (*responsible for, remind someone of*).

Question   Can you think of five or six examples of items in the language you teach whose grammatical characteristics are not obviously covered by a regular grammatical rule, and which you would therefore need to teach when you teach the item?

3. Collocation

The collocations typical of particular items are another factor that makes a particular combination sound 'right' or 'wrong' in a given context. So this is another piece of information about a new item which it may be worth teaching. When introducing words like *decision* and *conclusion*, for example, we may note that you *take* or *make* the one, but usually *come* to the other; similarly, you *throw a ball* but *toss a coin*; you may talk about someone being *dead tired* but it sounds odd to say **dead fatigued*.

Collocations are also often noted in dictionaries, either by providing the whole collocation under one of the head-words, or by a note in parenthesis.

Question   Think of three or four typical collocations in the language you teach, and try translating them into another language. Do the collocations translate exactly? If not, what kinds of learning/teaching problems might this lead to, and what might you do about it?

4. Aspects of meaning (1): denotation, connotation, appropriateness

The meaning of a word is primarily what it refers to in the real world, its denotation; this is often the sort of definition that is given in a dictionary. For example, *dog* denotes a kind of animal; more specifically, a common, domestic carnivorous mammal; and both *dank* and *moist* mean slightly wet.

A less obvious component of the meaning of an item is its connotation: the associations, or positive or negative feelings it evokes, which may or may not be indicated in a dictionary definition. The word *dog*, for example, as understood by most British people, has positive connotations of friendship and loyalty; whereas the equivalent in Arabic, as understood by most people in Arab countries has negative associations of dirt and inferiority. Within the English language, *moist* has favourable connotations while *dank* has unfavourable; so that you could describe something as 'pleasantly moist' where 'pleasantly dank' would sound absurd.

A more subtle aspect of meaning that often needs to be taught is whether a particular item is the appropriate one to use in a certain context or not. Thus it is useful for a learner to know that a certain word is very common, or relatively rare, or 'taboo' in polite conversation, or tends to be used in writing but not in speech, or is more suitable for formal than informal discourse, or belongs to a certain dialect. For example, you may know that *weep* is virtually synonymous in denotation with *cry*, but it is more formal, tends to be used in writing more than in speech, and is in general much less common.

Question   How would you present the meanings of the words *swim, fame, childish, political, impertinence, kid, guy* and *bastard*? For which would you mention their connotations? And their appropriate contexts? (Some possible answers may be found in the Notes, (1).)

5. Aspects of meaning (2): meaning relationships

How the meaning of one item relates to the meaning of others can also be useful in teaching. There are various such relationships: here are some of the main ones.

– Synonyms: items that mean the same, or nearly the same; for example, *bright, clever, smart* may serve as synonyms of *intelligent*.
– Antonyms: items that mean the opposite; *rich* is an antonym of *poor*.
– Hyponyms: items that serve as specific examples of a general concept; *dog, lion, mouse* are hyponyms of *animal*.
– Co-hyponyms or co-ordinates: other items that are the 'same kind of thing'; *red, blue, green* and *brown* are co-ordinates.
– Superordinates: general concepts that 'cover' specific items; *animal* is the superordinate of *dog, lion, mouse*.
– Translation: words or expressions in the learners' mother tongue that are (more or less) equivalent in meaning to the item being taught.

Besides these, there are other, perhaps looser, ways of associating meaning that are useful in teaching. You can, for instance, relate parts to a whole (the relationship between *arm* and *body*); or associate items that are part of the same real-world context (*tractor, farmer, milking* and *irrigate* are all associated with *agriculture*).

All these can be exploited in teaching to clarify the meaning of a new item, or for practice or test materials.

Question In any language you know, find at least one (more) example for each of the main categories of meaning relationships listed above.

6. Word formation

Vocabulary items, whether one-word or multi-word, can often be broken down into their component 'bits'. Exactly how these bits are put together is another piece of useful information – perhaps mainly for more advanced learners.

You may wish to teach the common prefixes and suffixes: for example, if learners know the meaning of *sub-*, *un-* and *-able*, this will help them guess the meanings of words like *substandard, ungrateful* and *untranslatable*. They should, however, be warned that in many common words the affixes no longer have any obvious connection with their root meaning (for example, *subject, comfortable*). New combinations using prefixes are not unusual, and the reader or hearer would be expected to gather their meaning from an understanding of their components (*ultra-modern, super-hero*).

Another way vocabulary items are built is by combining two words (two nouns, or a gerund and a noun, or a noun and a verb) to make one item: a single compound word, or two separate, sometimes hyphenated words (*bookcase, follow-up, swimming pool*). Again, new coinages using this kind of combination are very common.

Questions What prefixes and suffixes in the language you teach would you consider it useful for learners to know? (Some suggestions in English are provided in the Notes, (2).)

How does a language you know other than English combine words to make longer vocabulary items? Can you give examples?

A good modern dictionary should supply much of the information listed in this unit when you look up a specific item. English teachers might find it useful to look at the *Cambridge International Dictionary of English* (1995) or the *Longman Dictionary of Contemporary English* (1995).

▶ Unit Two: Presenting new vocabulary

This unit looks at the varied ways a new word can be presented to learners. If you prefer not to do the task, study Box 5.1 and then go straight on to the discussion questions in Box 5.2. Some possible answers to the latter are given later in the unit.

Task **Exploring different ways of presenting new vocabulary**

Stage 1: Ideas for presenting specific items

Select an item from the vocabulary taught in a foreign language textbook you know. Think how the meaning of this item would best be presented to learners who are encountering it for the first time, and note down some ideas.

If you are working in a group, three or four participants then get together, share ideas and contribute new ones to each other.

BOX 5.1: WAYS OF PRESENTING THE MEANING OF NEW ITEMS

- concise definition (as in a dictionary; often a superordinate with qualifications: for example, a cat is an animal which…)
- detailed description (of appearance, qualities…)
- examples (hyponyms)
- illustration (picture, object)
- demonstration (acting, mime)
- context (story or sentence in which the item occurs)
- synonyms
- opposite(s) (antonyms)
- translation
- associated ideas, collocations

© *Cambridge University Press 1996*

Stage 2: Studying further techniques

Putting your practical suggestions aside for the moment, study a list of different techniques of presenting the meaning of new vocabulary. In a group, this list may be compiled by a brainstorm among participants, or derived from Box 5.1; or a combination of the two.

Stage 3: Application and comparison

Identify which one or more of the techniques were used in your own idea(s) for presentation. If you are in a group: were there any techniques which tended to be more 'popular', others which were barely used? On second thoughts: would you/could you have used other techniques to supplement your original idea for presentation?

Stage 4: Discussion

On the basis of the information gathered in Stage 3, or your own reflection, discuss orally or in writing generalizations that can be made about the usefulness of the different techniques. Specific questions to consider appear in Box 5.2; of these, some possible answers to Questions 1–3 are presented below.

BOX 5.2: QUESTIONS FOR DISCUSSION: VOCABULARY PRESENTATION TECHNIQUES

1. Some techniques are more popular than others. What are they, and can you account for their popularity?
2. Are there techniques that are particularly appropriate for the presentation of certain types of words?
3. Are there techniques which are likely to be more, or less, appropriate for particular learner populations (young/adult, beginner/advanced, different background cultures)?
4. Do you, as an individual, find that you prefer some kinds of techniques and tend to avoid others? Which? And why?

© Cambridge University Press 1996

Comments on the questions in Box 5.2

1. Answers to this will vary; on the whole, definition, synonym and description tend to be the most popular, perhaps because they are the most obvious and conventional. The use of the others demands more awareness and originality, but can be more rewarding in terms of effective teaching and interest.
2. Yes. A concrete object, for example, is more easily illustrated visually, an action can be mimed. Concepts that are very difficult to explain in the target language because the learners are not yet sufficiently proficient to understand the explanation may be more conveniently presented through mother-tongue translation or explanation. You can probably think of further examples.
3. Yes. For example, younger learners react well to concrete illustration, older ones can cope better with more abstract explanation or definition.

▷ **Unit Three: Remembering vocabulary**

There are various reasons why we remember some words better than others: the nature of the words themselves, under what circumstances they are learnt, the method of teaching and so on. The following is an interesting way to examine some of these factors. It is actually a memory experiment, involving the recall of as many items as possible on a learned list. Obviously, we do not usually do this in the classroom, but its results have clear relevance for conventional vocabulary learning and teaching. If you have time, and are working in a group, it is worthwhile trying it yourself: work according to the Stages laid out below, and only read the Comments section afterwards to compare your own results and conclusions with mine. If you are not able to do the experiment yourself, read through the instructions and go straight on to the *Comments*.

The experiment takes about an hour, including instructions and discussion. There should be at least eight participants, and may be as many as 30. If there is no trainer, one participant should be prepared to take on the role of timekeeper, telling people when to start and finish the different rounds.

Task **Group experiment: Memorizing words**

Stage 1: Preparation

Prepare: one copy of the lists in Box 5.3 for each participant; a results sheet, as in Box 5.4; and have ready a pocket calculator.

Stage 2: Process

First round: half the pairs in the class work on List A, half on List B; partners help each other learn by heart the items on their list. After three minutes

---

BOX 5.3: WORD-LEARNING EXPERIMENT

A	B
WHO	ARM
DOT	LEG
ASH	PEG
LAR	PIG
SEX	TON
OCT	FOX
FOR	DOG
AWE	CAT
ION	MAN
CAN	BOY
OWN	SON
DIG	MUM
OBI	DAD
HUT	BAD
THE	SAD

© *Cambridge University Press 1996*

they conceal the lists and try to write down as many items as they can remember. Their results (the number of words they remembered) are recorded on a sheet or OHP film (Box 5.4).

Second round: each pair does the same thing again with the list they did not work on the first time; but this time they work for a minute and stop for a minute, work for a minute and stop for a minute, work for a minute; then write down what they remember. The 'stopping' minutes should be filled with an activity that takes their minds off the lists: counting backwards from 100, for example. The results are recorded as before.

Stage 3: Results

Work out the average results for:

– Each list (in the bottom row of the table): was there a difference? Can you account for it?
– Each round (in the extreme right-hand column of the table): was there any difference between 'massed' learning (doing all the learning in one block of time) and 'distributed' (having breaks between learning sessions)?

Stage 4: Conclusions

The average results probably show some significant differences. Discuss what the implications might be for teaching.

Stage 5: Further discussion

After looking at the numerical results, consider or discuss the following questions:

1. Were there any particular words that most people seemed to remember better? Can you account for this?
2. What strategies did people use or invent to help themselves remember?
3. Was there any significance in the placing of an item in a list? Were words from the beginning – or end – more easily remembered?

BOX 5.4: RESULTS SHEET

ROUNDS	LIST A	LIST B	AVERAGE
FIRST			
SECOND			
AVERAGE			

© Cambridge University Press 1996

Comments

Results

List B often produces near-perfect scores; List A noticeably less. This difference can be attributed to two main factors: the uniform (fairly low) level of difficulty of the items in List B, as opposed to the very mixed level of List A; and the fact that the words in List B are grouped according to meaning- or sound-association, whereas in List A there is no such grouping. The results would indicate not only that we learn words better when we can easily assign meaning to them, but also that it is much easier to learn words in groups, where one can be associated with, or 'hung onto' another. It is interesting that an association through rhyme (*sad–bad*) can be just as effective as an aid to memory as one through meaning (*mum–dad*), though of course this varies from learner to learner.

A comparison between massed and distributed learning usually shows a difference in favour of the distributed.

Implications for teaching

There are various interesting practical conclusions to be drawn.

1. You will get better results if the words you teach have clear, easily comprehensible meanings.
2. You will get better results if items can be linked with each other, or with ones already known, through meaning- or sound-association.
3. It is better to teach vocabulary in separated, spaced sessions than to teach it all at once. In other words, words will be learnt better if, for example, they are taught briefly at the beginning of a lesson, reviewed later in the same lesson, and again in the next than if the same total amount of time is used for learning the words all at once. This needs careful lesson-planning, but will repay the effort.

Further questions

Some possible answers to the questions asked at Stage 5 above are:

1. Particular words that were remembered: people tend to remember words that have personal or emotive significance (*mum, dad, sex*).
2. Strategies: people commonly attempt to link items together in sense units, or find some reason to associate them, or look for personal significance. All these can be harnessed in teaching.

   Another point worth thinking about here is the wide variety of strategies used by different learners. A strategy found useful by one learner may be quite useless to another.

   We cannot, of course, teach a whole class in a way that will fit every student's learning strategies! – but we can encourage individual students to find what 'works' for them and to approach a learning task in an appropriate way.
3. The placing of words in a list: words at the beginning of a list tend to be remembered better, all things being equal. This may affect your planning: teach your more important new words first, or at the beginning of a lesson.

See Stevick (1976) for further discussion of similar issues.

▶ Unit Four: Ideas for vocabulary work in the classroom

Unit One dealt with ways of presenting specific individual items; this one looks at procedures that involve interaction with a whole set of items, in order both to consolidate learning of ones the learners have previously encountered, and to provide a context for the introduction of new ones.

Group task   **Sharing ideas**

Stage 1: Preparation

Each participant prepares a vocabulary activity which they think is effective. Teachers with some experience may bring activities they have used; others may recall ideas from their own language-learning experience or that they have observed, or find suggestions in books (see *Further reading* at the end of this module); or simply create new ones.

Stage 2: Presentation

The activities are presented to the group. This is best done by actually performing them, the presenter role-playing the teacher and the others the students; in this way you get the 'feel' of the procedure and remember it well. But doing it this way is very time-consuming, so in a large group some people may have to simply describe their activities, or present them in written form.

Stage 3: Discussion

A discussion should follow each presentation, on questions such as: What was the main objective of the activity (awareness-raising/presentation of new vocabulary/review and practice)? What particular aspects of vocabulary did the activity focus on? How effective was it, and why? How interesting/enjoyable was it? For what sort of class, or situation, is it appropriate? Were there any unusual or original aspects of it which you would like to discuss?

Two activities of my own are described below.

Ideas for vocabulary activities

1. Brainstorming round an idea

Write a single word in the centre of the board, and ask students to brainstorm all the words they can think of that are connected with it. Every item that is suggested is written up on the board with a line connecting it to the original word, so that the end result is a 'sun-ray' effect. For example, the word *tree* might produce something like the sketch below.

This activity is mainly for revising words the class already knows, but new ones may be introduced, by the teacher or by students. Although there are no sentences or paragraphs, the circle of associated items is in itself a meaningful context for the learning of new vocabulary. The focus is on the meaning of isolated items.

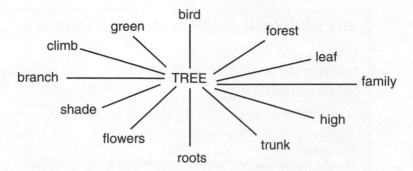

This kind of association exercise is useful when introducing a poem or other literature: a key concept can be placed in the centre, and the brainstorm used as a 'warm-up' to the theme, as well as a framework for the introduction of some of the new vocabulary.

You may, of course, use other sorts of stimulus-words or connections: put a prefix (say *sub-*) in the centre and invite the class to think of words that begin with it; or a transitive verb (like *push*) and think of objects to go with it; or any verb, and think of possible adverbs; or a noun, and think of adjectives; or vice versa. You can probably think of further possibilities: the basic technique is very versatile.

2. Identifying words we know

As an introduction to the vocabulary of a new reading passage: the students are given the new text, and asked to underline, or mark with fluorescent pens, all the words they **know**. They then get together in pairs or threes to compare: a student who knows something not known to their friend(s) teaches it to them, so that they can mark it in on their texts. They then try to guess the meaning of the remaining unmarked items.

Finally the teacher brings the class together to hear results, checking guesses and teaching new items where necessary.

This activity tends to be morale-boosting, in that it stresses what the students know rather than what they do not; it encourages student cooperation and peer-teaching; it also entails repeated exposure to the text and vocabulary items, through individual, group and teacher-led stages.

▷ Unit Five: Testing vocabulary

There are many different types of vocabulary-testing techniques, selected examples of which are shown in Box 5.5. Some are written out as they would be presented to the learner; others are described. If you do not wish to do the task, study Box 5.5 and then go on to read the following Comments.

Task **Looking at vocabulary-testing techniques**

For each example, define for yourself what aspects of the item(s) are being tested, and – just as important – what is **not** being tested! You may wish to

BOX 5.5: VOCABULARY-TESTING TECHNIQUES

Example 1
Choose the letter of the item which is the nearest in meaning to the word in italics:

He was *reluctant* to answer.

a) unprepared   b) unwilling   c) refusing   d) slow

Example 2
Choose the letter of the definition which comes closest in meaning to the word *elated*.

a) ready and willing   b) tense and excited
c) tending to talk a lot   d) in high spirits

Example 3
Draw lines connecting the pairs of opposites.

A	B
brave	awake
female	expensive
cheap	succeed
asleep	cowardly
fail	male

Example 4
Which of the prefixes in Column A can combine with which of the words in Column B? Write out the complete words.

A	B
over	human
trans	national
super	flow
dis	form
inter	infect

Example 5
Underline the odd one out: goat, horse, cow, spider, sheep, dog, cat.

Example 6
For each of the following words, write a sentence that makes its meaning clear.

1. wealth   2. laughter   3. decision   4. brilliant

Example 7
(The teacher dictates the words from Example 6, the students write them down.)

Example 8
(The teacher dictates the mother-tongue equivalents of the words in Example 6, the students write down the target-language versions.)

Example 9
Fill in the gaps:

In the seventeenth _____ Spanish ships sailed _____ to Central and

_____. America to fetch gold for the Spanish _____. The ships were

often attacked by _____, who infested the 'Spanish Main' (the sea

_____ north-east of Central and South America).

> Adapted from *The Cambridge English Course 2 Student's Book* Michael Swan and
> Catherine Walter, 1985

Example 10

Complete the passage using the words from the list:

   area, century, pirates, government, regularly, South

In the seventeenth_____ Spanish ships sailed _____ to Central and

_____ America to fetch gold for the Spanish_____. The ships were

often attacked by_____, who infested the 'Spanish Main' (the sea

_____ north-east of Central and South America).

Example 11
(Students are given sentences in the mother tongue to translate into the target
language; or vice versa.)

Example 12

Finish the following sentences:

1. I feel <u>depressed</u> when…
2. I never have an <u>appetite</u> when…
3. It was a great <u>relief</u> when…

© Cambridge University Press 1996

refer back to Unit One for a summary of various aspects of vocabulary
items that need to be taught and therefore, in the present context, tested.
Add any further remarks you wish on the advantages or disadvantages of
the technique, and how, or whether, you would use it.

   After discussion of these examples, you may wish to suggest further
useful techniques which have not been shown here.

   Teachers learning in a group might like to come together later to
compare notes; and/or refer to my own comments below.

Comments

Examples 1 and 2: Multiple-choice
Note that only denotative meaning is tested, the testee does not need to know
the words' connotations, spelling, pronunciation, grammar, or how they would
be used in context. Multiple-choice questions are tricky and time-consuming to
compose, but, if the answers are clear, very quick and easy to mark. Note that a

testee who does not know the answer has a 25 per cent chance of being right by guessing!

The second example allows for more careful and subtle distinctions in meaning.

Example 3: Matching
As in the previous examples, only meaning is tested; and is knowledge of an opposite a proof that the testee knows the meaning of the original word? Matching items are quicker and easier to compose than multiple-choice; but note that the last option – if the learner has all the others right – becomes obvious. This problem can be corrected by the provision of more items in Column B than in A.

Example 4: Matching
Here the only thing that is being tested is whether the testee is aware of the existence of the (combined) word! Which probably means they also know its meaning, but this fact is not actually being tested. See also the last comment on matching exercises above.

Example 5: Odd one out
Again, only meaning is being tested, and you have no way of being sure that all the items are known. But this is at least more interesting to do, and usually easy to mark.

Example 6: Writing sentences
Spelling and pronunciation of the items are not tested, but most other aspects are. This is a bit boring to do, and difficult to mark objectively, but does check the testee's knowledge fairly well.

Example 7: Dictation
Dictation tests aural recognition and spelling only. However, if learners can recognize and spell an item correctly they probably also know what it means: it is extremely difficult to perceive, let alone spell, words you do not know. A relatively easy test to administer and check.

Example 8: Dictation-translation
This checks if students know meaning and spelling only. There is the problem that the mother-tongue translation may be inexact or misleading; but if it is a reasonable equivalent, then this is a very quick, easy and convenient test to administer and check.

Example 9: Gap-filling
This tests meaning, spelling, to some extent grammar and collocation. But testees may write down possibly acceptable items that are not in fact the originals, or what you intended; will you accept them?

Example 10: Gap-filling with a 'pool' of answers
Meaning is tested here, also to some extent grammar and collocation. This version is easier to do and mark than Example 9.

Example 11: Translation
Translation can test all aspects of an item, but there is the usual difficulty of finding exact equivalents across languages, and it may be tricky to mark.

Example 12: Sentence completion
This tests (denotative) meaning only; but is 'personalized' and interesting to do and read!

Notes

Meaning: denotation, connotation, appropriateness

Swim means the action of propelling oneself through the water by moving the body; *fame* means the state of being well known to the public, with connotations of favour and popularity; *childish* means like a child, usually applied to an adult, or an adult's behaviour, with negative connotations; *political* means to do with public or national affairs, often connoting cynical power-play; *impertinence* is impoliteness, usually used of an inferior behaving with lack of respect to a superior. *Kid* means the same as 'child', and *guy* means 'man', but both are used almost exclusively in informal, spoken speech; note that *guy* in the singular usually refers to a male, but the plural commonly includes both males and females. *Bastard* is a child of parents who are not married; usually used as an insult or an expression of contempt in informal spoken language (the word *illegitimate* would be substituted if no offence is intended).

Word formation

Some common, useful prefixes in English are:
a-/ab-, ante-, anti-, auto-, co-/con-/com-, circum-, dis-, e-/ex-, inter-, mis-, non-, per-, pre-, re-, sub-, super-, trans-;
and suffixes: *-able, -er/-or, -ic, -ify, -ism, -ist, -ise/-ize, -ment, -ness, -tion.*

Further reading

BACKGROUND

Carter, R. and McCarthy, M. (1988) *Vocabulary and Language Teaching*, London: Longman.
(A collection of articles on applied-linguistics aspects of the topic; see particularly the Introduction, and articles by Nattinger and by Sinclair and Renouf)
Hurford, J. R. (1983) *Semantics: A Coursebook*, Cambridge: Cambridge University Press.
(Easy to follow and comprehensive, with self-checking exercises and tests; an excellent way to teach yourself the subject)

Leech, G. (1974) *Semantics*, Harmondsworth: Penguin.
(A compact account of the subject; more advanced and detailed than the Hurford and Heasley)

McCarthy, M. (1990) *Vocabulary*, Oxford: Oxford University Press.
(Comprehensive and readable discussion of theoretical and practical issues in teaching vocabulary)

Nation, I. S. P. (1990) *Teaching and Learning Vocabulary*, New York: Newbury House.
(Comprehensive coverage of background theory and research, as well as practical teaching techniques)

Richards, J. C. (1976) 'The role of vocabulary teaching', *TESOL Quarterly*, **10**, 1, 77–89.
(What it means to 'know' a word, and implications for teaching)

Stevick, E. (1976) *Memory, Meaning, Method*, Rowley, Mass.: Newbury House.
(See Chapters 2 and 3 on how we remember words)

TEACHER'S HANDBOOKS

Allen, V. F. (1983) *Techniques in Teaching Vocabulary*, New York: Oxford University Press.
(A sensible and simply written treatment of practical vocabulary teaching, with examples and tasks)

Gairns, R. and Redman, S. (1986) *Working with Words*, Cambridge: Cambridge University Press.
(Summary of theoretical background, then practical guidelines on how to teach vocabulary; plenty of examples of activities)

Morgan, J. and Rinvolucri, M. (1986) *Vocabulary*, Oxford: Oxford University Press.
(A collection of lively and imaginative activities for learning and practising vocabulary)

Module 6: Teaching grammar

▶ ## Unit One: What is grammar?

Grammar in general

Grammar is sometimes defined as 'the way words are put together to make correct sentences'. This is, as we shall see presently, an over-simplification, but it is a good starting-point (and an easy way to explain the term to young learners). Thus in English *I am a teacher* is grammatical, **I a teacher*, and **I are a teacher* are not.

We can, however, apply the term 'grammatical' to units smaller than sentences. A brief phrase said or written on its own can be grammatically acceptable or unacceptable in its own right: *a tall woman* sounds right; **a woman tall* does not. The same may be true of single words: compare *went* with **goed*.

Further: the minimal components to be combined may not be whole words; for example, the *-ed* suffix indicating the past tense of a regular verb in English, or the *-s* plural of nouns. And sometimes it is not even a question of putting 'bits' before or after other 'bits'; words may actually change their spelling and pronunciation in certain grammatical contexts: irregular forms of the past tense, for example, in English, and many common plural forms in Arabic.

Question   Can you formulate a more precise definition of 'grammar', in the light of the above discussion? Compare your definition with a dictionary's, or with that suggested in the Notes, (1).

Grammatical structures

A specific instance of grammar is usually called a 'structure'. Examples of structures would be the past tense, noun plurals, the comparison of adjectives, and so on. Not all languages, of course, have the same structures: the English verb has 'aspects' (such as the progressive: *she is going* for example) which many other languages do not; German ascribes masculine, feminine or neuter gender to its nouns, which English does not. It is largely such discrepancies which cause problems to the foreign language learner; though quite how difficult these problems will be it is often hard to predict, even if you are familiar with the learner's mother tongue. Occasionally foreign structures that look strange may be surprisingly easy to master, and vice versa.

Question   Think of two languages you know. Can you suggest an example of a structure that exists in one but not in the other? How difficult is the structure to learn for the speaker of the other language?

Grammatical meaning

Grammar does not only affect how units of language are combined in order to 'look right'; it also affects their meaning. The teaching of grammatical meaning tends, unfortunately, to be neglected in many textbooks in favour of an emphasis on accuracy of form; but it is no good knowing how to perceive or construct a new tense of a verb if you do not know exactly what difference it makes to meaning when it is used. It is very often the meanings of the structures which create the difficulties for foreign learners mentioned above.

The meaning of a grammatical structure may be quite difficult to teach. It is fairly simple to explain that the addition of a plural -*s* to the noun in English and French indicates that you are talking about more than one item, and there are parallels in other languages. But how would you explain to the foreigner when to use the present perfect (*I have gone*, for example) in English, and when the past simple (*I went*)? If you are a grammarian or an experienced English language teacher, you may have the answer at your fingertips; but most English speakers who have not previously studied this question will have to stop and think, and may find it difficult to answer.

Question Choose a structure in your own native language. How would you explain its meaning to learners? How would you get them to understand when this particular structure would be used rather than others with slightly different meanings?

▷ Unit Two: The place of grammar teaching

The place of grammar in the teaching of foreign languages is controversial. Most people agree that knowledge of a language means, among other things, knowing its grammar; but this knowledge may be intuitive (as it is in our native language), and it is not necessarily true that grammatical structures need to be taught as such, or that formal rules need to be learned. Or is it?

In Box 6.1 are some extracts from the literature relating to the teaching of grammar, which express a variety of opinions on this question. They are necessarily decontextualized and over-simplified versions of their writers' opinions: nevertheless the issues they raise are basic and interesting.

Task **Critical reading**

Read the extracts in Box 6.1, and, if you are working in a group, discuss your reactions. If you are on your own, you may find it helpful to observe the following sequence for each extract:

1. Summarize in your own words what the writer is saying.
2. State whether you agree or disagree in principle.
3. In the light of your own experience as teacher or learner, add further criticisms, positive or negative, of the writer's point of view. Where you

---

BOX 6.1: OPINIONS ABOUT THE TEACHING OF GRAMMAR

Extract 1

The important point is that the study of grammar as such is neither necessary nor sufficient for learning to use a language.

> (from L. Newmark 'How not to interfere with language learning' in Brumfit, C. J. and Johnson, K. (eds.) *The Communicative Approach to Language Teaching*, Oxford University Press, 1979, p. 165)

Extract 2

The student's craving for explicit formulization of generalizations can usually be met better by textbooks and grammars that he reads outside class than by discussion in class.

> (*ibid.*)

Extract 3

The language teacher's view of what constitutes knowledge of a language is...a knowledge of the syntactic structure of sentences... The assumption that the language teacher appears to make is that once this basis is provided, then the learner will have no difficulty in dealing with the actual use of language...
There is a good deal of evidence to suggest that this assumption is of very doubtful validity indeed.

> (from H. G. Widdowson, 'Directions in the teaching of discourse' in Brumfit, C. J. and Johnson, K. (eds.) *The Communicative Approach to Language Teaching*, Oxford University Press, 1979, pp. 49–60)

Extract 4

The evidence seems to show beyond doubt that though it is by communicative use in real 'speech acts' that the new language 'sticks' in the learner's mind, insight into pattern is an equal partner with communicative use in what language teachers now see as the dual process of acquisition/learning. Grammar, approached as a voyage of discovery into the patterns of language rather than the learning of prescriptive rules, is no longer a bogey word.

> (from Eric Hawkins, *Awareness of Language: An Introduction*, Cambridge University Press, 1984, pp. 150–1)

© *Cambridge University Press 1996*

---

can, quote evidence from your own or others' experience to back up your point of view.

My own comments follow.

Comments: The place of grammar teaching

Extract 1

The writer is saying that you do not need to learn grammar, as such, in order to learn a language. This statement is probably true: one learns one's mother tongue without studying grammar. But it is, perhaps, a little misleading, and misses the point. The important question is not whether teaching and learning grammar is necessary and/or sufficient for language learning, but whether it **helps** or not. And my own opinion is that yes, it does help, provided it is taught consistently as a means to improving mastery of the language, not as an end in itself.

Extract 2

It is better, says the writer, for the learner to study grammar individually and independently than as a part of the classroom lesson. The interesting thing about this quotation (which occurs in the same paragraph as Extract 1, but a few lines earlier) is that it presupposes that the learner does **want** to study rules ('The student's craving...'). The writer gives no reasons to support his claim that grammar is better studied outside class; and if learners see the study of grammar as desirable as a part of their learning, I would think this is surely sufficient justification for the teacher to help them by providing information and practice in the classroom.

Extract 3

The writer's claim is that teaching learners how to construct grammatical sentences does not enable them to produce real-life discourse. The implication is that the learners need to learn how to make meanings within real contexts, and how to create longer units of language than single sentences. This is fair enough, but we should not, I think, conclude that the writer thinks grammar teaching is useless: the point is that grammatical accuracy on its own is a dead end, unless used to receive and produce interesting and purposeful meanings within the context of real-life language use.

Extract 4

Here, the writer is affirming the usefulness of grammar for effective language learning. He also implies that grammar can be interesting ('a voyage of discovery') in itself: apparently a reaction against traditional prescriptive rule-teaching, which he describes as a 'bogey'. I agree with him in principle, though I am not sure that all students can find an intrinsic interest in grammar as such. The main point is an affirmation of its value as a means to help language learning.

▷ Unit Three: Grammatical terms

If you do decide to do any formal, conscious teaching of grammar, it is useful to have at your fingertips the various common terms that are used in explanations of grammatical structures. If you are not familiar with them already, you may find the following definitions useful.

(Note, however that these definitions are based on English grammar, and may not be accurate representations of categories in some other languages; they are, moreover, only brief summaries, and not comprehensive. Fuller and more precise descriptions can be found in the grammar books referred to under *Further reading*.)

Units of language

Linguists usually define the largest unit of language as 'discourse' or 'text'; but for most practical teaching purposes, the sentence is probably the most convenient 'base' unit. Smaller units are the clause, the phrase, the word, the morpheme.

The **sentence** is a set of words standing on their own as a sense unit, its conclusion marked by a full stop or equivalent (question mark, exclamation mark). In many languages sentences begin with a capital letter, and include a verb.

The **clause** is a kind of mini-sentence: a set of words which make a sense unit, but may not be concluded by a full stop. A sentence may have two or more clauses (*She left because it was late and she was tired.*) or only one (*she was tired.*).

The **phrase** is a shorter unit within the clause, of one or more words, but fulfilling the same sort of function as a single word. A verb phrase, for example, functions the same way as a single-word verb, a noun phrase like a one-word noun or pronoun: *was going, a long table*.

The **word** is the minimum normally separable form: in writing, it appears as a stretch of letters with a space either side.

The **morpheme** is a bit of a word which can be perceived as a distinct component: within the word *passed*, for example, are the two morphemes *pass*, and *-ed*. A word may consist of a single morpheme (*book*).

Question   Look at the first sentence of this unit ('If you do decide…') and try to find two or more examples of each of the above sentence components. You might then like to check with the Notes, (2).

Alternatively, analyse another sentence similarly, possibly in another language.

Parts of the sentence

We may also analyse the sentence according to the relationships between its component phrases: these are called parts of the sentence. The most common parts of the sentence are **subject**, **verb** and **object**, which may be combined into a basic pattern like *I saw the man*: *I* being the subject, *saw* the verb and *the man* the object. The object may be direct or indirect; thus in *I sent him a letter*, *him* is the indirect object, *a letter* the direct.

The **complement** looks like an object, except that it refers to the same thing as the subject; so that it would come after verbs like *be, become, seem*; in the sentence *She is a good doctor.*, the phrase *a good doctor* is the complement.

Finally there is the **adverbial**: another word or phrase which adds further information: words or phrases like *yesterday, at home, on his own*.

Question   Using the first sentence of this section ('We may also analyse…'), find at least one of each of the categories described above: subject, verb, object, complement and adverbial (Notes, (3)). Again, you may prefer to use a different sentence in another language.

Parts of speech

Different parts of the sentence may be realized by various kinds of words (or phrases): these are called parts of speech.

Nouns are traditionally characterized as naming a 'person, place or thing'; but in fact they may refer to activities or events (*conversation, battle*), abstracts (*beauty, theory*) and various other kinds of things. They usually function, as do pronouns, as the subject, object or complement of a verb, or follow prepositions. They may be preceded by determiners (*the, some*, for example) or by adjectives, and may take the plural -*s*.

   Most nouns are 'common' (*finger, meeting*); 'proper' nouns (*Queen Victoria, Syria*) signify the name of a specific person, place, event, etc., and are written in English with a capital letter. Another useful distinction is between 'countable' nouns (items which can be counted and may appear in the plural: *horse, cup*, for example) and 'non-countable' or 'mass' nouns (certain uncountable substances or abstracts: *coffee, dust, wisdom*).

Verbs are often called words of 'doing' (*swim, sit*), but they may also indicate a state of 'being', 'feeling', 'being in relationship to' (*remain, regret, precede*). Verbs can be used in different tenses, and in active and passive voices.

   It is useful to distinguish between transitive verbs (those that take a direct object: *hit, feed*) and intransitive ones (those that do not: *laugh, fall*), though many verbs can be either, depending on context (*fight, relax*).

Adjectives normally describe the things referred to by nouns or pronouns (*black, serious*); they may function as complements or be attached to a noun.

Adverbs describe the concepts defined by verbs (*quickly, alone*), adjectives or other adverbs (*extremely, quite*) or an entire sentence or situation (*unfortunately, perhaps*).

Pronouns usually function as substitutes for nouns or noun phrases (*he, him, who, those*) and like them may function as subject, object, complement or follow a preposition.

Auxiliary verbs may be attached to main verbs in a verb phrase: *is*, for example, in *is going*.

Modal verbs (such as *can, must, may*) are a particular type of auxiliary verb; they express ideas such as possibility, ability, compulsion, probability, willingness.

Determiners are (usually short) items that introduce a noun or a noun phrase (*the, a, all, some, many*).

Prepositions define time, space and more abstract relationships, and precede nouns or pronouns (*in, before, of, according to, despite*).

Question   Open a newspaper. Can you find and underline examples of some or all of the above categories?

▶ Unit Four: Presenting and explaining grammar

It is surprisingly difficult to present and explain a foreign-language grammatical structure to a class of learners. The problem is first to understand yourself what is involved in 'knowing' the structure (its written and spoken forms, its nuances of meaning), and in particular what is likely to cause difficulties to the learners; and second, how to present examples and formulate explanations that will clearly convey the necessary information. This is a place where clear thinking and speaking are of paramount importance: although you may elicit suggestions from the learners and encourage their participation in the presentation, it is essential for you to know how to present the structure's form and meaning yourself in a way that is clear, simple, accurate and helpful. Note that there is often a conflict between 'simple' and 'accurate'; if you give a completely accurate account of a structure, it may be far from simple; if you simplify, you may not be accurate. One of the problems of grammar presentations is to find the appropriate balance between the two.

The task provides a framework for utilizing your own experience in order to learn more about effective grammar presentation and improve practice. If you do not do it, go straight on to the Guidelines section at the end of the unit.

Task **Classroom or peer-teaching**

Stage 1: Presentation

Present and explain a grammatical structure to a class; the presentation should not take longer than five minutes. (You may or may not wish to consult a grammar book to help you prepare.)

If you are engaged in professional teaching, do this in one of your own classes, and teach a structure that is from your textbook, or that fits in with your programme. If you are not at present teaching, choose a structure you feel fairly confident about, and present it to a group of colleagues. (If you are on your own, write down the text of a presentation you might give a class.)

The presentation should be recorded in some way; you might tape-record it or ask a colleague to observe and take notes. If neither of these is possible, then write down as accurate an account as possible immediately after the lesson.

Stage 2 (optional)

If you did not do so before, look up a grammar book (see *Further reading* for some references) to check your explanation: was there anything important you omitted or misrepresented?

Stage 3: Feedback

Ask a colleague or student to tell you immediately afterwards how clear they thought your presentation was, and if they have any particular comments.

You may find it useful to use the questions in Box 6.2 as points of reference. Some comments in the form of general recommendations may be found below.

Stage 4

In the light of the critical discussion of your presentation, write out for yourself a set of guidelines for presenting and explaining grammar.

Stage 5

Compare what you have written with my suggested guidelines as laid out below, or with what others have said (for example, Harmer, 1989; Doff, 1988: Ch.3). Is there anything further you would like to add to your own guidelines in the light of your reading?

Stage 6

Do Stage 1 again, using another structure. Note briefly any changes you notice in your own teaching as a result of the process you have been through in this unit.

BOX 6.2: QUESTIONS ON GRAMMAR PRESENTATIONS

1. **The structure itself**. Was the structure presented in both speech and writing, both form and meaning?
2. **Examples.** Were enough examples provided of the structure in a meaningful context? Are you sure the students understood their meanings?
3. **Terminology.** Did you call the structure by its (grammar-book) name? If so, was this helpful? If not, would it have helped if you had? What other grammatical terminology was (would have been) useful?
4. **Language.** Was the structure explained in the students' mother tongue, or in the target language, or in a combination of the two? Was this effective?
5. **Explanation.** Was the information given about the structure at the right level: reasonably accurate but not too detailed? Did you use comparison with the students' mother tongue (if known)? Was this/would this have been useful?
6. **Delivery.** Were you speaking (and writing) clearly and at an appropriate speed?
7. **Rules.** Was an explicit rule given? Why/why not? If so, did you explain it yourself or did you elicit it from the students? Was this the best way to do it?

© Cambridge University Press 1996

Guidelines on presenting and explaining a new grammatical structure

1. In general, a good presentation should include both oral and written forms, and both form and meaning.
2. It is important for learners to have plenty of contextualized examples of the structure and to understand them. Visual materials can also contribute to understanding.
3. The answers to this will depend on your situation and learners. On the whole older or more analytically-minded learners will benefit more from the use of terminology.
4. Again, this very much depends on your own situation and judgement.
5. This is the problem about striking the right balance between accuracy and simplicity referred to earlier in this unit. Your explanation should cover the great majority of instances learners are likely to encounter; obvious

exceptions should be noted, but too much detail may only confuse. As a rule, a simple generalization, even if not entirely accurate, is more helpful to learners than a detailed grammar-book definition.

6. These are basic and important points; your observer will help you here.
7. Here you have to decide whether a rule would be helpful or not; then, whether to elicit it from the learners on the basis of examples (sometimes called the 'inductive' method), or give it yourself, and invite them to produce examples ('deductive'). Like grammatical terminology, explicit rules are helpful to older or more analytically-minded learners. As regards inductive or deductive methods: you have to ask yourself which is more effective in this situation. If the learners can perceive and define the rule themselves quickly and easily, then there is a lot to be said for letting them do so: what they discover themselves they are more likely to remember. But if they find this difficult, you may waste a lot of valuable class time on sterile and frustrating guessing, or on misleading suggestions; in such cases it is better to provide the information yourself.

▶ Unit Five: Grammar practice activities

The aim of grammar practice is to get students to learn the structures so thoroughly that they will be able to produce them correctly on their own. But it is unsatisfactory for students to be able to produce correct samples of a structure only when they are being specifically tested on it: many of us are familiar with the phenomenon of learners who get full marks on all the grammar exercises and tests, but then make mistakes in the same structures when they are composing their own free speech or writing. The problem in such a case is that the structures have not been thoroughly mastered; the learner still depends on a measure of conscious monitoring in order to produce them correctly.

One of our jobs as teachers is to help our students make the 'leap' from form-focussed accuracy work to fluent, but acceptable, production, by providing a 'bridge': a variety of practice activities that familiarize them with the structures in context, giving practice both in form and communicative meaning.

Look at Box 6.3, which consists of descriptions of a number of practice activities for various English structures. They are laid out in sequence: from a very controlled and accuracy-oriented exercise at the beginning to a fluency activity giving opportunities for the free use of the grammar in context at the end.

It is not suggested that such a sequence be rigidly followed in classroom teaching, though on the whole the more controlled procedures tend to come earlier; but rather that our lessons should include a fairly representative selection of activities that provide both form-focussed and meaning-focussed practice.

BOX 6.3: TYPES OF GRAMMAR PRACTICE: FROM ACCURACY TO FLUENCY

Type 1: Awareness

After the learners have been introduced to the structure, (see Unit Four above), they are given opportunities to encounter it within some kind of discourse, and do a task that focusses their attention on its form and/or meaning.

Example: Learners are given extracts from newspaper articles and asked to find and underline all the examples of the past tense that they can find.

Type 2: Controlled drills

Learners produce examples of the structure: these examples are, however, predetermined by the teacher or textbook, and have to conform to very clear, closed-ended cues.

Example: Write or say statements about John, modelled on the following example:

John *drinks tea* but he *doesn't drink* coffee.
a) like: ice cream/cake   b) speak: English/Italian
c) enjoy: playing football/playing chess

Type 3: Meaningful drills

Again the responses are very controlled, but learners can make a limited choice of vocabulary.

Example: Again in order to practise forms of the present simple tense:
Choose someone you know very well, and write down their name. Now compose true statements about them according to the following model:

He/She *likes ice cream*; OR He/She *doesn't like ice cream*.
a) enjoy: playing tennis   b) drink: wine   c) speak: Polish

Type 4: Guided, meaningful practice

Learners form sentences of their own according to a set pattern, but exactly what vocabulary they use is up to them.

Example: Practising conditional clauses, learners are given the cue *If I had a million dollars*, and suggest, in speech or writing, what they *would* do.

Type 5: (Structure-based) free sentence composition

Learners are provided with a visual or situational cue, and invited to compose their own responses; they are directed to use the structure.

Example: A picture showing a number of people doing different things is shown to the class; they describe it using the appropriate tense.

Type 6: (Structure-based) discourse composition

Learners hold a discussion or write a passage according to a given task; they are directed to use at least some examples of the structure within the discourse.

Example: The class is given a dilemma situation ('You have seen a good friend cheating in an important test') and asked to recommend a solution. They are directed to include modals (*might, should, must, can, could*, etc.) in their speech/writing.

Type 7: Free discourse

As in Type 6, but the learners are given no specific direction to use the structure; however, the task situation is such that instances of it are likely to appear.
Example: As in Type 6, but without the final direction.

© Cambridge University Press 1996

Application   Look at the grammar exercises in a locally-used foreign language coursebook, and classify them roughly according to the types listed in Box 6.3. Many coursebooks provide plenty of exercises that suit the descriptions of Types 2–3, but tend to neglect the others. Is this true of the book you are looking at?

▷ Unit Six: Grammatical mistakes

Note: This module does not include a section on grammar testing; for some practical testing techniques that may be used for grammar as well as vocabulary see Unit Five of the previous module; and for a discussion of language testing in general, see Module 3: *Tests*. I prefer to concentrate here on one of the most important products of such tests: the information they give us on common learner errors.

Terminology

Applied linguistics theory commonly distinguishes between **errors** (which are consistent and based on a mis-learned generalization) and **mistakes** (occasional, inconsistent slips). However, when you come across instances during a lesson it is usually difficult to tell the difference with any degree of certainty; I have, therefore, not insisted on rigorous distinction between the two terms in the following discussion.

What is a mistake?

Usually, language teachers perceive a mistake intuitively: something sounds or looks 'wrong'. It may actually interfere with successful communication, or simply 'jar' – produce a slight feeling of discomfort in the reader or hearer. We have to be careful, however, not to define as mistakes slightly deviant forms which may not accord with some grammar-book prescriptions, but are quite acceptable to competent or native speakers of the language.

Mistakes within the learning process

If we present new structures carefully and give plenty of varied practice in using them, we may hope that our students will make relatively few mistakes. But some will inevitably appear.

Mistakes may be seen as an integral and natural part of learning: a symptom of the learner's progress through an 'interlanguage' towards a closer and closer approximation to the target language. Some would say that it is not necessary to correct at all: as the learner advances mistakes will disappear on their own.

Even if you think – as most learners do – that grammar mistakes need to be corrected, it is important to relate to them not as a sign of inadequacy (you have failed to teach something, the student has failed to learn it), but rather as a means to advance teaching and learning ('here is some useful information about what we need to pay attention to, let's now consider how to use this information in order to make progress'). The following Inquiry task is based on this approach to correction.

Inquiry   **Learner errors**

Stage 1: Gathering samples

Gather a few samples of learners' writing that does not consist of answers to grammar exercises: answers to comprehension questions, essays, letters, short paragraphs. Alternatively, record foreign learners speaking. (If you did Unit Two of Module 4: *Teaching pronunciation* then you will already have recordings you might be able to use here; if not, the same unit will provide you with some hints on how to make such recordings. See page 50.)

Stage 2: Classifying

Go through the samples you have collected, noting mistakes. Can you categorize them into types? What are the most common ones?

Stage 3: Ordering

Together with colleagues, make a list of the most common mistakes, in rough order of frequency.

Stage 4: Reordering

There are, of course, all sorts of other factors, besides frequency, which may affect the level of importance you attach to an error. It may be, for example, less urgent to correct one which is very common but which does not actually affect comprehensibility than one that does. In English, learners commonly omit the third-person *-s* suffix in the present simple, and slightly less commonly substitute a present verb form when they mean the past; on the whole, the second mistake is more likely to lead to misunderstanding than the first and therefore is more important to correct. Another error may be considered less important because a lot of very proficient, or native, speakers often make it. And so on.

Rearrange your list of errors, if necessary, so that they are in order of importance for correction.

Using the information

The information you have gained may be used for three main purposes:

1. As a guide for the presentation and practice of new structures

If you know that a certain structure is particularly difficult to produce without mistakes, you will try to invest more time and effort next time you present it. Learners who like to think analytically may appreciate your sharing the problem with them frankly even at the earliest stages: 'This is the mistake a lot of people make: look out for it!' Conversely, if you know that your learners' use of another structure is usually mistake-free, maybe you can afford to teach it more briefly, and skip lengthy explanations.

2. As a guide for correction

It is possible to correct every single mistake in learners' oral or written work; but then they may be unable to cope with the sheer quantity of information, let alone learn it with any degree of thoroughness. It is probably better to be selective: to concentrate on the 'important' errors, and direct the learner's attention towards them only. (On the question of correction in general, see Module 17: *Giving feedback*.)

3. As a guide for remedial work

Having diagnosed that a certain structure is particularly problematic for your students, it is a good idea to give a review and extra practice of the structure, detached from the mistake-making event itself. You may start by telling them frankly what the frequent error is that you are trying to correct; or you may feel it better (particularly with more intuitive, or younger learners) to go straight into practice of correct forms.

Notes

(1) Definition

One possible definition might be: Grammar is a set of rules that define how words (or parts of words) are combined or changed to form acceptable units of meaning within a language.

(2) Units of language

The sentence is:

> If you do decide to do any formal, conscious teaching of grammar, it is useful to have at your fingertips the various common terms that are used in explanations of grammatical structures.

Clauses
   The main clause of the sentence is: *it is useful to have at your fingertips the various common terms*. There are two subordinate clauses: *If you do decide to do any formal, conscious teaching of grammar* and *that are used in explanations of grammatical structures*.
Phrases
   Some noun phrases are: *you*; *any formal, conscious teaching of grammar*; *it*; *your fingertips*; *the various common terms*; *explanations of grammatical structures*. (Note that *grammatical structures* is another noun phrase within a prepositional phrase within a noun phrase!)
   Verb phrases are: *do decide, is, are used*.
   Prepositional phrases are: *of grammar, at your fingertips, of grammatical structures*.

Words
These are simply: *If, you, do, decide*, etc.
Morphemes
Most of the words are also single morphemes. Some that can be broken down into more than one morpheme are: *teach+ing*; *use+ful, finger+tips*.

(3) Parts of the sentence

The sentence is:

> We may also analyse the sentence according to the relationships between its component phrases: these are called parts of the sentence.

Subject: In this sentence the subjects are pronouns: *we, these*.
Verb: There are two verbs: *analyse* and *are called*.
Object: the sentence is the object of the verb *analyse*.
Complement: parts of the sentence is the complement of the verb *are called*.
Adverbial: The phrase *according to the relationships between its component phrases* functions as an adverbial.

Further reading

ENGLISH GRAMMARS AND BACKGROUND (based on British English, except for the Celce-Murcia, which is based on American)

Celce-Murcia, M. and Larsen-Freeman, D. (1983) *The Grammar Book*, Rowley, Mass.: Newbury House.
(A fairly detailed account of English grammar for the teacher)
Leech, G., Deuchar, M. and Hoogenraad, R. (1983) *English Grammar for Today*, London: Macmillan.
(Less thorough than the *University Grammar* listed below but more readable; for improving your own general grammatical knowledge)
Quirk, R. and Greenbaum, S. (1973) *A University Grammar of English*, London: Longman.
(A very comprehensive reference book – perhaps too detailed to be often used by a busy teacher)
Sinclair, J. (1992) *Collins COBUILD English Usage*, Birmingham University with London: HarperCollins.
(A comprehensive but accessible grammar for teacher or learners, based on the COBUILD corpus of language samples)
Swan, M. (1980) *Practical English Usage*, Oxford: Oxford University Press.
(Good for looking up specific points you need for teaching; clearly set out, with common mistakes explained and corrected. There is also a simpler version, *Basic English Usage*)
Swan, M. and Smith, B. (1987) *Learner English*, Cambridge: Cambridge University Press.
(Articles on common interference mistakes produced in English by speakers of other languages)

TEACHER'S HANDBOOKS

Bygate, M., Tonkyn, A. and Williams, E. (eds.) (1994) *Grammr and the Language Teacher*, Hemel Hempstead: Prentice Hall International.
(A collection of articles on various aspects of grammar and grammar teaching, with a practical classroom orientation)

Celce-Murcia, M. and Hilles, S. L. (1988) *Techniques and Resources in Teaching Grammar*, New York: Oxford University Press.
(Guidelines and practical suggestions, with examples; readable)

Close, R. A. (1992) *A Teachers' Grammar: The Central Problems of English*, Hove: Language Teaching Publications.
(A summary of some of the grammar problems of English, and how to cope with them)

Doff, A. (1988) *Teach English: A Training Course for Teachers* (Teacher's Workbook and Trainer's Handbook), Cambridge: Cambridge University Press: Chapters 3 and 6.
(Very practical advice and activities for the (student) teacher)

Harmer, J. (1989) *Teaching and Learning Grammar*, London: Longman.
(A slim, readable volume: useful suggestions and advice)

Ur, P. (1988) *Grammar Practice Activities*, Cambridge: Cambridge University Press.
(A collection of communicative and game-like activities, with general guidelines for effective activity design)

Module 7: Topics, situations, notions, functions

▶ **Unit One: Topics and situations**

Language has traditionally been segmented, as shown in the last three modules, into sounds, vocabulary and grammatical structures, but it may equally well be taught through larger meaningful segments based on whole 'chunks' of discourse. It would seem logical to group such chunks round a common topic and many courses are planned in such a way. Unit 1 of a coursebook might, for example, deal with the home, Unit 2 with the family, and so on.

Another possibility is to base the language round situations: these are topics 'brought alive' as it were, and integrated into some kind of communicative event. Thus the Unit 1 mentioned above might integrate into the topic of 'home' a situation where someone is showing a visitor round their home, describing the different rooms and furniture; similarly the topic of 'family' might be contextualized by showing the same host introducing the visitor to members of the family.

In some ways topics and situations are more difficult to teach than isolated items like words or structures, in that they involve whole discourse, with longer and more complicated language constructs. On the other hand, the learner is immediately engaging with language that expresses meanings in context, and these may be seen as more interesting and clearly relevant for communicative purposes.

Many coursebooks base their units on topics or situations as described above.

Question Have a look at a locally-used coursebook. Is each unit in fact based on a clearly definable topic, or situation, or both? Is there a general 'base' situation which is maintained throughout the book (for example, the doings of a particular set of people)?

Introducing a new topic or situation

New topics and situations need to be presented in much the same way as new language items or texts (see Module 1: *Presentations and explanations*). That is to say, learners have to perceive and understand both the underlying theme and the language which is used to express it. The presentation of topics or situations may be approached from different directions; for example:

1. Take the topic or situation, do a task based on it, eliciting from the learners or teaching any necessary new language, possibly going on later to study a text; or

2. Teach the new language, and through it approach the topic/situation and/or an appropriate text; or
3. Go straight into a text, using it both to teach new language and to explore the relevant topic/situation.

Some practical techniques implementing these ideas are shown in Box 7.1.

Question Look through the techniques suggested in Box 7.1. Are there any you would not use? Can you add more?

Task: **Peer-teaching**

Choose one of the following topics or situations: the first two are appropriate for a relatively young, elementary class, the next two for an older, more advanced one.

1. School
2. Two children discussing their favourite lessons
3. Education
4. A teachers' meeting about a problem student

In small groups, plan how you would introduce your chosen item to your class, perhaps utilizing some of the ideas in Box 7.1; then one representative actually presents it to the rest of the full group. Continue until each small group has 'taught' its topic.

Then discuss the presentations: how interesting were they? How well do you think the learners would have understood the material?

BOX 7.1: SOME IDEAS FOR PRESENTATION OF NEW TOPICS OR SITUATIONS

- Write the name of the topic in the middle of the board and invite the class to brainstorm all the associated words they can think of (see pp.68-69).
- Write the name of the topic in the middle of the board and ask the class what they know about it and/or what they would like to know.
- Describe a communicative situation and characters and invite the class to suggest orally what the characters will say.
- Give the title of a text and invite the class to write down sentences or expressions they expect will occur within it.
- Define briefly the opening event and characters in a communicative situation and ask the class to imagine what will happen next.
- Present a recorded dialogue and ask the class to tell you where they think it is taking place and who the characters are.
- Present a text, ask for an appropriate title.
- Express your own, or someone else's, opinions about a topic, invite discussion.
- Teach a selection of words and expressions, ask the class what they think the situation or topic is.

© Cambridge University Press 1996

▶ **Unit Two: What ARE notions and functions?**

Notions and functions are rather more precise categories than 'topics' and 'situations'. The latter define general themes or communicative events, whereas notions and functions are the ways particular meanings are realized in language. Thus, as discussed in the previous unit, a topic may be 'the family' and a situation may be 'visiting a friend's home', whereas notions and functions may be things like 'time past' or 'inviting'. 'Time past' may include past tenses, phrases like *a month ago, in 1990, last week*, and utterances using temporal clauses beginning with *when..., before..., after...* and so on; 'inviting' may include phrases like *Would you like to...?, I suggest..., How about...?, Please... .*

The number of possible topics and communicative situations is virtually infinite, whereas the number of functions and notions is in principle finite. It has therefore been suggested that syllabuses for language courses should be based on a taxonomy of functions and notions, since they represent the basic units underlying a communicative system more realistically than the categories of lexis and grammar which may be taught detached from particular communicative contexts. The rationale behind the design of such syllabuses has been discussed by Wilkins (1976) among others; perhaps the most well-known example (in English) is Van Ek (1990).

The difference between a notion and a function

If you look up some of the references listed under *Further reading* at the end of this unit, and read what people have to say about notions and functions you will find that the two terms are not used very consistently. Sometimes they seem to refer to the same thing; sometimes one is seen as a subset of the other; and the issue is further complicated by the introduction of other overlapping terms such as 'conceptual categories', 'speech acts', 'performatives', etc. It is all very confusing.

It is probably not very useful for us as teachers to invest time and energy in sorting out and defining all these concepts, although you may enjoy doing so: the subject of communicative acts is a fascinating one in its own right! For professional purposes, however, we may perhaps focus on only one interesting distinction: that between notions and functions as defined, for example, in Van Ek (1990).

A **notion** is a concept, or idea: it may be quite specific, in which case it is virtually the same as vocabulary (*dog, house*, for example); or it may be very general – *time, size, emotion, movement* – in which case it often overlaps with the concept of 'topic'. A comprehensive list of notions may be found in a thesaurus (for example, *Roget's Thesaurus* in English): the headings of the different sections are 'general' notions, whereas the items listed within these are more likely to be 'specific'.

A **function** on the other hand is some kind of communicative act: it is the use of language to achieve a purpose, usually involving interaction between at least two people. Examples would be *suggesting, promising, apologizing, greeting.* Very often functions are 'binary'; that is to say, the performance of one implies a certain response or set of responses which take the form of another, complementary function. Suggestions or invitations, for example, are typically followed by acceptance or rejection; greeting by acknowledgement or further greeting; and so on. 'Unitary' functions may occur on their own – *informing*, for example – with no necessary expected response. However, whether a specific instance of a function is binary or unitary would, of course, depend on its actual context.

To check under-standing Have a look at the items listed in Box 7.2. Can you sort them into separate lists of notions and functions? And can you then suggest which of the functions would be likely to be 'binary', i.e. followed or preceded by a complementary further function? A solution is provided in the Notes, (1) at the end of the module.

BOX 7.2: NOTIONS AND FUNCTIONS

location	offer	request
obligation	promise	spatial relations
advise	the future	food
threat	crime	instruction
apology	the body	remind
probability	expression of opinion	

© Cambridge University Press 1996

▶ Unit Three: Teaching chunks of language; from text to task

Topics, situations, notions and functions may differ in the ways outlined in the previous two units, but in principle the idea uniting them is a 'holistic' view of how bits of language should be presented to learners. Such a view emphasizes the importance of dealing with whole, meaningful chunks of language in context, rather than decontextualized items such as lists of vocabulary, or isolated examples of grammatical structures. It is, of course, possible to present notions and functions 'phrase-book' fashion as lists of isolated items (just as it is possible – and desirable – to teach grammar and vocabulary as used in communication); but it is, on the whole, more effective to teach them as samples of language used by people within a specific interactive situation.

This unit looks at some techniques of teaching such samples contextualized within texts.

Learning by heart

Learning by heart has been until recently rather frowned upon by teachers and educationists – and not only in the field of language teaching. This has been partly a reaction against the mindless rote-learning of previous generations of schoolchildren, associated with the discouragement of creative or original thinking and stress on the memorization of data such as multiplication tables, dates in history and passages from literature. Within language teaching, learning by heart has been associated with the audio-lingual methodology popular in in the 1960s but later rejected by most methodologists, which also emphasized learning through unthinking habit-forming and relied heavily on mimicry and memorization.

More recently, however, both within language teaching and in other areas of education, people are beginning to realize that learning by heart has value, and that it is quite compatible with creativity and originality of thought. Just as an automatic knowledge of the multiplication tables enables the young mathematician to progress faster into interesting problem-solving, so memorized chunks of language or formulaic utterances associated with particular communicative contexts furnish the learner with a rich and reliable 'vocabulary' of ready-made expressions which contribute significantly to his or her overall mastery of the language (Widdowson, 1989).

Thus if we present our learners with samples of functions incorporated into situational dialogues, it makes sense to ask them to learn some of these by heart: provided, of course, that we consistently maintain their awareness of the meaning and purpose of what they are saying.

BOX 7.3: OFFERING HELP

A: Can I help?
B: Oh yes, please, I don't know what to do…
A: What's the matter?
B: He doesn't understand what I'm telling him!
A: Would you like me to explain?
B: Please do!

(adapted from Alan Maley and Alan Duff, *Variations on a Theme*, Cambridge University Press, 1978, p. 46)

© *Cambridge University Press 1996*

Task **Different interpretations of the same text**

Imagine you are teaching the function of offering help and accepting. You have selected the dialogue shown in Box 7.3 to exemplify it. Having learned it by heart, what sorts of different interpretations would you or your students suggest in order to consolidate learning and vary its performance? For example, you might wish to suggest different situations or contexts for the dialogue; different kinds of characters; different relationships between them; different attitudes to the problem about which help is being offered.

Some ideas of my own are given below.

Some ways of varying the dialogue in Box 7.3

The situation: foreign tourists are trying to buy some necessary equipment in a
  shop; a student teacher is trying to explain something to a child, helped by

the class teacher; a driver has been stopped by a police officer for a traffic offence and is trying to explain why he or she is innocent…

The characters: excited, apathetic, annoyed, pleased, tired, nervous, embarrassed, assertive, good-humoured…

The relationships: authoritative–deferential; aggressive–defensive; affectionate; formal…

Attitude to the problem: the problem may be seen as: trivial; distressing; a matter of life or death; irritating; funny…

Varying a theme

Learning texts by heart and then delivering them according to different interpretations is one way of engaging with samples of written or spoken language functions or situations. Another possibility – which may or may not be combined with learning by heart – is to take the basic text and elaborate on it.

Let us take the situation of two people meeting at some kind of social gathering and getting to know one another. The situation is presented to learners through an introductory spoken or written text: a dialogue between the new acquaintances, for example, or a narrative account of their meeting, or a diary entry by one of them describing the encounter. Language functions may include things like introducing oneself, informing, requesting information, expressing interest; topics and notions might include family, work, tastes, travel.

Rather than simply learning or answering comprehension questions on such texts, the class may be invited to vary and extend them, leading to further exploration of the kind of language being learned. They might, for example, either on their own or in collaboration with you, do one or more of the following:

– create a new text on a similar topic;
– suggest other ways the characters could have expressed the same notions or functions; what difference would these changes have made?
– suggest other ways the meeting might have developed, and how the characters might have expressed themselves;
– re-present the original text in a different way: if it was a diary entry, for example, then reconstruct the dialogue, or vice versa.

Task **Looking at a coursebook**

Select a coursebook you know that uses texts based on communicative events or situations. What are some of the tasks through which the book gets the learners to engage with the topics, situations, notions and functions within the texts? Do these tasks limit learner activity to the actual words of the text, or do they lead into further variations, other ways of expressing similar themes? Have you any suggestions of your own for supplementing the tasks set by the book?

▷ # Unit Four: Teaching chunks of language: from task to text

Teaching topics, situations, notions and functions through tasks and learner-initiated language rather than through ready-made texts is another possible strategy. Methodologies based on this idea have been described by Prabhu (1987) and Willis (1990).

In such a methodology, the teacher has a syllabus of topics, but may or may not have ready-made texts or lists of actual language samples that are to be taught. The main initiative comes from the students. Thus in a lesson on personal appearance, for example, learners might be asked to start by working in pairs describing pictures of people before them; each participant has to draw people from the description provided by their partner. If they need new bits of language they teach each other or ask the teacher. (Notice that the teacher presentation of new language, as described in the first module, is still inevitably with us, but the items to be presented grow out of learner need within a communicative situation rather than being predetermined by teacher, syllabus or textbook.) Later, the activity may be reported in the full class and the necessary language summarized, polished and elaborated – and later reviewed and practised. Also at a later stage, listening and reading texts may be brought in, but these are to consolidate or enrich the original task-based learning, rather than as a starting-point themselves.

One advantage of doing it this way is that the minds of teacher and students are from the outset firmly focussed on the 'holistic' language topic, whereas the use of a text as starting-point can lead to neglect of meaning and purpose in favour of analysis of grammar and vocabulary items – as you may have found if you did the task at the end of the previous unit. Another advantage is the 'authentic' flavour of the language-learning process: this is arguably how people learn languages when they are plunged into a foreign society, having to function in communicative situations, and learning as they go along, coping with a certain unpredictability of the language content that will be needed and learned.

This unpredictability, however, can be a disadvantage: many teachers and learners like the sense of structure provided by a programme of language content which has been planned in advance and which they know they are going to have to work on. Also, a lot of initiative and sheer hard work is demanded of both teachers and learners in suggesting and then recalling or noting down the new language.

Task ## Role play

One member of the group role-plays the teacher; the rest are not very advanced learners who have been studying the foreign language for, say, a year or two at school.

Stage 1: Role play
The 'learners' divide into pairs and do the describing-people task mentioned above: each member of the pair has a different pair of characters before them (either Box 7.4.1 or Box 7.4.2), and describes each

in turn; the partner has to try to draw the people from the description. As you work, remember how limited you are in your knowledge: ask the 'teacher' for new language as you need it.

Stage 2: Discussion

Discuss the following questions.

1. How did you feel doing this activity? Do you have any particular comments, positive or negative, as teacher or learners?
2. The objective of the task was to produce and use language growing out of topics and notions connected to parts of the body, clothes and accessories and of situations and functions connected with describing and explaining. Did the task in fact achieve this objective?
3. Was this language noted down – or could it have been – by the teacher or students and used as a basis for further practice?
4. What would you suggest doing next in order to engage further with the target language functions, notions, etc.?
5. Do you feel the need for a prepared written or spoken text? If so, what sort of text might you use? Would you prefer to use it before the task or after?

BOX 7.4.1: PEOPLE TO DESCRIBE

© *Cambridge University Press 1996*

BOX 7.4.2: PEOPLE TO DESCRIBE

© *Cambridge University Press 1996*

▷ ## Unit Five: Combining different kinds of language segments

Probably the teaching of larger 'holistic' language components such as functions or topics is most effective when combined with some teaching of other smaller segments such as vocabulary or grammar (Long and Crookes, 1992). Thus task-based activity aimed at focussing on chunks of language-in-context may be integrated with the presentation or practice of specific items that are relevant to the target theme, and will help learners engage more intensively with the language associated with it. Conversely, the learning of pronunciation, vocabulary and grammar is probably most effective when these are also integrated into activities that use the target items meaningfully for some communicative purpose.

If this is accepted, then the question arises: where should we start? Teach the smaller bits first (the words *pen, pencil*, etc.; the use of *have, has*, possessive adjectives) and then get learners to communicate information about the ownership of different objects? Or get them to try to communicate such information, teaching them the items as they need them? Or provide them with a ready-made text exemplifying a situation where ownership of objects needs to be identified and later analyse it into components for intensive study?

I do not think the answer to this question is necessarily very important. Probably all these methods are practicable and may be effective. Which one you choose will depend to some extent on your own preferences and those of your students; perhaps even more so, in practice, on the approach adopted by your coursebook. What is important is the principle that the different language segments should be combined: that we should not lose sight of the importance of the communicative acts and overall interactive context of language use by over-stressing accurate pronunciation or grammar; and conversely, that we should not spend all our time on 'holistic' communication, neglecting useful intensive study of specific language problems.

What goes with what?

But if we are going to combine pronunciation, vocabulary and grammar with more communicative language segments such as functions and notions, how do we select what to study with what? Some associations may seem quite straightforward: the general topic of 'people's appearance' will entail notions such as parts of the body and clothing, and vocabulary such as *head, hand, dress, shoes* and *coat*. A more problematic association is that between functions and grammar. It may on the face of it seem obvious that some functions have neat opposite numbers in grammar; for example, one might think that the function of inviting would go with the imperative: *Have a cup of coffee!, Come to my party!* However a little more thought will produce utterances that are clearly invitations, but equally clearly not imperatives: *We should love you to come to our party., Would you like another piece of cake?*

In principle, any grammatical structure or vocabulary item may be used within a variety of notions, functions, topics and situations – and vice versa: there are few, if any, 'one-to-one' relationships. The notion of possibility may be expressed by the modal *can*; but also by words like *perhaps* and *feasible*, and expressions like *would not exclude the possibility that*. Conversely, *can* may also be used for requests, where actual possibility is not in question (*Can you open the window, please?*), personal abilities (*She can play the piano beautifully.*), and so on.

Question Try making similar comparisons in another language you know. Is the same general principle – that there are no one-to-one correspondences between grammar and function – true?

Thus, even if you accept in principle that a grammatical structure should be practised within the context of an appropriate function or situation, or that the teaching of a topic should include the teaching of relevant vocabulary, the selection of actual items may not be so simple. Your coursebook may do this for you, coordinating different categories of language within each teaching unit; but it may not. In any case, it is worth being aware yourself, as a teacher, of the relationships between the different categories and possible ways of combining them. The following task invites you to work out some combinations of your own.

Task **Coordinating different categories of language in a teaching programme**

In the table shown in Box 7.5 each column represents a different basis for selection of language: situation, function, vocabulary, etc. In each row one of these is filled in; can you fill in some suggestions for the others? Note that

---

BOX 7.5: COORDINATING DIFFERENT LANGUAGE CATEGORIES

Situations	Topics	Notions and Functions	Grammar	Vocabulary
Getting to know someone				
	Road accidents			
		Making requests		
			Future tense	
				farmer, secretary, etc. (jobs)

© Cambridge University Press 1996

pronunciation has been omitted, since any specific aspect of pronunciation can be linked to a very wide range of other categories, and the decision about which to concentrate on will be to some extent arbitrary. In the vocabulary column put only a sample of the kinds of words and expressions you would teach, or a definition; you do not have to list them all.

You do not, of course, have to fill in every single box; but try to fill in as many as you can, in say, twenty minutes. Then perhaps compare your table with a colleague's.

Some suggestions for ways the table could be filled in are given in the Notes, (2).

Notes

(1) Notions and functions

The functions in the list would be: *offer, request, promise, advise, threat, instruction, apology, remind, expression of opinion*. The rest are notions.

Of the functions, the obviously binary ones are: *offer* (followed by acceptance or rejection); *request* (followed by positive or negative response); *instruction* (usually responded to by some expression of comprehension); *apology* (usually followed by acknowledgement). *Promises, advice, reminders* and *threats* may or may not be followed by explicit responses: in any case these may vary widely in nature. Expressions of opinion in writing are often not responded to at all; in speech, they may be followed by further expressions of (different) opinions.

(2) Ideas for coordinating different language categories

Situations	Topics	Notions and Functions	Grammar	Vocabulary
Getting to know someone	Tastes, hobbies	Inquiring Informing Greeting	Interrogative forms Verb (e.g. *enjoy*) *+-ing*	*swimming, sports*, etc. (pastimes, leisure activities)
Reporting an accident	Road accidents	Time past Narrating Describing	Past tense	*road, car, drive,* etc. (to do with street scene or accident)
Shopping	Clothes	Making requests	Modals *would, could, might*	clothes, adjectives of colour, size, etc.
Planning a holiday	Travel, accommodation	Future time Predicting Suggesting	Future tense	*train, plane,* etc. (transport) *hotel, camping,* etc. (accommodation)
Asking about or describing a profession	Professions Activities Equipment	Requesting information Describing activity	Yes/no questions Present tense	*farmer, secretary,* etc. (jobs)

Further reading

Long, M. H. and Crookes, G. (1992) 'Three approaches to task-based syllabus design', *TESOL Quarterly*, **26**, 1, 27–56.
(Suggests that teaching programmes based on communicative tasks are most effective when combined with explicit teaching of grammar, vocabulary, etc.)

Maley, A. and Duff, A. (1978) *Variations on a Theme*, Cambridge: Cambridge University Press.
(A collection of dialogues exemplifying different functions and notions)

Prabhu, N. S. (1987) *Second Language Pedagogy: A Perspective,* Oxford: Oxford University Press.
(Rationale and description of a teaching programme based on communicative tasks)

Ur, P. (1988) *Grammar Practice Activities*, Cambridge: Cambridge University Press.
(Ideas for practising grammar within appropriate situations, or to express notions or functions)

Van Ek, J. A. (1990) *The Threshold Level in a European Unit-Credit System for Modern Language Learning by Adults,* Strasbourg: Council of Europe.
(A well-known example of a functional-notional syllabus in use)

Widdowson, H. G. (1989) 'Knowledge of language and ability for use', *Applied Linguistics*, **10**, 2, 128–37.
(On the importance of learning 'chunks' of complete utterances or 'formulae' for effective language learning)

Wilkins, D. A. (1976) *Notional Syllabuses*, Oxford: Oxford University Press.
(A classic, fairly brief introduction to the rationale behind basing syllabuses on functions and notions rather than grammar or vocabulary)

Willis, D. (1990) *The Lexical Syllabus*, London: Collins: Ch. 5.
(Describes how a lexical syllabus would be taught through a task-based methodology)

Language proficiency can be defined in terms of **accuracy** and **fluency**; if a learner has mastered a language successfully, that means that he or she can understand and produce it both accurately (correctly) and fluently (receiving and conveying messages with ease). Thus in planning a unit of teaching, it is useful to separate the two aspects, and define clearly the learning objective at any given point in a lesson. When the objective is accuracy, teacher and learners are chiefly concerned with 'getting the language right': forming correct sounds, words, sentences. When it is fluency, they are concentrating on the 'message': communicating or receiving content. (For a more detailed discussion of the accuracy/fluency dichotomy, see Brumfit, 1984.)

On the whole, the teaching of pronunciation, vocabulary and grammar will tend to be accuracy-oriented: in these we are mainly interested in getting learners to say the sounds right, to use the words to express the appropriate meanings, or to construct their sentences in a way that sounds acceptable. In the teaching of language content within the more 'holistic' categories of topics or functions we are beginning to move over towards fluency, with more emphasis on producing appropriate language in context: equal importance is attached to form and message.

In teaching the so-called 'four skills' – listening, speaking, reading and writing – the emphasis will usually be firmly on fluency. What we are interested in here – and what is emphasized in the following four modules – is the development of learners' facility in receiving and conveying messages, with a corresponding lowering of emphasis on accuracy. Where 'listening' or 'reading' texts are used in coursebooks for accuracy, it will be found that they are in fact being used to teach grammar or vocabulary, not listening or reading communication as such. Not that this is necessarily a bad thing! – but it is important for the teacher to know what is in fact being learned in any specific language task.

To clarify this distinction, look at the following table which shows some ways accuracy and fluency activities in the classroom typically differ:

Accuracy activities	Fluency activities
The texts are usually composed of separate ('discrete') items: sentences or words.	The texts are usually whole pieces of discourse: conversations, stories, etc.
Performance is assessed on how few language mistakes are made.	Performance is assessed on how well ideas are expressed or understood.
Texts may be used in any mode (skill), regardless of how they are used in real life (dialogues may be written, written texts used for listening).	Texts are usually used as they would be in real life: dialogues are spoken, articles and written stories are read.
Tasks do not usually simulate real-life situations.	Tasks often simulate real-life situations.

Sometimes an activity that stresses accuracy leads into one that is based on fluency, or vice versa; and in many cases activities combine both to some extent. In most classroom procedures, however, a clear orientation one way or another is evident. Lack of awareness of such orientation can lead to confusion and frustration: as, for example, when the teacher gives a writing assignment whose ostensible aim is fluency-oriented (to tell a story, for example, or to answer a letter), and then assesses it on the basis of grammar and spelling.

Reference

Brumfit, C. J. (1984) *Communicative Methodology in Language Teaching: The Roles of Fluency and Accuracy*, Cambridge: Cambridge University Press.

Module 8: Teaching listening

▶ ## Unit One: What does real-life listening involve?

In principle, the objective of listening comprehension practice in the classroom is that students should learn to function successfully in real-life listening situations. This being so, it makes sense to examine first of all what real-life listening is, and what sorts of things the listener needs to be able to do in order to comprehend satisfactorily in a variety of situations.

Task **Real-life listening situations**

Stage 1: Gathering samples

Make a list of as many situations as you can think of where people are listening to other people in their own mother tongue. These include, of course, situations where they may be doing other things besides listening – speaking, usually – but the essential point is that they need to be able to understand what is said in order to function satisfactorily in the situation. One way of doing this task is to talk yourself through a routine day and note all the different listening experiences that occur.

Now compare your list with that given in Box 8.1. Are there any items there which you had not thought of? Are there any items you had which this list does not include? In any case, if you put the two lists together – yours and mine – you should have a fairly representative selection of listening situations.

BOX 8.1: LISTENING SITUATIONS

interview	theatre show
instructions	telephone chat
loudspeaker announcements	lesson, lecture
radio news	conversation, gossip
committee meeting	watching television
shopping	story-telling

© Cambridge University Press 1996

Stage 2: Finding typical characteristics

Looking at the list you have compiled, can you find some features that seem to be common to most of the situations? Such features might be associated with: the kind of language that is usually used; the kind of interaction; what the listener is doing. For example, in most situations the speaker is improvising as he or she speaks, which results in a rather informal, disorganized kind of language; and in most situations the listener is responding to what is being said as well as listening. Can you think of other such common characteristics?

This is a rather difficult task, and you may not be able to find many ideas. Share your ideas with colleagues, if possible, and then compare them with the suggestions given in the next section.

Characteristics of real-life listening situations

1. Informal spoken discourse

Most of the spoken language we listen to is informal and spontaneous: the speaker is making it up as he or she goes along rather than reading aloud or reciting from memory. (You might like to refer to the transcription of a sample of such language shown in Box 10.1; though this lacks, of course, illustrations of purely auditory characteristics such as changes in vocal pitch or volume.) Informal speech has various interesting features:

Brevity of 'chunks'. It is usually broken into short chunks. In a conversation, for example, people take turns to speak, usually in short turns of a few seconds each.

Pronunciation. The pronunciation of words is often slurred, and noticeably different from the phonological representation given in a dictionary. There are obvious examples such as *can't*, in English for *cannot*, which have made their way even into the written language. Less obvious examples include such changes as 'orright' for *all right* or 'Sh'we go?' for *Shall we go?* (For a detailed discussion of this see Brown, 1977.)

Vocabulary. The vocabulary is often colloquial; in English you might, for example, use *guy* where in writing you would use *man*, or *kid* for *child*.

Grammar. Informal speech tends to be somewhat ungrammatical: utterances do not usually divide neatly into sentences; a grammatical structure may change in mid-utterance; unfinished clauses are common.

'Noise'. There will be a certain amount of 'noise': bits of the discourse that are unintelligible to the hearer, and therefore as far as he or she is concerned are meaningless 'noise'. This may be because the words are not said clearly, or not known to the hearer, or because the hearer is not attending – any number of reasons. We usually comprehend somewhat less than 100 per cent of what is said to us, making up for the deficit by guessing the missing items or simply ignoring them and gathering what we can from the rest.

Redundancy. The speaker normally says a good deal more than is strictly necessary for the conveying of the message. Redundancy includes such things as repetition, paraphrase, glossing with utterances in parenthesis, self-correction, the use of 'fillers' such as *I mean*, *well*, *er*. This to some extent compensates for the gaps created by 'noise'.

Non-repetition. The discourse will not be repeated verbatim; normally it is heard only once, though this may be compensated for by the redundancy of the discourse, and by the possibility of requesting repetition or explanation.

2. Listener expectation and purpose

The listener almost always knows in advance something about what is going to be said: who is speaking, for example, or the basic topic. Linked to this is his or her purpose: we normally have some objective in listening beyond understanding for its own sake – to find out something, for example. And we expect to hear something relevant to our purpose.

3. Looking as well as listening

Only a very small proportion of listening is done 'blind' – to the radio or telephone for example. Normally, we have something to look at that is linked to what is being said: usually the speaker him- or herself, but often other visual stimuli as well – for example a map, scene or object, or the environment in general.

4. Ongoing, purposeful listener response

The listener is usually responding at intervals as the discourse is going on. It is relatively rare for us to listen to extended speech and respond only at the end. The responses, moreover, are normally directly related to the listening purpose, and are only occasionally a simple demonstration of comprehension.

5. Speaker attention

The speaker usually directs his or her speech at the listener, takes the listener's character, intentions etc. into account when speaking, and often responds directly to his or her reactions, whether verbal or non-verbal, by changing or adapting the discourse.

Application   Think of a situation where you yourself have recently been listening. How many of the above features in fact apply?

▶ Unit Two: Real-life listening in the classroom

The title above is, of course, a contradiction in terms: classroom listening is not real-life listening. However, in order to provide students with training in listening comprehension that will prepare them for effective functioning outside the classroom, activities should give learners practice in coping with at least some of the features of real-life situations. For example: it would seem not very helpful to base listening exercises mainly on passages that are read aloud and followed by comprehension questions, when we know that very little of the discourse we hear in real life is read aloud, and we do not normally respond by answering comprehension questions.

It is worth noting also that listening activities based on simulated real-life situations are likely to be more motivating and interesting to do than contrived textbook comprehension exercises. If you did not do Unit One, look now at the section *Characteristics of real-life listening situations* on pages 106–107. Below are some guidelines for the design of listening texts and tasks that are based on these ideas.

Guidelines

1. Listening texts

Informal talk. Most listening texts should be based on discourse that is either genuine improvised, spontaneous speech, or at least a fair imitation of it. A typical written text that is read aloud as a basis for classroom listening activity is unlikely to incorporate the characteristics of informal speech as described above, and will thus provide the learners with no practice in understanding the most common form of spoken discourse.

Speaker visibility; direct speaker–listener interaction. The fact that in most listening situations the speaker is visible and directly interacting with the listener should make us think twice about the conventional use of audio recordings for listening comprehension exercises. It is useful to the learners if you improvise at least some of the listening texts yourself in their presence (or, if feasible, get another competent speaker of the language to do so). Video also makes a positive contribution to the effectiveness of listening practice, in that it supplies the aspect of speaker visibility and the general visual environment of the text.

Single exposure. If real-life discourse is rarely 'replayed' then learners should be encouraged to develop the ability to extract the information they need from a single hearing. The discourse, therefore, must be redundant enough to provide this information more than once within the original text; and where possible hearers should be able to stop the speaker to request a repeat or explanation.

2. Listening tasks

Expectations. Learners should have in advance some idea about the kind of text they are going to hear. Thus the mere instruction 'Listen to the passage ...' is less useful than something like: 'You are going to hear a husband and wife discussing their plans for the summer ...'. The latter instruction activates learners' relevant schemata (their own previous knowledge and concepts of facts, scenes, events, etc.) and enables them to use this previous knowledge to build anticipatory 'scaffolding' that will help them understand.

Purpose. Similarly, a listening purpose should be provided by the definition of a pre-set task, which should involve some kind of clear visible or audible response. Thus, rather than say simply: 'Listen and understand ...' we should give a specific instruction such as: 'Listen and find out where the family are going for their summer holidays. Mark the places on your map.' The definition of a purpose enables the listener to listen selectively for significant information – easier, as well as more natural, than trying to understand everything.

Ongoing listener response. Finally, the task should usually involve intermittent responses during the listening; learners should be encouraged to respond to the information they are looking for as they hear it, not to wait to the end.

Practical classroom application

The guidelines given above are, I believe, valid and useful as general bases for the design of effective listening materials and tasks. They are not, however, rules: they do not, as we have seen, apply to every real-life situation; moreover, there may be very good pedagogical reasons for deviating from some of them in the classroom.

Putting aside, for the moment, the criterion 'nearness to real-life listening', let us consider these guidelines from the point of view of practical classroom teaching. The latter involves pedagogical considerations no less important than authenticity of the listening experience, such as classroom management, cost-effective use of time, student motivation, interest and learning preferences.

For example: one pedagogical advantage of 'real-life' listening situations as a basis for comprehension exercises is, as previously noted, that these are motivating to do – far more than artificial texts-with-questions. On the other hand, a disadvantage of the guideline 'single exposure' is that it might conflict with your desire to let your students listen more than once in order to give them more practice, prevent frustration and give them another chance to succeed in doing the task.

Question   **What practical advantages or problems can you foresee, or have you experienced, that might derive from applying any of the guidelines listed earlier?**

My own answers to this follow.

Implementing the guidelines: some specific practical implications

1. Listening texts

The implication of this guideline is that at least some of your students' listening practice should be based on a text which you yourself improvise for your class, and which is heard only once.

Advantages. Less recorded material means less of the expense, inconvenience and occasional breakdown that the frequent use of tape-recorders entails. You can also adapt the level and speed of the text to your specific students and respond directly to their needs.

Problems or reservations. Many teachers lack confidence in their own ability to improvise fluently in the target language, or are worried their spoken language is not a good enough ('native') model for students to listen to; such teachers prefer to rely, if not on recordings, then at least on a written text they can read aloud. However, most foreign language teachers, even if not native speakers of the target language, can present a perfectly competent improvised speech model; though many find this difficult to believe and are unnecessarily apprehensive!

Another problem is that if learners only hear you, they will not have the opportunity to practise listening to different voices and accents.

Finally, on the point of single-exposure listening: even if learners can do the task after one listening, you may wish to let them hear the text again, for the sake of further exposure and practice and better chances of successful performance.

Conclusion. In general, it is important for foreign language teachers to be able to improvise speech in the target language. Few, however, can do so without prompts or notes of some kind; it helps to have before you a list of the main points you want to mention, or the picture or diagram you have to describe, or the answers you plan to elicit from the class.

Having said this, there certainly is room for the occasional use of recordings, in order to give practice in situations where we listen 'blind', and in order to expose learners to different voices and accents.

We shall also often wish to let our students listen to the text more than once, for the reasons given above. Perhaps a good compromise might be to ask them to try to do as much as they can on the first listening, and check results; and then let them listen again for the sake of further practice and improved answers.

2. Listening tasks: expectations and purpose

Advantages. Providing the students with some idea of what they are going to hear and what they are asked to do with it helps them to succeed in the task, as well as raising motivation and interest. A visual focus can often provide this: for example, if the task involves marking a picture, diagram, or map – or even a written text.

Problems or reservations. Occasionally we may wish to ask students to find out what the passage is about without any previous hint: for the sake of the fun and challenge, and to encourage them to use real-world knowledge to help interpretation. Also, there are some excellent listening activities that need no clear task at all beyond the comprehension itself: listening to stories for example, or watching exciting films.

Conclusion. If there is no pre-set task we should be careful to ensure that the text itself is stimulating enough, and of an appropriate level, to ensure motivated and successful listening on the part of the learners.

3. Ongoing listener response

Advantages. The fact that learners are active during the listening rather than waiting to the end keeps them busy and helps to prevent boredom.

Problems or reservations. The most naturally-occurring response – speech – is usually impractical in the classroom: you cannot hear and monitor the spoken responses of all the class together! Thus most answers will have to be in the form of physical movements, which can be monitored visually, or by written responses which can be checked later.

A more serious problem is that materials writers often overload the task: too many responses are demanded of the learners, information is coming in too fast (not enough 'redundancy') and there is no time to respond during the listening. The result is frustration and irritation: even if the listening text is repeated the initial feeling of failure is something that should be avoided.

Conclusion. Check the activity by doing it yourself or with colleagues before administering it: make sure the task is do-able! If necessary, reduce the demands, at least the first time round.

▷ **Unit Three: Learner problems**

The topic of listening practice as a preparation for real-life listening comprehension has been examined in Units One and Two. Here, we shall be looking at some problems from the point of view of the learner. What aspects of listening to a foreign language are particularly difficult for learners to cope with, and what can we as teachers do about them?

Inquiry   **Learner problems**

Stage 1: Defining some problems

Read through the list given in Box 8.2 of some difficulties that learners have with listening to a foreign language. Add more if you wish.

Stage 2: Interview

Interview some learners to find out which of these they consider particularly problematic, whether there are any others they can suggest, and what sort of practice they find helpful.

Stage 3: Summary

On your own or with colleagues, try to summarize the main problems and make some suggestions as to what the teacher can do to help solve them.
Some comments follow.

BOX 8.2: LEARNER DIFFICULTIES IN LISTENING

1. I have trouble catching the actual sounds of the foreign language.
2. I have to understand every word; if I miss something, I feel I am failing and get worried and stressed.
3. I can understand people if they talk slowly and clearly; I can't understand fast, natural native-sounding speech.
4. I need to hear things more than once in order to understand.
5. I find it difficult to 'keep up' with all the information I am getting, and cannot think ahead or predict.
6. If the listening goes on a long time I get tired, and find it more and more difficult to concentrate.

© *Cambridge University Press 1996*

Comments on the learner problems described in Box 8.2.

1. Trouble with sounds

Since most listeners rely mostly on context for comprehension, they are often themselves unaware of inaccurate sound perception. See Module 4: *Teaching pronunciation* for some ideas on how to diagnose these kinds of problems.

2. Have to understand every word

This is a very common problem, often unconsciously fostered by teachers and/or listening comprehension materials which encourage the learner to believe that everything that is said bears (equally) important information. The effort to understand everything often results in ineffective comprehension, as well as feelings of fatigue and failure. We may need to give learners practice in selective ignoring of heard information – something they do naturally in their mother tongue. We should explain this point to the learners, and set them occasional tasks that ask them to scan a relatively long text for one or two limited items of information.

3. Can't understand fast, natural native speech

Learners will often ask you to slow down and speak clearly – by which they mean pronounce each word the way it would sound in isolation; and the temptation is to do as they ask. But if you do, you are not helping them to learn to cope with everyday informal speech. They should be exposed to as much spontaneous informal talk as they can successfully understand as soon as possible; and it is worth taking the time to explain to them why. One of the advantages of teacher-produced talk is that you can provide them with this sort of discourse at the right level for them, getting faster and more fluent as their listening skills develop.

4. Need to hear things more than once

As noted in Unit Two above there may be very good pedagogical reasons for exposing learners to texts more than once. But the fact remains that in real life they are often going to have to cope with 'one-off' listening; and we can certainly make a useful contribution to their learning if we can improve their ability to do so. We can for example, try to use texts that include 'redundant' passages and within which the essential information is presented more than once and not too intensively; and give learners the opportunity to request clarification or repetition during the listening.

5. Find it difficult to keep up

Again, the learner feels overloaded with incoming information. The solution is not (so much) to slow down the discourse but rather to encourage them to relax, stop trying to understand everything, learn to pick out what is essential and allow themselves to ignore the rest.

6. Get tired

This is one reason for not making listening comprehension passages too long overall, and for breaking them up into short 'chunks' through pause, listener response or change of speaker.

▶ Unit Four: Types of activities

This unit provides a fairly full – though not exhaustive – taxonomy of listening comprehension activity types you may find in coursebooks or listening comprehension books. There are various ways of classifying such a taxonomy:

by listening skill, by level of difficulty, and so on. I have chosen to do so by the amount and complexity of response demanded of the learner.

Study the list, and add any further types you can think of that I have omitted. Then perhaps try the task suggested at the end of the unit.

Types of listening activities

1. No overt response
The learners do not have to do anything in response to the listening; however, facial expression and body language often show if they are following or not.

Stories. Tell a joke or real-life anecdote, retell a well-known story, read a story from a book; or play a recording of a story. If the story is well-chosen, learners are likely to be motivated to attend and understand in order to enjoy it.

Songs. Sing a song yourself, or play a recording of one. Note, however, that if no response is required learners may simply enjoy the music without understanding the words.

Entertainment: films, theatre, video. As with stories, if the content is really entertaining (interesting, stimulating, humorous, dramatic) learners will be motivated to make the effort to understand without the need for any further task.

2. Short responses
Obeying instructions. Learners perform actions, or draw shapes or pictures, in response to instructions.

Ticking off items. A list, text or picture is provided: listeners mark or tick off words/components as they hear them within a spoken description, story or simple list of items.

True/false. The listening passage consists of a number of statements, some of which are true and some false (possibly based on material the class has just learnt). Learners write ticks or crosses to indicate whether the statements are right or wrong; or make brief responses ('True!' or 'False!' for example); or they may stay silent if the statements are right, say 'No!' if they are wrong.

Detecting mistakes. The teacher tells a story or describes something the class knows, but with a number of deliberate mistakes or inconsistencies. Listeners raise their hands or call out when they hear something wrong.

Cloze. The listening text has occasional brief gaps, represented by silence or some kind of buzz. Learners write down what they think might be the missing word. Note that if the text is recorded, the gaps have to be much more widely spaced than in a reading one; otherwise there is not enough time to listen, understand, think of the answer, and write. If you are speaking the text yourself, then you can more easily adapt the pace of your speech to the speed of learner responses.

Guessing definitions. The teacher provides brief oral definitions of a person, place, thing, action or whatever; learners write down what they think it is.

Skimming and scanning. A not-too-long listening text is given, improvised or recorded; learners are asked to identify some general topic or information (skimming), or certain limited information (scanning) and note the answer(s).

Written questions inviting brief answers may be provided in advance; or a grid, with certain entries missing; or a picture or diagram to be altered or completed.

3. Longer responses

Answering questions. One or more questions demanding fairly full responses are given in advance, to which the listening text provides the answer(s). Because of the relative length of the answers demanded, they are most conveniently given in writing.

Note-taking. Learners take brief notes from a short lecture or talk.

Paraphrasing and translating. Learners rewrite the listening text in different words: either in the same language (paraphrase) or in another (translation).

Summarizing. Learners write a brief summary of the content of the listening passage.

Long gap-filling. A long gap is left, at the beginning, middle or end of a text; learners guess and write down, or say, what they think might be missing.

4. Extended responses

Here, the listening is only a 'jump-off point' for extended reading, writing or speaking: in other words, these are 'combined skills' activities.

Problem-solving. A problem is described orally; learners discuss how to deal with it, and/or write down a suggested solution.

Interpretation. An extract from a piece of dialogue or monologue is provided, with no previous information; the listeners try to guess from the words, kinds of voices, tone and any other evidence what is going on. At a more sophisticated level, a piece of literature that is suitable for reading aloud (some poetry, for example) can be discussed and analysed.

Follow-up
task

Listening activities in coursebooks

Any one specific set of materials is unlikely, of course, to provide examples of all the types listed here, though if you look through the books listed under *Further reading* below, you should find most of them. But certainly teachers and learners have a right to expect a fair range and variety in the specific materials used in their course.

Go through the list of *Types of listening activities* again, marking activity types that seem to you particularly useful, or even essential. Then look at a coursebook or listening comprehension book that you are familiar with, and see how many of these are represented. Are there many that are totally neglected? Are there others that are over-used?

If the range and variety in a book you are using is very limited, you may be able to remedy this by improvising your own activities or using supplementary materials: English teachers will find some suggestions for such materials under *Further reading* below.

▷ **Unit Five: Adapting activities**

Most modern course materials include cassettes of listening texts, with corresponding listening tasks in the students' book. You can, of course, simply use these as they stand, but you may find that you wish to supplement them. The tasks may be too easy or difficult; they may give no useful preparation for real-life listening (see Unit Two); they may not seem to come to grips with some specific learner problem (see Unit Three); or some types of activity that you consider important (see Unit Four) may be missing.

   You will probably not, in the course of a busy teaching schedule, have much time to prepare many supplementary activities of your own. Perhaps the most useful and cost-effective action is to take your ready-made materials and, using either the text or the task as your basis, make alterations, involving minimal preparation, to make the activity more effective.

Task **Criticizing and adapting coursebook listening activities**

In Boxes 8.3.1–3 are descriptions of three listening tasks, with the listening texts that go with them. What might you do to improve or vary them to suit a class you teach or know of? Try doing them yourself before thinking about changes: one person reads or improvises the text(s), others do the tasks. This will not, of course, reproduce exactly learner experience with such activities, but it will give you a 'feel' for possible problems.

   My own suggestions follow.

BOX 8.3.1: LISTENING ACTIVITY 1

Instructions
1. Listen to the recording of someone giving instructions. What are they talking about?
2. Look at the words below. Use a dictionary to check the meaning of any you are not sure about.
   Nouns: *switch, slot, disk, handle, key, arrow, screen*
   Verbs: *lock, type*   Adjectives: *bent, capital*
3. Listen to the cassette again, and use the words to complete these notes:

   Turn it on, here is the _____ at the side. Then you'll see some words and numbers on the _____ and finally a _____ C.

   Take your _____ and put it in the _____, and _____ it in; you have to close this _____ . Now _____ in 'A' and press the _____ with the sort of _____ _____ at the side.

The listening text
   First you turn it on, here's the switch at the side. Then you'll see some words and numbers on the screen, and finally a capital C and a sort of V sideways on. OK, now take your disk, this one, and put it in the slot – it's called a 'drive' – and lock it in, you have to close this little handle here. Now type in 'A' and press the key with the sort of bent arrow at the side.

© *Cambridge University Press 1996*

115

BOX 8.3.2: LISTENING ACTIVITY 2

Instructions to student

Your worksheet shows a map of a zoo; write in the names of the animals in the appropriate cages as your teacher tells you.

Instructions to teacher

Using your filled-in map of the zoo, describe to the class where each animal lives; they may ask you to repeat or explain anything they did not catch or understand.

Student's map

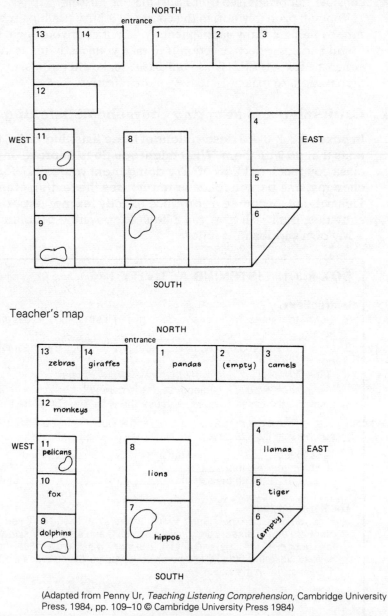

Teacher's map

(Adapted from Penny Ur, *Teaching Listening Comprehension*, Cambridge University Press, 1984, pp. 109–10 © Cambridge University Press 1984)

BOX 8.3.3: LISTENING ACTIVITY 3

Instructions
  Listen to the following recorded talk, and then answer the multiple-choice questions below.

The listening text
  Crash! was perhaps the most famous pop group of that time. It consisted of three female singers, with no band. They came originally from Manchester, and began singing in local clubs, but their fame soon spread throughout the British Isles and then all over the world. Their hairstyle and clothes were imitated by a whole generation of teenagers, and thousands came to hear them sing, bought recordings of their songs or went to see their films.

The questions
  1. Crash! was
     a) notorious   b) well-known   c) unpopular   d) local
  2. The group was composed of:
     a) three boys   b) two girls and a boy
     c) two boys and a girl   d) three girls
  3. The group was from:
     a) Britain   b) France   c) Brazil   d) Egypt
  4. A lot of young people wanted to
     a) sing like them   b) look like them
     c) live in Manchester   d) all of these

© *Cambridge University Press 1996*

Criticisms of the examples of listening activities in Boxes 8.3.1–3

Activity 1

The topic of this activity (a computer) limits its learner audience to some extent to middle-class 'Westernized' learners; it would be inappropriate for classes of students unfamiliar with computers.

Assuming that the audience has the necessary background knowledge, the first exercise (gist-getting) is a useful one, and the text sounds like authentic speech. We might, however, need to pre-teach some of the vocabulary in order to make sure the listening is successful. Note that the text, although an imitation of spontaneous speech, is in fact very dense, with little redundancy and not much opportunity to make up for anything you have missed; it is also 'blind' listening – which it obviously would not be in real life. It might be worth re-presenting the text through your own speech in order to correct some of these shortcomings, and/or providing a picture.

The second task is basically a vocabulary exercise, entailing learning or looking up words many of which they will already have needed for the previous activity: if they are only learning them now, they must have had unnecessary difficulty before. As mentioned above, it would probably be a good idea to pre-teach – or at least review – the vocabulary in advance.

The final exercise demands recycling of the words they have learned: useful for vocabulary practice, but not so good for listening. If they understand and have the items before them, and have already heard the text, then they can probably do the exercise by reading; there is no logical necessity for listening. If, however, they are asked to fill in the items while listening, as suggested, they are unlikely to be able to write fast enough to do so – as you will have found yourself if you tried this out. One solution here is to let learners fill in the gaps at their leisure on the written text, and then use the listening to check their answers.

Activity 2

Here, I would say the activity is child-oriented, and perhaps less suitable for adults; but the necessary background knowledge is perhaps easier, so it could be used in a wider variety of classes than the previous example.

This is an example of the teacher-improvised type of exercise previously recommended, where the actual words of the text can be adapted to the level of the class, and where the listeners can request repetition of information they missed or clarifications. It involves more work for the teacher, but is easier on the learners, and arguably provides a more authentic type of listening text than recorded passages. Resist the temptation to write out the text you are going to say! – though it can be helpful to supplement the sketches with notes.

Note, however, that this is not a particularly 'authentic' type of interaction: it is more of a game, perhaps, than a real attempt at simulation of a natural communicative situation.

Activity 3

This is a very common kind of listening task: used mostly for testing since it is very easy to mark objectively. It is probably, however, less effective in giving listening practice than the previous two examples. It lacks most of the common characteristics of real-life listening (see Units One and Two), is based on a dense, obviously written text, and does not give much help with learner problems such as those suggested in Unit Three. There is a heavy reading component; in fact, this gives practice in reading as much as in listening.

It can be improved to some extent as a listening activity if you go through the questions with the class first, checking comprehension: this lightens the reading load when they are answering the questions and gives some previous information, expectation and purpose with which to approach the listening. Sometimes I even ask a class to guess what the answers will be before listening: this activates their background knowledge, and adds extra challenge and motivation: was I right or wasn't I?

To practise selective listening, learners can be asked to answer only one or two specific questions each time they hear the text.

Further reading

BACKGROUND

Brown, G. (1977) *Listening to Spoken English*, London: Longman.
(A detailed and comprehensive analysis; theoretical orientation, but the application to teaching is clear)

Rost, M. (1990) *Listening in Language Learning*, London: Longman.
(Comprehensive coverage of background issues, clear and interesting to read: plenty of examples and discussion questions)

TEACHER'S HANDBOOKS

Anderson, A. and Lynch, T. (1988) *Listening*, Oxford: Oxford University Press.
(Very accessible guidance for teachers: an analysis of listening skills, plenty of examples of activities; particular emphasis on problems of grading)

Rost, M. (1991) *Listening in Action: Activities for Developing Listening in Language Education*, Hemel Hempstead: Prentice Hall International.
(A series of suggested activities, classified according to the type of listening, with guiding notes and suggestions)

Underwood, M. (1989) *Teaching Listening*, London: Longman.
(A readable, practical teacher's handbook: discusses pre-, while- and post-listening activities, and some key problems)

Ur, P. (1984) *Teaching Listening Comprehension*, Cambridge: Cambridge University Press.
(Theoretical topics similar to those treated here; with a number of suggestions for listening activities)

Module 9: Teaching speaking

▶ Unit One: Successful oral fluency practice

Of all the four skills (listening, speaking, reading and writing), speaking seems intuitively the most important: people who know a language are referred to as 'speakers' of that language, as if speaking included all other kinds of knowing; and many if not most foreign language learners are primarily interested in learning to speak.

Classroom activities that develop learners' ability to express themselves through speech would therefore seem an important component of a language course. Yet it is difficult to design and administer such activities; more so, in many ways, than to do so for listening, reading or writing. We shall come on to what the problems are presently, but first let us try to define what is meant by 'an effective speaking activity'.

Question Imagine or recall a successful speaking activity in the classroom that you have either organized as teacher or participated in as student. What are the characteristics of this activity that make you judge it 'successful'?

Compare your ideas with those shown in Box 9.1.

BOX 9.1: CHARACTERISTICS OF A SUCCESSFUL SPEAKING ACTIVITY

1. **Learners talk a lot.** As much as possible of the period of time allotted to the activity is in fact occupied by learner talk. This may seem obvious, but often most time is taken up with teacher talk or pauses.
2. **Participation is even.** Classroom discussion is not dominated by a minority of talkative participants: all get a chance to speak, and contributions are fairly evenly distributed.
3. **Motivation is high.** Learners are eager to speak: because they are interested in the topic and have something new to say about it, or because they want to contribute to achieving a task objective.
4. **Language is of an acceptable level.** Learners express themselves in utterances that are relevant, easily comprehensible to each other, and of an acceptable level of language accuracy.

© Cambridge University Press 1996

In practice, however, few classroom activities succeed in satisfying all the criteria shown in Box 9.1.

Question   What are some of the problems in getting learners to talk in the classroom? Perhaps think back to your experiences as either learner or teacher.

Now look at Box 9.2, and see if any of the problems I have come across in my teaching are the same as yours.

BOX 9.2: PROBLEMS WITH SPEAKING ACTIVITIES

1. **Inhibition.** Unlike reading, writing and listening activities, speaking requires some degree of real-time exposure to an audience. Learners are often inhibited about trying to say things in a foreign language in the classroom: worried about making mistakes, fearful of criticism or losing face, or simply shy of the attention that their speech attracts.
2. **Nothing to say.** Even if they are not inhibited, you often hear learners complain that they cannot think of anything to say: they have no motive to express themselves beyond the guilty feeling that they should be speaking.
3. **Low or uneven participation.** Only one participant can talk at a time if he or she is to be heard; and in a large group this means that each one will have only very little talking time. This problem is compounded by the tendency of some learners to dominate, while others speak very little or not at all.
4. **Mother-tongue use.** In classes where all, or a number of, the learners share the same mother tongue, they may tend to use it: because it is easier, because it feels unnatural to speak to one another in a foreign language, and because they feel less 'exposed' if they are speaking their mother tongue. If they are talking in small groups it can be quite difficult to get some classes – particularly the less disciplined or motivated ones – to keep to the target language.

© *Cambridge University Press 1996*

Follow-up discussion

Consider what you might do in the classroom in order to overcome each of the problems described in Box 9.2. You may wish to supplement your ideas with those suggested below.

What the teacher can do to help to solve some of the problems

1. Use group work
This increases the sheer amount of learner talk going on in a limited period of time and also lowers the inhibitions of learners who are unwilling to speak in front of the full class. It is true that group work means the teacher cannot supervise all learner speech, so that not all utterances will be correct, and learners may occasionally slip into their native language; nevertheless, even taking into consideration occasional mistakes and mother-tongue use, the amount of time remaining for positive, useful oral practice is still likely to be far more than in the full-class set-up.

2. Base the activity on easy language
In general, the level of language needed for a discussion should be **lower** than that used in intensive language-learning activities in the same class: it should be easily recalled and produced by the participants, so that they can speak fluently

with the minimum of hesitation. It is a good idea to teach or review essential vocabulary before the activity starts.

3. Make a careful choice of topic and task to stimulate interest
On the whole, the clearer the purpose of the discussion the more motivated participants will be (see Unit Two).

4. Give some instruction or training in discussion skills
If the task is based on group discussion then include instructions about participation when introducing it. For example, tell learners to make sure that everyone in the group contributes to the discussion; appoint a chairperson to each group who will regulate participation.

5. Keep students speaking the target language
You might appoint one of the group as monitor, whose job it is to remind participants to use the target language, and perhaps report later to the teacher how well the group managed to keep to it. Even if there is no actual penalty attached, the very awareness that someone is monitoring such lapses helps participants to be more careful.

However, when all is said and done, the best way to keep students speaking the target language is simply to be there yourself as much as possible, reminding them and modelling the language use yourself: there is no substitute for nagging!

▶ Unit Two: The functions of topic and task

This unit looks at some key components that make for successful oral fluency activities. A good way to study these is through the group experiment suggested below; or simply look briefly at Box 9.3, and then read on to the following sections.

Group experiment: Comparing two activities

Stage 1: Experience

In Box 9.3 is a description of two oral fluency activities. Try them out in small groups, one after the other, allowing about five minutes for each. You can do this with colleagues, or with a class of learners whose English is fairly advanced. During the activities, try – even if you are participating yourself – to keep an eye on how things are going: how much people are talking, the kind of language they are using, how interested and motivated they seem to be.

Stage 2: Comparing

Now compare the two: which was more successful in producing good oral fluency practice? If you felt that one was noticeably more successful than the other, can you put your finger on some of the reasons why? Was it the topic? The task? The organization?

BOX 9.3: TYPES OF ORAL FLUENCY ACTIVITIES

Activity 1
Discuss the following conflicting opinions.

Opinion 1. Children should be taught in heterogeneous classes: setting them into ability groupings puts a 'failure' label onto members of the lower groups, whereas putting more and less able learners together encourages the slower ones to progress faster, without penalizing the more able.
Opinion 2. Children should be divided into ability groupings for most subjects: this enables the less able ones to be taught at a pace suitable for them, while the better students do not need to wait for the slower ones to catch up.

Activity 2
A good schoolteacher should have the following qualities. Can your group agree together in what order of priority you would put them?

sense of humour	enthusiasm for teaching
honesty	pleasant appearance
love of children	fairness
knowledge of subject	ability to create interest
flexibility	ability to keep order
clear speaking voice	intelligence

© *Cambridge University Press 1996*

The results I usually get from this experiment are described under *Which is better?* overleaf.

Topic- and task-based activities

The main difference between the two activities in Box 9.3 is that the first is topic-based and the second task-based. In other words, the first simply asks participants to talk about a (controversial) subject, the main objective being clearly the discussion process itself; the second asks them actually to perform something, where the discussion process is a means to an end.

Topic. A good topic is one to which learners can relate using ideas from their own experience and knowledge; the 'ability-grouping' topic is therefore appropriate for most schoolchildren, schoolteachers or young people whose school memories are fresh. It should also represent a genuine controversy, in which participants are likely to be fairly evenly divided (as my own classes tend to be on this one). Some questions or suggested lines of thought can help to stimulate discussion, but not too many arguments for and against should be 'fed' to the class in advance: leave room for their own initiative and originality.

A topic-centred discussion can be done as a formal debate, where a motion is proposed and opposed by prepared speakers, discussed further by members of the group, and finally voted on by all. (This technique is used in the task of Unit Six below.)

Task. A task is essentially goal-oriented: it requires the group, or pair, to achieve an objective that is usually expressed by an observable result, such as brief notes or lists, a rearrangement of jumbled items, a drawing, a spoken summary. This result should be attainable only by interaction between participants: so within the definition of the task you often find instructions such as 'reach a consensus', or 'find out everyone's opinion'.

A task is often enhanced if there is some kind of visual focus to base the talking on: a picture, for example.

Some examples of discussion tasks are presented in Unit Three.

Which is better?

When I have done the above experiment with teachers the task-centred activity scores higher with most groups on all criteria: there is more talk, more even participation, more motivation and enjoyment. When asked why, participants say things like: 'I knew where I was going, there was some purpose in speaking'; 'It was a challenge – we were aware that time was running out and we had to get a result'; 'It was more like a game, we enjoyed it'.

Thus, as a generalization, it is probably advisable to base most oral fluency activities on tasks.

However, having said this, it is important to note that there is usually a small but significant minority who do prefer a topic-centred discussion: 'I found it more interesting: you can go into things more deeply without the pressure of having to reach a decision'; 'I like debating, exploring issues in free discussion'. Such learners also need to be catered for so occasional topic-centred discussions should be included in a balanced programme.

▶ Unit Three: Discussion activities

This unit presents a selection of discussion activities suitable for various levels. The study of their strong and weak points as classroom procedures is best done through experience, as suggested in the teaching task below. Alternatively, you may find it interesting simply to read and think about the ideas in Box 9.4 and then look at the following comments.

Task **Classroom- or peer-teaching: trying out activities**

Stage 1: Preparation

The activities in Box 9.4 are laid out more or less in order of difficulty (of both language and task), the simplest first. Select one that seems appropriate for a class you teach, or may be teaching in the future, and, alone or with a colleague, discuss and note down how you expect this to work with them. How will you present it? Will all your students participate? Will they enjoy it? Can you foresee any particular problems?

Stage 2: Experience

Do the activity. If you cannot conveniently do so with learners, then try it out with a group of colleagues, where one of you role-plays the teacher and the rest are students. If you are doing it with a class of students, try to get a colleague to come and observe and take notes, relating particularly to the points listed in Box 9.1.

Stage 3: Reflection

After finishing, discuss (with your observer if you had one) or think about your students' and your own performance. If you did it with a group of learners, base your discussion on the questions under Stage 1 above and your anticipatory answers: how accurate were your predictions? Otherwise, relate to the points listed in Box 9.1.

Note that not all the ideas listed in Box 9.4 are necessarily good ones: some may have interesting weaknesses!

Conclusions from my own experience with these activities are described below.

BOX 9.4: DISCUSSION ACTIVITIES

1. Describing pictures
Each group has a picture (one of the two shown below) which all its members can see. They have two minutes to say as many sentences as they can that describe it; a 'secretary' marks a tick on a piece of paper representing each sentence. At the end of the two minutes, groups report how many ticks they have. They then repeat the exercise with the second picture, trying to get more ticks than the first time.

© *Cambridge University Press 1996*

---

2. Picture differences

The students are in pairs; each member of the pair has a different picture (either A or B). Without showing each other their pictures they have to find out what the differences are between them (there are ten). (Solution on p.127.)

3. Things in common

Students sit in pairs, preferably choosing as their partner someone they do not know very well. They talk to one another in order to find out as many things as they can that they have in common. These must be things that can only be discovered through talking – not obvious or visible characteristics like 'We are in the same class' or 'We both have blue eyes'. At the end they share their findings with the full class.

4. Shopping list

Imagine there is a miracle store that actually sells the commodities shown in the table below. The owners of this store will, however, only stock the items if they are convinced there is a demand. Students each choose three items they want to buy, and try to find for each at least three other 'buyers' – that is, students who have also chosen it. They mark the names of the other students in the appropriate column; if four people want an item, this is enough 'demand' to justify the owners of the store acquiring the stock. The aim is to get the owners to stock all the items you have chosen.

Name of commodity	Second buyer	Third buyer	Fourth buyer
1. More free time			
2. An automatic house-cleaning robot			
3. Popularity			
4. A job that involves travel abroad			
5. Fame			
6. More patience			
7. A perfect figure			
8. More excitement in my life			
9. Perfect health			
10. A talent for making money			

5. Solving a problem

The students are told that they are an educational advisory committee, which has to advise the principal of a school on problems with students. What would they advise with regard to the problem below? They should discuss their recommendation and write it out in the form of a letter to the principal.

> Benny, the only child of rich parents, is in the 7th Grade (aged 13). He is unpopular with both children and teachers. He likes to attach himself to other members of the class, looking for attention, and doesn't seem to realize they don't want him. He likes to express his opinions, in class and out of it, but his ideas are often silly, and laughed at. He has bad breath.
>
> Last Thursday his classmates got annoyed and told him straight that they didn't want him around; next lesson a teacher scolded him sharply in front of the class. Later he was found crying in the toilet saying he wanted to die. He was taken home and has not been back to school since (a week).

© *Cambridge University Press 1996*

Solution to differences between the pictures in *Picture differences* in Box 9.4
1. In picture A the baby is crying.
2 In picture A the mother has a black sweater; in Picture B she has a white sweater.
3. In picture A a woman is driving the car; in picture B a man is driving.
4. In picture A the building in the background has four windows; in picture B it has seven windows.
5. In picture A the man in the foreground has a hat.
6. In picture A the man directing the car has striped trousers; in picture B he has white trousers.
7. In picture A the woman in the foreground has long hair; in picture B she has short hair.
8. In picture B there is a wheelbarrow on the scaffolding in the background.
9 In picture A the number on the door is 118; in picture B it is 119.
10 In picture A the man on the ladder has a T-shirt; in picture B he has a long-sleeved shirt.

Comments on the activities in Box 9.4

1. Describing pictures
This is a simple but surprisingly productive activity for beginner classes. Make sure participants understand that it is only necessary for the secretary to put a tick for each contribution; some tend to assume that every sentence has to be written out – but this cuts down drastically the amount of talk possible. The second time round, with a new picture, the groups almost invariably break their previous record.

2. Picture differences
A well-known activity which usually produces plenty of purposeful question-and-answer exchanges. The vocabulary needed is specific and fairly predictable; make sure it is known in advance, writing up new words on the board, though you may find you have to add to the list as the activity is going on. The problem here is the temptation to 'peep' at a partner's picture: your function during the activity may be mainly to stop people cheating! You may also need to drop hints to pairs that are 'stuck'.

3. Things in common
An 'ice-breaking' activity, which fosters a feeling of solidarity by stressing shared characteristics of participants. At the end if all pairs tell the class everything they found, then the feedback gets a little tedious; it is better to ask a few volunteers to suggest selected ideas that they think are particularly original or pleasing.

4. Shopping list
An imaginative, fun activity – but, as you will have found if you did it, actually rather sterile in the amount of talk it produces. Participants may simply ask each other 'One?' or 'Seven?', and answer 'Yes' or 'No'. One thing that helps is simply to delete the numbers on the left; another is to suggest to participants that they try to persuade each other to change their choices in order to agree on which to buy. The teacher can role-play the store-owner.

5. Solving a problem
This is particularly suitable for people who are themselves adolescents, or involved with adolescent education, and is intended for fairly advanced learners. It usually works well, producing a high level of participation and motivation; as with many simulation tasks, participants tend to become personally involved: they begin to see the characters as real people, and to relate to the problem as an emotional issue as well as an intellectual and moral one. At the feedback stage, the resulting letters can be read aloud: this often produces further discussion.

▷ # Unit Four: Other kinds of spoken interaction

Structured task- or topic-based activities with clear goals are a good basis for classroom talk in the foreign language, particularly at elementary and intermediate levels. However, the kind of talking they give practice in is in some respects limited: more advanced learners may need a wider range of activity types.

Question   **Look (again) at the activities described in Box 9.4. What kinds of speaking (situations) can you think of that they do not give practice in?**

The extracts in Box 9.5 suggest some more kinds of oral interaction; study and perhaps discuss them, and then read on to the following Comment.

Comment: Different kinds of interaction

Discussion tasks tend to be based on transactional talk, short turns and fairly detached argument or persuasion. The main types of interaction which are discussed in the extracts in Box 9.5 and which tend to be neglected are: interactional talk; long turns; talk which is based on (non-classroom) situations, emotions and personal relationships.

1. Interactional talk
This is to some extent a matter of learning conventional formulae of courtesy: how to greet, take leave, begin and end conversations, apologize, thank and so on. But even more than this it is culture-linked: how the interactional function of speech is realized in different languages depends as much on cultural convention as on knowledge of the words of the language.

2. Long turns
The ability to speak at length is one which adult, more advanced or academic students will perhaps need and therefore needs cultivating; for other types of classes it may be less important.

3. Varied situations, feelings, relationships
It is certainly arguable that learners will need to function in a wide variety of such contexts, and it makes sense to give them opportunities to try using the target language in simulations of at least a selection of them. Conventional task-based discussions do not provide such opportunities; but, as the extract quoted here claims, role-play activities do – which is a cogent argument for including them in a language course. (For a more precise definition and discussion of simulation and role play, see Unit Five.)

Follow-up questions for discussion

Which of the above kinds of interaction are important for your students? For those kinds you think important, can you suggest activities that give practice in them?
    Some ideas of my own follow.

BOX 9.5: TYPES OF SPOKEN DISCOURSE

Extract 1

Interactional uses of language are those in which the primary purposes for communication are social. The emphasis is on creating harmonious interactions between participants rather than on communicating information. The goal for the participants is to make social interaction comfortable and non-threatening and to communicate goodwill. Although information may be communicated in the process, the accurate and orderly presentation of information is not the primary purpose. Examples of interactional uses of language are greeting, making small talk, telling jokes, giving compliments, making casual 'chat' of the kind used to pass time with friends or to make encounters with strangers comfortable.

Brown and Yule (1983) suggest that language used in the interactional mode is *listener oriented* …

Transactional uses of language are those in which language is being used primarily for communicating information. They are 'message' oriented rather than 'listener' oriented. Accurate and coherent communication of the message is important, as well as confirmation that the message has been understood. Explicitness and directness of meaning is essential, in comparison with the vagueness of interactional language … Examples of language being used primarily for a transactional purpose include news broadcasts, lectures, descriptions and instructions.

(from Jack C. Richards, *The Language Teaching Matrix*, Cambridge University Press 1990, pp. 54–5, 56)

Extract 2

A short turn consists of only one or two utterances, a long turn consists of a string of utterances which may last as long as an hour's lecture … What is demanded of a speaker in a long turn is considerably more demanding than what is required of a speaker in a short turn. As soon as a speaker 'takes the floor' for a long turn, tells an anecdote, tells a joke, explains how something works, justifies a position, describes an individual, and so on, he takes responsibility for creating a structured sequence of utterances which must help the listener to create a *coherent* mental representation of what he is trying to say. What the speaker says must be coherently structured …

The general point which needs to be made … is that it is important that the teacher should realise that simply training the student to produce short turns will not automatically yield students who can perform satisfactorily in long turns.

(from Gillian Brown and George Yule, *Teaching the Spoken Language*, Cambridge University Press, 1983, pp. 12, 14)

Extract 3

The use of role play has added a tremendous number of possibilities for communication practice. Students are no longer limited to the kind of language used by learners in a classroom: they can be shopkeepers or spies, grandparents or children, authority figures or subordinates; they can be bold or frightened, irritated or amused, disapproving or affectionate; they can be in Buckingham Palace or on a ship or on the moon; they can be threatening, advising, apologising, condoling. The language can correspondingly vary along several parameters: according to the profession, status, personality, attitudes or mood of the character being role-played, according to the physical setting imagined, according to the communicative functions or purpose required.

(from Penny Ur, *Discussions that Work*, Cambridge University Press, 1981, p. 9)

© Cambridge University Press 1996

Teaching these kinds of interaction in the classroom

1. Interactional talk

The way interactional talk is carried out in different languages is very culture-linked, and it is difficult to explain the conventions that govern it in a foreign language; it is dubious therefore whether it is worth investing very much effort in teaching and practising them. My own opinion is that given general language proficiency and a knowledge of the more obvious courtesy conventions, most learners will be able to cope adequately with interactional speech on the basis of their own cultural knowledge and common sense. Some kinds of role play (see Unit Five) can give opportunities for practising it.

2. Long turns

Some activities that help students to practise speaking in long turns are:

– telling stories (well-known tales or personal anecdotes)
– telling jokes
– describing a person or place in detail
– recounting the plot of a film, play or book
– giving a short lecture or talk
– arguing a case for or against a proposal.

3. Varied situations, feelings, relationships

The obvious classroom activities to use here are those based on role play. This topic is discussed more fully in Unit Five.

▷ # Unit Five: Role play and related techniques

It was suggested in one of the extracts quoted in the previous unit that one way to vary the kinds of spoken interaction that learners can experience in the classroom is the use of what is called 'role play'. Role play, in the above context, is used to refer to all sorts of activities where learners imagine themselves in a situation outside the classroom (as for example in Box 9.4, Activity 5), sometimes playing the role of someone other than themselves, and using language appropriate to this new context. (The term can also be used in a narrower sense, to denote only those activities where each learner is allotted a specific character role, as in the section headed *Role play* below.)

Dialogues

This is a traditional language-learning technique that has gone somewhat out of fashion in recent years. The learners are taught a brief dialogue which they learn by heart. For example:

> A: *Look, it's stopped raining!*
> B: *So it has! Do you want to go out?*
> A: *Yes, I've got a lot of shopping to do.*

131

> B: *Right, let's go. Where do you want to go first?*

They then perform it; privately in pairs, or publicly in front of the whole class.

Learners can be asked to perform the dialogue in different ways: in different moods (sad, happy, irritated, bored, for example); in different role-relationships (a parent and child, wife and husband, wheelchair patient and nurse, etc.). Then the actual words of the text can be varied: other ideas substituted (by teacher or learners) for 'shopping' or 'it's stopped raining', and the situation and the rest of the dialogue adapted accordingly. Finally, the learners can suggest a continuation: two (or more) additional utterances which carry the action further.

Particularly for beginners or the less confident, the dialogue is a good way to get learners to practise saying target-language utterances without hesitation and within a wide variety of contexts; and learning by heart increases the learner's vocabulary of ready-made combinations of words or 'formulae'.

Plays

These are an expansion of the dialogue technique, where a class learns and performs a play. This can be based on something they have read; or composed by them or the teacher; or an actual play from the literature of the target language.

Rehearsals and other preparations are rather time-consuming, but the results can contribute a great deal both to learning and to learner confidence and morale. The production of a class play is perhaps most appropriate for the end of a course or a year's study, performed at a final party or celebration.

Simulations

In simulations the individual participants speak and react as themselves, but the group role, situation and task they are given is an imaginary one. For example:

> *You are the managing committee of a special school for blind children. You want to organize a summer camp for the children, but your school budget is insufficient. Decide how you might raise the money.*

They usually work in small groups, with no audience.

For learners who feel self-conscious about acting someone else, this type of activity is less demanding. But most such discussions do not usually allow much latitude for the use of language to express different emotions or relationships between speakers, or to use 'interactive' speech.

Role play

Participants are given a situation plus problem or task, as in simulations; but they are also allotted individual roles, which may be written out on cards. For example:

> *ROLE CARD A: You are a customer in a cake shop. You want a birthday cake for a friend. He or she is very fond of chocolate.*

ROLE CARD B: *You are a shop assistant in a cake shop. You have many kinds of cake, but not chocolate cake.*

(Porter-Ladousse, 1987: 51)

Very often the role play is done in pairs, as in the above example; sometimes it involves interaction between five or six different roles.

Normally, the groups or pairs improvise their role play between themselves, simultaneously, with no audience. Sometimes, however, volunteers may perform their role plays later in front of the class.

This is virtually the only way we can give our learners the opportunity to practise improvising a range of real-life spoken language in the classroom, and is an extremely effective technique if the students are confident and cooperative; but more inhibited or anxious people find role play difficult and sometimes even embarrassing. Factors that can contribute to a role play's success are: making sure that the language demanded is well within the learners' capacity; your own enthusiasm; careful and clear presentation and instructions. A preliminary demonstration or rehearsal by you together with a student volunteer can be very helpful.

Follow-up discussion or writing

Have you experienced any of the above techniques as teacher or learner? Choose the one that you think most useful, and write down or share with colleagues your experiences and reflections.

▷ # Unit Six: Oral testing

When testing the oral proficiency of learners we may simply interview them and assess their responses; or use other techniques like role play, group discussion between learners, monologue, picture-description and so on (more ideas for oral testing techniques can be found in Underhill, 1987).

But choosing an appropriate elicitation technique is only part of the problem; there are many other difficulties associated with design, administration and assessment. So serious are these difficulties, in fact, that most language exams either do not include oral testing techniques or give them very low weighting in the final grade.

Question   Does a final language proficiency examination you are familiar with (a state school-leaving exam, for example) include an oral component (as distinct from listening comprehension)? If so, how much weighting is it given in the final grade?

This unit deals mainly with the question: to test or not to test? The main arguments for and against are displayed in Box 9.6, and the Debating task suggested below can help you clarify your own thinking about them. My own conclusions are summarized briefly at the end of the unit.

133

Task **Debate**

Stage 1: Preparation

Think about what your own arguments would be for, or against, testing oral proficiency. Perhaps look at those laid out in Box 9.6 and decide what your reaction is to each as you read it. Do you agree or disagree? Would you add any further comment?

Stage 2: Debate

If you are working with other teachers, divide into two groups; one prepares the case in favour of oral testing, the other against. (It does not matter, for the moment, which side you are really on; prepare the case for your group as convincingly as you can for the sake of the argument.) One or two main speakers present the case for each group, and the discussion is then thrown open for free participation.

At the end of the debate, you might like to put the issue to the vote. At this point you may abandon the views of 'your' group if you do not really accept them, and vote according to your own inclination.

If you are working on your own, discuss the issues in writing and come to your own conclusion. You may be interested in comparing your conclusion with mine as expressed at the end of this unit.

BOX 9.6: FOR AND AGAINST TESTING ORAL FLUENCY

For

1. In principle, a language test should include all aspects of language skill – including speaking.
2. Speaking is not just 'any skill' – it is arguably the most important, and therefore should take priority in any language test.
3. If you have an oral proficiency test at the end of a course, then this will have a 'backwash' effect: teachers and students will spend more time on developing speaking skills during the course itself. Conversely, if you do not have such a test they will tend to neglect them.
4. Students who speak well but write badly will be discriminated against if all, or most, of the test is based on writing.

Against

1. It is very difficult to design tests that get learners to improvise speech in the foreign language.
2. When answers to a test are written, assessors can check them carefully at their leisure; but speech flits past, and is very difficult to judge quickly, objectively and reliably. Recordings can be made; but this is liable to be prohibitively expensive and time-consuming.
3. There are no obvious criteria for assessment. Are you going to judge testees only on fluency? Or is accuracy going to play a part? And what about listening comprehension?
4. Even if you agree on criteria, some testers will be stricter in applying them, others more lenient. It will be difficult to get reliable, consistent assessment.
5. In oral testing each candidate has to be tested separately and individually, in real time; few institutions can afford the necessary investment of time and money.

© *Cambridge University Press 1996*

My conclusion

I think that oral testing is worth the investment: not so much for the sake of the overall validity of the proficiency test of which it is part, as for the sake of the backwash. An example: some years ago an oral component was introduced into the Israeli school-leaving exam, with a 20% weighting in the final grade; the immediate effect was a very noticeable rise in the emphasis on oral work in school classrooms and a corresponding improvement in learners' speaking skills.

This is not to say that there are not serious difficulties and criticisms of the test. One of the main problems is, of course, inter-rater (tester) reliability: the fact that since you need a very large number of testers, and it is difficult to ensure appropriate training for all of them, you are likely to get some variation in their assessments of testees' proficiency. This problem can, however, be mitigated by requiring testers to grade according to very explicit criteria (for an example, see the *Notes*).

More detailed information gained from professional research and materials development can be found in the literature: look at some of the articles and books listed under the last section of *Further reading* below.

Notes

Scale of oral testing criteria

The following scale is loosely based on that actually used in the Israeli exam mentioned in Unit Six. The candidates are tested on fluency and accuracy, and may get a maximum of five points on each of these two aspects, ten points in all.

Accuracy		*Fluency*	
Little or no language produced	1	Little or no communication	1
Poor vocabulary, mistakes in basic grammar, may have very strong foreign accent	2	Very hesitant and brief utterances, sometimes difficult to understand	2
Adequate but not rich vocabulary, makes obvious grammar mistakes, slight foreign accent	3	Gets ideas across, but hesitantly and briefly	3
Good range of vocabulary, occasional grammar slips, slight foreign accent	4	Effective communication in short turns	4
Wide vocabulary appropriately used, virtually no grammar mistakes, native-like or slight foreign accent	5	Easy and effective communication, uses long turns	5
TOTAL SCORE OUT OF 10: _____			

Further reading

BACKGROUND

Brown, G. and Yule, G. (1983) *Teaching the Spoken Language*, Cambridge: Cambridge University Press.
(A comprehensive summary of theoretical issues underlying practical teaching decisions)
Richards, J. C. and Schmidt, R. W. (eds.) (1983) *Language and Communication*, London: Longman.
(Applied linguistics: research-based discussion of aspects of verbal interaction; see particularly articles by Canale and by Richards and Schmidt)

TEACHER'S HANDBOOKS, ARTICLES

Byrne, D. (1986) *Teaching Oral English* (2nd edn.), London: Longman.
(A basic, readable teacher's guide, relating to oral work in a progression from presentation to practice to production; plenty of examples and teaching ideas)
Byrne, D. (1987) *Techniques for Classroom Interaction*, London: Longman.
(Simple, practical guidelines and a variety of ideas for games and fluency activities; provides some useful teacher awareness tasks)
Dörnyei, Z. and Thurrell, S. (1992) *Conversations and Dialogues in Action*, Hemel Hempstead: Prentice Hall International.
(Practical ideas for using and developing dialogues for conversation practice)
Hyland, K. (1991) 'Developing oral presentation skills', *English Teaching Forum*, **29**, 2, 35–7.
Porter-Ladousse, G. and Noble, T. (1991) 'Oral presentations: Group activity or one-man show?', *English Teaching Forum*, **29**, 2, 31–2.
(Two useful articles – conveniently in the same issue of the journal – on teaching 'long-turn' speech in the classroom)
Klippel, F. (1984) *Keep Talking*, Cambridge: Cambridge University Press.
(A collection of imaginative discussion activities, mostly for fairly advanced, adult students)
Nolasco, R. and Arthur, L. (1987) *Conversation*, Oxford: Oxford University Press.
(Brief summaries of some basic issues accompanied by plenty of illustrative and useful classroom tasks)
Pattison, P. (1987) *Developing Communication Skills*, Cambridge: Cambridge University Press.
(Plenty of ideas for oral communication activities, with examples in French, German and English)
Porter-Ladousse, G. (1987) *Role Play*, Oxford: Oxford University Press.
(Brief practical guidelines; and an excellent collection of role play and simulation techniques)
Ur, P. (1981) *Discussions that Work*, Cambridge: Cambridge University Press.
(Guidelines, followed by a number of task-based discussion activities, mostly for intermediate to advanced learners)

TESTING ORAL PROFICIENCY

Hayward, T. (1983) 'Testing spoken English – an introduction', *Practical English Teaching* **4**, 2, 37–9.
  (A clear, brief introduction to the issues: some ideas on how to test)
Lombardo, L. (1984) 'Oral testing: getting a sample of real language', *English Teaching Forum*, **22**, 1, 2–6.
  (An account of an oral test actually carried out with students: problems, solutions, conclusions)
Underhill, N. (1987) *Testing Spoken Language*, Cambridge: Cambridge University Press.
  (Readable, interesting; particularly good on elicitation techniques)

Module 10: Teaching reading

Preliminary definition. For the purposes of this module, **reading** means 'reading and understanding'. A foreign language learner who says, 'I can read the words but I don't know what they mean' is not, therefore, reading, in this sense. He or she is merely decoding – translating written symbols into corresponding sounds.

▶ Unit One: How do we read?

This unit attempts to clarify and illustrate some aspects of the nature of reading, as defined above. It consists mainly of a task which examines assumptions through experiment.

BOX 10.1: SOME ASSUMPTIONS ABOUT THE NATURE OF READING

1. We need to perceive and decode letters in order to read words.
2. We need to understand all the words in order to understand the meaning of a text.
3. The more symbols (letters or words) there are in a text, the longer it will take to read it.
4. We gather meaning from what we read.
5. Our understanding of a text comes from understanding the words of which it is composed.

© Cambridge University Press 1996

Task **Examining how we read**

Stage 1: Preliminary thinking

Look at the statements shown in Box 10.1. Do you agree with them? Disagree? Agree, but with reservations?

Think about or discuss these statements, and perhaps note down your responses.

Stage 2: Short experimental readings

Now try reading some short texts, and see whether the results make any difference to, or confirm, your answers.

1. Can you read the English words shown in Box 10.2.1?

BOX 10.2.1: CAN YOU READ IT? (1)

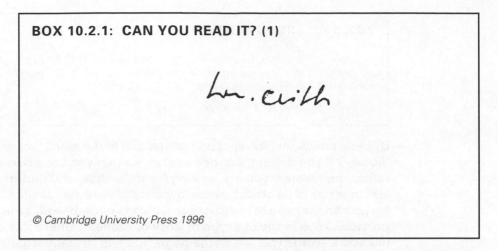

You might guess various possibilities; but you cannot be sure you are right. If, however, you look at Box 10.2.2 on page 140, you will probably be able to read the same words with little difficulty.

The conclusion would be that we can read words without necessarily being able to identify and decode single letters; in this case, you read a word by fitting its general visual 'shape' into a sense context.

2. Read carefully the three texts in Box 10.3. Which takes you most time to read and which least? Read on only after you have tried this.

BOX 10.3: HOW LONG DOES IT TAKE YOU TO READ?

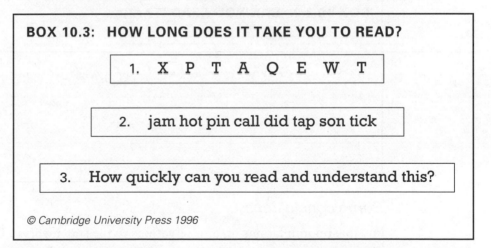

1. X P T A Q E W T

2. jam hot pin call did tap son tick

3. How quickly can you read and understand this?

Most people find that the first two texts take about the same time to read, the third is noticeably quicker. This is a fairly clear indication that it is not accurate to say that there is a simple one-to-one relationship between the amount of text (words, letters) and the speed of reading. What appears to be more significant is the number of sense units: letters combined into meaningful words, or words combined into meaningful sentences. Roughly speaking, a text will take more or less time to read according to the number and coherence of these kinds of units, rather than simply according to the amount of words and letters.

3. Finally, read the text in Box 10.4 as quickly as you can.

BOX 10.4: READ QUICKLY

The handsome knight mounted his horse, and galloped off to save the beautiful princess. On and on, over mountains and valleys, until his galloping house was exhausted. At last he dismounted … Where was the dragon?

© Cambridge University Press 1996

Did you notice that the second occurrence of the word 'horse' was spelled 'house'? If you did not, this does not mean that you are a bad reader, but rather the reverse: you are looking for meanings, and understanding the text in terms of its overall sense. Successful reading results from the understanding you bring to a text, which is often based, as here, on previous knowledge of a type of story or context; where this conflicts with the actual words you see on the page, you will (usually rightly) prefer to rely on your general understanding.

For a more thorough treatment of these issues, see Smith (1978).

Stage 3: Drawing conclusions

In the light of the above experiments, do you need to revise your original responses to the statements in Box 10.1?

My own conclusions follow.

BOX 10.2.2: CAN YOU READ IT? (2)

She's a "natural" teacher! (And it was a pleasure to have her with us)

Some conclusions

Possible reformulations of, or reservations to the statements in Box 10.1 might be:

1. When beginning to read a text, or where there is little or no helpful context, we depend on decoding letters to understand words; but as soon as there is a meaningful context we tend to bring our own interpretation to the word according to its general 'shape' and the sense of the text rather than according to its exact component letters. Thus, reading activities should probably stress reading for understanding rather than exact decoding of letters.
2. We need to understand some words in order to understand the meaning of a text, but by no means all: we often 'skip' or misread words in order to make sense of the whole more quickly or conveniently. The implication of this for

teaching is probably that we should not insist too strongly on our learners understanding every word, but rather encourage them to go for the overall meaning of a text.

3. Very roughly, the more sense units there are in a text, the longer it will take to read it. If smaller sense units (words, sentences) are combined into bigger, coherent ones (sentences, paragraphs), the whole is much faster to read than if they are separate or incoherent. Learners therefore will probably read more successfully if given whole meaningful units of text to read rather than disconnected 'bits'.

4. and 5. The word 'gather' implies that somehow the meaning of a text is there in the words and all we need to do is pick it up. However, our understanding is based on far more than simple reception of the words themselves, and the process of reading would be better defined as 'constructing' meaning from a written text. The 'construction' of meaning that occurs in reading is a combination of 'bottom–up' processes (decoding and understanding words, phrases and sentences in the text) and 'top–down' ones (our expectations, previous knowledge constructs (schemata) of the text content and genre). It is very difficult, sometimes impossible, to read successfully a text where our own schemata cannot be brought to bear. Thus, learners should be encouraged to combine top–down and bottom–up strategies in reading, which means in practice doing such things as discussing the topic of a text before reading it, arousing expectations, eliciting connections between references in the text and situations known to the learners.

▷ **Unit Two: Beginning reading**

Note: This unit is relevant for situations where the learners' mother tongue has a different alphabet from that of the foreign language being taught.

For many learners, beginning to read the foreign language involves learning an entire new set of written symbols. And for the teacher, some preliminary decisions need to be made about how to teach them. Some of the problems are shown in Box 10.5.

Task **Thinking about teaching the beginning of reading**

Look at the questions in Box 10.5 and note for yourself, or discuss with colleagues, what your own answers would be. Then compare these with my ideas as laid out under *Guidelines* below. How far are the latter acceptable and appropriate in your situation?

Beginning reading: some guidelines

1. It is generally preferable to begin reading only after the learners have some basic knowledge of the spoken language, so that reading becomes as quickly as possible a matter of recognizing meanings rather than deciphering

> **BOX 10.5: SOME QUESTIONS ABOUT BEGINNING READING**
>
> 1. Should I teach my students only orally for a while, so that they have basic oral proficiency in the foreign language before tackling reading? Or start reading and writing from the beginning?
> 2. Should I teach them single letters, and gradually build these up into words? Or teach the written form of meaningful words first, letting them come to the different component letters by analysis later?
> 3. If I decide to teach single letters, should I teach them by name first, or by (usual) sound?
> 4. If there are various forms to each letter (such as the capital and lower-case forms in the Roman alphabet, the beginning, middle and end forms in Arabic), at what stage should I teach each?
> 5. At what stage should I teach the conventional order of the alphabet?
>
> *© Cambridge University Press 1996*

symbols. Such knowledge also enables us to give much more varied and interesting tasks for reading practice.

2. I have found it most practical and productive to begin with single letters (the conventional 'phonic' method), starting with the most common and useful. A collection of known, common letters very quickly enables students to cope with a large number of words, whereas learning specific words as such does not readily generate further combinations. Having said this however, there are two important reservations. First, it is worth teaching some very common words globally very early on – for example: *the*, *he*, *she*, *this*, *is*, *are* in English – and practising their recognition through tasks like identifying them in a newspaper extract. Second, some learners do actually prefer to learn 'globally', having a good memory for full-word combinations. In any case, whole words in tasks that involve understanding meanings should be used as soon as possible; phonetics learning is only an entry stage, and our aim is proficient reading that involves recognition of whole sense units.

3. It is, surely, more useful for reading purposes if the learner knows the most common sound of the letter; its name can be left until later.

4. My own preference is to teach the different forms of the letters together. This slows down the process a little, but means that the letters the learners do know can immediately be recognized in the context of a text.

5. Alphabetical order can be learned later when the learners need to know it for dictionary use.

If you are interested in seeing how these guidelines may be implemented in materials, have a look at the sample tasks for the beginning of reading/writing shown in the *Notes*.

▶ # Unit Three: Types of reading activities

Text + comprehension question activities

A conventional type of reading activity or test consists of a text followed by comprehension questions. In this unit, we shall look at some examples of this kind of material, consider what makes it more, or less, effective, and suggest variations.

Task ## Answering comprehension questions (1)

Try doing the activity shown in Box 10.6.

BOX 10.6:   COMPREHENSION TEXT AND QUESTIONS (1)

READ THE TEXT AND ANSWER THE FOLLOWING QUESTIONS.

Yesterday I saw the palgish flester golling begrunt the bruck. He seemed very chanderbil, so I did not jorter him, just deapled to him quistly. Perhaps later he will besand cander, and I will be able to rangel to him.

1. What was the flester doing, and where?
2. What sort of a flester was he?
3. Why did the writer decide not to jorter him?
4. How did she deaple?
5. What did she hope would happen later?

© *Cambridge University Press 1996*

You probably had no difficulty in answering the questions; however, this obviously did not show that you had understood the passage! In other words, you did not in fact 'read' the text successfully at all, in the sense in which the word is understood here (see the definition at the beginning of the module). The conclusion has to be that answering 'comprehension' questions, as such, may not encourage, or provide proof of, successful reading.

Question **What is it about these questions which makes them answerable in spite of the incomprehensibility of the source text? Try to answer before reading on!**

The answer, perhaps, is that their vocabulary simply echoes the text, while the grammar of both text and questions is fairly obvious and corresponds neatly, so that if you recognize the grammar context, you can simply slot in the appropriate vocabulary.

Task ## Answering comprehension questions (2)

The text and questions in Box 10.7 are different. Try answering them, and then think about the question that follows.

BOX 10.7: COMPREHENSION TEXT AND QUESTIONS (2)

READ THE TEXT AND ANSWER THE FOLLOWING QUESTIONS:

Yesterday I saw the new patient hurrying along the corridor. He seemed very upset, so I did not follow him, just called to him gently. Perhaps later he will feel better, and I will be able to talk to him.

1. What is the problem described here?
2. Is this event taking place indoors or outside?
3. Did the writer try to get near the patient?
4. What do you think she said when she called to him?
5. What might the job of the writer be?
6. Why do you think she wants to talk to the patient?

© *Cambridge University Press 1996*

Question   Here, the reader would have to understand the content of the passage in order to answer these questions (similar ones would be unanswerable if applied to the previous 'nonsense' text). Can you put your finger on why? In other words, in what ways – apart from the fact that they are in normal English – do these questions differ from those given in Box 10.6? Try answering before reading on.

The questions here are different in that they do not quote verbatim from the text but paraphrase it, or request paraphrases, or invite some measure of interpretation and application of the reader's background knowledge. They thus demand real comprehension, and encourage an interactive, personal 'engaging' with the text, as well as being more interesting to do. Interpretative questions often have more than one possible answer and can be used as a basis for discussion.

However, one disadvantage of the conventional text-plus-questions remains: the reader has no particular motive to read the text in the first place.

Task   **Answering comprehension questions (3)**

Stage 1: Trying a task (1)

Try doing the activity in Box 10.8.1.

BOX 10.8.1: QUESTIONS GIVEN BEFORE THE TEXT

Read the questions and guess what the answers are going to be. Later, you will read the text and be able to check how many you got right.

1. Where was Jane walking?
2. What did she hear behind her?
3. What was her necklace made of?
4. What did the thief steal (two things)?
5. What did he do next?

© *Cambridge University Press 1996*

Stage 2: Reflection

Before reading on, try answering the following questions (assuming that you did not cheat and read the source passage first!): Were your guesses as to what the answers would be completely random? Or did you base them on some kind of evidence or knowledge?

A suggested answer will be found under Comments below.

Stage 3: Trying a task (2)

Now look at Box 10.8.2, which is the text on which the questions are based. Try as you do so to compare your motivation to read and ease of comprehension with those you felt when reading the 'new patient' passage.

Comments

You probably felt more motivated to read, and the reading itself was more purposeful, because of the challenge of finding out whether you had got your answers right or not. Probably at least some of your answers were in fact right; you will have based them both on information given within the questions themselves (the necklace, for example, was obviously one of the things stolen) and on your own 'schemata' (your previous knowledge, for example, of thieves and theft; thus you would be likely to guess that having stolen something the thief would run away).

Whether you found the reading text easier to understand is more difficult to judge, since your level of English is obviously too high for this example; but for a learner, the passage would probably have been easier simply because of the preparation of topic and vocabulary which was provided through the questions.

Guessing the answers to comprehension questions before reading is only one way of motivating learners to read a text. There are, of course, many others, and these can often be based on the learners' own previous ideas on the topic rather than the teacher's or textbook writer's. For example, you might tell them what the topic of the text is going to be and invite them to frame their own questions (what do they want to find out?) or suggest vocabulary that they think will come up in the course of the text (what sorts of things do they think the text will say?).

Reading tasks other than questions

Setting questions to answer, whether before or after the text, is not, of course, the only way to get learners to engage with the meaning of a reading passage. Sometimes no actual task is necessary, if the passage is easy and motivating to read: the learner reads, as in his or her own mother tongue, for enjoyment or information. But a task is useful for two reasons: first, it may provide the learners with a purpose in reading and make the whole activity more interesting and effective; second, we need to know how well our learners are reading, and we can get this information conveniently through looking at the results of comprehension tasks. An example of a task not based on comprehension questions might be: giving the learners a set of titles together with a set of extracts from different newspaper articles or stories and asking them to match the titles to the appropriate extracts.

BOX 10.8.2: PASSAGE FOLLOWING QUESTIONS

As Jane was walking down the street, sh6e heard someone walking quietly behind her. She began to feel afraid. Suddenly a large hand touched her neck: her gold necklace broke and disappeared. In another moment, her bag too was gone, and the thief was running away.

© Cambridge University Press 1996

Task **Thinking of alternative reading activities**

Make a list of further possible reading activities, using different kinds of texts. These can be for different kinds of learners, or for a specific class you are acquainted with. A locally-used textbook may be one source of ideas, as well as your own and your colleagues' experience and creativity. Some suggestions of my own appear in Box 10.9.

BOX 10.9: IDEAS FOR READING ACTIVITIES

1. **Pre-question.** A general question is given before reading, asking the learners to find out a piece of information central to the understanding of the text.
2. **Do-it-yourself questions.** Learners compose and answer their own questions.
3. **Provide a title.** Learners suggest a title if none was given originally; or an alternative, if there was.
4. **Summarize.** Learners summarize the content in a sentence or two. This may also be done in the mother tongue.
5. **Continue.** The text is a story; learners suggest what might happen next.
6. **Preface.** The text is a story; learners suggest what might have happened before.
7. **Gapped text.** Towards the end of the text, four or five gaps are left that can only be filled in if the text has been understood. Note that this is different from the conventional cloze test (a text with regular gaps throughout) which tests grammatical and lexical accuracy and actually discourages purposeful, fluent reading.
8. **Mistakes in the text.** The text has, towards the end, occasional mistakes (wrong words; or intrusive ones; or omissions). Learners are told in advance how many mistakes to look for.
9. **Comparison.** There are two texts on a similar topic; learners note points of similarity or difference of content.
10. **Responding.** The text is a letter or a provocative article; learners discuss how they would respond, or write an answer.
11. **Re-presentation of content.** The text gives information or tells a story; learners re-present its content through a different graphic medium. For example:
    - a drawing that illustrates the text
    - colouring
    - marking a map
    - lists of events or items described in the text
    - a diagram (such as a grid or flow chart) indicating relationships between items, characters or events.

© Cambridge University Press 1996

▶ **Unit Four: Improving reading skills**

Getting our learners to understand a simple text, as discussed in the previous unit, is only the beginning. Reading skills need to be fostered so that learners can cope with more and more sophisticated texts and tasks, and deal with them efficiently: quickly, appropriately and skilfully. The following task invites you to look at characteristics of efficient reading and think for yourself about how they would affect teaching. But you may if you prefer simply read each item of Box 10.10, and then continue immediately to the Comments and Summary sections below.

Task **Characteristics of efficient reading, and implications for teaching**

Look at the list of ideas on efficient and inefficient reading in Box 10.10; cross out or change any you do not agree with, and add any further items you wish.

Next, note for each what the implications are for teaching. In other words, try to put your finger on what you as a teacher could, or should, do to help to foster the 'efficient' quality: what types of texts or tasks you might select, what kinds of instructions and advice you might provide.

Having done this, you might like to compare your ideas with mine as discussed in the Comments. When you have finished, summarize for yourself a list of main recommendations for teaching, and/or look at the Summary section at the end of the unit.

Comments on the items in Box 10.10

1. and 2. The texts should be accessible: if learners cannot understand vital information without looking up words or being given extra information from elsewhere then the activity may improve their vocabulary and general knowledge, but will be less useful as an aid to improving their reading skills as such. Note that the appropriateness of language level depends to some extent on the task: quite a difficult text may provide useful reading for an intermediate class if the task demands understanding only of those parts that are readily comprehensible to them.

3. There is some controversy over whether you can in fact improve reading speed as such through training; and in any case different reading purposes demand different speeds. In my opinion, the most useful thing we can do as teachers is to provide our students with the opportunities to do as much (successful) reading as possible, including a varied diet of types of reading (fast, slow, skimming, scanning, studying). The aim is to encourage 'automatization' of recognition of common words or word-combinations, this being in general the crucial contributory factor to reading speed.

4. Scanning tasks (where the student is asked in advance to look out for a specific item of information while reading) are very useful for getting learners to read selectively. Careful selection of texts (see (1) above) is also important. Finally, this is a place where frank explanation of efficient

147

BOX 10.10: EFFICIENT AND INEFFICIENT READING

	Efficient	*Inefficient*
1. **Language**	The language of the text is comprehensible to the learners.	The language of the text is too difficult.
2. **Content**	The content of the text is accessible to the learners; they know enough about it to be able to apply their own background knowledge.	The text is too difficult in the sense that the content is too far removed from the knowledge and experience of the learners.
3. **Speed**	The reading progresses fairly fast: mainly because the reader has 'automatized' recognition of common combinations, and does not waste time working out each word or group of words anew.	The reading is slow: the reader does not have a large 'vocabulary' of automatically recognized items.
4. **Attention**	The reader concentrates on the significant bits, and skims the rest; may even skip parts he or she knows to be insignificant.	The reader pays the same amount of attention to all parts of the text.
5. **Incomprehensible vocabulary**	The reader takes incomprehensible vocabulary in his or her stride: guesses its meaning from the surrounding text, or ignores it and manages without; uses a dictionary only when these strategies are insufficient.	The reader cannot tolerate incomprehensible vocabulary items: stops to look every one up in a dictionary, and/or feels discouraged from trying to comprehend the text as a whole.
6. **Prediction**	The reader thinks ahead, hypothesizes, predicts.	The reader does not think ahead, deals with the text as it comes.
7. **Background information**	The reader has and uses background information to help understand the text.	The reader does not have or use background information.
8. **Motivation**	The reader is motivated to read: by interesting content or a challenging task.	The reader has no particular interest in reading.
9. **Purpose**	The reader is aware of a clear purpose in reading: for example, to find out something, to get pleasure.	The reader has no clear purpose other than to obey the teacher's instruction.
10. **Strategies**	The reader uses different strategies for different kinds of reading.	The reader uses the same strategy for all texts.

reading strategy (for example, where the teacher 'legitimizes' skipping insignificant parts of a text for certain tasks) can help learners help themselves.

5. Again, tasks aimed at encouraging learners to guess or 'do without' words can help to habituate them to using these strategies. The dictionary is often over-used, resulting in slower, less fluent reading, as well as frequent misunderstanding through the selection of the wrong definition. Learners should, of course, know how to use the dictionary, but they should also learn when it is necessary and when an intelligent guess is preferable. On the whole, the dictionary is best used as a means to confirm or disprove a preliminary guess of their own, based on understanding of the context.

6. There are tasks which specifically encourage prediction, such as 'What do you think will happen next?' or 'What do you think the next few words will be?'

7. Tasks should encourage learners to apply their own background knowledge and experience to the reading of texts.

8. and 9. On the whole, it is best to give the task in advance, so that learners know what their purpose is in reading. The exception is the case of extensive reading (novels or stories, for example) when the reading material is motivating in itself and a task may actually distract and spoil the reader's enjoyment.

10. We should make sure that our learners are provided with a variety of different kinds of reading tasks, and encourage them explicitly to use different strategies ('Just skim through this quickly and get the main idea'; 'You'll find you have to study this fairly carefully to grasp the author's prejudices; look for …').

A summary of the above in the form of brief practical recommendations is given in Box 10.11.

BOX 10.11: RECOMMENDATIONS

1. Make sure your students get a lot of successful reading experience: through encouraging them to choose their own simplified readers, for example, and giving them time to read them.
2. Make sure that most of the vocabulary in reading texts is familiar to your students, and that words that are unknown can be either easily guessed or safely ignored.
3. Give interesting tasks before asking learners to read, so that they have a clear purpose and motivating challenge. Or use texts that are interesting enough to provide their own motivation.
4. Make sure that the tasks encourage selective, intelligent reading for the main meaning, and do not just test understanding of trivial details.
5. Allow, and even encourage, students to manage without understanding every word: by the use of scanning tasks, for example, that require them to focus on limited items of information.
6. Provide as wide a variety of texts and tasks as you can, to give learners practice in different kinds of reading.

© Cambridge University Press 1996

Application   Look at the reading texts and tasks supplied in a foreign language textbook you know. How far do they accord with the recommendations in Box 10.11? And what might you do to compensate for any weaknesses you discover?

▷ Unit Five: Advanced reading

Activities for more advanced readers are more sophisticated in various ways: the texts and tasks probably approximate more closely to the kind of texts and tasks that people tackle in their mother-tongue reading; the tasks tend to involve more complex thinking than mere comprehension of information; and the activities more often involve extended speaking, listening and writing as well as reading. (Note the repeated use of the word *more*; I am not implying that all these things may not also occur in less advanced reading materials.)

Authenticity of text and task

With less proficient learners, we usually use simplified texts in order to make them appropriate in level for our learners; and tasks also may not represent any kind of real-life reading purpose. This is because such materials on the whole are more effective at earlier stages of learning; indeed, the use of 'authentic' texts with less proficient learners is often frustrating and counter-productive.

However, ultimately we want our learners to be able to cope with the same kinds of reading that are encountered by native speakers of the target language. As they become more advanced, therefore, it would seem sensible to start basing their reading practice on a wide variety of authentic (or near-authentic) texts, and on tasks that represent the kinds of things a reader would do with them in real life rather than on conventional comprehension exercises. Answering multiple-choice questions on a poem, for example, or filling in words missing from a letter would seem a fairly irrelevant response to these types of discourse: discussing the interpretation of the poem or writing an answer to the letter would be more appropriate. Obviously completely authentic performance cannot always be provided for – we are not going to turn our classroom into a kitchen, for example, in order to respond authentically to a recipe! – but we can, and should, make some attempt to select tasks that approximate to those we might do in real life.

Beyond understanding

Our aims in (real-life) reading usually go beyond mere understanding. We may wish to understand something in order to learn from it (in a course of study, for example), in order to find out how to act (instructions, directions), in order to express an opinion about it (a letter requesting advice), or for many other purposes. Other pieces of writing, into which the writer has invested thought and care (literature, for example) demand a personal response from the reader to the ideas in the text, such as interpretation, application to other contexts, criticism or evaluation. Advanced reading activities should therefore see the understanding of a text only as a preliminary step on the way to further learning or other personal purposes.

Combining skills

Tasks that are based on more complex thinking are likely to involve a more complex process. Also, in general, more advanced language work of any kind tends to involve longer, multi-stage activities, in order to explore to the full the opportunities to engage with the language in different ways. It is therefore very likely that activity before, during and after the reading itself will entail extended speaking, listening and writing.

Task **Criticizing reading materials**

In Boxes 10.12.1–5 are five examples of texts in English for intermediate to advanced readers. The first three are accompanied by tasks; the last two are not. What would be your comments on the first three? And can you design your own tasks for the others? Some suggested answers to these questions appear after the boxes.

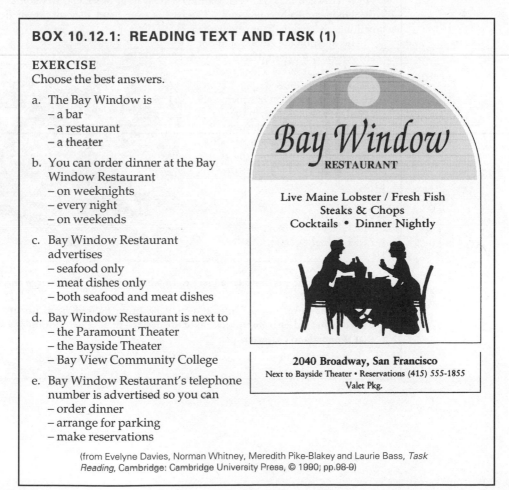

BOX 10.12.1: READING TEXT AND TASK (1)

EXERCISE
Choose the best answers.

a. The Bay Window is
   – a bar
   – a restaurant
   – a theater

b. You can order dinner at the Bay Window Restaurant
   – on weeknights
   – every night
   – on weekends

c. Bay Window Restaurant advertises
   – seafood only
   – meat dishes only
   – both seafood and meat dishes

d. Bay Window Restaurant is next to
   – the Paramount Theater
   – the Bayside Theater
   – Bay View Community College

e. Bay Window Restaurant's telephone number is advertised so you can
   – order dinner
   – arrange for parking
   – make reservations

Bay Window
RESTAURANT

Live Maine Lobster / Fresh Fish
Steaks & Chops
Cocktails • Dinner Nightly

2040 Broadway, San Francisco
Next to Bayside Theater • Reservations (415) 555-1855
Valet Pkg.

(from Evelyne Davies, Norman Whitney, Meredith Pike-Blakey and Laurie Bass, *Task Reading*, Cambridge: Cambridge University Press, © 1990; pp.98-9)

BOX 10.12.2: READING TEXT AND TASK (2)

The following excerpt is taken from *Alice in Wonderland*. The Dodo (a kind of bird) is suggesting a way in which the whole party, who are very wet, can get dry. What is ridiculous about this excerpt?

A Caucus Race

"What I was going to say," said the Dodo in an offended tone, "was that the best thing to get us dry would be a caucus race."

"What *is* a caucus race?" said Alice; not that she much wanted to know, but the Dodo had paused as if it thought that *somebody* ought to speak, and no one else seemed inclined to say anything.

"Why," said the Dodo, "the best way to explain it is to do it." (And as you might like to try the thing yourself, some winter day, I will tell you how the Dodo managed it.)

First it marked out a race-course, in a sort of circle ("the exact shape doesn't matter," it said), and then all the party were placed along the course, here and there. There was no "One, two, three, and away," but they began running when they liked and left off when they liked so that it was not easy to know when the race was over. However, when they had been running half an hour or so, and were quite dry again, the Dodo suddenly called out, "The race is over!" and they all crowded round it, panting, and asking, "But who has won?"

This question the Dodo could not answer without a great deal of thought, and it sat for a long time with one finger pressed upon its forehead (the position in which you usually see Shakespeare, in the pictures of him); while the rest waited in silence. At last the Dodo said, "*Everybody* has won, and all must have prizes."

(from Alice in Wonderland by Lewis Carroll)

- We all have concepts of what "a race" is. In what ways does this passage challenge the usual concepts?
- Look up the word "caucus" in your dictionary. In the light of the dictionary definition, can you offer a deeper interpretation of the passage than "a description of a silly game that Wonderland characters play"?

(from Amos Paran, *Points of Departure*, Israel: Eric Cohen Books, 1993: p.74)

BOX 10.12.3: TEXT AND TASK (3)

Beat the Burglar

Don't invite crime – take basic, sensible precautions. Your house and property are valuable and must be properly protected. When you buy a lock, you buy time – and this is the one thing a burglar can't afford. Most thieves are casual opportunists to whom the best deterrents are delay and noise which could mean discovery.

When you leave it – lock it!

First of all, fit security locks to all doors and windows and a safety chain on the front door. Secondly, use them! And use them every time you go out, even if it's only for a short time. If you have any ladders or tools, don't leave them lying about in the garden, lock them away or at least immobilise them.
Don't rely on "safe" or "secret" places for keys and valuables – nine times out of ten, they are the first place a thief will look.

When you move house ....

When you move into a new home, even if it is fitted with security locks, change them. You don't know who may have duplicate keys. When you are new to a district, you are particularly vulnerable. Never let anyone that you don't know into your house. An official-looking cap is not enough, ask for proof of identity and look at it carefully – if you are still not satisfied, don't let the person in.

Valuables need special protection

Really valuable items, such as jewellery, should be given special protection – preferably by leaving them with your bank. But a small security safe, properly installed, should protect you against all but the most determined burglar. It is also most important to maintain an up-to-date list of valuables and their descriptions. In the case of fine art, paintings, ceramics or jewellery, colour photographs can sometimes be of assistance to the police should you be unfortunate enough to have them stolen. Enter the details on the back of the pictures. But don't keep such documents in your house, keep them at the bank or with your insurance company.

Going on holiday?

Don't advertise the fact that your house is empty. Do remember to cancel the milk and newspapers and also to draw curtains back. Don't leave notes for tradesmen and try not to talk about your holidays and future plans loudly in public.
Operate a "Good Neighbour" scheme to ensure that mail is taken in, the house checked regularly and that lights are put on. If you plan to be away for a long time, make sure that your lawn is cut.
Call at your local police station and tell them you are going away. Make sure that they know who has your spare key and how you can be contacted in case of trouble.
Especially at holiday time, don't leave cash or valuables in the house – take them with you or lodge them with the bank.

(Metropolitan Police: *Beat the Burglar*)

(from Simon Greenall and Michael Swan, *Effective Reading: Skills for Advanced Students*, © Cambridge University Press, 1986, pp. 38–9)

BOX 10.12.4: TEXT (4)

Human rights for everyone

The main Declaration of Rights, covering human rights for all people, was proclaimed by the United Nations in 1948. *The Universal Declaration of Human Rights, 1948*, has thirty articles. These are some of the most important.

All human beings are born free and equal in dignity and rights.
Everyone is entitled to all the rights and freedoms set forth in the
    Declaration without distinction of any kind, such as race, colour, sex,
    language, religion, political or other opinion, national or social origin,
    property, birth or other status.
Everyone has the right to life, liberty and security of person.
No one shall be held in slavery or servitude.
No one shall be subjected to torture or to cruelty, inhuman or degrading
    treatment or punishment.
Everyone has the right to recognition everywhere as a person before the law.
No one shall be subjected to arbitrary arrest, detention or exile.
Everyone charged with a penal offence has the right to be presumed innocent
    until proved guilty according to law in a public trial at which
    he has had all the guarantees necessary for his defence.
No one shall be subjected to arbitrary interference with his privacy, family,
    home or correspondence, nor attacks upon his honour and reputation.
Everyone has the right to seek and to enjoy in other countries asylum from
    persecution.

(Nan Berger, *Rights*)

(quoted in Michael Swan (ed.), *Kaleidoscope*, © Cambridge University Press, 1979, pp. 154–5)

BOX 10.12.5: TEXT (5)

Good marriages

I know some good marriages. Second marriages mostly. Marriages where both people have outgrown the bullshit of me-Tarzan, you-Jane and are just trying to get through their days by helping each other, being good to each other, doing the chores as they come up and not worrying too much about who does what. Some men reach that delightfully relaxed state of affairs about age forty or after a couple of divorces. Maybe marriages are best in middle age. When all the nonsense falls away and you realize you have to love one another because you're going to die anyway.

(Erica Jong, *Fear of Flying*)

(quoted in Michael Swan (ed.), *Kaleidoscope*, © Cambridge University Press, 1979, p. 71.)

Comments on the material in Boxes 10.12.1–5

Text and task 1

This is an authentic-looking text, made accessible to not very advanced learners by its shortness, supporting graphic devices (different typefaces, illustration), and carefully focussed following questions. Note that these questions do not just test 'technical' comprehension of content: they elicit the kind of information that a reader of the advertisement looking for somewhere to eat might really want to know. Not all the text needs to be read and understood by the reader in order to answer the questions, which require selective scanning – again, the way one would approach such a text in real life. This sort of exercise is a good introduction to more advanced authentic reading tasks using unsimplified texts.

Text and task 2

This is an excerpt from a classic of children's literature, published and read in translation in many parts of the world: many students may therefore already know the story. There is a special kind of extra interest in reading a text like this: it is familiar, yet seen from a new angle – and there is the satisfaction of knowing that you are reading it in its original form; it is authentic unsimplified writing, yet not too difficult; and students are able to apply previous knowledge while reaping the benefit from the reading of a 'new' passage. There is also the sheer literary value: plenty to talk about and enjoy beyond the mere comprehension of information.

The tasks are appropriate to this kind of text: the pre-reading task directs attention to the absurdity of the race described; and the following question goes more deeply into the same issue, inviting analysis and application to other life situations. Note that there are no 'comprehension questions' as such (compare this to the previous example), but rather an invitation to consider the story as a whole, and go straight into written or oral discussion of its events and ideas. Learners are, indeed, directed to look up a word: but it is clear that this is not for the sake of reading comprehension as such (the children for whom the book was written were surely not expected to know what the word means), but as a way into another angle from which to consider and analyse what the writer might be getting at.

A side benefit of using such texts is that they may stimulate students to go on and read more of the original from which the excerpt was taken.

Text and task 3

The learner is asked to read, pick out particular types of information, draw conclusions and formulate written questions: these are then used as a basis for interview-type discussion and further writing. This is a relatively lengthy, multi-stage activity, involving analytic and logical thought and extended speaking and writing as well as the basic reading. The task as well as the text has an authentic flavour, in the sense of being based on an imaginable real-life situation.

The directive to 'write down five questions' is perhaps disproportionately limiting, considering the length and amount of varied information in the text. Alternatives might be: 'Write at least five questions' or 'Write as many questions as you can in fifteen minutes'.

Text 4

The text sets forth a series of principles, which are presented in a format similar to that of laws. It would make sense therefore to study them as if they were a series of laws and consider questions such as the following, through discussion and/or writing:

– Can you define in simple language what each item is saying that you can or cannot do?
– Can you suggest other similar items?

- Can you suggest examples from your own knowledge of cases where one or more of them have been violated? Or maintained?
- Choose one which seems to you difficult to implement in practice. What are the difficulties, and how might they be overcome?
- Can you think of any circumstances where you would think it **right** to disobey any of them?
- Can you suggest a series of perhaps more detailed rights that would be appropriate for your own particular community or institution?

Text 5

This passage is expressing an opinion about marriage – specifically 'good marriages'. Thus an appropriate response might be a reasoned, critical expression of a counter-opinion on the part of the reader. Having made sure my class understood exactly what kind of 'good marriage' Erica Jong is in fact describing (mature, relaxed, etc.), I might invite students to exchange different points of view in open discussion: in what ways do they agree or disagree with the ideas put forward here, and can they support their ideas with examples, anecdotes, quotes. A good summing-up activity might be a piece of writing, of similar length to the original, expressing the individual student's notion of what a good marriage is.

Notes

Beginning-of-reading workcards and worksheets

The workcards and worksheets shown on this and the next page are designed for beginner learners of English who are learning the Roman alphabet for the first time. They implement the suggestions given in the last section of Unit Two, and can be used as self-access tasks, or as a basis for class- or homework. Note that they are presented here as illustrations of tasks for the teaching of reading, but in fact many of them are also directed at the learning of writing. They can be made specifically reading-oriented by changing the 'copy' instructions to 'circle', 'mark' or 'delete'.

Each 'set' shows two samples of tasks, which are models for a whole set of similar short worksheets or cards; each such set may serve as the basis for a reading/writing practice session. The instructions, given here for the reader's convenience in English, would in the original have been given in the learners' mother tongue.

Set one

TASK 1
Draw lines linking the English letter with the Russian one which sounds the same.
p   n   R   o   T   L
К   з   т   щ   Д   Е

TASK 2
Draw lines linking small with capital letters.
F   Y   D   f
t   T   y   d

156

Set two

TASK 1
Which letter begins which word? Write the two forms of the letter under the picture.

E   p   D   t   p   c   d   e   H   C   T   h

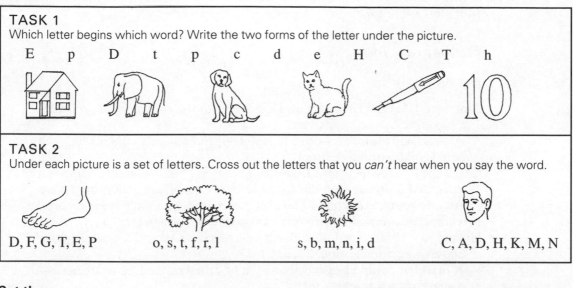

TASK 2
Under each picture is a set of letters. Cross out the letters that you *can't* hear when you say the word.

D, F, G, T, E, P   o, s, t, f, r, l   s, b, m, n, i, d   C, A, D, H, K, M, N

Set three

TASK 1
From the extract from the newspaper alongside, copy out (and translate) any words that you can read and understand.

AMONG the unexpected pleasures of the Caribbean are the contrasting characters of islands standing just a few miles apart: some are low-lying, with white sand beaches set in startling blue seas, others are rainforested mountains that soar majestically from a coastline of secluded coves. Some are ideal for an action-packed vacation, others comatose and perfect for a quiet escape.

Set four

TASK 1
Copy out words that are the names of animals.

head   dog   table

cow

pencil   horse

TASK 2
Which words go togther?
Copy out the words in pairs.

woman

table   man   hand   foot

up   down   chair

Set five

TASK 1
Copy out only the sentences that are relevant to the picture.

1. There is a table here.
2. They are under the tree.
3. They are not happy.
4. They are eating.
5. They are drinking.

More details on the use of workcards and worksheets can be found in Module 13: *Materials*.

Further reading

BACKGROUND

Alderson, J. C. and Urquhart, A. H. (eds.) (1984) *Reading in a Foreign Language*, London: Longman.
(Articles on research on various aspects of foreign language reading, with critical discussion by editors)
Carrell, P. L., Devine, J. and Eskey, D. E. (eds.) (1988) *Interactive Approaches to Second Language Reading*, Cambridge: Cambridge University Press.
(An interesting collection of articles on research and underlying theory on reading as interaction with text in a second or foreign language)
Hyland, K. (1990) 'Purpose and strategy: teaching extensive reading skills', *English Teaching Forum*, **28**, 2, 14–17.
(A brief but comprehensive discussion of different reading strategies, with suggestions for teaching them)
Smith, F. (1978) *Reading*, Cambridge: Cambridge University Press.
(A very lively and readable, sometimes provocative, introduction to the topic of learning to read in the first or second language)
Williams, R. (1986) '"Top ten" principles for teaching reading', *ELT Journal*, **40**, 1, 42–5.
(Brief, readable summary of some important guidelines)

TEACHER'S HANDBOOKS

Greenwood, J. (1988) *Class Readers*, Oxford: Oxford University Press.
(A collection of activities to use before, during and after reading a book or story with a class)
Grellet, F. (1981) *Developing Reading Skills,* Cambridge: Cambridge University Press.
(Analysis of reading skills, suggested activities that give practice in them; guidelines and plenty of examples)
Nuttall, C. (1983) *Teaching Reading Skills in a Foreign Language*, London: Heinemann.
(A thorough and sensible introduction to the subject; plenty of practical teaching suggestions, with underlying rationale)
Wallace, C. (1992) *Reading*, Oxford: Oxford University Press.
(An analysis of learner activity and task design, including tasks for the (teacher) reader, mainly based on materials for advanced language learners)
Williams, E. (1984) *Reading in the Language Classroom*, London: Macmillan.
(A fairly brief, clearly written summary of the topic)

Module 11: Teaching writing

Note: This module does not deal with the very early stages of teaching to read and write a foreign alphabet; for this topic, see Module 10: *Teaching reading*, Unit Two.

▷ ## Unit One: Written versus spoken text

One of the reasons that teaching writing is so different from teaching speech is that the two types of discourse differ in some basic characteristics. This unit studies some of these differences, and their implications for teaching. If you do not wish to do the task, look at Box 11.1, and then go straight on to the *Differences* section below.

Task ## Defining the differences between spoken and written discourse

Stage 1: Listing differences

Can you define and note down some of the differences between spoken and written discourse? These may refer to vocabulary, style, grammar, content, the activity of the producers and receivers of the different kinds of discourse – anything you can think of. It may help to look at the samples of speech and writing shown in Box 11.1.

Do not go on to Stage 2 until you have done this.

Stage 2: expanding

Now compare your list of differences with mine as given below. Check if there are items in my list that are missing in yours, and vice versa. Putting the two together, you should have a fairly comprehensive comparison.

Differences between written and spoken discourse

(The following are some generalizations, to which there are certain exceptions: see the Notes, (1).)

1. Permanence
Written discourse is fixed and stable so the reading can be done at whatever time, speed and level of thoroughness the individual reader wishes. Spoken text

159

BOX 11.1: SAMPLES OF WRITTEN AND SPOKEN TEXTS

The written text (refers to a diagram of a cassette recorder with different components numbered)
- For recording from the built-in microphone ensure that no equipment is connected to socket (1)
- For other recordings connect the separate microphone or the equipment from which you wish to record to socket (11)
- Insert a cassette
- Press record (2) and start key (4) at the same time
- To stop, press stop key (6)

The spoken text

Marion: Could you explain to me how to make a recording with this cassette recorder?

Ron: (er) Yes certainly. (um) First of all you (er) open the (er) place where the cassette goes, press down the button marked eject, then you put the cassette in and close the lid. (um) Then (um) to record you have to press down two buttons simultaneously (er) the one marked rec for record and the one marked start. So you press those two down like that—

Marion: Uhuh

Ron: and it starts recording (er) automatically ...

Marion: Ummm. And what if I want to record with a different microphone, not the built-in one here?

Ron: There's a, a place, a socket here—

Marion: Oh yes

Ron: on the bottom left, and you can put an outside microphone into that and record from another source.

(from Ronald V. White, *Teaching Written English*, Heinemann Educational Books, 1980, pp. 11–12)

© *Cambridge University Press 1996*

---

in contrast is fleeting, and moves on in real time. The listener – though he or she may occasionally interrupt to request clarification – must in general follow what is said at the speed set by the speaker.

2. Explicitness

The written text is explicit; it has to make clear the context and all references. The written text in Box 11.1, for example, is apparently clarified by a diagram with numbered items. In speech, however, the real-time situation and knowledge shared between speaker and listener means that some information can be assumed and need not be made explicit: in Box 11.1, what is referred to by words like *this* and *here* is apparently clear to both speaker and hearer.

3. Density

The content is presented much more densely in writing. In speech, the information is 'diluted' and conveyed through many more words: there are a lot of repetitions, glosses, 'fillers', producing a text that is noticeably longer and with more redundant passages.

4. Detachment

The writing of a text is detached in time and space from its reading; the writer normally works alone, and may not be acquainted with his or her readers. Speaking usually takes place in immediate interaction with known listeners, with the availability of immediate feedback.

5. Organization

A written text is usually organized and carefully formulated, since its composer has time and opportunity to edit it before making it available for reading. A speaker is improvising as he or she speaks: ongoing alterations, in the shape of glosses, self-corrections and so on produce an apparently disorganized 'stream-of-consciousness' kind of discourse. Thus a written text conforms more to conventional rules of grammar, and its vocabulary is more precise and formal.

6. Slowness of production, speed of reception

Writing is much slower than speaking. On the other hand, we can usually read a piece of text and understand it much faster than we can take in the same text if we listen while someone reads it aloud to us.

7. Standard language

Writing normally uses a generally acceptable standard variety of the language, whereas speech may sometimes be in a regional or other limited-context dialect. In some languages (Chinese, for example), the various spoken dialects may even be mutually incomprehensible, while the written language is universally understood.

8. A learnt skill

Most people acquire the spoken language (at least of their own mother tongue) intuitively, whereas the written form is in most cases deliberately taught and learned.

9. Sheer amount and importance

Spoken texts are far longer, normally (in the sense that they contain more words), than a representation of the same information in writing; this is largely because of the phenomenon called 'redundancy', discussed in (3) above and in Module 8: *Teaching listening*, Unit One. It is also, I think, true to say that most people speak far more than they write. Associated with this point is a third: that speech is more important for survival and effective functioning in society than writing is.

Question   How far would you think it necessary or useful to make your own – present or prospective – students aware of some or all of these points? (My answer to this is given in the Notes, (2).)

▶ # Unit Two: Teaching procedures

This unit is based on the assumption that the objective of the teaching of writing in a foreign language is to get learners to acquire the abilities and skills they need to produce a range of different kinds of written texts similar to those an educated person would be expected to be able to produce in their own language. If the objectives in your teaching situation, or as expressed in your syllabus, are different (to pass a certain exam, for example, or to write specific kinds of texts), it is worth taking a moment to define what they are; you may find that you need to adapt some of the material in this unit.

Some of the characteristics of written texts in general were considered in Unit One; this unit studies the objectives and content of textbook procedures that teach writing: what is, or should be, their content? We shall look at some writing tasks and examine what each in fact does for the learner. First, does it really teach writing, or just use writing as a means to teach some other aspect of language (grammar, for example)? Second, if it does focus on writing itself, what sort of a balance does it maintain between 'micro' aspects (spelling, punctuation, etc.) and 'macro' (content, organization)?

Writing as a means or as an end

1. As a means
Writing is widely used within foreign language courses as a convenient means for engaging with aspects of language other than the writing itself. For example: learners note down new vocabulary; copy out grammar rules; write out answers to reading or listening comprehension questions; do written tests. In these examples, writing is simply used either as a means of getting the students to attend to and practise a particular language point, or – even more frequently – as a convenient method of testing it: providing information as to how well something has been learned in a form which the teacher can then check at his or her leisure.

2. As an end
Other activities take as their main objective the writing itself. At the 'micro' level they practise specific written forms at the level of word or sentence (handwriting or typing, spelling, punctuation); at the 'macro' level the emphasis is on content and organization: tasks invite learners to express themselves using their own words, state a purpose for writing, and often specify an audience. Examples of such activities would be: narrating a story, writing a letter.

3. As both means and end
A third kind of activity combines purposeful and original writing with the learning or practice of some other skill or content. For example, a written response to the reading of a controversial newspaper article (combines writing with reading); the writing of anecdotes to illustrate the meaning of idioms (combines writing with vocabulary practice).

Task **Classifying writing activities**

In Box 11.2 are a series of instructions introducing 'writing' activities in textbooks. Where would you put each on the scale shown here?

WRITING AS AN END IN ITSELF	WRITING AS MEANS AND END	WRITING AS A MEANS

See the Notes, (3) for my own suggested classification.

BOX 11.2: INSTRUCTIONS FOR WRITING ACTIVITIES

A. The sentences in the following paragraph have been jumbled. Write them out in the correct order.
B. Finish the following sentences in a way that makes the underlined word clear. For example:

An <u>expert</u> is someone who …

C. The following story is written in the present tense. Rewrite it in the past.
D. We have come to an exciting point in the story. Write down what you think will happen next, and why.
E. For a survey on child education in this country: could you please state your main criticisms of the way you were brought up?

© *Cambridge University Press 1996*

Writing for content and/or form

The purpose of writing, in principle, is the expression of ideas, the conveying of a message to the reader; so the ideas themselves should arguably be seen as the most important aspect of the writing. On the other hand, the writer needs also to pay some attention to formal aspects: neat handwriting, correct spelling and punctuation, as well as acceptable grammar and careful selection of vocabulary. This is because much higher standards of language are normally demanded in writing than in speech: more careful constructions, more precise and varied vocabulary, more correctness of expression in general. Also, the slow and reflective nature of the process of writing in itself enables the writer to devote time and attention to formal aspects during the process of production – something it is difficult to demand in the course of the real-time flow of speech.

One of our problems in teaching writing is to maintain a fair balance between content and form when defining our requirements and assessing. What this 'fair balance' is depends, of course, to some extent on your own teaching situation and opinion.

Application Look at a textbook you know, or a book that explicitly sets out to teach writing, and identify two or three activities that do, in your opinion, really teach writing as an 'end' not just as a 'means', as defined in the first part of this unit. Do these activities maintain a balance between content and form that seems to you appropriate for your own teaching situation? If there is a bias, which way does it tend?

163

▶ # Unit Three: Tasks that stimulate writing

Tasks given in textbooks to stimulate writing do not always do so very effectively. When you are selecting activities or designing your own for a class you are teaching, what are your chief considerations? In Box 11.3 are some of my own, expressed as questions.

Question   Are the criteria shown in Box 11.3 acceptable to you? Would you omit or change any of them, add more?

BOX 11.3:   SOME CRITERIA FOR THE EVALUATION OF TEXTBOOK WRITING ACTIVITIES

1. Would my students find the activity motivating, stimulating and interesting to do?
2. Is it of an appropriate level for them? Or would they find it too easy/difficult/childish/sophisticated?
3. Is the kind of writing relevant to their needs?
4. Would I need to do some preliminary teaching in preparation for this activity?
5. In general, do I like this activity? Would I use it?

© *Cambridge University Press 1996*

The task below asks you to criticize various types of writing activities as vehicles for promoting writing skills. An alternative to the task is simply to study the list of activities in the light of the following *Comments*.

Task   **Evaluating writing activities**

In Box 11.4 are some writing activities of types commonly found in coursebooks. How would you evaluate them for use in a particular class? The class can be one you are teaching or have taught; or one you remember participating in as a student; or even a hypothetical one, which you can imagine teaching. If you answered the question above, then you have a list of appropriate criteria ready; otherwise you might find it useful to refer to those provided in Box 11.3.

When you have finished, you might find it interesting to compare your comments with mine below.

Comments: Writing tasks

1. Book report
Can be a fairly routine, rather boring, exercise; usually done in order to check that students have read a book, rather than for the sake of the writing. Some preliminary guidance is sometimes needed on content and organization.

2. Book review
About the same level as (1), also needing some preliminary guidance; but the writing is more purposeful, audience-oriented and interesting to do. There is

---

BOX 11.4:   SOME TEXTBOOK WRITING ACTIVITIES

1. Write a report of a book you have just read.
2. Write a review of a book you enjoyed and would like to recommend to other people in the class.
3. Write an instruction sheet for something you yourself know how to do well (e.g. prepare some kind of food).
4. Write a narrative based on a picture or series of pictures.
5. Describe an occasion when you were disappointed (or afraid, surprised, relieved ...).
6. Look out of the window, and describe the view you see.
7. Describe someone you know very well.
8. Write imaginary descriptions of five people, based on photographs and some information about their professions.
9. Write an answer to a (given) letter of complaint.
10. Write a letter applying for a job as babysitter, stating your qualifications for the job.
11. Think of a change you would like to see introduced in your country, home community or place of work/study. Write a recommendation to the authorities, explaining why it is desirable and suggesting how it might be effected.
12. Read a newspaper article reporting a piece of news, and notice the kinds of information provided. Write a similar article of your own on an imaginary event.
13. Imagine your ideal school. Describe it.
14. Describe the process represented in a flowchart or other kind of diagram.
15. Listen to a piece of music. Describe the plot and atmosphere of the film for which it is to be the background music.

© Cambridge University Press 1995

---

some point in rewriting and polishing the reviews for publishing within the class (on a class noticeboard, for example).

3. Instruction sheet

Students usually find this interesting to do, and a little easier than (1) and (2). You may wish to give some advice on the layout of instructions.

4. Narrative

A fairly interesting task that can be adapted for most levels. It does depend on preparation of suitable pictures, perhaps cut from magazines.

5. Personal story

On the whole students are motivated to write (and read) about personal experiences; also, each can write at his or her own level of proficiency. Preparation: perhaps a brief sample of a personal story contributed by the teacher or a volunteer student.

6. Describe a view

This can be interesting, but should be kept fairly short; it can be done at various levels of proficiency. If no window with a view is available, students can be asked to recall and describe a view they are familiar with.

7. Describe someone
Fairly easy to do, and straightforward to present; can be interesting both to write and read.

8. Describe people
Of about the same level as (7); can also be interesting, because of the stimulus to the imagination – but of course demands more preparation.

9. Answer a letter
Usually a highly motivating task, fairly advanced, with a clear audience and purpose. As it stands, you need to prepare the original letter; an alternative is to ask all the students to write letters of complaint, and later answer each other's letters. Some pre-teaching of conventional letter formalities and layout in the target language is necessary.

10. Job application
Again, some conventions about letters like this will need to be taught, and perhaps some details about the exact job being applied for.

11. Propose change
Advanced writing, involving the organized and convincing presentation of an argument. You may or may not feel it necessary to read a similar piece of writing with the students in advance, to supply a model.

12. News report
This is clear 'model-imitation' writing, which is perhaps useful, but not very interesting to do. It may be more interesting if it is a report of a genuine local event. In preparation, you may need to draw learners' attention to the typical features of this genre of written discourse.

13. Ideal school
A task which is interesting and relevant for schoolchildren. Little preparation is necessary, apart from, perhaps, some preliminary brainstorming of the kinds of topics they may wish to include.

14. Describe process
A more sophisticated task, requiring precise and orderly representation of facts: suitable particularly for learners in science or technology.

15. Film music
A stimulating, fun task for imaginative students, but it may take time to select and prepare a suitable piece of music.

▷ # Unit Four: The process of composition

When we are teaching advanced composition, it is sometimes difficult to decide what kind of teacher intervention can be most productive. One thing that can help is to study how people write: how a writer thinks, feels and acts at the various stages of composing a text.

Experience ## The writing process

Stage 1: Writing

Choose one of the two problems described in Box 11.5, and compose a written answer in the form of a short text of about 200–300 words. Do this on paper, not on a word processor, crossing out rather than erasing parts you wish to delete, so that all versions of the draft are preserved, though you may start a new version on a fresh piece of paper as often as you like. As you compose your answer, try to be aware of how you are thinking and what you are doing. You may keep a piece of paper at your elbow to note down things that you notice about your own thinking and action, as they come up; or describe your thoughts into a cassette recorder as you write; or simply keep notes in your head, and write down what you remember as soon as you finish the composition process. (My own responses to the problems themselves are given at the end of this unit.)

BOX 11.5: PROBLEMS TO RESPOND TO IN WRITING

Problem 1
If the immediate objective of the students in a specific class is to pass a school-leaving exam which does not include any extended writing, and if after leaving school very few of them will need to do much writing in the foreign language – how much writing should be taught, if any?

Problem 2
If not-very-proficient students are asked to write freely, they produce work that is full of language mistakes. What should be done about this? Not let them write freely? Not correct mistakes? …

© *Cambridge University Press 1996*

Stage 2: Reflection

If you are in a group, compare your results with those of other participants. What were the similarities and differences in your writing process? If you are alone, reflect and note down your conclusions.

In either case, you might find the questions shown in Box 11.6 help to focus your thinking.

BOX 11.6: REFLECTING ON THE WRITING PROCESS

1. Preparation

Did you make preliminary notes? If so, were these in the form of a brainstorm? A series of numbered points? A skeleton outline? A combination of these? Or did you just think for a bit and then launch straight into the writing?

2. Process

How far did you get without crossing out / inserting / changing anything? In general, how much rewriting did you do? Did you finish one part to your own satisfaction before going on to the next? Or did you find yourself writing a later part, conscious that you had not yet done an earlier one? Did you find yourself writing something that you felt was not quite satisfactory, with a mental note to come back to it later? Did you change the order of 'chunks' of writing as you went on? At what stage did you edit formal aspects such as punctuation or grammar?

How did you feel during the writing process? Was it interesting? Absorbing? Tedious? Enjoyable? Uncomfortable?

Would you have liked help or advice from an experienced writer, or teacher, at any stage? If so, when and how?

3. Product

If you made preliminary notes, how closely did the final result in fact accord with the plan? How satisfied did you feel with it? Did you feel you wished someone to read it? Were you interested in reading what others had written on the same topic?

© Cambridge University Press 1996

If you are interested in reading my own introspective responses to some of the above questions, see the Notes, (4).

Stage 3: Conclusion

Try to draw some practical teaching conclusions from the results of your introspection and discussion. Compare these with the suggestions in the following section. Would you agree with them?

The writing process: Summary and implications for teaching

1. Individuals vary. Different writers may produce equally good results through widely different processes. This means that there is probably no one 'right' system of writing that we should recommend; rather, we should suggest and make available various possible strategies, encouraging individuals to experiment and search for one that is personally effective.

2. Writing is a messy business. Most people progress through a number of untidy drafts before reaching a final version. Nor do they always follow what might seem a rational order of priority: it is true that on the whole good writers think about content first and form later, but this order is not consistently observed. Actual content may be altered at quite late stages in the drafting, and changes to sentence or paragraph organization relatively early. So while it may be useful to advise learners not to worry too much about spelling and grammar at the beginning, and to get down their ideas first, it may not be wise to try to impose this as a rigid rule. More helpful, perhaps, is

to encourage learners to work through a number of revisions; to accept messy drafts as a positive, even essential, stage in writing; to treat early drafts as transition stages to be criticized but not formally assessed.

3. Writing is potentially satisfying. If you are writing on a topic about which you feel you have something worthwhile or interesting to say, the process of writing can be absorbing and enjoyable; and if it is worked through to a final product, most people feel pride in their work and want it to be read. It is therefore worth investing thought in the selection of topics and tasks that motivate learners to write; and extremely important to provide an appreciative reader audience, whether teacher or co-learners.

4. You learn to write through writing. This may seem obvious – the same can be said of all the other skills – nevertheless it needs to be emphasized. Reading, of course, helps, since it familiarizes learners with the conventions governing various kinds of texts and in general improves their language, but it is not enough, and is no substitute for hands-on writing experience. One of our main tasks then, as teachers, is to get our students to write a lot, thinking as they do so and learning from their own writing experience.

Postscript: The problems themselves

The 'problems' used in Box 11.5 as a basis for writing are of course genuine ones; here are some of my own thoughts on them.

Problem 1

With a class such as that described here I would do less writing than with other classes, but I would still do some, for two main reasons. First, neither we nor our students can be quite sure about the future, and some of the students might find themselves in a situation where they do need to write. Second, I believe that learning how to write effectively has value in itself as part of the long-term education process, and should not be evaluated only on whether it is immediately profitable or not.

Problem 2

The two suggestions at the end of this 'problem' can both contribute to solving it. We can certainly decide to correct only the more basic or serious mistakes in order to lessen the discouraging effect of too many corrections. And we can partially control student writing by, for example, giving a part of what they are to write ready-formulated in advance; or by prescribing certain limits or frameworks.

But to over-control writing so that there are few or no mistakes would, I feel, be a pity; students should have opportunities to spread their wings and be ambitious. Our responses to free writing, even if this is full of mistakes, can mitigate discouragement and encourage learning: we can, for example, draw students' attention in our feedback to things they have got right as well as things they have got wrong; and we can even explain frankly that writing-with-mistakes is not something to be ashamed of but rather a helpful and important stage in learning – which it is.

▶ # Unit Five: Giving feedback on writing

This unit describes various problems associated with the giving of feedback on original writing in the foreign language, and gives some advice as to how to deal with them. This advice is to be related to critically, as suggested in the Discussion task below.

Task ## Critical discussion

After reading each section think or discuss: how far do you agree with the advice? Would you (or do you) use the recommended feedback strategies?

1. What should feedback be mainly on: language? Content? Organization?

The problem

When a student submits a piece of original writing, the most important thing about it is, arguably, its content: whether the ideas or events that were written about were significant and interesting. Then there is the organization and presentation: whether the ideas were arranged in a way that was easy to follow and pleasing to read. Finally, there is the question of language forms: whether the grammar, vocabulary, spelling and punctuation were of an acceptable standard of accuracy.

Many teachers are aware that content and organization are important, but find themselves relating mainly to language forms in their feedback, conveying the implicit message that these are what matters. This is for various reasons:

1. Mistakes in spelling or grammar catch the eye and seem to demand to be corrected; they are very difficult to ignore.
2. Students also want their language mistakes to be corrected. (Ask them! And see Leki, 1991.)
3. Language mistakes are far more easily and quickly diagnosed and corrected than ones of content and organization.

Advice

We should, I think, correct language mistakes; our problem is how to do so without conveying the message that these are the only, or main, basis for evaluation of a piece of writing. One possibility is to note corrections within the body of the text, and devote comments at the end to matters of content and organization, followed by the evaluation. Alternatively, we may correct mistakes and make suggestions as to content and organization, but not evaluate; and give the evaluation only on the basis of the rewritten, polished version.

2. Should all mistakes be corrected?

The problem

If we accept that language (including punctuation) should be corrected, another problem arises: should *all* language mistakes be noted, even if there are so many that the page will be covered with corrections? If not, how do we judge which to relate to and which not?

Advice

The problem is one of potential conflict between two of our functions as teachers: language instruction versus support and encouragement of learning. The correcting of mistakes is part of the language instruction, but too much of it can be discouraging and demoralizing. Also, over-emphasis on language mistakes can distract both learners' and teachers' attention from the equally important aspects of content and organization.

Some kind of compromise is obviously called for, which will vary according to context. In principle, it would seem reasonable to say that language mistakes should be ignored if there is a danger that to correct them would hinder learning more than help it. We might correct only mistakes that actually affect meaning (that is, might lead to misunderstanding or confusion on the part of the reader), and/or those which are very basic; or, of course, vary our response according to individual need.

3. Should learners rewrite, incorporating corrections?

The problem

When we receive written work, we normally correct and comment on it and give it back. The question is whether to insist on the students rewriting the compositions, incorporating our suggestions for improvements. This can be tedious, and students do not like doing it; on the other hand, it does probably help to reinforce learning of the correct forms.

Advice

I think rewriting is very important: not only because it reinforces learning, but also because rewriting is an integral part of the writing process as a whole. However, if we demand rewriting on the part of the students, they have a right to demand from us that we reread – and value – what they have done. It makes sense to see the first version as provisional, and to regard the rewritten, final version as 'the' assignment, the one that is submitted for formal assessment. This helps to motivate learners to rewrite and to appreciate the value of doing so.

4. Should we let students correct or give feedback on each other's written work?

The problem

Correcting written work is very time-consuming, particularly if we have large classes. One possible solution is to let students correct and edit each other's writing. They may not be able to see or define all the good qualities or shortcomings of an assignment, but they will detect at least some of them. The problem is: will students feel uncomfortable correcting, or being corrected by, their peers? Will they accept criticism (positive or negative) from each other?

Advice

In general, yes, peer-correction can be a time-saving and useful technique; also, critical reading for style, content and language accuracy is a valuable exercise in itself. This does not release us from the duty of checking and evaluating student writing; but it can be a substitute for first-draft reading. Students can work together on their first drafts, giving each other feedback on content, language and organization; they then rewrite and give in the final version to the teacher.

The question of personal relationships, trust and willingness to accept criticism and help from one another remains. This is not a problem that can be solved by particular teaching techniques; it depends on the general classroom climate, which in its turn is created by the attitudes of both students and teachers.

Notes

(1) Differences between written and spoken discourse

The essential difference is, strictly speaking, between formal, detached discourse and informal, interactive discourse: usually, it is true, the first is writing and the second speech, but not always. For example, passing notes between participants during a meeting or lecture is writing but displays many of the characteristics of informal speech as described in this unit; and the reading of a paper at a conference, a news broadcast, a poetry recitation, are instances of speech with many of the characteristics of formal writing. This has led some writers to prefer to distinguish between 'autonomous' (usually corresponding to formal written) versus 'non-autonomous' (usually corresponding to informal spoken) prose (see Tannen, 1982). In rare cases we may even find mixed genres in either writing or speech: informal, non-interactive (a comic monologue), or formal, interactive (a Shakespeare play). However, in the vast majority of cases the differences are, as suggested in this unit, applicable to writing as opposed to speech and as such, I think, provide helpful terms of reference for teaching.

(2) Should students be aware of the differences?

More advanced, adult students – particularly those who are studying the language for academic or business purposes and may need to do extensive writing themselves – may well benefit from a formal presentation of such information. Other learners may simply be made aware of differences at the level of individual language item: that colloquial expressions, such as *cop* or *glitzy*, are not usually used in writing; that contractions such as *don't* and *he's* are usually written out in full, and so on.

(3) Suggested solution to 'Classifying writing exercises' task

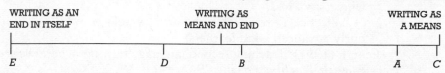

(A) is essentially reading comprehension; it provides little practice in writing beyond the copying. (B) is a vocabulary exercise which also requires brief creative writing. (C) is a grammar exercise (transformation of present tenses into pasts), contextualized into a story. (D) involves a combination of reading and writing. (E) is clearly a writing activity.

(4) Writing: My own composition process

Preparation

I think for a while, make very brief notes on a slip of paper in no particular order, and then launch straight into the writing, ordering and organizing as I go.

Process

I get nowhere without deleting or changing; do so constantly, as I write, and then again during subsequent rereadings. I frequently leave an unsatisfactory section and come back to it later; deliberately write later sections before earlier ones; change the order of sections. I edit both form and content throughout the writing process, including spelling, punctuation and typing errors, though the final editing sessions usually concentrate on 'micro'-aspects: changing words, letters and punctuation marks rather than whole sections.

I find writing absorbing and satisfying; often I get more satisfaction from rewriting and polishing than from the initial composition. Comments and suggestions from critical, knowledgeable readers during rewriting are sometimes painful at first, but eventually very helpful, in some cases essential.

Product

The final result is often quite different from the original conception, but usually I feel pride in it, and want people to read it. I like reading what others have written on the same topic, and am interested in hearing their reactions to my writing.

Further reading

BACKGROUND

Freedman, A., Pringle, I. and Yalden, J. (eds.) (1983) *Learning to Write: First Language/Second Language*, London: Longman.
(A series of articles on various aspects of learning to write: accounts of research, discussions of problems)
Hedge, T. (1988) *Writing*, Oxford: Oxford University Press.
(A summary of some main issues, followed by discussion of the teaching of various types and levels of writing, with plenty of illustrative tasks)

Kroll, B. (ed.) (1990) *Second Language Writing*, Cambridge: Cambridge University Press.
(A collection of research-based articles: relates mainly to writing done by fairly advanced adult learners)

Leki, I. (1991) 'Teaching second language writing; where we seem to be', *English Teaching Forum*, **29**, 2, 8–11, 26.
(A brief, readable overview of issues in the teaching of writing)

Smith, F. (1982) *Writing and the Writer*, London: Heinemann.
(On the process of (first-language) writing in general; informal, readable)

Tannen, D. (1982) 'Oral and literate strategies in spoken and written narrative', *Language* 58, 1, 1–21.
(On the differences between 'autonomous' and 'non-autonomous' text, as distinct from the written/spoken dichotomy)

TEACHER'S HANDBOOKS

Byrne, D. (1988) *Teaching Writing Skills* (2nd edn.), London: Longman.
(A guide to teaching writing from early to advanced stages; plenty of practical teaching ideas)

Raimes, A. (1983) *Techniques in Teaching Writing*, Oxford: Oxford University Press.
(A simple exposition of a number of varied techniques, mainly focusses on production of acceptable written language forms)

White, R. V. (1980) *Teaching Written English*, London: Heinemann Educational Books.
(A readable, not too long introduction to the basics of the topic)

White, R. V. and Arndt, V. (1992) *Process Writing*, London: Longman.
(Discusses various strategies and techniques used during the writing process, and suggests appropriate teaching procedures)

The content of language courses may be divided into two components: the language itself (its pronunciation, grammar, how to read it, etc.), and the ideas, or subject matter which the language is used to express. Part IV deals mainly with the organization of this content within language courses, and a preliminary question which obviously needs to be asked is: why is such organization necessary in the first place? The answer to this question as stated below recaps some points made earlier, in the introduction to Part II: *Teaching the language (1): The 'what'*.

In the context of 'natural' or 'immersion' learning learners have almost unlimited exposure to random samples of the language, often one-to-one 'teaching' and high motivation to learn in order to survive. Under such conditions there is little necessity – or indeed opportunity – to order or organize language content. In formal language courses, however, these conditions do not obtain, and therefore we need to do all we can to make the limited language content available as 'learnable' as possible. One way we can do this is by analysing the language, breaking it up into segments and ordering the segments into a sequence of gradually increasing difficulty. The objective is that any text or task learners are asked to engage with (a reading passage, a discussion activity, an isolated word) should be accessible and contribute to learning at a level 'right' for that learner; and that the whole series of such segments should come together in a rational and convenient progression.

The first two modules of Part IV are concerned with this kind of organization of language content. Module 12 deals with the **syllabus**: an overall specification or programme of what is to be learned (or at least taught) in a particular course or series of courses; and Module 13 deals with **materials**: textbooks, audio cassettes, computer programmes and so on, through which the content is 'packaged' into sets of learning texts and tasks.

The learning of language content may be the main goal of a course, but language itself is not, ultimately, a goal; it is normally a means: specifically, a means of communicating messages. Thus Module 14 deals with the **subject matter that is communicated**: the ideas or information whose expression may furnish a basis for language use and hence language learning, and which themselves may also lead to some different, but also valuable, learning. Such subject matter may include such things as culture (of the target language, or that of the learners' own background); literature of the target language; another subject of study; general world-knowledge; the learners themselves. A particularly problematic and interesting aspect of such content is the target-language literature, which is the topic of three out of the five units of this module.

Module 12: The syllabus

▶ ## Unit One: What is a syllabus?

Preliminary questions

How would you define the term 'syllabus'? What should, or may, a syllabus contain?

Compare your ideas with those presented below.

The courses you teach, or intend to teach, are very likely to be based on some kind of written syllabus. This unit looks at the typical content of syllabuses; and you will get most benefit out of it if you have an example of one at your elbow – preferably one that is used locally, or that you know something about – to refer to for illustration or comparison, or in order to do the Application task at the end of the unit.

Note that a syllabus may consist of an independent publication – a book or booklet – if it is intended to cover all the courses in a particular context regardless of the actual materials used: a country's national syllabus for schools, for example, or the syllabus of a group of language colleges. However, a textbook that is designed to cover an entire course should also provide its own syllabus through the introduction and contents page or index. This unit relates mostly to the first kind: an 'official' and comprehensive document that usually includes the word 'syllabus' in its title.

Common characteristics of a syllabus[1]

A syllabus is a document which consists, essentially, of **a list**. This list specifies all the things that are to be taught in the course(s) for which the syllabus was designed (a beginner's course, for example, or a six-year secondary-school programme): it is therefore **comprehensive**. The actual components of the list may be either **content** items (words, structures, topics), or **process** ones (tasks, methods). The former is the more common: see Unit Two for some of the possibilities. The items are **ordered**, usually having components that are considered easier or more essential earlier, and more difficult and less important ones later. This ordering may be fairly detailed and rigid, or general and flexible.

The syllabus generally has **explicit objectives**, usually declared at the beginning of the document, on the basis of which the components of the list are selected and ordered.

Another characteristic of the syllabus is that it is a **public document**. It is

---

[1] The description given here is relevant to most conventional syllabuses; there are, however, some innovative types to which it may not apply. For these, see Unit Two.

available for scrutiny not only by the teachers who are expected to implement it, but also by the consumers (the learners or their parents or employers), by representatives of the relevant authorities (inspectors, school boards), by other interested members of the public (researchers, teacher trainers or textbook writers). Underlying this characteristic is the principle of accountability: the composers of the syllabus are answerable to their target audience for the quality of their document.

There are other, optional, features, displayed by some syllabuses and not others. A **time schedule** is one: some syllabuses delimit the time framework of their components, prescribing, for example, that these items should be dealt with in the first month, those in the second; the class should have completed this much by the end of the year. A particular preferred **approach** or **methodology** to be used may also be defined, even in a syllabus that is essentially content-based. It may list recommended **materials** – coursebooks, visual materials or supplementary materials – either in general, or where relevant to certain items or sections.

BOX 12.1: CHARACTERISTICS OF A SYLLABUS

1. Consists of a comprehensive list of:
   - content items (words, structures, topics);
   - process items (tasks, methods).
2. Is ordered (easier, more essential items first).
3. Has explicit objectives (usually expressed in the introduction).
4. Is a public document.
5. May indicate a time schedule.
6. May indicate a preferred methodology or approach.
7. May recommend materials.

© *Cambridge University Press 1995*

Application   In Box 12.1 is a summary of the items listed in the previous section. Which of these apply to your own syllabus (or one that is commonly used locally)? Put a tick by ones that apply, a cross by ones that do not. Can you, perhaps, comment on the significance of the presence or absence of any of the items?

▶ Unit Two: Different types of language syllabus

A number of different kinds of syllabuses are used in foreign language teaching. A list of these is provided below; it is not, of course, exhaustive, but includes the main types that you may come across in practice or in your reading. Each is briefly explained; some also include references to sources of more detailed information on content or rationale.

Types of syllabuses

1. Grammatical
A list of grammatical structures, such as the present tense, comparison of adjectives, relative clauses, usually divided into sections graded according to difficulty and/or importance.

2. Lexical
A list of lexical items (*girl, boy, go away* . . .) with associated collocations and idioms, usually divided into graded sections. One such syllabus, based on a corpus (a computerized collection of samples of authentic language) is described in Willis, 1990.

3. Grammatical–lexical
A very common kind of syllabus: both structures and lexis are specified: either together, in sections that correspond to the units of a course, or in two separate lists.

4. Situational
These syllabuses take the real-life contexts of language uses as their basis: sections would be headed by names of situations or locations such as 'Eating a meal' or 'In the street'.

5. Topic-based
This is rather like the situational syllabus, except that the headings are broadly topic-based, including things like 'Food' or 'The family'; these usually indicate a fairly clear set of vocabulary items, which may be specified.

6. Notional
'Notions' are concepts that language can express. General notions may include 'number', for example, or 'time', 'place', 'colour'; specific notions look more like vocabulary items: 'man', 'woman', 'afternoon'. For an introduction to the topic of notional syllabuses see Wilkins, 1976.

7. Functional–notional
Functions are things you can **do** with language, as distinct from notions you can express: examples are 'identifying', 'denying', 'promising'. Purely functional syllabuses are rare: usually both functions and notions are combined, as for example in Van Ek, 1990.

8. Mixed or 'multi-strand'
Increasingly, modern syllabuses are combining different aspects in order to be maximally comprehensive and helpful to teachers and learners; in these you may find specification of topics, tasks, functions and notions, as well as grammar and vocabulary.

9. Procedural
These syllabuses specify the learning tasks to be done rather than the language itself or even its meanings. Examples of tasks might be: map reading, doing

scientific experiments, story-writing. The most well-known procedural syllabus is that associated with the Bangalore Project (Prabhu, 1987).

10. Process

This is the only syllabus which is not pre-set. The content of the course is negotiated with the learners at the beginning of the course and during it, and actually listed only retrospectively (Candlin, 1984; Clarke, 1991).

Task: **Classifying syllabuses**

Look at the syllabuses of two or three coursebooks, not necessarily those used locally. (Coursebook syllabuses are normally defined in the introduction and/or in a listing of the content provided at the front or back of the book.) Which of the types listed above do they belong to?

▶ Unit Three: Using the syllabus

Assuming the course you are to teach has a syllabus separate from your coursebook, composed or ratified by some recognized authority – how will, or would, you use it? For example: will you keep to it carefully, consulting it regularly? Or will you refer to it only rarely, to check yourself? Or will you adapt or even rewrite it completely?

Task: **Thinking about how to use the syllabus**

In Box 12.2 five teachers describe how they use their syllabuses. Consider on your own or discuss with colleagues: with whom do you identify most closely?

With regard to the teacher you feel you identify with most closely: what is it about his or her statement that you feel in sympathy with? What alterations would you need to introduce to make it express your own position more precisely? With regard to the others: what is it about their approaches that you reject, or that is irrelevant to your own teaching context? If you found yourself in their situation, how would you use the syllabus?

Some comments follow.

Comments on Box 12.2: Using the syllabus

How teachers use the syllabus varies very widely between different countries and institutions, and depends on financial resources as well as on teaching approach.

Where there is no lack of resources to invest in the drawing-up of very detailed syllabuses and the purchase of a wide variety of teaching materials teachers may find it most effective to work mainly from the syllabus as the basis of their programme, drawing on specific materials as they need them, as Anna does.

BOX 12.2: USING THE SYLLABUS

Anna: The syllabus of the language school where I teach is very comprehensive: it includes grammar, vocabulary, functions, notions, situations; and gives references to material I can use. I use it all the time and could not do without it. When preparing a teaching session or series of sessions I go first to the syllabus, decide what it will be appropriate to teach next according to its programme, plan how to combine and schedule the components I have selected, and take the relevant books or materials from the library as I need them.

Joseph: There is a syllabus, but we don't have to use it; nor is there any fixed coursebook, although the college recommends certain ones. Personally, I simply ignore the syllabus, since I prefer to do my own thing, based on the needs of my [adult] students. I use materials and activities from different sources (teacher's handbooks, textbooks, enrichment materials, literature) which are available in my institution's library in order to create a rich and varied programme that is flexible enough to be altered and adapted to student needs during the course.

Maria: They made us read the national syllabus in my teacher-training course, but I haven't looked at it since. What for? In my [state] school we use a class coursebook which lays out all the language I have to teach, as well as giving me texts, exercises and ideas for activities. I assume the Ministry would not have authorized the book if it didn't accord with the syllabus, so there's no reason for me to double-check if I'm teaching the right things.

Lilly: I possess the syllabus, and look at it occasionally, but mostly I work from the coursebook that my school chose for the class. It's just that sometimes I get a bit fed up with the coursebook and want to do something different: so then I 'do my own thing' for a bit, using the syllabus as a retrospective checklist, to make sure I'm still reasonably on target with the content . . . after all, I am being employed to teach a certain syllabus, I can't stray too far.

David: The school where I work cannot afford to buy coursebooks for the children, so I have the only book; I also have an officially authorized syllabus. Everything I teach I take either from the syllabus or from the coursebook. I don't add material of my own; for one thing, the authorities do not approve; for another, I am not confident enough of my knowledge of the language I am teaching – I might make mistakes.

© *Cambridge University Press 1996*

In other relatively affluent settings there may be a policy of allowing teachers complete freedom in designing their teaching programme; in such a case the syllabus may be non-existent or ignored, and teachers like Joseph may develop new, independent programmes, based mainly on the teacher's preferences and learners' needs. With a competent and creative teacher working with mature learners, this kind of situation can also generate a unique, exciting and satisfying teaching/learning experience. However, in most contexts the disadvantages outweigh the advantages: apart from a possibly prohibitive amount of work for the teacher, the abandonment of a carefully pre-planned syllabus may result in significant gaps in the language content taught. This may not matter so much in a situation where the target language is used predominantly outside the classroom (if the class is composed of immigrants learning English in Australia, for example); in other situations, however, it may seriously impair learning.

Also, the lack of clear structure may make it difficult for either teacher or learners to feel a sense of progress or evaluate learning outcomes.

When only one coursebook can be afforded per student, the book often tends to take over the function of a syllabus, particularly if, as in the case of Maria, the book has been recommended for use by the same authority that drew up the syllabus. Here the use or non-use of the syllabus to supplement the book depends to some extent on the personality of the teacher, and his or her willingness to put in extra effort – as exemplified by Lilly.

There are some situations where even one book per student is an unknown luxury, as described by David; in this case the teacher may base the course on the coursebook or syllabus or a combination of the two. Note that sometimes, as here, the syllabus has an extra role to play: as a source of information and reassurance for teachers who are not confident of their own knowledge of the target language.

Further reading

LANGUAGE SYLLABUSES IN GENERAL

Brumfit, C. J. (ed.) (1984) *General English Syllabus Design, (ELT Documents 118)*, Oxford: Pergamon Press.
(A collection of articles on different kinds of English language syllabuses: useful summaries by Brumfit and Stern)
Dubin, F. and Olshtain, E. (1986) *Course Design*, Cambridge: Cambridge University Press.
(On the planning and development of English language teaching syllabus and materials in different contexts)
Nunan, D. (1988) *Syllabus Design*, Oxford: Oxford University Press.
(Mostly a series of tasks helping the reader to engage with and understand different issues)
White, R. V. (1988) *The ELT Curriculum: Design, Innovation and Management*, Oxford: Basil Blackwell.
(A fairly detailed and comprehensive survey of various current types of syllabus and how they are used)
Yalden, J. (1987) *Principles of Course Design for Language Teaching*, Cambridge: Cambridge University Press.
(Discusses different options in course and syllabus design, and the theories underlying them; illustrated by case studies)

SPECIFIC TYPES OF SYLLABUS

Candlin, C. N. (1984) 'Syllabus design as a critical process' in Brumfit, C. J. (ed.) (1984b) *General English Syllabus Design (ELT Documents 118)*, Oxford: Pergamon Press.
(Rationale and description of the 'process' syllabus)
Clarke, D. F. (1991) 'The negotiated syllabus: what is it and how is it likely to work?', *Applied Linguistics*, 12, 1, 13–28.
(Also about the 'process' syllabus: some reservations about its application in practice and practical suggestions)

Long, M. H. and Crookes, G. (1992) 'Three approaches to task-based syllabus design', *TESOL Quarterly*, **26**, 1, 27–56.
(Discusses syllabuses based on communicative tasks, and concludes that learning is most effective when these are combined with explicit language-learning (form-focussed) tasks)

Prabhu, N. S. (1987) *Second Language Pedagogy*, Oxford: Oxford University Press.
(Rationale and description of the procedural (task-based) syllabus)

Van Ek, J. A. (1990) *The Threshold Level in a European Unit-Credit System for Modern Language Learning by Adults*, Strasbourg: Council of Europe.
(A well-known example of a functional–notional syllabus in use)

Willis, D. (1990) *The Lexical Syllabus*, London: Collins.
(Describes briefly what a lexical syllabus would look like; goes on to discuss a methodology for its use in teaching)

Wilkins, D. A. (1976) *Notional Syllabuses*, Oxford: Oxford University Press.
(An introduction to notional syllabuses, as compared to 'traditional' grammatical–lexical)

Module 13: Materials

Note: The term 'coursebook' is used here to mean a textbook of which the teacher and, usually, each student has a copy, and which is in principle to be followed systematically as the basis for a language course.

▶ ## Unit One: How necessary is a coursebook?

Question What would your own answer be to the question asked in the title of this unit? And what would be your arguments to support it? Try answering this before reading on.

In some places coursebooks are taken for granted. In others they may not be used at all: the teacher works according to a syllabus, or according to his or her own programme, using textbooks and supplementary materials as the need arises. A third, 'compromise', situation is where a coursebook is used selectively, not necessarily in sequence, and is extensively supplemented by other materials.

Task **Thinking about advantages and disadvantages of using a coursebook**

In Boxes 13.1.1 and 13.1.2 are some of the arguments for and against the use of a coursebook. Read through them, ticking off those you agree with, and noting your criticisms of those you disagree with or have reservations about.

Question Were any of the ideas expressed in the 'for' or 'against' arguments in Boxes 13.1.1 and 13.1.2 new to you? If they were, and if they seem acceptable, would you now modify at all your answer to the question asked at the beginning of this unit as a result? Or do you find your previous opinion unchanged? Or even reinforced?

Comment

You may, of course, find that you agree with some of the 'against' points while overall supporting the 'for' position, or vice versa. The question then arises: having established your own position in principle, what will you do to compensate for problems or disadvantages you have perceived? This issue is tackled in Unit Three.

My own position on this issue is summarised in the Notes, (1).

> **BOX 13.1.1: IN FAVOUR OF USING A COURSEBOOK**
>
> **1. Framework**
> A coursebook provides a clear framework: teacher and learners know where they are going and what is coming next, so that there is a sense of structure and progress.
>
> **2. Syllabus**
> In many places the coursebook serves as a syllabus: if it is followed systematically, a carefully planned and balanced selection of language content will be covered.
>
> **3. Ready-made texts and tasks**
> The coursebook provides texts and learning tasks which are likely to be of an appropriate level for most of the class. This of course saves time for the teacher who would otherwise have to prepare his or her own.
>
> **4. Economy**
> A book is the cheapest way of providing learning material for each learner; alternatives, such as kits, sets of photocopied papers or computer software, are likely to be more expensive relative to the amount of material provided.
>
> **5. Convenience**
> A book is a convenient package. It is bound, so that its components stick together and stay in order; it is light and small enough to carry around easily; it is of a shape that is easily packed and stacked; it does not depend for its use on hardware or a supply of electricity.
>
> **6. Guidance**
> For teachers who are inexperienced or occasionally unsure of their knowledge of the language, the coursebook can provide useful guidance and support.
>
> **7. Autonomy**
> The learner can use the coursebook to learn new material, review and monitor progress with some degree of autonomy. A learner without a coursebook is more teacher-dependent.
>
> © *Cambridge University Press 1996*

► **Unit Two: Coursebook assessment**

Whether or not you elect to base your course on a coursebook, it is worth thinking about how you recognize a good one when you see it, and on what grounds you might reject or criticize it: in other words, what the main criteria are for coursebook assessment. Such criteria may be **general**, applicable to any language-teaching coursebook, or **specific**, relating to the appropriateness of the book for a certain course or learner population. An example of a general criterion might be: 'clear layout and print', or 'provides periodic review or test sections'; whereas a specific one might be: 'attractive and colourful illustrations' (if it is meant for younger learners), or 'vocabulary and texts relevant to topic' (if it is for students of science or technology).

BOX 13.1.2: AGAINST USING A COURSEBOOK

1. Inadequacy
Every class – in fact, every learner – has their own learning needs: no one coursebook can possibly supply these satisfactorily.

2. Irrelevance, lack of interest
The topics dealt with in the coursebook may not necessarily be relevant or interesting for your class.

3. Limitation
A coursebook is confining: its set structure and sequence may inhibit a teacher's initiative and creativity, and lead to boredom and lack of motivation on the part of the learners.

4. Homogeneity
Coursebooks have their own rationale and chosen teaching/learning approach. They do not usually cater for the variety of levels of ability and knowledge, or of learning styles and strategies that exist in most classes.

5. Over-easiness
Teachers find it too easy to follow the coursebook uncritically instead of using their initiative; they may find themselves functioning merely as mediators of its content instead of as teachers in their own right.

© Cambridge University Press 1996

The general criteria suggested in Box 13.2 have been selected from ideas given in a number of books and articles on the subject; if you would like to study these in more depth, look up the references given under *Further reading*.

Task **Assessing a coursebook**

Stage 1: Deciding on criteria

Study the list of criteria for assessing language-learning coursebooks shown in Box 13.2. In the left-hand column, note how important you think each criterion is: a double tick for 'very important', and a single tick for 'fairly important', a question mark for 'not sure'; and a cross or double cross for 'not important' or 'totally unimportant' respectively. Then add any further criteria you feel are significant (either general, or specific to your own context) in the spaces left at the end, and mark in their importance. Ignore the extreme right-hand column for the moment.

In deciding on the rating of each item, it might help to ask yourself: if this quality were missing, would I therefore not use the book? If so, then you obviously think the quality essential or very important. If, however, the quality is desirable, but its absence would not necessarily stop you using the book if all the other criteria were fulfilled, then perhaps a single tick may be enough.

If you are working in a group, compare your ideas with those of colleagues. My own ratings may be found in the Notes, (2).

185

```
┌─────────────────────────────────────────────────────────────────┐
│ BOX 13.2:  CRITERIA FOR COURSEBOOK ASSESSMENT                     │
└─────────────────────────────────────────────────────────────────┘
```

Importance	Criterion	
	Objectives explicitly laid out in an introduction, and implemented in the material	
	Approach educationally and socially acceptable to target community	
	Clear attractive layout; print easy to read	
	Appropriate visual materials available	
	Interesting topics and tasks	
	Varied topics and tasks, so as to provide for different learner levels, learning styles, interests, etc.	
	Clear instructions	
	Systematic coverage of syllabus	
	Content clearly organized and graded (sequenced by difficulty)	
	Periodic review and test sections	
	Plenty of authentic language	
	Good pronunciation explanation and practice	
	Good vocabulary explanation and practice	
	Good grammar presentation and practice	
	Fluency practice in all four skills	
	Encourages learners to develop own learning strategies and to become independent in their learning	
	Adequate guidance for the teacher; not too heavy preparation load	
	Audio cassettes	
	Readily available locally	

© Cambridge University Press 1996

Stage 2: Applying criteria

Now take a locally-used coursebook and examine it, applying the criteria you have in your list; note your ratings in the extreme right-hand column of the table. You might use a similar code to the one employed in Stage 1: a single or double tick indicates that the book scores high, or very high, on this criterion; a cross or double cross that it scores low or very low; and a question mark shows that you are not sure, or that the criterion applies only partially.

Again, you might compare notes with colleagues who have looked at the same materials, and see if you can come to a consensus on most or all of the items.

Stage 3: Summary

Can you now make some overall evaluation of the coursebook? Note that for this you need to compare the two columns you have filled; it is not enough simply to 'add up' the right-hand column. For example, if the book has scored very high on a criterion which you rated unimportant, this is less in its favour than a fairly high rating on a criterion you see as essential.

If you have been working on the same coursebook as other teachers in doing this unit, then it is probably most useful and enjoyable to work on this summary together.

▶ Unit Three: Using a coursebook

A coursebook should be related to critically: we should be aware of its good and bad points in order to make the most of the first and compensate for or neutralize the second. Some general critical questions to be asked about the coursebook as a whole will already have emerged if you have done the previous unit; in this one we shall be looking at more specific, detailed aspects: the components of a single unit, or chapter, and what we might need to do in order to make the best use of it.

Below are some critical questions which might be asked about the material, with following comments. These are grouped under the headings: *Coverage, Texts, Tasks (activities, exercises), Administration.*

Coverage

Any single unit of a coursebook should cover a fair range of language content and skills. Some categories of content are shown in Box 13.3.

Questions   Which categories in Box 13.3 do you think are most important? Does your coursebook cover these satisfactorily? Are there some that are neglected? Are there others that it spends too much time or space on in your opinion? You may need to provide content that is missing using supplementary materials; or deliberately omit sections that you feel are redundant.

Texts

Questions   Are the (reading or listening) texts of an appropriate level? Are they interesting? Varied?

> **BOX 13.3: COURSEBOOK COVERAGE**
>
> – pronunciation practice
> – introduction of new vocabulary and practice
> – grammar explanations and practice
> – recordings for listening practice
> – listening and speaking communicative tasks
> – reading and writing communicative tasks
> – mixed-skills communicative tasks
> – short and long reading texts
> – dictionary work
> – review of previously learnt material
> – some entertaining or fun activities
>
> © *Cambridge University Press 1996*

If the texts are too easy, you may need to substitute, or add, further texts. If, on the other hand, they are too difficult you may still be able to use them: by careful pre-teaching of vocabulary, by introductory discussion of the topic, by preliminary explanation of key sections, by careful omission of difficult bits.

The texts may be unsatisfactory, even if of the right level, because they are boring or trivial in content; or because all the texts in the book seem to be the same genre, style and overall topic. Interest may be added by challenging or original tasks; but the problem of sameness of genre can only be solved by providing supplementary texts.

Tasks (activities, exercises)

Questions **Do the tasks provide opportunities for plenty of use of the target language? Are they heterogeneous, allowing for responses at different levels? Do they cover a satisfactory range of language items and skills? Are they interesting? Are they relevant and useful for your class(es)? Is there a balance between accuracy and fluency practice: that is to say, activities whose objective is the production of correct language forms, and those whose objective is communicative language use?**

Some coursebook exercises are more like tests: brief checks to see whether the learner knows something or not, rather than frameworks for extended and interesting rehearsals of different aspects of language (see Module 2: *Practice activities* for the characteristics of good practice activities; see also the table on p. 336 for a summary of some of the differences between tests and practice activities).

If the tasks are too short and do not provide for very much learner activity, they can be extended by, for example, adding further similar items, or by making items open-ended instead of closed-ended so that each can trigger a number of learner responses; or by simply supplementing with further activities of your own. You may need to supplement also in order to provide more heterogeneous or interesting tasks for your class; or in order to provide material which is more relevant to their individual or group needs.

Administration

Questions   With regard to a specific component of the coursebook: would this be most effectively administered through teacher-led question-and-answer? Or perhaps learners should tackle it individually, through reading and writing? Or might it be most effective if they work on it collaboratively, in pairs or groups? Or use a combination of these strategies? Does the coursebook provide you with guidance on these questions?

When preparing to teach coursebook material, it is worth devoting a little thought as to how best to activate learners in a particular task in order to get optimum learning benefit out of it and make it interesting; and this is a point on which many coursebooks fail to provide guidance. For a more detailed study of this issue, see Module 16: *Classroom interaction*, Unit Five.

Application   Select one unit from a coursebook you are familiar with, and make a copy of it. Study it, using the questions and comments suggested in this unit, and note in the margins of your copy which components you might omit, change or supplement, and why; and how you think those you have retained would be most effectively administered in class. If there is a Teacher's Book, look at what it says after you have done the above, and compare its ideas with your own.

▷ Unit Four: Supplementary materials

Most language-teaching coursebooks probably need supplementing to some extent, if only in order to tailor them to the needs of a particular class or to offer richer options. This unit describes briefly various types of supplementary materials, their contribution to language learning, advantages and disadvantages, and invites you to consider which are most useful and important to you.

Task   **Simulation**

Imagine that you are to be given a grant of enough money to buy a 'package' of supplementary materials for your institution out of the catalogue given in Box 13.4, assuming, for the sake of argument, that each package costs about the same. You will be given a similar grant every half-year, so eventually you will be able to buy all the packages. The question is: in what order will you buy them, and how will you decide? Work out for yourself an order of priority, or do so together with colleagues. (You may, of course, add further packages if you wish, or alter the contents of the present ones, before beginning the task.)

It is assumed that the institution has a reasonable supply of standard stationery and office equipment, such as paper, pencils, felt-tipped pens, staplers, scissors, etc., and that classrooms are equipped with black- or whiteboards.

Some comments on the contents of the packages follow; you may find it helpful to read these before making your decisions about priorities.

My own priorities are described in the Notes, (3).

BOX 13.4: PACKAGES OF SUPPLEMENTARY MATERIALS

Package 1: A set of computers for learners' use, with accompanying language-learning programs on floppy disk.

Package 2: A set of reference books for the teachers, including: grammars, dictionaries; various specialized textbooks; handbooks of activities; and a subscription to a teachers' journal of your choice.

Package 3: A number of overhead projectors and slide projectors, with all necessary film, slides and markers.

Package 4: Video equipment, with assorted cassettes, including language-learning material and films in the target language.

Package 5: Computers and printers for teachers' use; each computer has a hard disk with the latest word processor and various programs that enable you to compose your own computer tasks for learners.

Package 6: Several cassette recorders with accompanying earphones (so that several learners can listen quietly to one machine); a selection of accompanying cassettes for language learning.

Package 7: A wide variety of posters and sets of coloured pictures, plus board and card games for language learning.

Package 8: A library of simplified readers in the target language, ranging from very simple to advanced. There would be enough books in this library to enable all students to borrow freely.

© Cambridge University Press 1996

Comments

Computers

Computers are seen by many as an important teaching aid. These days learners need to be 'computer literate', and since computers use language it would seem logical to take advantage of them for language learning. They enable individual work, since learners can progress at their own pace, and many programs include a self-check facility. Also, younger and adolescent learners in particular find the use of computers attractive and motivating. However, it takes time to train both teachers and students in their use; and in practice a lot of time in a computer lesson often goes on setting up programs, getting students into them, and then solving problems with moving from one stage, or one program, to another.

For teachers who are familiar with their use computers can be invaluable for preparing materials such as worksheets or tests.

Books

Books are very user-friendly 'packages' of material: they are light, easily scanned, easily stacked and do not need hardware or electricity. They are still the most convenient and popular method of packaging large texts, and a library of them is arguably the best way for learners to acquire a wide experience of foreign language reading.

It is very useful to have a collection of reference books, extra textbooks and teachers' handbooks easily available to the teaching staff; and regular reading of a professional journal can inject new ideas and update teachers on current thinking.

Overhead projectors

These are useful for presenting visual or written material to classes: they are more vivid and attention-catching than the black- or whiteboards. They also save lesson time, since you can prepare the displays in advance. However, this does mean added work in preparation! Another disadvantage is the need to carry the OHP from class to class, unless each classroom has its own – which is true only of the more affluent institutions. And of course, like any other electrical equipment, OHPs are vulnerable to breakdowns: electricity failure or bulbs burning out.

Video equipment

Video is an excellent source of authentic spoken language material; it is also attractive and motivating. It is flexible: you can start and stop it, run forward or back, 'freeze' frames in order to talk about them. And there are many good programmes on the market. A disadvantage is their lack of mobility: few video sets are portable, which means that classes need to be specially scheduled for video rooms; and of course there is the problem of occasional breakdowns and technical problems. When planning a video lesson, always have a 'back-up' alternative lesson ready!

Audio equipment

Cassette recorders and cassettes are relatively cheap, and easy to use; and they are the main source (other than the teacher) of spoken language texts in most classrooms. They are more mobile and easier to use than video recorders, but lack, of course, the visual content. Again there may be problems with electricity; on the other hand, most portable cassette recorders – unlike video and most computers – also work on batteries. When buying cassette recorders, make sure that there is a counter, and then use it to identify the desired entry-point; otherwise, if you want to replay during the lesson, you may waste valuable time running the tape back and forth to find it.

Posters, pictures, games

Materials of this kind are invaluable particularly for younger learners, and teachers of children find that they constantly use them. However, if you have time, this type of material can be largely home-made: glossy magazines in particular are an excellent source of pictures.

▷ # Unit Five: Teacher-made worksheets and workcards

Even with an excellent coursebook and a wide variety of other materials available, there comes a point at which many teachers find they have to make their own occasional supplementary workcards or worksheets: because they can find what they need nowhere else, because they want to provide for the needs of a specific class, or simply for the sake of variety.

Good teacher-made materials are arguably the best there are: relevant and personalized, answering the needs of the learners in a way no other materials can.

Differences between worksheets and workcards

A **worksheet** is a page (or two) of tasks, distributed to each student to do either in class or at home, intended to be written on, and usually taken in by the teacher to be checked. Teacher-made tests can be seen as a specific kind of worksheet. **Workcards** are made in sets, each card offering a different, fairly short task (see, for example, the set of tasks in the Notes to Module 10: *Teaching reading*). They are not written on: a student does one card, writing answers on a separate piece of paper or in a notebook, and then exchanges it for another, working through as many of the set as there is time for. Answers are often available for self-checking at some central location in the room, or on the back of the card itself. Workcards are permanent and re-usable; worksheets are disposable – though of course further copies can be made. Workcards take more effort and time to produce, but they are also more attractive to look at and work on (colours and cut-out pictures can be used), and more individualized: students have a choice as to which cards they do, and in which order; and the range of tasks available can be much more varied. In fact, the workcard lesson is a rudimentary self-access session, and can be developed into a fully individualized programme by varying the number and type of tasks provided.

For some examples of simple workcards and worksheets see the first section of the Notes to Module 10 on p. 156.

Task ## Making materials

Stage 1: Preparation

Choose a language point for which you want to make your own learner tasks, preferably having in mind a course or class you know. If you wish to make workcards, prepare cards, coloured pens and perhaps magazine pictures, scissors and glue. Worksheets may be written by hand, or on a typewriter or word processor.

Stage 2: First draft

Make a sample worksheet or workcard, preferably for a class you know on language they are learning.

Stage 3: Feedback

If you are working in a group, exchange your resulting materials and discuss. You may find the points listed in Box 13.4 helpful as a basis for feedback.

BOX 13.4: GUIDELINES FOR TEACHER-MADE MATERIALS

Worksheets and workcards should:
– be neat: clean, with level lines of neat writing, clear margins, different components well spaced;
– begin with short and clear instructions (if appropriate, in the learners' mother tongue), usually including an example;
– be clear and attractive to look at: have a balanced and varied layout, using underlining and other forms of emphasis to draw attention to significant items; possibly using colour and graphic illustration;
– be clearly do-able by the learners on their own;
– (optionally) include a self-check facility.

© *Cambridge University Press 1996*

Stage 4: Second draft

Remake your worksheet or workcard – or make a totally new one – implementing ideas you received from feedback on the first draft.

Notes

(1) How necessary is a coursebook?

The answer to this question necessarily depends on your own teaching style, the resources available to you and on the accepted way of doing things in your institution.

Personally, I very much prefer to use a coursebook. I find that a set framework helps me to regulate and time my programme; and, perhaps paradoxically, provides a firm jumping-off point for the creation of imaginative supplementary teaching ideas. Moreover, in my experience learners too prefer to have one; those classes which I have tried to teach on the basis of a selection from different sources have complained of a sense of lack of purpose, and, interestingly, that they feel that their learning is not taken seriously. It seems that the possession of a coursebook may carry a certain prestige.

(2) Coursebook assessment

The following are my ratings of the criteria, relevant, of course, to my own teaching situation.

Importance	Criterion	
✓✓	Objectives are explicitly laid out in an introduction, and implemented in the material	
✓	Approach is educationally and socially acceptable to target community	
✓✓	Clear attractive layout; print is easy to read	
✓	Appropriate visual materials are available	
✓✓	Interesting topics and tasks	
✓✓	Varied topics and tasks, so as to provide for different learner levels, learning styles, interests, etc.	
✓✓	Clear instructions	
✓✓	Systematic coverage of syllabus	
✓✓	Content is clearly organized and graded (sequenced by difficulty)	
✓	Periodic review and test sections	
✗	Plenty of authentic language	
?	Good pronunciation explanation and practice	
✓✓	Good vocabulary explanation and practice	
✓✓	Good grammar presentation and practice	
✓✓	Fluency practice in all four skills	
✓	Encourages learners to develop own learning strategies and to become independent in their learning	
✓	Adequate guidance for the teacher; not too heavy preparation load	
✓	Audio cassettes	
✓✓	Readily available locally	

(3) Priorities in acquiring supplementary materials

The following is the order in which I would buy the packages; but remember that my decisions are dictated at least partly by my specific teaching environment (teaching adolescents a foreign language in a state secondary school), and I might make different choices in a different situation.

I would buy first a library of readers for students (Package 8): there is, I think, no substitute for extensive reading of books personally chosen by students for enriching language and advancing reading skills. Then I would indulge the teachers in a library of our own (Package 2): an important professional resource.

Audio materials (Package 6) would come next: video arguably provides better language data (visual, attractive, etc.), but this is offset by the portability, relative reliability and simple operation of cassette recorders, not to mention their cheapness.

Next on my list would be overhead projectors (Package 3), provided I can buy enough so that teachers have no trouble getting and using one whenever they want. OHP displays are attention-catching, the preparation of transparencies saves teacher writing time during a lesson, and the classroom does not have to be darkened in order to use them. This last condition is not true of most slide projectors; also, slides cannot be written on during the course of a lesson. I would therefore prefer to spend most of this budget on OHPs.

I would then buy computers and printers for teachers' use (Package 5): a computer is an excellent means of preparing neat and professional-looking tests and worksheets and a convenient, space-saving way of storing them later.

Video equipment (Package 4) would be next on my list: I think it provides richer and more readily absorbed language data than, say, computers, and can be used very flexibly in a lesson. Computers for learners (Package 1) – the next item – are fun, but my experience using them in classes has not (yet?) convinced me that they are as cost-effective as audio and visual equipment, in terms of the learning outcomes as against investment in money and time.

The last package (Package 7) would be pictures, posters and games: I use pictures in the form of magazine cut-outs backed on card, and find these quite adequate for my needs; published materials would be a luxury. However, when I was teaching younger learners I used posters, published sets of picture cards and board games extensively: if I were in such a situation today, this item would probably come a good deal higher in my list.

Further reading

Allwright, R. L. (1981) 'What do we want the teaching materials for?', *ELT Journal*, 36, 1, 5–18.
   (A challenging, unconventional approach to materials, suggesting needs and purposes other than those implemented by most coursebooks)
Cunningsworth, A. (1984) *Evaluating and Selecting EFL Teaching Materials*, London: Heinemann.
   (Discussion of what we want from a coursebook, with analysis of examples)
O'Neill, R. (1982) 'Why use textbooks?', *ELT Journal*, 36, 2, 104–11.
   (Partly a reply to Allwright, a rationale for the use of the conventional coursebook, and suggestions for improvement of coursebook design and use)
Madsen, H. and Bourn, J. D. (1978) *Adaptation in Language Teaching*, Rowley, Mass.: Newbury House.
   (See articles by Burden and Tucker on criteria for coursebook evaluation)

VISUAL MATERIALS

Bowen, B. M. (1982) *Look Here!: Visual Aids in Language Teaching*, London: Macmillan.
   (A brief, very practical overview of different kinds of visual materials and their use in language teaching)

Wright, A. and Haleem, S. (1991) *Visuals for the Language Classroom*, London: Longman.
(A more thorough discussion of the topic, exploring classroom techniques associated with the various types of materials)

Gerngross, G. and Puchta, H. (1992) *Pictures in Action*, Englewood Cliffs: Prentice Hall.
(A set of recipes on how to use various kinds of pictures for different language-teaching objectives: simple and practical)

VIDEO

Allan, M. (1988) *Teaching English with Video*, London: Longman.
(Basic technical information, and different ways of using video recordings: very practical)

Cooper, R., Lavery, M. and Rinvolucri, M. (1991) *Video*, Oxford: Oxford University Press.
(Useful classroom activities for language learning using video)

COMPUTERS

Fortescue, S. and Jones, C. (1987) *Using Computers in the Language Classroom*, London: Longman.
(Clear, basic guidelines on different computers and programmes; organizing computer rooms; training students and teachers in computer use)

Kenning, M. J. and Kenning, M.-M. (1983) *An Introduction to Computer Assisted Language Teaching*, Oxford: Oxford University Press.
(A comprehensive introduction to the subject, including some guidance on writing your own programs)

Leech, G. and Candlin, C. (1986) *Computers in English Language Teaching and Research*, London: Longman.
(A selection of articles on different aspects of the use of computers in language teaching)

Module 14: Topic content

▶ ## Unit One: Different kinds of content

The topic content of courses (topics the language talks about, as distinct from the language content itself) may be of various types. Some main ones are shown in Box 14.1.

Why different courses tend to stress some types of content and not others depends very much, of course, on the objectives of the course. If your students are immigrants whose purpose in learning is to integrate into the target culture, then topics that are based on the latter will be very important. If, on the other hand, they are learning a foreign language in their home environment in order to function better in commerce or the tourist industry you will probably find topics that have to do with their own cultural background more appropriate. If you are teaching a class of mixed ethnic and religious backgrounds, you may feel safer with neutral 'zero-content' topics. As a teacher of schoolchildren, however, you may see yourself as educator at least as much as language teacher, and will wish to include general cultural knowledge and materials and activities that encourage intellectual or moral development.

Task **Thinking about different kinds of content**

Stage 1: Deciding on relative importance

Look through the list in Box 14.1, and decide which of the types of subject matter you think it is more, or less, important to include in the language course(s) you teach or may teach in the future. Some comments of my own, relating to my own teaching environment, may be found in the Notes, (1).

Stage 2 (optional): Inquiry

Ask some learners what kinds of content they would like to see included in an ideal language course. Do their ideas agree, on the whole, with yours? (See Prodromou, 1992a for a description of a similar inquiry.)

Stage 3: Application

Look at a local syllabus or a coursebook commonly used in the course(s) you have been thinking of. Does it include the kinds of content you think it should? Does it have too much of some other kinds which you consider inappropriate? In either case, what might you do in teaching to improve the balance?

BOX 14.1: TYPES OF NON-LINGUISTIC CONTENT

1. Zero or trivial content
Bland, fairly neutral characters and events, or superficially interesting topics with no cultural or other information or engagement with real-world issues. For example: sentences about fictional 'John and Mary' doing everyday activities; stereotype family stories; many pop songs, trivial anecdotes, 'soap-opera' style narrative or video.

2. The language
Aspects of the target language treated as topics of study in themselves: its history, for example, etymology or morphology.

3. Another subject of study
Other subjects on the school or university curriculum, such as science or history, taught through the medium of the foreign language.

4. Home culture
Discussion of institutions, people, places, events, writing, etc. pertaining to the learners' own culture. For example, Greek learners might discuss places they would recommend that tourists should visit in Greece.

5. Culture associated with the target language
Discussion of institutions, etc. pertaining to the culture of the target language. Materials for learners of English might take as topics the American Civil War, or British social customs.

6. Literature of the target language
In a sense a part of (5) above, but important enough to warrant a separate heading: stories, novels, plays, poetry written in the target language.

7. World or general knowledge
Culture or literature that is known in many countries, such as some folk tales, the Bible; geographical, historical or political information about any part of the world; general scientific or philosophical topics.

8. Moral, educational, political or social problems
Content that presents, or requires participants to take, a stance on some issue: for example, a dilemma to which learners suggest a solution.

9. The learners themselves
Exploration of learners' own experiences, knowledge, opinions and feelings: for example, activities that ask learners to write about someone they know, or compare tastes in food and drink.

© Cambridge University Press 1996

▶ Unit Two: Underlying messages

Course content often conveys a 'hidden curriculum': underlying messages that go beyond factual information. These may have to do with religious or political beliefs, or with attitudes towards certain kinds of people, nationalities, or cultures. It is very important for you to be aware of such 'subtext', for two major reasons. First, for the sake of your own professional integrity: you want to be sure you are teaching what you want to teach, and not unconsciously expressing support for attitudes you do not approve of, or denigrating those you do. Second, because learners who identify with groups who are discriminated against in course content may actually feel disadvantaged and learn less well: for example, female learners using materials which consistently present the male as superior.

Favourable or unfavourable attitudes may be expressed through various means. One is insidious slanting of coursebook content: for example, if the characters learners are asked to identify with in a book belong to a particular ethnic group, or express opinions that reflect a particular political stance. Another is sheer invisibility: of opinions that are disapproved of, or of a discriminated-against group; for example, if your samples of language in the classroom are consistently based on male protagonists (check yourself! – it can happen to all of us). A third – rarer, but easier to detect – is explicitly discriminatory remarks: for example, statements that imply that one language is 'superior' to another (see Phillipson, 1992 for some interesting comments on what he calls 'linguicism' applied to English).

Many prejudices which intellectually we reject are very deeply ingrained in our thinking: so much so that we may betray them without even realizing it (as in the example of using male subjects in language samples, mentioned above). Thus it often actually takes a conscious effort to counteract them; and indeed both teachers and coursebook writers these days are far more aware of the hidden curriculum of course content, and make efforts to see that the messages coming across are ones they feel comfortable with.

Task **Checking out underlying messages in a coursebook**

Take a coursebook – preferably one you are fairly familiar with – and try some or all of the following experiments.

1. Sexism

a) If your book is illustrated, look at the first 30 pictures. Count the number of men and the number of women featured in them. If there are no pictures, look at the grammar or vocabulary exercises, and do the same count on pronouns or nouns with clear gender. In either case, was there a significant difference? If so, what is the implication?

b) Again, using either illustrations or texts, look at the occupations which are assigned to men and women. Was there a consistent 'type' of occupation assigned to either? If so, do you find such a division acceptable?

2. Ageism

If your book is illustrated, look through the pictures and count the number of adults clearly over the age of 40 as compared with 'young' adults (not counting pictures of children). Does the division reflect what you would estimate to be the proportion of young/older adults in society? If not, do you approve or disapprove of the book's distorted picture? If you approve, can you justify your approval?

3. Social orientation

Read a selection of texts and exercises. What kinds of people are shown in them? Look at aspects such as wealth, social class, ethnic affiliation, occupation, cultural background. Do the kinds of people shown in these texts reflect more or less the social background of most of your students? If not, is the picture shown misleading or disturbing? Or positive, in that it presents acceptable role models for your students?

4. Values

Again look at texts and try to assess the kinds of things seen as desirable by the characters or writer. For example, are the characters mainly interested in material benefits (travel, cars, clothes, entertainment)? Or are they mostly concerned with personal relationships? Or do they care about social or moral issues such as the environment, peace, justice/injustice? Or do they have some other consistent dominant aspiration? (In some cases you may even be able to discern a clear political orientation.) Whatever you find: ask yourself if you approve of the values the book conveys and – particularly if you are a schoolteacher – if the educational message is an acceptable one for your students.

▷ # Unit Three: Literature (1): should it be included in the course?

Question What would be your own answer to the question asked in the title of this unit?

This will, of course, depend to some extent on the kind of classes you are teaching and what the course objectives are; but not only. There are certainly some overall advantages and disadvantages to the teaching of the literature of the target language in any course whose main objective is proficiency in the language itself.

Task **Considering advantages and disadvantages of literature teaching**

Look at the lists of advantages of literature teaching listed in Box 14.2.1, add any further items you can think of in the space provided, and then put a tick by those you consider most significant and influential. Then do the same for the list of disadvantages or problems shown in Box 14.2.2.

BOX 14.2.1: ADVANTAGES OF LITERATURE TEACHING

- Literature can be very enjoyable to read.
- It provides examples of different styles of writing, and representations of various authentic uses of the language.
- It is a good basis for vocabulary expansion.
- It fosters reading skills.
- It can supply an excellent jump-off point for discussion or writing.
- It involves emotions as well as intellect, which adds to motivation and may contribute to personal development.
- It is a part of the target culture and has value as part of the learners' general education.
- It encourages empathetic, critical and creative thinking.
- It contributes to world knowledge.
- It raises awareness of different human situations and conflicts.
-
-

© *Cambridge University Press 1996*

BOX 14.2.2: DISADVANTAGES OF, OR PROBLEMS WITH LITERATURE TEACHING

- Much literature is written in language that may be difficult for foreign language learners to read.
- We can use simplified versions, but these are a poor representation of the original.
- Many literary texts are long and time-consuming to teach.
- The target-language culture on which the literature is based is alien to learners and may be difficult for them to relate to.
- By using texts as a basis for language teaching we may spoil learners' enjoyment and appreciation of them as literature.
- Students of science and technology may find literature irrelevant to their needs.
-
-

© *Cambridge University Press 1996*

Task **Summarizing discussion or writing**

Could you now summarize in more detail your own approach to literature teaching in a language course, either through discussion with other participants in your group or through writing on your own? Think about which were the main considerations that led you to decide whether you are for or against literature teaching, and also how you would answer some of the opposing arguments. My own approach is summarized below.

An approach to literature teaching

I am, in principle, in favour of including literature in courses, not only as a rich source of language, but also because of its intrinsic educational and aesthetic value and its contribution to motivation and enjoyment. The problems of length, difficulty and alien content are very real ones: I attempt to solve them by careful selection of texts or, occasionally, by using only part of a long text. In some cases I use simplified or abbreviated versions, in spite of the 'watered-down' quality, if I think that enough of the literary value of the original is preserved and that my students will get worthwhile learning from them.

It is true that there is a danger of spoiling literature by 'over'-teaching it. However, if we take care not to over-emphasize the language teaching aspect but focus on enjoyment and appreciation of the composition itself, on the whole the gain is likely to be greater than the loss.

Finally: literature may be strictly speaking irrelevant for the learning of science and technology, but students of those subjects may still enjoy and ultimately benefit from studying it.

▶ Unit Four: Literature (2): teaching ideas

It is helpful to think of the learning and teaching of a piece of literature as a process containing three main stages:

1. encounter and impact;
2. understanding and familiarization;
3. analysis and interpretation.

Encounter and impact

The teaching objective here is to get learners to perceive the basic form and meaning of the text, and for it to make some kind of real impact on them, both intellectually and emotionally. It does not matter at this point if they do not understand every single word; but they do have to understand enough in order to have an overall perception of meanings.

Task **Thinking about how to introduce a literary text**

Some questions are shown in Box 14.3. Try to decide, preferably in negotiation with other teachers, what your answers would be. My own answers follow.

Some answers to the questions in Box 14.3

1. As a rule, I pre-teach all new words that are essential for basic understanding. My priority is that the text should be understood and make a real impact on the learners: and I am not prepared to risk these objectives for the sake of extra practice in inferencing skills.
2. and 3. Many teachers see 'warm-up' activities as an essential preliminary to the teaching of any literature: they raise curiosity and motivation, and provide some orientation of thinking and mood. But such activities can also have negative effects: they may dilute the direct impact of the literature itself,

---

BOX 14.3:   FIRST ENCOUNTER WITH A LITERARY TEXT: SOME QUESTIONS

1. Should you pre-teach new words or let learners try to guess them from context?
2. Should you do some preparatory work on content or atmosphere before presenting the text itself?
3. Should you provide some information about the author or the cultural or historic background before presenting the text itself?
4. Should you try to get through as much of the text as possible first time for the sake of immediate impact, or take it more gradually, making sure one bit is thoroughly studied before going on to the next?
5. Is the best way to manage learners' first encounter with a text by getting them to read it silently on their own? Or by asking them to read it aloud round the class? Or by reading it aloud yourself?
6. How can you check initial understanding?

© Cambridge University Press 1996

---

which is a pity; and, possibly prejudice the learners so that their perception of it is coloured by what they have been led to expect.

Usually, I prefer to do only so much introductory work as is needed to ensure understanding, such as an indication of the general topic, or any necessary cultural information; from then on, I prefer to let the literature speak for itself. Further background information and exploration come later.

4. I try to get through as much text as possible as quickly as possible, for the sake of the impact, momentum and enjoyment: after all, most literature is meant to be read, heard or seen as continuous text. It may be necessary to pause occasionally to explain, or check that everyone is 'with' me and understanding; but detailed study I postpone until we have finished a first reading.

5. Usually I read aloud literary texts to the class the first time (with the learners following in their texts), unless the text is too long for this to be practicable; on the whole this seems to be the best way to convey a clear first impression of the content and 'shape' of the literature. Learners' reading aloud is usually less clear; and texts may be more difficult to understand through silent reading, especially for the less proficient. With more advanced classes, however, silent reading, or well-prepared reading aloud by learners may be satisfactory options.

6. The most usual technique is to ask closed-ended comprehension questions: who is speaking, what are they saying, where is this happening, and so on. I prefer more open-ended ideas such as: ask learners to give a quick summary in their own words, possibly in their mother tongue; to ask them to tell me anything they understood, in any order; to ask for 'gut' reactions, anything they would like to say in response to the first reading, and develop brief discussions, focussing on content; to invite questions, to be written on the board and discussed.

Understanding and familiarization

The next stage is to get learners to interact with the text thoroughly and repeatedly so that they become familiar with the words and ideas, are confident they know the sequence of events and characters; and to help them to understand and appreciate the text in more depth and detail. How can we provide opportunities and motivation for repeated purposeful interaction with the text? And how can we check that the desired understanding and appreciation have in fact occurred?

Task **Studying and suggesting ideas for familiarizing learners with a text**

Some ideas are shown in Box 14.4. Read through and tick ones that seem useful to you; can you add more?

BOX 14.4:   UNDERSTANDING AND FAMILIARIZATION: TEACHING IDEAS

1. Reread, differently from the first time (if the first time was reading aloud, then this time silently, or vice versa).
2. Read through looking for bits you didn't understand: note them for later discussion.
3. Look through the text, pick out bits you particularly liked, or that stick in your memory; copy them out if they are short, otherwise just note the page reference. Then share.
4. Look through the text for a quotation which could serve as an alternative title.
5. Rewrite some or all of the text from someone else's point of view.
6. Rewrite some or all of the text in a different genre or style: for example, report the events of a short story for a newspaper.
7. Present the text, or particular aspects of it in a different visual format: as a flowchart, as a diagram, as a graph, as a list of events, as a grid . . .
8. Draw an illustration; or design a book-cover or advertisement for the text.
9.
10.

© Cambridge University Press 1996

Analysis and interpretation

Not all classes go very deeply into the interpretation of a text: not all teachers feel confident they can lead discussions on literary analysis. A deeper probing into the meanings and implications of a text does not necessarily demand a knowledge of the terminology of literary criticism, though this can help; it is essentially an attempt to discover new levels of meaning or perspectives, or to deepen appreciation of style or structure. Usually the main tool for such probing is the class discussion, initiated by an open-ended stimulus cue such as 'Let's compare . . .', 'What would have happened if . . .', 'Why do you think . . .?'

Different teachers have different ideas about their own role in such discussions. In Box 14.5 are some teacher statements. Which do you identify with? Which do you find problematical? My own comments follow.

BOX 14.5:   LEADING INTERPRETATIVE DISCUSSION: THE TEACHER'S ROLE

Miri: 'I read this poem often, love it, and have a clear idea of its underlying meanings: I try to lead the students towards a similar understanding, sometimes expressing my own ideas about it.'

Bella: 'I intervene as little as possible in discussions on literature, only pose questions; I would certainly never express my own opinions.'

Ali: 'I try to encourage students to develop their own interpretations, even if I think they are "wrong".'

Mat: 'On the whole, I stand aside and let the students build their own ideas; but if I see them going wildly wrong, I'll step in and show them why.'

Sylvie: 'I see my function in the discussion as prober, challenger, getting students to examine ideas critically, bring evidence. Sometimes I'll throw in outrageous ideas for the sake of provocation.'

© Cambridge University Press 1996

Comments on Box 14.5: The teacher's role in discussions on literature

The advantages of Miri's approach are that she is very likely to infect her students with her own love for the literature, and leave them with a clear and coherent conception of what it is saying and how. A disadvantage is that she may inhibit their own spontaneous responses and original interpretations. Bella is the opposite: learners may develop their own independent interpretations; but those who have no particular interest in the literature may be left 'cold'; she does little to raise their enthusiasm or help them to develop appreciation. Perhaps a compromise is possible, where you communicate your own enthusiasm and make your ideas available to the learners while allowing them room to disagree and develop different perspectives.

The difference between Ali and Mat focusses on one aspect of teacher intervention in discussions: what happens if the learners construct an interpretation that, it seems clear to you, is in total disagreement with the author's intention? If you are particularly attached to the piece of literature in question, you may find it extremely difficult, if not impossible, to allow learners to get away with such 'wrong' conceptions; you will find it easier if you are less involved with the literature, or if you are more committed to allowing free learner interpretations on the grounds that this results in ultimate personal enrichment and more valuable learning. One approach that can help is that expressed by Sylvie, since mistaken interpretations are very often exposed as such when examined carefully in the light of textual evidence.

▷ # Unit Five: Literature (3): teaching a specific text

In this unit you are asked to think about the teaching of a specific piece of literature, and if possible to try out your ideas in practice. You may like to work on one of the examples shown in Box 14.7, or on a different one of your own choosing.

Task ## Teaching a text

Stage 1: Planning

Prepare a lesson or two on the text, having in mind a specific class you know. Some points you may need to relate to are shown in Box 14.6.

BOX 14.6: PREPARING TO TEACH A LITERARY TEXT

– Will I do any pre-text teaching of language or content? If so, what?
– Will I do any other 'warm-up' activities? If so, what?
– How will the text be presented the first time?
– What should I do immediately after the first reading to encourage and check comprehension?
– What activities or tasks might encourage interaction and engagement with the text?
– What sorts of questions or tasks might get students to probe and explore more subtle meanings, aspects of style or structure?
– What might be a good way to 'round off' the study of this text?

© Cambridge University Press 1996

Stage 2 (optional): Experience and reflection

If feasible, try teaching the literature to a class, using your plan as a basis. Immediately afterwards, note down for yourself how things went, which ideas seemed to succeed and which not, and why.

Stage 3: Sharing and summarizing

If you are working with other teachers, share and compare your ideas and (if relevant) your experiences trying them out. Finally, summarize for yourself the main conclusions from the experience, as you may have done at the end of Stage 2, but taking into account also what you have learned from exchanging ideas with others: what kinds of literature-teaching techniques seemed to work well, which not so well, and why.

My ideas on the teaching of the texts shown in Box 14.7 are shown in the Notes, (2); if you worked on one of these you might find it interesting to compare your ideas with mine.

BOX 14.7: SAMPLE TEXTS FOR TEACHING

Teevee

In the house
of Mr and Mrs Spouse
he and she
would watch teevee
and never a word
between them spoken
until the day
the set was broken.

Then 'How do you do?'
said he to she,
'I don't believe we've met yet.
Spouse is my name.
What's yours?' he asked.
'Why, mine's the same!'
said she to he,
'Do you suppose that we could be —?'

But then the set came suddenly right about
And so they never did find out.

Eve Merriam

He Treats them to Ice-cream

Every Sunday they went for a walk together
He, she
And the three children.

One night
when she tried to stop him going
to his other woman,
he pulled out a flick-knife
from under the mattress.

They still go for a walk
every Sunday,
he, she and the three children.
He treats them to ice-cream and they all laugh.
She too.

Anna Swirszczynskia

Notes

(1) Types of topic content

I teach schoolchildren English as a foreign language, which they may use when travelling in English-speaking countries, in their own country for purposes of study, tourism or business, or in any country as a language of international communication.

The only type of non-linguistic content I have no personal experience of teaching is other school subjects taught through the medium of the foreign language, since this is not accepted practice in the schools where I am employed. However, it has been found a useful and productive method, particularly where the students are likely to need the language for the subject in question (in schools oriented towards academic study for example) or for immigrants.

'Zero content' material is often seen as pointless and boring by students, though some superficially attractive songs and stories may engage their attention. I do not like using such material as a basis for extended language work, since it lacks substantial content and wastes opportunities for engaging with real information or issues. However, as a schoolteacher I am perhaps more concerned with the educational aspects of my material than colleagues teaching in other situations. And we all probably use this type of material sometimes, as a basis for short improvised samples of language items!

Home-culture content is acceptable, not only because my students may need to know how to talk about it in the future, but also because it supplies subjects for discussion that are familiar, interesting and motivating. The target-language culture and literature, other countries' culture and general knowledge I think are important for my students' education in principle, as is some treatment of general and specific controversial issues leading to values' clarification. The language as a topic of study itself is not appropriate to most of my students, but can be used occasionally with some of the older classes who may find it intellectually challenging. I occasionally use the students themselves as a focus: I am interested in their ideas and experiences and want to show it, and they usually find these topics motivating, up to a point. However, I find caution and sensitivity are needed here: some students object to what they see as an invasion of privacy, or feel uncomfortable with 'touchy-feely' activities.

(2) Teaching a text

Teevee

This is a fairly easy poem, both in language and content, suitable for not too advanced classes; and it can be enjoyed both by adults and children. The only words I would pre-teach would be *spouse* and *set* (as a synonym for 'television').

For warm-up activities, it is tempting to do something on the influence of television on people's lives, and how it affects their ability to communicate with one another – but this is 'giving away' the main message of the poem, and I would rather have students discover this for themselves from direct interaction with the text. I might, however, do some casual discussion of television in general while eliciting or teaching various synonyms for it (*TV, the set, the box, the telly* . . .).

The text is easy enough to be read silently for the first time and understood by the students; but I think they will enjoy and appreciate the humour more if I read it aloud, while they follow it in their own texts. I would then ask them to recap the situation and events in their own words to check they have understood.

With younger students, I might ask them in threes to act out, or even mime, the events of the poem (the third actor being the television); or to draw a picture, or series of pictures, to illustrate it. Older students might discuss what style of illustration (e.g. photograph?/drawing? monochrome?/coloured?) would be appropriate to the poem and why. For any age: students might be asked to prepare and perform a 'dramatic reading' in small groups, possibly having previously learnt the text by heart.

For further study: students can be asked to divide the poem into three sections or chapters, and to compare the middle section with the first and third: from the point of view of content, rhythm, rhyme, punctuation – whatever they can find.

If they see it as a humorous poem, why is it funny? Can they find a serious side to it? If the poet has a serious message, what is it? Do they have any experiences or ideas of their own on the subject? Older students might get into a general discussion of the use of humour to make a point in literature: wit, satire, parody.

I would finish with another reading, either of my own or of a good student reader: the main experience I want them to be left with is the literature itself, not what we said about it.

He Treats them to Ice-cream

This poem is also based on simple language, and could be taught to various age-groups; but it is rather more serious in content.

The impact of the poem is based largely on the unexpected shifts in mood and action; hence a good way to present it might be, as suggested by Lazar (1993: 112–13), to expose them only to the first three lines, and elicit expectations about what is to follow; read the next stanza, think about it and, again, predict; and finally read the ending.

A brief recap of who the characters are and what actually happens could be followed by more detailed speculation on such topics as: how long do you think this story really took? How old were the children? Did the man stop seeing the other woman or not? What were the relationships like within the family?

As a follow-up to the discussion, students could tell, in writing or orally, the story from the point of view of any of the characters; the husband, the wife, one of the children, the other woman. Then, returning to the poem, you might ask the key question: why does the poet in fact give none of the detail which one would expect in such a story?

At a more sophisticated level, it might be interesting to look at aspects of style and structure: in what ways do the sentence-structure, punctuation and so on reflect the dramatic development of the poem? Or to discuss ethical or social questions: what is the 'message' of the poem? What does it say about family life?

Again, I would like to wind up study of the poem with a final rereading.

An additional possibility is of course to study 'Teevee' and 'He Treats them to Ice-cream' one after the other, and then compare them: often further insights, learning and pleasure result from comparing both content and form of texts which are, like these, of similar length, structure and general topic.

Further reading

BACKGROUND AND TEACHER'S HANDBOOKS

Alptekin, C. (1993) 'Target-language culture in EFL materials', *ELT Journal*, 47, 2, 136–43.
(A discussion of the problems inherent in basing a foreign language course on target-culture content: pleads for an open, intercultural approach)

Cook, V. J. (1983) 'What should language teaching be about?', *ELT Journal*, 37, 3, 229–34.
(A more thorough treatment of the subject of Unit One: does not actually answer its own title question, but explores possibilities)

Harrison, B. (ed.) (1990) *Culture and the Language Classroom*, Hong Kong: Modern English Publications and the British Council.
(Various articles on aspects of the teaching of culture in the foreign language classroom; see particularly articles by Barrow and Harrison)

Kramsch, C. (1993) *Context and Culture in Language Teaching*, Oxford: Oxford University Press.
(Edifying and exciting, though not easy, reading: discusses the encounter with foreign culture in language learning, seen as an exploration of differences and diversities rather than acquisition of information)

Prodromou, L. (1992a) 'What culture? Which culture? Cross-cultural factors in language learning', *ELT Journal*, 46, 1, 39–50.
(An interesting survey of the opinions of Greek learners of English as a foreign language)

Tomalin, B. and Stempleski, S. (1993) *Cultural Awareness*, Oxford: Oxford University Press.
(Ideas for teaching cultural awareness: examples are based on English-speaking cultures, but can easily be adapted for others)

UNDERLYING MESSAGES

Clarke, J. and Clarke, M. (1990) 'Stereotyping in TESOL materials', in Harrison, B. (ed.), *Culture and the Language Classroom*, Hong Kong: Modern English Publications and the British Council.
(Interesting and readable discussion of stereotyping of various kinds in (English) language teaching materials)

Phillipson, R. (1992) *Linguistic Imperialism*, Oxford: Oxford University Press.
(Shows how the spread of English is contributing to the dominance of the culture and general influence of English-speaking nations)

Sunderland, J. (ed.) (1994) *Exploring Gender: Questions and Implications for English Language Education*, Hemel Hempstead: Prentice Hall International.
(Relevant to the teaching of all languages, not just English! A collection of articles and case studies looking at various gender-related topics in language learning)

TEACHING LITERATURE

Bassnett, S. and Grundy, P. (1993) *Language through Literature*, London: Longman.

(Imaginative ideas for getting students to engage with literary language and texts and to create their own)

Brumfit, C. J. and Carter, R. (eds.) (1986) *Literature and Language Teaching*, Oxford: Oxford University Press.
(A collection of articles on various aspects of approach and practice: no recipes, not light reading, but interesting background)

Carter, R. and Long, M. N. (1991) *Teaching Literature*, London: Longman.
(Various ways of approaching the use of literature, with examples of texts and activities; for background study rather than use as a resource book)

Collie, J. and Slater, S. (1987) *Literature in the Language Classroom*, Cambridge: Cambridge University Press.
(Discussion of some general issues followed by a variety of practical literature-teaching techniques, relating to various literary genres)

Duff, A. and Maley, A. (1992) *Literature*, Oxford: Oxford University Press.
(A collection of interesting and challenging activities for engaging with literary texts and learning language from them)

Ellis, G. and McRae, J. (1991) *The Extensive Reading Handbook for Secondary Teachers*, Harmondsworth: Penguin.
(Misleading title: actually consists of plenty of good ideas for teaching literature at both primary and secondary levels: examples based on well-known English texts)

Hill, J. (1986) *Using Literature in Language Teaching*, London: Macmillan.
(A compact, basic introduction to the subject, including practical classroom procedures; examples refer to English literature)

Lazar, G. (1993) *Literature and Language Teaching*, Cambridge: Cambridge University Press.
(A good text to use to teach yourself how to teach literature: comprehensive, readable, with plenty of illustrative tasks accompanied by suggested answers)

Up to now the topic of foreign language teaching has been approached mainly from the perspective of language as a subject of study: how to teach various linguistic contents or skills, aspects of (language) course materials and structure. However, this direction of thought can result in neglect of some essential topics: specifically, those that are relevant to all classroom teaching, not only that of foreign languages. This and the next part, therefore, take as their point of departure aspects of instruction and education in general and apply these to language teaching, rather than the other way round. Part V deals mainly with the lesson: planning, interaction and management.

Module 15 focusses on the **lesson itself**: what it is, how it may be most effectively organized, prepared and evaluated. Module 16 looks at **classroom interaction**: how teachers activate students, or students activate themselves, and what kinds of interaction are conducive to what kinds of learning. Module 17 has to do with **giving feedback,** whether in speech or writing: what its purposes are and how it may be used to promote learning and learner morale. Finally, Module 18 deals with the topic of **classroom discipline**; less important, perhaps, for those (relatively few, perhaps lucky) teachers who work with highly motivated adults in small groups, but a central cause of concern for the many who teach large classes of adolescents in schools.

Module 15: Lesson planning

▶ ## Unit One: What does a lesson involve?

The lesson is a type of organized social event that occurs in virtually all cultures. Lessons in different places may vary in topic, time, place, atmosphere, methodology and materials, but they all, essentially, are concerned with learning as their main objective, involve the participation of learner(s) and teacher(s), and are limited and pre-scheduled as regards time, place and membership.

There are additional characteristics or perspectives to a lesson which may be less obvious, but which are also significant. One way to become aware of these is to look at metaphors that highlight one or another of them.

BOX 15.1: METAPHORS FOR A LESSON

a variety show	a conversation
climbing a mountain	doing the shopping
eating a meal	a football game
a wedding	a symphony
a menu	consulting a doctor

© *Cambridge University Press 1996*

Group task **Exploring metaphors**

Stage 1: Choosing a metaphor

Which of the metaphors shown in Box 15.1 expresses best, in your opinion as a teacher, the essence of a lesson? There is, of course, no 'right' answer, but your choice will reflect your own conception. If you can find no metaphor here which suits you, invent your own.

Stage 2: Comparing choices

If you are working in a group, get together in pairs or threes and share your selections and reasons for making them. Since any one choice is as valid as any other, there is no need to try to reach any kind of group consensus as to which is the 'best'; the aim of the discussion is simply to become more aware of the different attributes different people feel are significant. If you are on your own, go straight to Stage 3 below.

Stage 3: Analysis

Some of the main elements that may have come up in your thinking and discussion about the various metaphors are discussed in the section

Aspects of the lesson below. Have a look at this section and try to relate it to your own choice(s).

Stage 4: Optional follow-up

In the Notes, (1) you will find analyses of each metaphor in terms of the interpretation of the concept of a lesson which it seems to embody. These are not necessarily the only possible interpretations, but you may be interested in looking up 'your' metaphor, and seeing if the analysis fits your own approach.

Aspects of the lesson

1. **Transaction,** or series of transactions. This is expressed in the metaphors of shopping, a wedding and a meal, with the emphasis on some kind of purposeful give-and-take which results in a product: an acquisition or a definable mental or physical change in the participants. If you care about the transactional element, then what is important to you is the actual learning which takes place in the lesson.
2. **Interaction.** This is most obvious in the metaphor of conversation, but is also expressed in the wedding, the variety show, and, in perhaps a rather different way, in the football game. Here what is important are the social relationships between learners, or between learners and teacher; a lesson is seen as something which involves relaxed, warm interaction that protects and promotes the confidence and happiness of all participants.

   For a more detailed discussion of the transactional and interactional aspects of a lesson, see Prabhu (1992).
3. **Goal-oriented effort,** involving hard work (climbing a mountain, a football game). This implies awareness of a clear, worthwhile objective, the necessity of effort to attain it and a resulting sense of satisfaction and triumph if it is achieved, or of failure and disappointment if it is not.
4. **A satisfying, enjoyable experience** (a variety show, a symphony, eating a meal). This experience may be based on such things as aesthetic pleasure, fun, interest, challenge or entertainment; the main point is that participants should enjoy it and therefore be motivated to attend while it is going on (as distinct from feeling satisfied with the results).
5. **A role-based culture,** where certain roles (the teacher) involve responsibility and activity, others (the learners) responsiveness and receptivity (consultation with a doctor, a wedding, eating a meal). All participants know and accept in advance the demands that will be made on them, and their expected behaviours. This often implies:
6. **A conventional construct,** with elements of ritual (a wedding, a variety show, a performance of a symphony). Certain set behaviours occur every time (for example, a certain kind of introduction or ending), and the other components of the overall event are selected by an authority from a limited set of possibilities. In contrast, there is:
7. **A series of free choices** (a menu, a conversation). Participants are free to 'do their own thing' within a fairly loose structure, and construct the event as it progresses, through their own decision-making. There is no obvious authority figure who imposes choices.

▷ ## Unit Two: Lesson preparation

How should a lesson be prepared? Is there a best method to do so?

One way of looking for answers to these questions is to ask competent professionals, and then try to discover some general principles that seem to be accepted by all, or most, of them.

Inquiry **Lesson preparation**

Stage 1: Preliminary study

In Box 15.2 are seven questions about lesson preparation. Start by answering them yourself, in writing. (If you are a trainee with limited experience, then note how you hope to prepare lessons yourself, or how you have done so in teaching practice.) After writing each response, leave two or three lines empty before going on to the next.

BOX 15.2: QUESTIONS ON LESSON PREPARATION

1. How long before a specific lesson do you prepare it?
2. Do you write down lesson notes to guide you? Or do you rely on a lesson format provided by another teacher, the coursebook, or a Teacher's Book?
3. If so, are these notes brief (a single page or less) or long (more than one page)?
4. What do they consist of?
5. Do you note down your objectives?
6. Do you actually look at your notes during the lesson? If so, rarely? Occasionally? Frequently?
7. What do you do with your lesson notes after the lesson?

© *Cambridge University Press 1996*

Stage 2: Interview

Now interview at least two language teachers who are experienced and (as far as you can tell) conscientious and competent professionals. Ask them the same questions, stressing that what you want to know is what **they actually do** in daily practice, not what they think they ought to do!

My own answers to these questions may be found in the Notes, (2). If you cannot find (enough) teachers to interview, you may find it helpful to refer to these at Stage 4 (*Conclusions*) below.

Stage 3: Results

If you are working in a group and have each interviewed different teachers, share your results; if not, put together the different answers you got from your own interviewees. Can you make any generalizations, or does lesson preparation seem to be entirely idiosyncratic?

Stage 4: Conclusions

Think about or discuss the evidence you have gathered from interviews, and/or from my responses in the Notes. What conclusions can you draw?

Try to assess critically the relevance and usefulness of these conclusions for your own practice.

Stage 5: Personal application

Finally, revert to the answers you wrote yourself at the beginning of this task, and add notes below each one, recording ideas you have learned from this inquiry that may be helpful to you in future lesson planning.

▶ Unit Three: Varying lesson components

The teaching/learning tasks and topics which form the basis of different components of a language lesson have been discussed in earlier modules: presentation of new material, practice activities or tests; accurate reception or production of the language's pronunciation, vocabulary or grammar; or more fluency-oriented work such as discussing or writing essays. In this unit we shall be looking at the 'packaging' of such components: how they may be combined with each other and presented as a varied and effective lesson programme.

In a lesson which is entirely taken up with one kind of activity, interest is likely to flag: learners will find it more difficult to concentrate and may get bored and irritable which will detract from learning and may produce discipline problems in some classes. A varied lesson, besides being more interesting and pleasant for both teacher and learners, is also likely to cater for a wider range of learning styles and strategies, and may delay onset of fatigue by providing regular refreshing changes in the type of mental or physical activity demanded.

Task **Brainstorm**

How many different ways of varying language-learning activity within a lesson can you think of? It helps to think in terms of contrasts: for example, rapid-moving versus leisurely activities; or individuals versus pair/group versus full-class organization. Write down, or pool ideas in groups; then check with Box 15.3 to see if it adds any further suggestions.

Selection and organization

Variation of components within the programme of a lesson is a good principle, but it is not enough. Varied activities flung together in random order can result in a feeling of restlessness and disorder; it is therefore worth defining some principles of selection and organization of components to construct a smooth, coherent programme. Which components should come earlier, which later in a lesson? Which are likely to fit together well to form a coherent sequence? And so on.

Below are some guidelines for the combination of different components that I have found useful and relevant in my own teaching.

BOX 15.3: WAYS OF VARYING A LESSON

1. Tempo
Activities may be brisk and fast-moving (such as guessing games) or slow and reflective (such as reading literature and responding in writing).

2. Organization
The learners may work on their own at individualized tasks; or in pairs or groups; or as a full class in interaction with the teacher.

3. Mode and skill
Activities may be based on the written or the spoken language; and within these, they may vary as to whether the learners are asked to produce (speak, write) or receive (listen, read).

4. Difficulty
Activities may be seen as easy and non-demanding; or difficult, requiring concentration and effort.

5. Topic
Both the language teaching point and the (non-linguistic) topic may change from one activity to another.

6. Mood
Activities vary also in mood: light and fun-based versus serious and profound; happy versus sad; tense versus relaxed.

7. Stir–settle
Some activities enliven and excite learners (such as controversial discussions, or activities that involve physical movement); others, like dictations, have the effect of calming them down (see Maclennan, 1987).

8. Active–passive
Learners may be activated in a way that encourages their own initiative; or they may only be required to do as they are told.

© Cambridge University Press 1996

Guidelines for ordering components of a lesson

1. Put the harder tasks earlier

On the whole, students are fresher and more energetic earlier in the lesson, and get progressively less so as it goes on, particularly if the lesson is a long one. So it makes sense to put the tasks that demand more effort and concentration earlier on (learning new material, or tackling a difficult text, for example) and the lighter ones later. Similarly, tasks that need a lot of student initiative work better earlier in the lesson, with the more structured and controlled ones later.

2. Have quieter activities before lively ones

It can be quite difficult to calm down a class – particularly of children or adolescents – who have been participating in a lively, exciting activity. So if one of your central lesson components is something quiet and reflective it is better on the whole to put it before a lively one, not after. The exception to this is when you have a rather lethargic or tired class of adults; here 'stirring' activities early on can actually refresh and help students get into the right frame of mind for learning.

3. Think about transitions

If you have a sharp transition from, say, a reading–writing activity to an oral one, or from a fast-moving one to a slow one, devote some thought to the transition stage. It may be enough to 'frame' by summing up one component in a few words and introducing the next; or it may help to have a very brief transition activity which makes the move smoother (see Ur and Wright, 1992, for some ideas).

4. Pull the class together at the beginning and the end

If you bring the class together at the beginning for general greetings, organization and introduction of the day's programme, and then do a similar full-class 'rounding-off' at the end, this contributes to a sense of structure. On the whole, group or individual work is more smoothly organized if it takes place in the middle of the lesson, with clear beginning and ending points.

5. End on a positive note

This does not necessarily mean ending with a joke or a fun activity – though of course it may. For some classes it may mean something quite serious, like a summary of what we have achieved today, or a positive evaluation of something the class has done. Another possibility is to give a task which the class is very likely to succeed in and which will generate feelings of satisfaction. The point is to have students leave the classroom feeling good.

Discussion task Think about or discuss the questions:
- How far do you agree with these guidelines?
- Are they appropriate for your own teaching context as they stand, or would you wish to omit, add to or change any of them?

Follow-up observation task Observe one or two foreign language lessons, noting down in detail what the components are and how they are organized. The lessons should preferably be given by a teacher you do not know, or a video recording can be used. If these options are not available, use the lesson description given in Box 15.5.

Afterwards, think about your notes, or discuss them with colleagues, analysing the way the lesson was constructed. You may find it useful to refer to the points listed in Box 15.3. What possible alternatives, or improvements, can you think of?

▷ # Unit Four: Evaluating lesson effectiveness

It is important to stop and think after giving a lesson whether it was a good one or not, and why. This is not in order to indulge in self-congratulation or vain regrets, but in order to have a basis for your own learning from reflection on experience: this lesson was unsatisfactory, what could I have done to improve it? Or: this lesson was good, what was it exactly that made it so? Other units in this module have dealt with criteria that can be applied to the design or assessment of particular procedures; this one concentrates on overall evaluation of the lesson event: effective, or not?

Task ## Evaluating criteria

Imagine you have just come out of a lesson – whether your own, or one that you have observed – and wish to assess how effective it was. By what criteria will you evaluate it?

In Box 15.4 is a list of criteria I have heard suggested by teachers; you may wish to add more. Can you put them in order of priority: the most important, in your opinion, first, the least important last? You may, of course, put two or more at the same level if you think they are of the same importance.

Below are some notes on the criteria that you may find useful; and my own solution to the task, with explanations, is given at the end of the unit.

BOX 15.4: CRITERIA FOR EVALUATING LESSON EFFECTIVENESS

a) The learners were active all the time.
b) The learners were attentive all the time.
c) The learners enjoyed the lesson, were motivated.
d) The class seemed to be learning the material well.
e) The lesson went according to plan.
f) The language was used communicatively throughout.
g) The learners were engaging with the foreign language throughout.
h)
i)
j)

© *Cambridge University Press 1996*

Notes on the criteria

1. The learners were active, attentive, enjoying themselves

If learners are active, attentive, enjoying themselves and motivated they are likely to be learning better. On the other hand it is very possible to activate learners effectively and enjoyably and hold their attention for long periods of time in occupations that have little learning or educational value.

2. The class seemed to be learning the material well

The main goal of a lesson, when all is said and done, is to bring about learning; the problem is how to judge whether learning is in fact taking place.

3. The lesson went according to plan

On average, I would guess that a lesson that went on the whole according to plan is more likely to have been effective; but this does beg the question of whether the plan was a good one in the first place! Also, a sensitive and flexible teacher may well deviate from an original plan in response to changing circumstances or learner needs, with positive results.

4. The language was used communicatively throughout

It is certainly important to do activities that involve communication; but non-communicative activities (for example, grammar explanations) also have their place and assist learning.

5. The learners were engaging with the foreign language throughout

The engaging with the material to be learnt (in this case the language) is surely a prerequisite for learning that material. Learning, however, will result from this process only if the material and task are of appropriate level.

Suggested order of priority

My order would be the following:

1. c) The class seemed to be learning the material well.
2. g) The learners were engaging with the foreign language throughout.
3. b) The learners were attentive all the time.
4. d) The learners enjoyed the lesson, were motivated.
5. a) The learners were active all the time.
6. e) The lesson went according to plan.
7. f) The language was used communicatively throughout.

Comments

This order will quite probably be different from yours; and I found some decisions about the ranking – as I am sure you will have done – very difficult to make! Here are some of my considerations.

The first criterion has to be the learning; that is the main objective of a lesson. The fact that it is difficult to judge how much learners have learned does not let us off the duty of trying our best to do so! We can usually make a fairly good guess, based on our knowledge of the class, the type of activity they were engaged in, and some informal test activities that give feedback on learning (see Module 3: *Tests*).

The amount of learning is very likely to correlate highly with the amount of the foreign language the class engages with in the course of a lesson. If the foreign language material is too difficult, or the task too slow, or too much time is spent on organization or mother-tongue explanation, the amount of learning will lessen.

Learners who are really engaging with the language must be attentive; loss of attention means loss of learning time. However, this attention may be directed at activities which produce little learning! – which is why this item is not higher up the list.

Enjoyment and motivation are important because they make it more likely that learners will attend; they also contribute to learners' holding a long-term positive attitude towards language lessons and learning in general. But it is, of course, possible to have participants thoroughly enjoying a lesson without learning anything.

Active learning is usually good learning; however, learners may be apparently passive (quietly listening or reading) and actually learning a lot; and, conversely, may be very active and learning nothing. It is common – and dangerous – for teachers to over-estimate the importance of learners being active all the time.

Most teachers plan carefully, and if the plan was a reasonably good one, then a lesson that accorded with it was probably also good. However, a specific plan may turn out to be not so good; in such a case following it may be disastrous, and inspired improvisation more successful. Also, occasionally, unexpected circumstances or learner demand may result in changes, with similarly positive results.[1] In summary: yes, a criterion that has some use, but too dubious to be put very high.

Communication is important for language learning, but non-communicative activities can also teach; for some learners lesson time spent on the latter may actually be a better long-term investment. The higher you rank this criterion, the more crucial you feel the communicative character of the lesson to be; obviously I personally do not feel this to be as important a factor as the others.

Follow-up task ## Practice and/or observation

The aim of this task is to try to evaluate the effectiveness of a lesson. The lesson itself could be one of the following possibilities:

1. Most usefully: one you yourself have planned and taught, based on a unit in a coursebook or syllabus you use or are familiar with.
2. One taught by a colleague or another teacher.
3. Less effective: a video recording of a lesson.
4. As a final resort: the observation notes shown in Box 15.5.

(My comments on this version are given in the Notes, (3).)

Try to evaluate how good the lesson was, using the criteria and priorities you have worked on in this unit. If you have observed together with other teachers, come together after the lesson to compare notes.

---

[1] But an interesting piece of research on pupil appraisals of teachers indicates that school-age pupils consider the description 'This teacher would do something else if that's what the class wants' as a characteristic of the **bad** teacher! (Wragg, E. C. and Wood, E. K. (1984) 'Pupil appraisals of teaching' in Wragg, E. C. (ed.) *Classroom Teaching Skills*, London and Sydney: Croom Helm: 79–96)

BOX 15.5: DESCRIPTION OF A LESSON

This was a heterogeneous class of 35 fifteen-year-olds.

9.15   The teacher (T) enters, students (Ss) gradually quieten, sit, take out books.

9.20   T elicits the topic Ss had been asked to prepare for today ('conformism'), elicits and discusses some key words, does not write them up.

9.25   T distributes cartoons, asks Ss to work in pairs and suggest captions that have to do with the topic. Some Ss work, most do not.

9.30   T elicits results: only three pairs are willing to suggest ideas. T suggests they carry on for homework.

9.32   T tells Ss to open books at p.35: an article on conformism. T: 'What would you do if you wanted to get the general idea of the article?' Suggests they read only first sentence of each paragraph.

9.35   Silent reading

9.38   T does true/false exercise from book based only on these first sentences, using volunteer responders for each item, correcting and commenting. Some questions are not yet answerable.

9.45   T gives homework: read the entire article, finish finding the answers to the T/F questions.

9.47   T invites individual student to perform a prepared monologue (about Stalin) before the class. The class applauds. T approves warmly, refrains from commenting on language mistakes.

9.52   T initiates discussion on the topic of the monologue; about seven students participate, most of the rest are listening.

10.00   The lesson ends, some Ss come up to talk to T.

© Cambridge University Press 1996

▶ Unit Five: Practical lesson management

'If only you'd told me before,' complained a young teacher to me recently. She had found herself with extra time on her hands at the end of a lesson, and nothing with which to fill it, and I had suggested that she should make a habit of having a reserve activity ready as part of her regular lesson plan. She adopted the idea gladly, but reproached me – perhaps rightly – for not having suggested it earlier.

In Box 15.6 is a set of such hints, which you may find useful – and which may, hopefully, help to prevent you finding yourself in a similar situation! If you are yourself experienced, you may be able to add more.

Discussion task   **If you are yourself experienced, find an inexperienced colleague to sit with, and vice versa; or form mixed groups of more and less experienced participants. The experienced teacher(s) should first talk their inexperienced colleague(s) through the list in Box 15.6, adding further comment and illustration, and answering questions; and then add any other practical advice that they feel can be helpful.**

BOX 15.6: HINTS FOR LESSON MANAGEMENT

1. Prepare more than you need: it is advisable to have an easily presented, light 'reserve' activity ready in case of extra time (see Ur and Wright, 1992 for some ideas).
2. Similarly, note in advance which component(s) of the lesson you will sacrifice if you find yourself with too little time for everything!
3. Keep a watch or clock easily visible, make sure you are aware throughout how time is going relative to your programme. It is difficult to judge intuitively how time is going when you are busy, and the smooth running of your lesson depends to some extent on proper timing.
4. Do not leave the giving of homework to the last minute! At the end of the lesson learners' attention is at a low ebb, and you may run out of time before you finish explaining. Explain it earlier on, and then give a quick reminder at the end.
5. If you have papers to distribute and a large class, do not try to give every paper yourself to every student! Give a number of papers to people at different points in the class, ask them to take one and pass the rest on.
6. If you are doing group work, give instructions and make sure these are understood **before** dividing into groups or even, if practicable, handing out materials; if you do it the other way round, students will be looking at each other and at the materials, and they are less likely to attend to what you have to say.

© *Cambridge University Press 1996*

Postscript

The problem is, of course, that the young teacher mentioned at the beginning of this unit may well have in fact been told previously, by me or by someone else, to prepare reserve activities. But frequently such advice is not in fact remembered and used until you actually experience the need for it – more often than not, as here, through encountering a problem which its implementation could have prevented! Perhaps each of us has to discover the usefulness of such hints for ourselves? But at least their provision in advance may accelerate and facilitate such discovery when the time comes.

Notes

(1) Metaphors

a) **A variety show** is essentially pleasing and involves mixed, stimulating components; if you chose it you see variety and enjoyment as key factors in a lesson. You probably see the learners as an audience to be motivated and stimulated rather than made to work.
b) **Climbing a mountain** is essentially a challenge. The corresponding lesson involves, therefore, an investment of effort on the part of learners and teacher, may not be particularly pleasurable while in process, but provides rewards in the form of successful achievement of the aim. However, there is the corresponding danger of failure and disappointment if this aim is not attained.

223

c) **Eating a meal** is like a lesson if the latter is seen basically as the performance of some important or necessary function, combined with some feelings of satisfaction and pleasure. Learning is perhaps seen as essentially receptive, a matter of intake rather than of effort and initiative.

d) **A wedding** is a largely ritual, though meaningful, event. The corresponding lesson is therefore to some extent structured, with certain set routines and conventions; the roles and relationship are also predetermined and fairly rigid. It is to a large extent the adequate performance of these routines and maintenance of roles which determines its success.

e) **A menu,** in contrast, involves choice and flexibility; it is not, however, concerned with outcomes. If you chose this one, you are more interested in possibilities, options and process than in the final product in terms of successful learning.

f) If you chose **conversation**, you probably see the lesson as a rather informal social event, where what is important is communication, and the formation and maintenance of good relationships between participants. The teacher would be seen as the facilitator of interaction, and much of the initiative would be taken by the learners.

g) **Doing the shopping** is the successful performance of a series of necessary business transactions, where the shopper has usually pre-planned a list of things to do and an itinerary. The lesson, therefore, would be essentially a systematic and goal-oriented progression through a prepared set of items, with the emphasis on efficiency and completion of tasks.

h) **A football game**, like a mountain climb, involves the investment of effort in order to achieve a defined aim; but here the effort is made as a team, and social interaction, whether cooperative or competitive, is important. There are also elements typical of such games – such as the existence of rules and a referee, challenge, tension – which you may find applicable.

i) If you see a lesson as **a symphony**, then what interests you perhaps is the aspect of aesthetic variation and order: the combination of different themes, tempo, volume, tone and so on that go to make a full and balanced programme and make it likely that learners will enjoy the lesson. There is also the aspect of harmonious cooperation, of working together to create a shared, satisfying result.

j) The lesson seen as **a consultation with a doctor** implies a certain relationship between teacher and learner that parallels that between doctor and patient, where the first is authoritative and takes most of the responsibility and initiative in interaction, and the second is mainly receptive and obedient. Another facet of the same relationship is the caring attitude of the professional towards the client, and the trust of the client in the professional.

(2) Lesson preparation

1. Some component tasks or texts may have been prepared days or weeks in advance, but I prepare the specific lesson usually not more than a day or two in advance, so that it can be linked to the one before and the programme of activities is fresh in my mind.
2. Yes, I always write down lesson notes.
3. These notes are usually very brief: less than a page.

4. The notes consist of brief headings and abbreviations (probably largely incomprehensible to anyone else) reminding me what I wanted to do and in what order; page numbers, if I am using a book; notes of specific language items I intend to teach, or cues or questions for tasks; a reserve activity for use if I find myself with extra time.
5. I am aware of my teaching objectives, but do not write them down.
6. I look at my notes only very occasionally during the lesson: usually only for specific information like page numbers or vocabulary items. It is the writing itself which is important and helps me organize myself; once the plan is there, it is usually fresh enough in my memory not to have to refer to it during the lesson. However, I like to have it there, just in case!
7. I keep the notes for a while. Periodically, when I have time, I go through them and note down and file ideas that were successful and that I therefore want to remember and re-use; the rest I throw away.

(3) Comments on the lesson description in Box 15.5

On the whole, I would say this was a satisfactory lesson; students were on-task most of the time, probably learning; the lesson was varied and progressed at a brisk pace. There were, however, some lost opportunities, and some procedures may not be to the taste of some teachers.

Some specific points:

– It took five minutes for the students to quieten: time wasted for language learning; perhaps more assertive demand on the part of the teacher could have shortened this initial transition?
– The fact that the teacher elicited topic and words was good, since the students were prepared, and at least some of them knew the words. But what about those who did not? To promote 'intake' it might have been better to put them on the board and tell students to write them in their notebooks.
– The pair work did not really work; virtually no learning was taking place. Probably the task was too difficult and not clearly enough defined: I am not sure I could have done it myself. And would they be able to do it for homework, if they could not do it in class?
– The teacher was deliberately guiding students towards developing reading strategies, and making them use one: a good idea. The students read well, obviously concentrating and focussed.
– The true/false exercise was done 'ping-pong' fashion: many students were not involved. There would have been a higher proportion of student activity if the teacher had let them try answering in writing for two or three minutes before checking in the full class.
– It was good that the teacher gave homework at this stage so that it was not left to the last minute.
– The speech: obviously something students were used to and treated as routine; though many teachers, and students, dislike this procedure. The rest of the class was sympathetic and attentive – clearly listening and understanding.
– The discussion: if the objective here was oral fluency practice then not many students benefited from it! A common, perhaps not optimally cost-effective, use of class time.

Further reading

Maclennan, S. (1987) 'Integrating lesson planning and class management', *ELT Journal*, **41**, 3, 193–7.
(Lesson planning, with particular reference to the 'stir–settle' factor)
Prabhu, N. S. (1992) 'The dynamics of the language lesson', *TESOL Quarterly*, **26**, 2, 225–41.
(An interesting analysis of various facets of the lesson, principally comparing the contribution of transactional and interactional elements)
Underwood, M. (1987) *Effective Classroom Management*, London: Longman.
(Various aspects of classroom management and lesson planning: practical and comprehensive)
Ur, P. and Wright, A. (1992) *Five-Minute Activities*, Cambridge: Cambridge University Press.
(A collection of short activities which can be used to ease transitions, as reserves, or to introduce or round off lessons)

Module 16: Classroom interaction

▶ ## Unit One: Patterns of classroom interaction

Observation has shown that the most common type of classroom interaction is that known as 'IRF' – 'Initiation–Response–Feedback': the teacher initiates an exchange, usually in the form of a question, one of the students answers, the teacher gives feedback (assessment, correction, comment), initiates the next question – and so on (Sinclair and Coulthard, 1975).

There are, however, alternative patterns: the initiative does not always have to be in the hands of the teacher; and interaction may be between students, or between a student and the material.

Task **Classifying forms of interaction**

Look at the various patterns of interaction described in Box 16.1, and note for each one how active the teacher and students are in their participation, using the following code:

TT = Teacher very active, students only receptive
T = Teacher active, students mainly receptive
TS = Teacher and students fairly equally active
S = Students active, teacher mainly receptive
SS = Students very active, teacher only receptive

Can you add any further ideas for interaction patterns, and attach appropriate codes?

If you wish, look up the Notes, (1) for my own answers.

Follow-up
observation
and
discussion
Observe one or two lessons, and note down the types of interaction you saw, using your own list or that shown in Box 16.1. After the observation, discuss or reflect on the following questions:
1. Was there one particular type of interaction that seemed to predominate?
2. Did teacher activity predominate? Or student activity? Or was the interaction more or less balanced?
3. How appropriate did you think the chosen interaction patterns were for the teaching objectives in the different activities? Perhaps look at one or two specific examples from your observation. This point is studied more fully in Unit Five.

BOX 16.1: INTERACTION PATTERNS

Group work
Students work in small groups on tasks that entail interaction: conveying information, for example, or group decision-making. The teacher walks around listening, intervenes little if at all.

Closed-ended teacher questioning ('IRF')
Only one 'right' response gets approved. Sometimes cynically called the 'Guess what the teacher wants you to say' game.

Individual work
The teacher gives a task or set of tasks, and students work on them independently; the teacher walks around monitoring and assisting where necessary.

Choral responses
The teacher gives a model which is repeated by all the class in the chorus; or gives a cue which is responded to in chorus.

Collaboration
Students do the same sort of tasks as in 'Individual work', but work together, usually in pairs, to try to achieve the best results they can. The teacher may or may not intervene. (Note that this is different from 'Group work', where the task itself necessitates interaction.)

Student initiates, teacher answers
For example, in a guessing game: the students think of questions and the teacher responds; but the teacher decides who asks.

Full-class interaction
The students debate a topic or do a language task as a class; the teacher may intervene occasionally, to stimulate participation or to monitor.

Teacher talk
This may involve some kind of silent student response, such as writing from dictation, but there is no initiative on the part of the student.

Self-access
Students choose their own learning tasks, and work autonomously.

Open-ended teacher questioning
There are a number of possible 'right' answers, so that more students answer each cue.

© Cambridge University Press 1996

▶ Unit Two: Questioning

Questioning is a universally used activation technique in teaching, mainly within the Initiation–Response–Feedback pattern described at the beginning of Unit One.

Note that teacher questions are not always realized by interrogatives. For example, the question:

    'What can you see in this picture?'

may be expressed by the statement:

    'We'll describe what is going on in this picture.'

or by the command:

    'Tell me what you can see in this picture.'

So perhaps a question, in the context of teaching, may be best defined as a teacher utterance which has the objective of eliciting an oral response from the learner(s).

Task **Reasons for questioning**

There are various reasons why a teacher might ask a question in the classroom. Read through the list of possible reasons shown in Box 16.2, and add any more that you can think of.

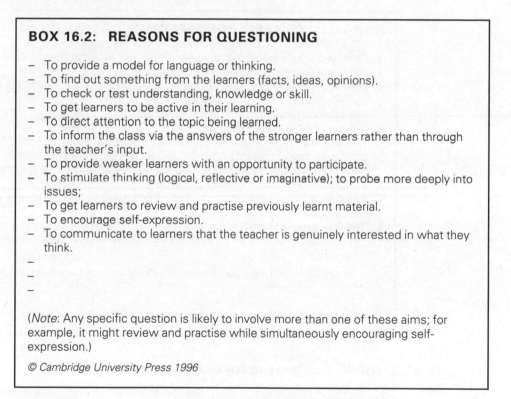

BOX 16.2: REASONS FOR QUESTIONING

- To provide a model for language or thinking.
- To find out something from the learners (facts, ideas, opinions).
- To check or test understanding, knowledge or skill.
- To get learners to be active in their learning.
- To direct attention to the topic being learned.
- To inform the class via the answers of the stronger learners rather than through the teacher's input.
- To provide weaker learners with an opportunity to participate.
- To stimulate thinking (logical, reflective or imaginative); to probe more deeply into issues;
- To get learners to review and practise previously learnt material.
- To encourage self-expression.
- To communicate to learners that the teacher is genuinely interested in what they think.
-
-
-

(*Note*: Any specific question is likely to involve more than one of these aims; for example, it might review and practise while simultaneously encouraging self-expression.)

© Cambridge University Press 1996

Effective questioning

There have been numerous attempts to identify characteristics of effective questioning techniques in the classroom. Questions have been classified according to various different criteria: what kind of thinking they try to elicit (plain recall, for example, analysis, or evaluation); whether they are 'genuine' or 'display' questions (does the teacher really want to know the answer, or is he or she simply checking if the student does?); whether they are closed- or open-ended (do they have a single right answer or many?); and many others. For some more detailed suggested methods of analysis, see references given under *Further reading* ('Questioning') below.

However, in the present context, I propose concentrating on a few basic principles that would seem to characterize effective questions within the conventional IRF structure, defining 'effective questions' in terms of the desired response. As language teachers, our motive in questioning is usually to get our students to engage with the language material actively through speech; so an effective questioning technique is one that elicits fairly prompt, motivated, relevant and full responses. If, on the other hand, our questions result in long silences, or are answered by only the strongest students, or obviously bore the class, or consistently elicit only very brief or unsuccessful answers, then there is probably something wrong.

Some useful criteria for effective questioning for language teachers are suggested in Box 16.3.

BOX 16.3: CRITERIA FOR EFFECTIVE QUESTIONING

1. **Clarity:** do the learners immediately grasp not only what the question means, but also what kind of an answer is required?
2. **Learning value:** does the question stimulate thinking and responses that will contribute to further learning of the target material? Or is it irrelevant, unhelpful or merely time-filling?
3. **Interest:** do learners find the question interesting, challenging, stimulating?
4. **Availability:** can most of the members of the class try to answer it? Or only the more advanced, confident, knowledgeable? (Note that the mere addition of a few seconds' wait-time before accepting a response can make the question available to a significantly larger number of learners.)
5. **Extension:** does the question invite and encourage extended and/or varied answers?[1]
6. **Teacher reaction:** are the learners sure that their responses will be related to with respect, that they will not be put down or ridiculed if they say something inappropriate?

1 Occasionally – for example, where the emphasis is on listening comprehension rather than speaking – brief single answers may be more appropriate; in such cases this criterion would not apply.

© Cambridge University Press 1996

Task   **Critical analysis of teacher questions**

Look at the exchanges in Box 16.4, which are loosely based on events actually observed in classrooms. Can you identify what the purpose of the teacher is in questioning, and comment on the way he or she went about it, perhaps applying the criteria suggested above? See the *Comments* section below for my own criticisms.

BOX 16.4: TEACHER QUESTIONING

Exchange 1

   T: Now today we are going to discuss circuses. Have you ever been to a circus?
   Ss: (immediately) Yes, yes.
   T: Yes. Where you see clowns, and horses and elephants and acrobats…

Exchange 2

   T: Yesterday we learned various words that express feelings. Can you tell me…What does 'relief' mean?
      (pause)
      Well, when might you feel relief?
      (pause)
      Can you remember a time when you felt relief? Yes, Maria?
   S1: When my friend was late, I thought he wasn't coming and then he came.
   T: Good…Fran?
   S2: I thought I will fail the exam, and then in the end I pass.
   T: Good. Now: 'fear'?

Exchange 3

   T: Right: what was the story about? Can anyone tell me? Claire?
   S: Man.
   T: Yes, a man. What did this man do? Can you tell me anything about him?
   S: He…married.

Exchange 4

   T: Here's a picture, with lots of things going on. Tell me some of them. For example: the policeman is talking to the driver, perhaps he's telling him where to go. What else?
   S1: The little girl is buying an ice-cream.
   S2: There's a woman, old woman, in the middle, she's crossing the road.
   S3: A man…sitting…on chair…
   T: OK, a man is sitting on a chair, there in the corner…What else?

© Cambridge University Press 1996

Comments

Exchange 1

There is a problem of 'double messages' here, since the declared objective is contradicted by the questioning technique used. The teacher says explicitly that the intention is to 'discuss'; but the introductory question, though clear, actually discourages discussion: it is a 'yes/no' question inviting a single, brief answer, lacking 'extension', and not forwarding the declared teaching objective. However, it is both interesting and 'available': the fact that the students answer promptly and apparently enthusiastically indicates that they probably have something to say – though they are given no opportunity to do so.

Either the teacher did not really intend to 'discuss' at all and prefers to hold the stage herself, or she is not aware of the inappropriate form of her questions; perhaps a combination of the two.

Exchange 2

The purpose of the exchange is, presumably, to review vocabulary learned the day before. The obvious question: 'What does X mean?' though apparently clear, is unsuccessful in eliciting answers, probably because it is too abstract and difficult; even a competent native speaker of the language might have trouble answering. It is, thus, not very 'available', and certainly does not elicit extended answers. This teacher, however, quickly realizes her mistake and rephrases, twice. The question that demands a concrete example from experience is much better on all counts, and predictably receives immediate and fairly full responses. But then, what is going to happen with the next item?

Exchange 3
There is no indication of pauses after the questions, and the answers are basically correct in content; the questions seem fairly clear, interesting and available to most of the class, but their value in providing for learning is lowered because of the difficulty of the learners in expressing their answers in the foreign language. The teacher might have been able to help by giving some 'scaffolding', or modelling answers, in her questions: 'Was it about a man, a woman, an animal…? It was…Yes, Claire?'

Exchange 4
Here the teacher makes it very clear what kinds of responses she is requesting by providing examples. She also implies that she expects a number of answers ('extension'). The combination of these two strategies makes the question far more 'available': the sheer number of student responses to the single cue looks like being relatively large, and the weak student (S3) ventures a response based on the examples (of the teacher and of previous speakers) which he or she would not have done if only one response, without illustration, had been requested. The sheer number of responses contributes significantly to the effectiveness of the desired practice of the target language as a whole (see Module 2: *Practice activities* for a discussion of the characteristics of good practice activities).

▶ Unit Three: Group work

In group work, learners perform a learning task through small-group interaction. It is a form of learner activation that is of particular value in the practice of oral fluency: learners in a class that is divided into five groups get five times as many opportunities to talk as in full-class organization. It also has other advantages: it fosters learner responsibility and independence, can improve motivation and contribute to a feeling of cooperation and warmth in the class. There is some research that indicates that the use of group work improves learning outcomes (see *Further reading*).

These potential advantages are not, however, always realized. Teachers fear they may lose control, that there may be too much noise, that their students may over-use their mother tongue, do the task badly or not at all: and their fears are often well founded. Some people – both learners and teachers – dislike a situation where the teacher cannot constantly monitor learner language.

The success of group work depends to some extent on the surrounding social climate, and on how habituated the class is to using it; and also, of course, on the selection of an interesting and stimulating task whose performance is well within the ability of the group. But it also depends, more immediately, on effective and careful organization. Some guidelines on organizing group work are given in Box 16.5, divided into four sections: presentation, process, ending, feedback. You might like to use the task as a way of studying them.

Note also that a class may not readily take to group work if it is used to being constantly teacher-directed. But this is something that can be learned through practice; do not give up if your first attempts at group work with a class are unsatisfactory.

Task **Evaluating guidelines**

The guidelines given in Box 16.5 are ones that I recommend, but may be of varying usefulness to you. As you read, tick ideas that seem in the light of your experience to be particularly important, delete any that you think trivial or unnecessary, and make notes in the margins of any queries, criticisms or other reactions that occur to you as you read.

Compare your notes with those of colleagues, and discuss the relevance of the guidelines to your own teaching situation.

▶ Unit Four: Individualization

The concept of individualization in language learning

The concept of 'individualization' in education is sometimes identified with the provision of a self-access centre, or even a full self-access learning programme. Materials of various kinds are made available, and the learners choose which to work on: the organization of these choices may be in the hands of either teacher or learner, and learners may be working on their own or in groups or pairs.

I would, however, define the term more modestly, as a situation where learners are given a measure of freedom to choose how and what they learn at any particular time (implying less direct teacher supervision and more learner autonomy and responsibility for learning), and there is some attempt to adapt or select tasks and materials to suit the individual. The opposite is 'lockstep' learning, where everyone in the class, in principle, is expected to do the same thing at the same time in the same way.

Individualized learning thus defined does not necessarily imply a programme based entirely on self-instruction, nor the existence of self-access centres (which are expensive to equip and maintain and therefore not available to most foreign-language learners). It does imply a serious attempt to provide for differing learner needs within a class and to place a higher proportion of responsibility for learning on the shoulders of the learners themselves. For most of us, it is perhaps more useful to devote thought to how we can achieve at least some degree of this kind of individualization within a conventional classroom than it is to give up on the attempt because we do not have the time or resources to organize full self-access facilities. This unit therefore looks at

---

BOX 16.5: GROUP-WORK ORGANIZATION

1. Presentation

The instructions that are given at the beginning are crucial: if the students do not understand exactly what they have to do there will be time-wasting, confusion, lack of effective practice, possible loss of control. Select tasks that are simple enough to describe easily; and in monolingual classes you may find it cost-effective to explain some or all in the students' mother tongue. It is advisable to give the instructions **before** giving out materials or dividing the class into groups; and a preliminary rehearsal or 'dry run' of a sample of the activity with the full class can help to clarify things. Note, however, that if your students have already done similar activities you will be able to shorten the process, giving only brief guidelines; it is mainly the first time of doing something with a class that such care needs to be invested in instructing.

Try to foresee what language will be needed, and have a preliminary quick review of appropriate grammar or vocabulary. Finally, before giving the sign to start tell the class what the arrangements are for stopping: if there is a time limit, or a set signal for stopping, say what it is; if the groups simply stop when they have finished, then tell them what they will have to do next. It is wise to have a 'reserve' task planned to occupy members of groups who finish earlier than expected.

(See Unit Three of Module 1 (pages 16–18) for a more detailed discussion of the giving of instructions in general.)

2. Process

Your job during the activity is to go from group to group, monitor, and either contribute or keep out of the way – whichever is likely to be more helpful. If you do decide to intervene, your contribution may take the form of:

– providing general approval and support;
– helping students who are having difficulty;
– keeping the students using the target language (in many cases your mere presence will ensure this!);
– tactfully regulating participation in a discussion where you find some students are over-dominant and others silent.

3. Ending

If you have set a time limit, then this will help you draw the activity to a close at a certain point. In principle, try to finish the activity while the students are still enjoying it and interested, or only just beginning to flag.

4. Feedback

A feedback session usually takes place in the context of full-class interaction after the end of the group work. Feedback on the task may take many forms: giving the right solution, if there is one; listening to and evaluating suggestions; pooling ideas on the board; displaying materials the groups have produced; and so on. Your main objective here is to express appreciation of the effort that has been invested and its results. Feedback on language may be integrated into this discussion of the task, or provide the focus of a separate class session later.

© Cambridge University Press 1996

---

individualization in the context of the teacher-fronted lesson.

If you are interested in studying more thoroughly individualized programmes, have a look at Dickinson (1987) and Sheerin (1989).

Procedures that allow for individual choice

In Box 16.6 there is a list of classroom procedures, listed in random order, that allow for differing degrees of individual learner choice. This choice may be in:

1. **Speed:** how fast or slowly each individual may work (everyone being engaged in the same basic task);
2. **Level:** tasks that are basically aimed at the same teaching point may be presented in easier or more difficult versions, so that the learner can choose the one that suits his or her level;
3. **Topic:** the learner may be able to select tasks that – while all are based on the same language skill or teaching point – vary in the subject or topic of the text as well as in level;
4. **Language skill or teaching point:** each learner may choose to work on a quite different aspect of language: listening, for example, or grammar, or reading literature.

Another way learning procedures can vary is in the amount of work demanded of the teacher in preparation.

The task below asks you to think about the degree of individualization provided by different practical classroom procedures, and the relationship between these and the degree of teacher work that needs to be invested. If you do not wish to do the task, read through it quickly and then go on to the Conclusions at the end of the unit.

Task **Assessing individualized procedures**

Stage 1: Categorization

Insert the names of the different procedures described in Box 16.6 into the appropriate squares in the grid shown in Box 16.7. It is possible to have procedures 'overflowing' across the lines, if you feel they do not fit neatly into a category.

Stage 2: Conclusions

When you have finished, look at your grid to see if any kind of systematic pattern emerges, and any conclusions can be drawn.

A suggested way of completing the grid is shown in the Notes, (2).

Some conclusions

If your filled-in grid looks similar to mine as shown in the Notes, (2), there are two conclusions we might draw from it.

1. The techniques higher up on our grid (that are more individualized) tend on average to be also more to the right (involve more teacher preparation): the conclusion would be that on the whole more choice for the learner means more work for the teacher.
2. Nevertheless, note that there is at least one item quite high up on the grid that is also on the left. It is possible, in spite of the generalization just made, to individualize to quite a high degree without a prohibitive amount of work. The crucial issue is perhaps careful planning rather than sheer work hours.

BOX 16.6:   CLASSROOM PROCEDURES

1. **Readers.** Students choose individual simplified readers, of varied level and topic, from a school library, and read quietly in class.
2. **Response to listening.** The teacher plays a recorded text on a topical issue, and asks the class to note down points they understood.
3. **Workcards.** A pile of workcards prepared by the teacher is put in the centre of the class, all practising the material the class has recently learned, but each different. Each student chooses one, completes it and then takes another.
4. **Textbook questions in class.** The class has been given a set of questions from the textbook to answer in writing; each student does them on his or her own.
5. **Worksheets.** The teacher distributes worksheets which all practise the same grammar point, but containing various sections with different kinds of practice tasks and topics. The students choose which sections they want to do, and do as much as they can in the time allotted.
6. **Textbook exercises for homework.** The teacher gives three sets of comprehension questions from the textbook, of varying difficulty, on a passage that has been read in class; each student is asked to select and do one set.
7. **Varied tasks.** The teacher has prepared a number of workcards based on different language skills and content. There is a cassette recorder in one corner with headsets for listening tasks, and another corner available for quiet talk. Students select, work on and exchange cards freely.

© *Cambridge University Press 1996*

BOX 16.7:   CATEGORIZING INDIVIDUALIZED PROCEDURES

Learner choice in:			
speed level topic language point			
speed level topic			
speed level			
speed			
	Little or no teacher preparation	*Some teacher preparation*	*A heavy load of teacher preparation*

© *Cambridge University Press 1996*

▷ # Unit Five: The selection of appropriate activation techniques

The 'Initiation–Response–Feedback' ('IRF') pattern described at the beginning of this module tends to be used most of the time in most classrooms, even if it is not in fact the most effective way of achieving the teaching objective at the time. This unit aims to raise awareness of the suitability of different patterns for different teaching objectives, and suggests some general considerations.

Task ## Matching

In Box 16.8 are some descriptions of materials and objectives in using them, expressed as teacher statements. Imagine you have been asked to advise the teachers what kind of classroom interaction would be most effective in producing learning in each context. To each description below (a–g) match one or more of the interaction patterns listed in Box 16.1 and note down, or discuss, your choice.

Some factors that might in general influence such choices are discussed in the *Comment* section below; specific possible 'matches' are suggested in the Notes, (3).

Comment

1. 'IRF' is a convenient and easily administered activation technique that quickly provides the teacher with some indication of what some of the class knows. Its results do not, however, provide a very representative sample of what most of the class know or do not know, since only a minority have a chance to express themselves, and these are usually the more advanced and confident. Individual work provides far more accurate and comprehensive feedback.
2. If the class is in the early stages of learning something, then the 'IRF' pattern is useful, since it allows the teacher to monitor immediately, and learners may also learn from each other's responses. Later, however, when they know the material better and simply need to consolidate it through rehearsal they are probably better served by individual, group or pair work which allows active participation of more students simultaneously.
3. Teacher speech or reading aloud is useful for presenting new language or texts; also for recycling material which the class has previously encountered through their own reading. The extra exposure contributes to the consolidation of learning, particularly if the teacher speaks expressively or dramatically.
4. Collaboration is invaluable when learners are producing considered, careful written language, and want to avoid mistakes or have them corrected as quickly as possible, but when you yourself cannot possibly monitor all of them at the same time. In collaboration, learners contribute to each other's writing and are made more aware of their own; they can in fact do a substantial proportion of the monitoring on their own.

BOX 16.8: TEACHER OBJECTIVES AND LEARNER ACTIVATION

a) Comprehension check
'We've just finished reading a story. I want to make sure the class has understood it, using the comprehension questions in the book.'

b) Familiarization with text
'We've just finished reading a story. I'm fairly sure they've understood the basic plot, but I want them to get really familiar with the text through reading, as they're going to have to pass an exam on it.'

c) Oral fluency
'I have a small [fifteen] class of business people, who need more practice in talking. I want them to do a discussion task where they have to decide which qualities are most important for a manager.'

d) Grammar check
'We've been working on the distinction between two similar verb tenses. I want to find out how far they've grasped it, using an exercise in the book where they have to allot the right tense to the right context.'

e) Writing
'They need to improve their writing. I want to ask them to write for a few minutes in class, but am worried they might just make a lot of mistakes and not learn anything.'

f) Grammar practice
'They need to practise forming and asking questions. I thought of using an interview situation; they might interview me or each other.'

g) New vocabulary
'I want to introduce some new vocabulary in preparation for a text we're going to read.'

© Cambridge University Press 1996

Notes

(1) Interaction patterns

I have listed the items below in order, from the most teacher-dominated (1) to the most student-active (9).

1. Teacher talk (TT)
2. Choral responses (T)
3. Closed-ended teacher questioning ('IRF') (T)
4. Open-ended teacher questioning (TS)
5. Student initiates, teacher answers (TS)
6. Full-class interaction (S)
7. Individual work (S)
8. Collaboration (S)
9. Group work (S)
10. Self-access (SS)

(2) Categorizing individualized procedures

Learner choice in:			
speed level topic language point			*varied tasks*
speed level topic	*readers*		*workcards worksheets*
speed level	*textbook exercises for homework*	*response to listening*	
speed	*textbook questions in class*		
	Little or no teacher preparation	*Some teacher preparation*	*A heavy load of teacher preparation*

(3) Suggested solutions to the task in Unit Five

a) Closed or open-ended teacher questioning is the usual solution; probably more effective is individual work. In full-class questioning only a minority of the class answers, and these will tend to be those who understand. Feedback on learner understanding will therefore be incomplete and inadequate. More detailed and reliable information can be obtained if learners are asked to do the questions individually in writing, while you move around the class to help and monitor. Notebooks can also be taken in for later inspection.

b) Teacher reading aloud (a form of teacher talk); or combined group and individual work. If the learners have read the text previously on their own, your reading it aloud might be an effective way of 'recycling'. Another possibility is to ask different learners to study different sections of the story in depth, and then get together to teach each other what they have studied.

c) Group work. A class of fifteen may seem small; but even so, dividing it into three groups of five for a task like this gives each participant, on average, three times as much practice in talking.

d) Individual work. The teacher's clear objective is to test, though he or she does not actually use the word (see Unit One of Module 3: *Tests* for a definition of a test). Therefore the objection to 'IRF' is the same as in (a) above; and the solution also similar.

e) Individual work and/or collaboration. This is a case where peer teaching can contribute. Learners can be asked either to write alone and then help each other improve, correct and polish their texts; or write collaboratively in the first place, pooling their efforts to produce the best joint result they can.

Teacher monitoring can take place during the writing – as far as time and class numbers permit – or after.

f) Open-ended teacher questioning, individual work and/or collaboration; followed by full-class interaction or group work. In order to make the interview produce as much practice in questions as possible, it is a good idea to let the learners prepare at least some of these in advance; individually, or in pairs, or through a full-class brainstorm of ideas. The interview may then be targeted at the teacher in the full class; or at (volunteer) students in full class or small groups.

g) Teacher talk, and/or teacher questioning; possibly choral responses. In general, the most efficient way to introduce new vocabulary is just to present and explain it frankly. If, however, you think that some of your class know some of the items, ask them, and give them the opportunity to teach (or review) them for you. If they do not know them, then such questioning is to be avoided: it is likely to result in silence or wrong answers and a general feeling of frustration and failure. After the new items have been introduced, repeating them in chorus can help learners to perceive and remember them.

Further reading

CLASSROOM INTERACTION IN GENERAL

Bloom, B. S. (1956) *Taxonomy of Educational Objectives*, Vol. I, New York: McKay.
(A classic hierarchical taxonomy of cognitive objectives, and by implication of types of questions and learning tasks)
Flanders, N. A. (1970) *Analyzing Teaching Behavior*, Reading, Mass.: Addison-Wesley.
(One well-known system of analysis of teacher–student interaction, which may be applied in observation)
Malamah-Thomas, A. (1987) *Classroom Interaction*, Oxford: Oxford University Press.
(Mainly a series of tasks defining and critically exploring various aspects of classroom interaction)
Sinclair, J. and Coulthard, R. M. (1975) *Towards an Analysis of Discourse*, Oxford: Oxford University Press.
(An analysis of classroom discourse into a hierarchy of categories of oral participation)

QUESTIONING

Brock, C. A. (1986) 'The effects of referential questions on ESL classroom discourse', *TESOL Quarterly*, **20**, 1, 47–59.
(An interesting piece of research on the effectiveness of 'genuine' questions in eliciting fuller answers)
Brown, G. A. and Edmondson, R. (1984) 'Asking questions', in Wragg, E. C. (ed.), *Classroom Teaching Skills*, London and Sydney: Croom Helm, pp. 97–120.

(Based on various pieces of research, a brief, useful summary of purposes and
types of classroom questions)

Long, M. H. and Sato, C. J. (1983) 'Classroom foreigner talk discourse: forms
and functions of teachers' questions', in Seliger, H. W. and Long, M. H.
(eds.), *Classroom Oriented Research in Second Language Acquisition*,
Rowley, Mass.: Newbury House.

(On the use of various kinds of questions in the foreign-language classroom)

GROUP WORK

Bejarano, Y. (1987) 'A cooperative small-group methodology in the language
classroom', *TESOL Quarterly* **21**, 3, 483–501.

Long, M. H. and Porter, P. A. (1985) 'Group work, interlanguage talk and
second language acquisition', *TESOL Quarterly*, **19**, 2, 207–28.

(Two articles on research on the effectiveness of group work in language
teaching)

INDIVIDUALIZATION

Dickinson, L. (1987) *Self-Instruction in Language Learning*, Cambridge:
Cambridge University Press.

(Discusses the rationale and organization of entire self-instructional
programmes: with examples of actual programmes and ideas how to design
or adapt materials)

Geddes, M. and Sturtridge, G. (eds.) (1982) *Individualization*, Oxford: Modern
English Publications.

(A collection of articles on various aspects of individualized learning, with a
very practical orientation)

McCall, J. (1992) *Self-access: Setting up a Centre*, Manchester: The British
Council.

(A slim booklet with very practical advice as to how to go about setting up
different kinds of self-access centres)

Sheerin, S. (1989) *Self-access*, Oxford: Oxford University Press.

(Guidance and plenty of ideas for self-access tasks at various levels)

Sturtridge, G. (1992) *Self-access: Preparation and Training*, Manchester: The
British Council.

(Another booklet in the same series as McCall's above, with some useful ideas
about how to prepare both teachers and learners for self-access work)

Module 17: Giving feedback

▶ Unit One: Different approaches to the nature and function of feedback

Preliminary definition: What is feedback?

In the context of teaching in general, feedback is information that is given to the learner about his or her performance of a learning task, usually with the objective of improving this performance. Some examples in language teaching: the words 'Yes, right!', said to a learner who has answered a question; a grade of 70% on an exam; a raised eyebrow in response to a mistake in grammar; comments written in the margin of an essay.

Feedback has two main distinguishable components: assessment and correction. In assessment, the learner is simply informed how well or badly he or she has performed. A percentage grade on an exam would be one example; or the response 'No' to an attempted answer to a question in class; or a comment such as 'Fair' at the end of a written assignment. In correction, some specific information is provided on aspects of the learner's performance: through explanation, or provision of better or other alternatives, or through elicitation of these from the learner. Note that in principle correction can and should include information on what the learner did **right**, as well as wrong, and why! – but teachers and learners generally understand the term as referring to the correction of mistakes, so that is (usually) how it is used here.

Question   Are the two components of assessment and correction completely separable? In other words, can you have assessment without correction, or correction without assessment?
Read on for a possible answer to this.

The relationship between assessment and correction

It is, of course, perfectly possible to give assessment without correcting, as when a final percentage mark on an exam is made known to a learner without the exam itself being returned or commented on. The other way round is very much less feasible: it is virtually impossible to comment on what is right or wrong in what a learner has done without conveying some kind of assessment. If a correction is supplied, the learner is very aware that this means the teacher thinks something was wrong; if comment is given on why something was appropriate, there is necessarily an underlying message of commendation.

Teachers are sometimes urged to be 'non-judgemental' when giving feedback; in my opinion this is unrealistic. Any meaningful feedback is going to involve some kind of judgement. It is more useful, perhaps, to accept that there is judgement involved, but to try to make the attitude to this more positive: that mistakes are a natural and useful part of language learning; that when the teacher gives feedback on them, the purpose is to help and promote learning; and that 'getting it wrong' is not 'bad', but rather a way into 'getting it right'.

Approaches to the giving of feedback

In Boxes 17.1 and 17.2 you will find expressions of selected opinions on the nature and functions of assessment and mistake correction; these are based on different theories of language learning or methodologies. It is not essential for you to be familiar with the names or details of the theories for the purposes of this bit of study; but if you are interested in reading further on any of them, see McLaughlin (1987) and/or Richards and Rodgers (1986); or references provided with specific items.

The opinions as stated here are obviously simplified, and expressed in 'strong' forms, as these are likely to provide more interesting and fruitful departure-points for discussion.

BOX 17.1:   THE PROVISION OF ASSESSMENT: DIFFERENT OPINIONS

Audio-lingualism
Negative assessment is to be avoided as far as possible since it functions as 'punishment' and may inhibit or discourage learning. Positive assessment provides reinforcement of correct responses, and promotes learning.

Humanistic methodologies
A crucial function of the giving of assessment is to preserve and promote a positive self-image of the learner as a person and language learner. Assessment therefore should be positive or non-judgemental.

Skill theory
For successful acquisition of a skill, the learner needs feedback on how well he or she is doing; hence the importance of the provision of constant and honest assessment (Johnson, 1995).

© *Cambridge University Press 1996*

Task   *Stage 1: Study*

As you read, think about or discuss how far you agree with the various statements.

Stage 2: Discussion

After reading: can you summarize your own opinion on the functions of assessment and correction? Write down your own statements in a format similar to that shown in Boxes 17.1/2; if you are working in a group, compare your ideas with those of colleagues.

If you are interested in comparing your own opinion with mine, look at the Notes, (1).

BOX 17.2:   THE CORRECTION OF MISTAKES: DIFFERENT OPINIONS

Audio-lingualism
Learner mistakes are, in principle, avoided by the limiting of progress to very small, controlled steps: hence there should be little need for correction. The latter is, in any case, not useful for learning; people learn by getting things right in the first place and having their performance reinforced.

Cognitive code-learning
Mistakes are regrettable, but an unavoidable part of learning: they should be corrected whenever they occur to prevent them occurring again.

Interlanguage

Mistakes are not regrettable, but an integral and important part of language learning; correcting them is a way of bringing the learner's 'interlanguage' closer to the target language (Selinker, 1972, 1992).

Communicative approach
Not all mistakes need to be corrected: the main aim of language learning is to receive and convey meaningful messages, and correction should be focussed on mistakes that interfere with this aim, not on inaccuracies of usage.

Monitor theory
Correction does not contribute to real acquisition of the language, but only to the learner's conscious 'monitoring' of speech or writing. Hence the main activity of the teacher should be to provide comprehensible input from which the learner can acquire language, not to correct (Krashen, 1982).

© Cambridge University Press 1996

▷ # Unit Two: Assessment

Note: In literature on education, a distinction is sometimes made between assessment (of learner performance), evaluation (of innovation or change in, for example, school organization or a course syllabus) and appraisal (of teacher performance). This unit is concerned only with feedback on learning, and the terms 'evaluation' and 'assessment' are used interchangeably.

Most of the feedback we give our learners is ongoing correction and assessment, directed at specific bits of learner-produced language with the aim of bringing about improvement; the type of evaluation involved here is sometimes called 'formative', since its main purpose is to 'form': to enhance, not conclude, a process. Distinct from this is the evaluation usually termed 'summative', where the teacher evaluates an overall aspect of the learner's knowledge in order to summarize the situation: how proficient he or she is at a certain point in time, for example, or how much he or she has progressed during a particular course.

Summative evaluation may contribute little or nothing to the ongoing teaching/learning process; but it is a part of the teacher's job, something we need to know how to do effectively.

Below are descriptions of various ways of gathering the information which will serve as a basis for assessment, and of some common criteria used for assessing it.

Gathering information (1): Tests

The most common way of gathering information for assessment is through tests (see Module 3); the usual criterion is an arbitrary level which the learner is expected to have reached; and the result is generally expressed through percentages.

Question **Can you remember taking an exam or test at the end of a programme of study, or in order to be accepted into a course or profession? What was the criterion for success, and how was your result expressed?**

Gathering information (2): Other sources

There, are, however, various problems with tests as a basis for summative evaluation: they are a one-off event which may not necessarily give a fair sample of the learner's overall proficiency; they are not always valid (actually testing what they say they are) or reliable (giving consistent results); and if they are seen as the sole basis for a crucial evaluation in the learner's career, they can be extremely stressful.

Other options do, however, exist. These are summarized below; or see Brindley (1989) for a more detailed discussion.

1. **Teacher's assessment.** The teacher gives a subjective estimate of the learner's overall performance.
2. **Continuous assessment.** The final grade is some kind of combination of the grades the learner received for various assignments during the course.
3. **Self-assessment.** The learners themselves evaluate their own performance, using clear criteria and weighting systems agreed on beforehand.
4. **Portfolio.** The learner gathers a collection of assignments and projects done over a long period into a file; and this portfolio provides the basis for evaluation.

Question **Have you yourself any experience of any of the above, as teacher or learner? How valid or useful were/are they, in your experience?**

Criteria

Having collected the 'evidence' of the learners' proficiency in one or more of the ways described above, what will be our yardstick in deciding how good it is? The following are some of the possibilities.

1. **Criterion-referenced:** how well the learner is performing relative to a fixed criterion, where this is based on an estimation of what it is reasonable or

245

desirable to demand from learners at the relevant point in their development (age, career, level, stage of a course).

2. **Norm-referenced:** how well the learner is performing relative to the group. In this case, a group of slow learners would be assessed according to different, easier, norms than a group of faster ones.

3. **Individual-referenced:** how well the learner is performing relative to his or her own previous performance, or relative to an estimate of his or her individual ability.

Question   **What criteria do/would you yourself use in assessing learners' performance? Would you combine different criteria? Would you take into account learners' effort, motivation and progress in deciding on a final grade?**

Assessment grades

Percentages are probably the most common way of expressing assessment grades, but there are others.

1. **Letters, words or phrases:** 'A' or 'B'; 'Good', 'Excellent'. These look a little less impersonal, less definitive than percentages; but in fact learners often 'read' them as definitive number-type grades, exactly as they read percentages.

2. **Profiles:** a totally different kind of expression of assessment, comprising a number of separate grades on different skills or sections of knowledge, so that there is a possibility of describing the performance of an individual learner in more detail, showing his or her various strengths and weaknesses.

Summary   **What is the most common way of gathering information, assessing**
question   **proficiency and awarding grades in your own teaching context? What changes or improvements would you like to see introduced?**

▶ Unit Three: Correcting mistakes in oral work

Preliminary note. On the whole, we give feedback on oral work through speech, on written work through writing; and although there are occasional situations where we might do it the other way round (for example, discuss an essay with a student in a one-to-one tutorial, or write a letter providing feedback on speech) these are very much the exceptions and will not be dealt with in this unit and the next.

There are some situations where we might prefer not to correct a learner's mistake: in fluency work, for example, when the learner is in mid-speech, and to correct would disturb and discourage more than help. But there are other situations when correction is likely to be helpful.

Question   Would you support the recommendation to refrain from correcting during fluency-oriented speech, and to do so only during accuracy-oriented exercises? Can you add any further comment?

Read on for my answer to this.

The recommendation not to correct a learner during fluent speech is in principle a valid one, but perhaps an over-simplification. There can be places where to refrain from providing an acceptable form where the speaker is obviously uneasy or 'floundering' can actually be demoralizing, and gentle, supportive intervention can help. Conversely, even where the emphasis is on getting the language right, we may not always correct: in a grammar exercise, for example, if the learner has contributed an interesting or personal piece of information that does not happen to use the target form; also, when they have got most of an item right we may prefer not to draw attention to a relatively trivial mistake.

Techniques of oral correction

Oral corrections are usually provided directly by the teacher; but they may also be elicited from the learner who made the mistake in the first place, or by another member of the class. Corrections may or may not include a clarification of why the mistake was made, and may or may not require re-production of the acceptable form by the learner.

The objective of the inquiry project suggested below is to ascertain which of these techniques are in fact most used in a selection of lessons taught locally, and which are preferred by learners. Some practical conclusions may be drawn from the results.

Inquiry   **Correction techniques in the classroom**

Stage 1: Preparation

Look at the set of oral correction techniques listed in Box 17.2. Reword, or add further items as you feel necessary. Think about and note down for yourself: which do you expect to be used most frequently in the classroom, and which do you imagine most learners actually prefer?

Make copies of the list for use at Stages 2 and 3.

Stage 2: Observation

Observe some lessons, taught, if possible, by different teachers; or watch video recordings of lessons. Every time you hear a correction, try to identify to which category it belongs and put a mark in the appropriate square. At the end, count your marks, and note down which kinds of correction are most often used and which least.

Stage 3: Interview

Interview some learners to find out which kinds of correction they find most useful. If you are working on your own try to find ten or so respondents; if you are working in a group, then each participant can interview one or two, pooling results later.

The same list of techniques as used for observation can function as a basis for the interviews. Plus or minus signs can be inserted in the appropriate squares to show which your respondents preferred or disliked.

The learners should be interviewed one by one, but the interview may be held in various ways. You may simply show them a copy of the list, and ask them to identify which techniques they prefer; or read out the options and ask them to comment; or ask them a general question like: 'Do you like the teacher to correct your mistakes, and if so, how?' – interpreting their answers yourself in order to fill in answers. The interview may, of course, be conducted in the learners' mother tongue, if you feel this is appropriate.

Summarize the most, and least, popular techniques in the same way as you did at the end of Stage 2.

Stage 4: Summary and conclusions

Discuss or think about what you have found out. Some interesting questions to consider might be the following:

- Did your results differ from your expectations as recorded at Stage 1? If so, how?
- Did the teachers you observed actually correct in the way learners say they prefer? If not, how would you account for the differences?
- As a general conclusion, which would seem to be the most helpful way(s) of correcting? And under what circumstances might you do something different?

Comments

One of the crucial issues which will emerge in this discussion is the discrepancy between what teachers think is best, or usually do, and what learners find most useful. Given that there is a discrepancy, whose opinion should be more respected? The learner has reliable intuitive knowledge about what kind of correction helps most; but teachers – especially experienced ones – have a different kind of knowledge which may be no less valid. My own feeling is that learner preferences are on the whole a reliable guide; and if I choose to disregard these I should be very clear in my mind why I am doing so.

How the correction is expressed

At least as important as what the correction consists of is **how** it is expressed: gently or assertively, supportively or as a condemnation, tactfully or rudely. On the whole, of course, we should go for encouraging, tactful correction; but it is less easy to generalize about gently/assertively: some learner populations respond better to the one, some to the other. In general, in fact, learner responses to different expressions of feedback are often surprising: a teacher correction that seems to an observer a humiliating 'put-down' may not be perceived as such by the learner to whom it was addressed; or an apparently gentle, tactful one may give offence. A good deal of teacher sensitivity is needed here.

BOX 17.2:   ORAL CORRECTION TECHNIQUES

*Class observed ....

*Learner interviewed ....

Teacher's responses to mistakes	*Observation / Learner opinions*
1. Does not react at all.	
2. Indicates there is a mistake, but does not provide any further information about what is wrong.	
3. Says what was wrong and provides a model of the acceptable version.	
4. Indicates something was wrong, elicits acceptable version from the learner who made the mistake.	
5. Indicates something was wrong, elicits acceptable version from another member of the class.	
6. (May go with any of 3–5 above) Asks the learner who made the mistake to reproduce the corrected version.	
7. (May go with any of 3–5 above) Provides or elicits an explanation of why the mistake was made and how to avoid it.	

*Delete or fill in as appropriate.

© *Cambridge University Press 1995*

Task **Observation and inquiry**

Pick out five or six instances of correction in a lesson, and for each note down briefly what happened and then add some adjectives you would use to describe the manner in which it was given (e.g. gentle/loud/hesitant/brisk/supportive?). If you were observing together with a colleague, compare your descriptions after the lesson: did your opinions tally? If not, is there any way of finding out whose perception was truer?

If feasible, find out from the learner(s) how they felt at the time, and compare their impressions with your own.

▶ **Unit Four: Written feedback**

Learners' written work includes not only written compositions, but also assignments on grammar or vocabulary, answers to comprehension questions, tests and so on; and teachers are expected, as part of their job, to respond to such work, providing appropriate (written) feedback.

How can this feedback be made optimally effective?

Question Can you remember how you felt about the ways teachers responded to your own written work when you were learning a foreign language (or even your own)? Try to recall particular instances, and perhaps share with colleagues.

The following task invites you to experiment with correcting written work yourself; if you do not actually do it, you may find it interesting and helpful simply to look at the examples of learner writing in Box 17.3 and then read straight on to the *Comments* below.

Experiential task **Correcting written work**

Stage 1: Reading

Look at the written assignments provided in Box 17.3. The first is a grammar exercise mainly on the present perfect tense, which the students did for homework. The second is a test on vocabulary, which is also intended to check their mastery of the use of relative clauses in definitions. The third is a short piece of writing done in class as an individual summary of a group discussion, and given in to the teacher at the end of the lesson.

Stage 2: Giving feedback

Imagine these are assignments done by your own students, and write in your corrections and other feedback either on the page itself or on a copy. Do this on your own rather than collaboratively.

Stage 3: Reflection

If you are in a group, come together with other participants when you have finished to compare your responses. Perhaps work in pairs, reading each other's corrections and discussing differences.

Whether working on your own or with others, you might find the set of questions shown in Box 17.4 useful to stimulate thinking. My own answers to these appear in the Notes, (2).

BOX 17.3: SAMPLES OF LEARNERS' WRITTEN WORK

1. Grammar exercise on the present perfect tense, given as homework

---

14.1 *You are asking someone about things he has done in his life. Use the words in brackets to make your questions.*
Example: (you ever / be / to Italy?)   <u>Have you ever been to Italy?</u>

1 (you ever / be / to / South America?)   <u>Have you ever been to south America?</u>
2 (you / read / any English books?)   <u>Have you ever read any English books?</u>
3 (you / live / in this town all your life?)   <u>Have you ever ____ in this town all your...</u>
4 (how many times / you / be / in love?)   <u>how many times have you been in love?</u>
5 (what's the most beautiful country you / ever / visit?)   <u>whats the most beautiful country have you ever visited?</u>
6 (you ever / speak / to a famous person?)   <u>have you ever spoken to a famous...?</u>

14.2 *Complete the answers to these questions. Use the verb in brackets.*
Example: Is it a beautiful painting? (see)   <u>Yes, it's the most beautiful painting I've ever seen.</u>

1 Is it a good film? (see)   Yes, it's the best <u>film I'ev ever seen</u>
2 Is it a long book? (read)   Yes, it's the <u>longer book I'ev ever read</u>
3 Is she an interesting person? (meet)   Yes, she's the most <u>interested gril I have ever met.</u>

(From Raymond Murphy, *English Grammar in Use*, Cambridge University Press, 1985, p. 29)

2. Test on vocabulary and relative clauses

Define the following words, using who/which/that/whose/when/where.

For example: a deserted house = a house where nobody lives

1. a temple: <u>a house where religious people lives in.</u>

2. a motionless tree: <u>a tree which not moving at all.</u>

3. an illusion: <u>a false sight.</u>

4. courage: <u>a man who not have any fear.</u>

5. sweat: <u>its like terrrble but more then dhis.</u>

6. a PR man: <u>a man who work on a public relations.</u>

7. a virus: <u>a thing which make people sick.</u>

8. an antibody: <u>a thing which help the man get over the sickness.</u>

9. a host: <u>a man who takes visitors to his haase</u>

10. a paw: <u>a proce of a animal.</u>

3. Writing following a discussion

```
Dear Helpful Harriet,
I have a problem with this teacher at school.
He is always shouting at me, though I don't
disturb more than lots of other pupils in the
class.  It's true that I sometimes don't do
my homework, but I know his subject very
well, always get high marks on the tests, so
there is no point doing silly homework.  He
gave me a much lower mark than I deserve at
the end of the term.  It's not fair.  And
it's no good saying go to the class teacher,
she always backs him up.  What can I do?

                Yours,
                        FRUSTRATED STUDENT
```

My advice to you is to talk with the problematic teacher and trying to expline him what do you fill and think about her and what do you think that you can do toyther to solve your problem toyther please tet me know what happend with your case

Follow-up discussion

Conclusions

Can you draw some conclusions as to what makes feedback on learner writing more or less effective? Try writing down what for you would be the three most important principles in giving written feedback, and share with colleagues.

If you wish to explore this topic further, you might like to look at Module 11: *Teaching writing*, Unit Five; for the topic of feedback on more advanced writing, see Zamel (1985).

BOX 17.4: CONSIDERING WRITTEN FEEDBACK

1. Did you use a red pen for your comments? Or another colour? Or a pen or pencil? Can you account for your choice?
2. For which of the assignments, if any, did you give some kind of assessment at the end ('Good', for example)? Why, or why not?
3. Did you correct all the mistakes? If so, why? If not, on what did you base your decision which to correct and which not?
4. Those mistakes you corrected: did you write in the correct form? Give a hint what it should be? Simply indicate it was wrong? Why?
5. Did you note only what was wrong, or did you give some kind of indication of what was right or particularly good?
6. Did you provide any kind of informative feedback other than mistake correction and overall assessment, designed to help the student improve? (e.g. 'This was good because...', or 'Take care when you...')
7. When responding to the assignment that entailed expression of personal opinion, did you provide a response of your own to the content? ('I agree with this point', 'Yes, but have you considered...?')
8. Did you require the student to redo any of the assignment? Can you say why, or why not?
9. Finally, try rereading your corrections imagining you are the student: what do you think the student will feel about them?

© Cambridge University Press 1996

▷ ## Unit Five: Clarifying personal attitudes

This unit asks you to define your own attitudes to various aspects of the topic of feedback; it focusses particularly on the feelings and relationships which may be affected by the giving and getting of feedback.

Task **Agree or disagree?**

In Box 17.5 there is a list of statements, with an 'Agree–Disagree' continuum below each. You may like to add more statements in the spaces provided.

Put a cross on the continuum for each statement to indicate how far you agree with it. Perhaps look first at the *Comments* section below, which may help (or complicate!) your thinking. My own opinions are expressed in the Notes, (3).

Comments on Box 17.5

1. In relating to this question try to free yourself from the superficial negative connotations often associated with the phrase 'power hierarchy'. Power hierarchies may in some circumstances be necessary, productive and fully compatible with good human relationships.
2. In answering this question, teachers often conveniently overlook the word 'potentially'! Note: the question is not whether assessment humiliates, but if

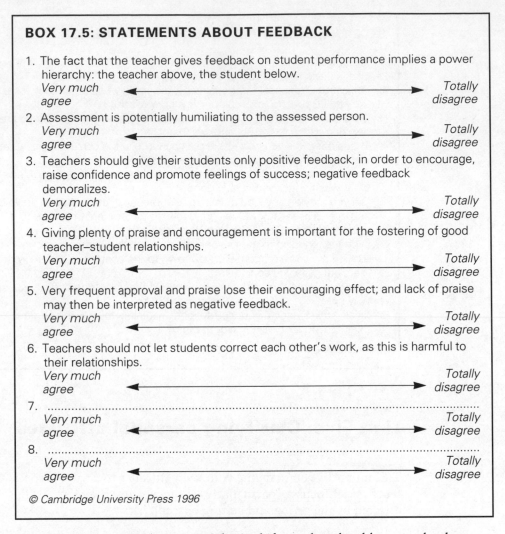

there is or is not such a **potential**. (And if so, what should or may be done about it?)

3. The main controversial feature in this statement is the word 'only' in the first line.

4. In considering this question it might help to ask yourself: can I conceive of (or recall) a good teacher–student relationship where the teacher gives or gave very little positive feedback? Can I conceive of (or recall) one where there is or was plenty of positive feedback but relationships are or were nevertheless bad?

5. Can you recall a situation where the teacher over-praised? Or is the opposite usually the case?

6. Again, your answer to this will very much depend on your own experience.

Notes

(1) The value of assessment and correction for learning

In general, both positive and negative assessments should, in my opinion, be made available to the learner, as honestly as possible: mainly because in my experience this is what learners feel, and say, they want. However, it is essential for such assessments to be given in an atmosphere of support and warm solidarity, so that learners feel that the teacher's motive is honestly to promote and encourage their learning, not to put them down. The problem in negative assessment is often not the assessment itself, but rather the accompanying implications of aggression on the side of the assessor and humiliation on the side of the assessed – which can, and should, be eliminated.

As to correction: I think there is certainly a place for correction. Again, most learners ask for it; and it does contribute to some extent to learning. However, we should not over-estimate this contribution; most experienced teachers are familiar with the phenomenon of recurring corrections of the same mistake which do not seem to lead to improvement. I would rather invest time and energy in creating opportunities for learners to get things right as much as possible than in painstaking work on correcting mistakes. This is one point on which I am in agreement with the presently unfashionable audio-lingual method.

(2) Comments on the questions in Box 17.4

1. I usually use a coloured pen for corrections, simply in order to make them maximally clear and visible to the learner. The exception to this is when providing feedback on advanced writing (essays, papers, other forms of self-expression); here, if the writer has printed or written in ink, I give comments in pencil in order to convey a less authoritative, more diffident message: I'm suggesting, not telling.
2. I provided an assessing comment on the grammar exercise, in order to let the student know how well I thought he or she had mastered the material. Similarly, I gave a grade on the test, partly because this is what people who do tests usually expect and want. For the third assignment, however, I did not: this is a piece of spontaneous composition where the main activity was discussion, the writer had little chance to reread or polish, and I did not think it fair to judge it as a sample of the learner's writing.
3. I corrected virtually all the mistakes in the test. In the grammar exercise I corrected all the mistakes which had to do with the target forms, but ignored most of the others: learners can only use just so much feedback information: to give too much may simply distract, discourage and actually detract from its value for learning. In the third assignment I did not mark in corrections in the body of the student's text, but noted below some points they might attend to for the future: this was because I see this kind of writing not, like the others, as a presentation of language samples for display, but mainly as a form of self-expression, to be respected as such.
4. I wrote in the full correct forms. I do not see much value in demanding that students focus again on the wrong form and try to work out what is wrong

about it – besides, many of them never bother to do so! I would rather confront them with the acceptable forms as quickly and clearly as possible. (However, in the case of a first draft of an essay which a student is to rewrite, I might simply indicate there is a mistake, knowing that they are going to take the trouble to find out how to correct in order to make the final draft as good as possible.)

5. Yes. I put in ticks here and there indicating my appreciation of a difficulty overcome, or a note such as 'well expressed' in the margin. These responses can draw learners' attention to their successes, thus boosting morale and reinforcing learning.

6. Yes. For example, I noted for the student who did the relative clause exercise that she needed to review the irregular third-person forms of the present tense. If we can give information that makes students aware of their particular problems and suggest what they might do about them, this is one of the most valuable kinds of feedback we can provide.

7. Again, yes. I think it is very important to respond to an expression of opinion with one of my own: 'Yes, I feel the same…', 'I'm not sure about this. What would happen if…?'. This kind of comment makes it clear that the message is important, and that I see it as valuable enough to respond to as interlocutor.

8. Asking learners to re-do all their corrected work as a routine can be tedious and discouraging. For these exercises I did not require rewriting, though I did give another very similar grammar exercise to the one shown here a week or two later, having reviewed what I saw as the main problems. One instance where I do consistently request rewriting is for longer compositions or essays. In this case, the first draft does not get graded, only corrected, with constructive suggestions for the second version. The student then knows that, if he or she incorporates all the corrections and suggestions, there is a very good chance of getting a high mark, and the procedure is immediately rewarding as well as learning-valuable.

(3) Statements about feedback

1. Feedback implies a power hierarchy.

Very much agree ←——**✗**————————————————————→ *Totally disagree*

In my opinion a power hierarchy in the classroom, with the teacher in charge and students subordinate, is inevitable: the right of the teacher to correct and assess is one expression of it. Underlying, and to some extent offsetting this apparent dominance, however, is the teacher's role as server and supporter of the learners: the two roles are not only compatible, but, I think, complementary and essential for healthy classroom relationships.

2. Assessment is potentially humiliating.

Very much agree ←————**✗**——————————————————→ *Totally disagree*

If you have recently undergone assessment yourself, you may recall the experience of real, or feared, humiliation. It is important to recognize that the potential exists in order to be able to ensure that it is not realized.

3. Teachers should give only positive feedback.

Very much ←——————————————— ✗ ——→ *Totally*
agree   *disagree*

It is true that positive feedback tends to encourage, but this can be overstated, as here. Negative feedback, if given supportively and warmly, will be recognized as constructive, and will not necessarily discourage.

4. Giving praise fosters good teacher–student relationships.

Very much ←————————— ✗ —————————→ *Totally*
agree   *disagree*

Yes, up to a point. But if there are good relationships, praise often becomes unnecessary; frank, friendly criticism is probably more appropriate and contributes more to the further strengthening of the relationship. And see the next question.

5. Very frequent approval loses its encouraging effect.

Very much ←— ✗ —————————————————→ *Totally*
agree   *disagree*

I have seen this happen: the giving of praise can easily be devalued through overuse. Students come to expect it as a matter of course, cease to be particularly encouraged by it, and are hurt if it is not forthcoming. In fact, overused, uncritical praise can begin to irritate.

6. Correcting each other can be harmful to student relationships.

Very much ←————————————— ✗ ———→ *Totally*
agree   *disagree*

If peer-correction causes conflict or tension between individuals, this probably means that relationships were not particularly warm or trusting in the first place. In other words, I do not think that peer-correction in itself can hurt if students feel good with one another in general; it may, however, do so if there was previous dislike or lack of trust between them.

Further reading

Bartram, M. and Walton, R. (1991) *Correction: Mistake Management – A Positive Approach for Language Teachers*, Hove: Language Teaching Publications.
(A compact, clear, systematic and, as it says, practical guide to the subject; interesting and relevant reader tasks help to clarify)
Brindley, G. (1989) *Assessing Achievement in the Learner-Centred Curriculum*, Macquarie University, Sydney: National Centre for English Language Teaching and Research.
(A comprehensive and readable overview of ways of assessment in language learning)
Edge, J. (1989) *Mistakes and Correction*, London: Longman.
(A simple, practical handbook: suggests various techniques for correcting in different situations)
Harmer, J. (1984) 'How to give your students feedback', *Practical English Teaching*, 5, 2, 39–40.
(Practical guidelines on ways of correcting in the classroom)

Johnson, K. (1988) 'Mistake correction', *ELT Journal*, **42**, 2, 89–96.
(Ways of correcting mistakes effectively within a skill model of language learning)

Leki, I. (1991) 'The preferences of ESL students for error correction in college-level writing classes', *Foreign Language Annals* (New York), **24**, 3, 203–18.
(An interesting piece of research, indicating that learners do, on the whole, want detailed correction of grammar, spelling, etc.)

Norrish, J. (1983) *Language Learners and their Errors*, London: Macmillan.
(A basic, sensible teacher's guide, clearly written, with plenty of practical examples and suggestions)

Raz, H. (1992) 'The crucial role of feedback and evaluation in language classes', *The Teacher Trainer*, **6**, 1, 15–17.
(Stresses the importance for the learner of ongoing supportive feedback rather than test-based evaluation)

Zamel, V. (1985) 'Responding to student writing', *TESOL Quarterly*, **19**, 1, 79–101.
(A thoughtful discussion of dilemmas in giving feedback on (advanced) student writing, and some practical solutions)

REFERENCES IN UNIT ONE

Johnson, K. (1995) *Language Teaching and Skill Learning*, Oxford: Basil Blackwell.

Krashen, S. D. (1982) *Principles and Practice in Second Language Acquisition*, Oxford: Pergamon Press.

McLaughlin, B. (1987) *Theories of Second-Language Learning*, London: Edward Arnold.

Richards, J. C. and Rodgers, T. S. (1986) *Approaches and Methods in Language Teaching*, Cambridge: Cambridge University Press.

Selinker, L. (1972) 'Interlanguage', *IRAL*, **10**, 219–31.

Selinker, L. (1992) *Rediscovering Interlanguage*, London: Longman.

Module 18: Classroom discipline

▶ ## Unit One: What is discipline?

Discussion task

Brainstorm and definition

The phrase 'classroom discipline' has for most teachers an immediate and clear meaning, but it is in fact quite a complex concept, and hard to define in words. One way into such a definition is to start by brainstorming all the ideas that seem to you to be comprised in it: 'control' for example, or 'rules'.

Try brainstorming a list of such words for yourself, or in your group, and then look at the one shown in Box 18.1. Add to the latter whatever items you think I have missed, delete any you think irrelevant; finally put a circle round the ones you think most basic and essential. Using these, you may now find it easier to formulate a satisfactory definition.

You may be interested in comparing your definition with that given in a dictionary, or with my own as suggested in the Notes, (1).

Optional follow-up study

There are, of course, more subtle and interesting distinctions to be discovered within the concept of 'discipline'. Try discussing the distinctions between the following pairs:

1. 'control' v. 'discipline';
2. 'authoritarian' v. 'authoritative';
3. 'power' v. 'authority'.

Simplified versions of the distinctions between the above pairs of concepts appear in the Notes, (2). For more detailed and careful discussion see: Wilson, 1971: 77–80; Widdowson, 1987: 83–8; Peters, 1966: 237–47.

BOX 18.1: THE CONCEPT OF DISCIPLINE

control	contract	(ground) rules
agree	accept	responsibility
rewards	routine	punishments
respect	smooth	behaviour
norms	power	authority
obey	consistent	authoritative
authoritarian	efficient	cooperation

© Cambridge University Press 1996

▶ # Unit Two: What does a disciplined classroom look like?

Task ## Examining assumptions

Stage 1: Assessing

Imagine an ideally disciplined classroom. Then have a look at the set of statements in Box 18.2. Put a double plus (++) by statements which seem to you to describe a characteristic which is always typical of the disciplined classroom, and a single one by those which describe a characteristic which is fairly typical but not inevitable. Where you think the characteristic is entirely irrelevant or not very important, put a double or single minus (–); and a question mark where you feel uncertain. You may, of course, make any other combinations you like, or note reservations in the margin.

Stage 2: Rethinking

Read the *Comments* section below, and share ideas with colleagues. Would you, as a result of reading and discussion, alter any of your responses?

My own opinions are given in the Notes, (3).

BOX 18.2: POSSIBLE CHARACTERISTICS OF THE DISCIPLINED CLASSROOM

1. Learning is taking place.
2. It is quiet.
3. The teacher is in control.
4. Teacher and students are cooperating smoothly.
5. Students are motivated.
6. The lesson is proceeding according to plan.
7. Teacher and students are aiming for the same objective.
8. The teacher has natural charismatic 'authority'.

© Cambridge University Press 1996

Comments

1. The question of the relationship between discipline and learning in a lesson is a crucial one. It seems fairly clear that in a disciplined classroom it is easier to activate students in the way the teachers want, and that time will be probably spent on-task, rather than wasted on organizational problems or disruptive behaviour. However, I have seen well-disciplined classes in which little or no learning was taking place, simply because the activities had themselves little learning value: see, for example the first scenario described in Box 2.2, on page 25, and the following comments. Thus, the existence of a disciplined classroom does not, in itself, necessarily imply that learning is taking place. There is, certainly, a link between the two: but it is not a consistent or inevitable one. (Note, however, that the converse is more likely to be consistently true: that is, that little or no learning will take place in a thoroughly undisciplined atmosphere.)

2. It is easy to claim that this criterion is irrelevant: what about well-disciplined classes where noisy pair or group work is going on?

But there are other relevant questions which might lead you to a different conclusion. For example: pair and group work involving noisy talk take up only a part of lesson time – what about the rest? Or: imagine yourself walking down the corridor of a school and listening at the door of each classroom. Half are noisy, half are quiet. If you had to guess which were the more disciplined ones, what would you say? I would go for the quiet ones (unless I knew that all the teachers used interactive group work at least half the time!).

A further argument: disciplined classes may or may not be quiet; undisciplined ones are usually noisy. There is, therefore, arguably some positive correlation between quietness and the level of discipline.

3. The fact that a teacher is in control of proceedings does not necessarily mean that he or she is standing in front of the class telling everyone what to do. The initiative may have been handed over to the students to do what they decide in a particular activity: nevertheless, it was the teacher who took and implemented the decision that there should be such a handover of initiative, and who may, at any point, take it back. However democratic the setup, the underlying responsibility for the control of any disciplined classroom has to be, surely, in the hands of the teacher: how authoritarian or liberal, rigid or flexible he or she is in the operation of this control is another question.

4. Smooth-running process is the main outward manifestation of discipline in the classroom, as it is in any other organization; and there has to be cooperation of participants in order to produce this. It must be noted however, that cooperation between students, or between students and teacher, is not necessarily either willing or democratic: it may well be a result of coercion or fear. There are all sorts of ways of bringing it about: you will have your own ideas about what methods are ethically, educationally, personally or practically acceptable and which are not.

5. Can you imagine a class of unmotivated students which is disciplined? Or a class of motivated students which is undisciplined? My answer to both of these is yes: which means that the correlation between the two is not absolute. The association is one of probability: if the class is motivated to learn, it is more likely to be easy to manage.

6. Again, we have here a case of probability rather than inevitable cause and effect. A lesson which is going according to plan is more likely to be disciplined: the teacher knows where he or she is going, activities are well prepared and organized; and the awareness that the process is clearly planned tends to boost teacher confidence and student trust, which in their turn also contribute to discipline. On the other hand, changes and improvisations do not necessarily lead to indiscipline, and may even prevent it.

7. Students may be quite unaware of the objective of the lesson, and yet be amenable to the control of the teacher, and the class as a whole disciplined. On the other hand, if they actually have and wish to implement opposing objectives of their own – for example, they want to discuss something in their own language when the teacher wants them to do so in the target language – the result may well be chaos, unless they can be persuaded to forgo their own objectives, and do as they are asked. The latter is what in fact happens in many classrooms, especially with younger or adolescent learners in schools.

A shared knowledge of and agreement on lesson objectives is not, therefore, absolutely necessary for a disciplined classroom, but it probably contributes to it, by raising motivation and the likelihood of cooperation.

8. There is no doubt, in my opinion, that there exists such a quality as charismatic 'authority'; that some teachers possess it while others do not; and that the possessors of this quality find it much easier to control classes. The good news is that the classes of teachers who do not possess natural 'authority' (and I speak as one such myself!) can be equally disciplined: we just have to work at it harder.

▷ # Unit Three: What teacher action is conducive to a disciplined classroom?

Factors that contribute to classroom discipline

The idea that some teachers have a kind of natural 'authority', as suggested at the end of the previous unit, is not very helpful to the rest of us: what may be helpful is a study of the kind of teacher behaviours that are available to anyone and that are likely to produce a state of discipline in the classroom. These are not limited to classroom management skills, such as knowing how to organize the beginning of a lesson, or how to get students to raise their hands instead of shouting out answers. The choice of an appropriate methodology, for example, is likely to ensure that students feel they are learning in a way that is 'right' and useful for them, and they will therefore be more willing to cooperate. The fostering of interpersonal relationships – feelings of respect and goodwill between individuals – is obviously another important factor. Then there is the question of good planning: a carefully and clearly organized lesson makes for purposeful and orderly process. Finally, student motivation is extremely important, and can be enhanced by teacher action: the more interesting and motivating the learning activity, the more likely it is that students will be cooperative and stay on-task.

To recap: some important factors that contribute to classroom discipline and are potentially within the control of, or influenced by, the teacher are:

– classroom management
– methodology
– interpersonal relationships
– lesson planning
– student motivation.

Question   Have a look at the hints for teachers in Box 18.3. Can you pick out at least one example that has to do with each of the above?

Task   **Practical hints**

Stage 1: Prioritizing

Read through the list of practical hints in Box 18.3, and decide which, for you, are the ten most important. You may, of course, add any you feel are missing.

Stage 2: Discussion

If you are working in a group, compare your answers with those of other participants and try to come to a consensus on the 'top ten'. If you are working alone find, if possible, an experienced teacher to compare notes with; and/or look at the following section, which gives some comments. My own selection appears in the Notes, (4).

BOX 18.3: PRACTICAL HINTS FOR TEACHERS ON CLASSROOM DISCIPLINE

1. Start by being firm with students: you can relax later.
2. Get silence before you start speaking to the class.
3. Know and use the students' names.
4. Prepare lessons thoroughly and structure them firmly.
5. Be mobile: walk around the class.
6. Start the lesson with a 'bang' and sustain interest and curiosity.
7. Speak clearly.
8. Make sure your instructions are clear.
9. Have extra material prepared (e.g. to cope with slower/faster-working students).
10. Look at the class when speaking, and learn how to 'scan'.
11. Make work appropriate (to pupils' age, ability, cultural background).
12. Develop an effective questioning technique.
13. Develop the art of timing your lesson to fit the available period.
14. Vary your teaching techniques.
15. Anticipate discipline problems and act quickly.
16. Avoid confrontations.
17. Clarify fixed rules and standards, and be consistent in applying them.
18. Show yourself as supporter and helper to the students.
19. Don't patronize students, treat them with respect.
20. Use humour constructively.
21. Choose topics and tasks that will activate students.
22. Be warm and friendly to the students.

Adapted from Wragg (1981:22)

© *Cambridge University Press 1996*

Comments

The original list on which this version is based was derived from the responses of student teachers when asked which hints from experienced teachers they had found most useful. The order of items 1–20 is the same as that in the original, and represents the respondents' overall order of importance. In other words, the most useful hint, for most people, was 'Start by being firm…', the least useful 'Use humour constructively'.

I added Item 21 (the activation value of tasks) as particularly relevant to language teaching, and worth discussing. I would not, however, include it in my top ten. It is necessary to be fairly rigorous here in your thinking: activation of students (particularly in an activity involving talk and/or physical movement) is certainly important for learning, but it is a double-edged weapon for classroom discipline as such. It may get students involved and thoroughly cooperative on the one hand, but can over-enliven and unsettle them on the other. (However, we might sometimes consider it justifiable to risk a little unsettling for the sake of the learning!)

Item 22 (which also did not appear in the original) is a misleadingly attractive one: teacher warmth and friendliness, while undoubtedly a positive attribute in itself from other points of view, makes no direct contribution to classroom discipline, and may in some circumstances detract from it.

The next step: learner self-discipline

Although the immediate responsibility for the maintenance of classroom discipline in most situations is the teacher's, the ultimate goal is to reach the point where learners take on or at least share this responsibility. The ability to self-discipline is to some extent a function of the maturity of the learner, but can be fostered by the teacher. The way to do this is not simply to try to hand over responsibility to the learners for running the lesson – this teaches little, and can be disastrous – but first to get them used to the 'feel' of orderly classroom process, then gradually to begin to share decision-making based on this.

 Unit Four: Dealing with discipline problems

Like the previous unit, this one deals with practical recommendations, but this time the focus is on the prevention and treatment of discipline problems as they arise in class, rather than, as up to now, on the creation of a disciplined atmosphere in the first place.

Below is some advice in the form of directions on how to deal with deviant student behaviour in class. These are based on my own experience as a teacher who had to learn the hard way how to teach unruly classes of adolescents in a foreign country. I hope you find them useful: try as you read to recall classroom events in your own experience, as learner or teacher, which are relevant to the different topics.

In spite of the prescriptive tone, do not treat these directions as any kind of objective 'truth'! They should be regarded as one possible expression of classroom realities, which can be tested against your own experience and may furnish a starting-point from which you may develop strategies that work for you.

Before the problem arises

The teachers who are most successful in maintaining discipline in class are not those who are good at dealing with problems, but those who know how to prevent their arising in the first place. I suggest three main preventative strategies:

1. Careful planning

When a lesson is clearly planned and organized there is likely to be a constant momentum and a feeling of purpose, which keep students' attention on the task in hand (or in anticipation of the next) and does not allow the formation of a 'vacuum' which may be filled by distracting or counterproductive activity. Moreover, the awareness that everything is planned and you know where you are going contributes a great deal to your own confidence, and to your ability to win the trust of the students.

2. Clear instructions

Problems sometimes arise due to student uncertainty about what they are supposed to be doing. Instructions, though they take up a very small proportion of lesson time, are crucial. The necessary information needs to be communicated clearly and quickly, courteously but assertively: this is precisely what the task involves, these are possible options, those are not (see Module 1: *Presentations and explanations*, Unit Three). This is not incompatible with the existence of student-teacher negotiation about what to do: but too much hesitation and mind-changing can distract and bore students, with obvious implications for discipline.

3. Keep in touch

You need to be constantly aware of what is going on in all quarters of the classroom, keeping your eyes and ears open: as if you have sensitive antennae, or a revolving radar dish constantly on the alert, ready to pick up 'blips'. This achieves two things: first, students know you are aware of them all the time which encourages participation and personal contact on the one hand, and discourages deviant activity on the other; second, you yourself are able to detect a student's incipient loss of interest or distraction and do something about it before it has become problematic.

When the problem is beginning

Inexperienced teachers tend to ignore minor problems, in the hope that they will go away by themselves. Occasionally they do; but more often they simply escalate. In principle, it is advisable to respond immediately and actively to any incipient problem you detect.

1. Deal with it quietly

The best action is a quiet but clear-cut response that stops the deviant activity, keeping the latter as low-profile as possible. For example: if a student has not opened his or her book in response to an instruction from you, it is better quietly to go up to them and open the book yourself than draw the attention of the whole class by a reprimand or loud, repeated instruction. Over-assertive reactions can lead to the very escalation you wish to avoid.

2. Don't take things personally

This is a difficult instruction to obey sometimes, but an important one. Inexperienced teachers of adolescents are often upset by remarks that were not intended personally; or allow incidents of unpleasant conflict to rankle long after the student has forgotten they ever happened. Try to relate to the problem, not the student, as the object to be attacked and dealt with. A more difficult piece of advice: even if you are quite sure the criticism **was** meant personally, do your best to relate to it as if it was not: don't let the student pull you into personal conflict.

3. Don't use threats

Threats are often a sign of weakness; use the formula 'if you...then...' only as a real, factual option that you are ready to put into practice, not as a weapon to make an impression or intimidate.

When the problem has exploded

The priority here is to act quickly in order to get the class to revert to smooth routine as fast as possible. Often it is preferable to take a decision, even if not a very good one, fast, than to hesitate or do nothing.

1. Explode yourself

Often a swift, loud command will do the trick, with a display of anger: provided, of course, that you do not really lose your temper or become personally aggressive! The trouble with displaying anger is that you cannot do it too often, or it loses its effect.

2. Give in

For example, if students refuse to do homework you might say, 'All right, don't'. This is a perfectly respectable option, which is unfortunately shunned by many teachers who feel they risk loss of face. Its advantage is that it immediately defuses the situation, and if done quickly and decisively, will not be seen as dishonourable surrender! It also puts you in a position to fairly demand something from them in return! But again, it cannot be used too often, for obvious reasons.

3. Make them an offer they can't refuse

If they are pushing you into a confrontation, and you cannot give in but do not wish to impose your will by getting over-assertive – look for a way of diverting or sidestepping the crisis. Some strategies are: postponement ('Let's come back to this tomorrow at the beginning of the day. Now, to get back to...'); or compromise ('I'll tell you what: you have to do all the assignments, but I'll give you extra time to finish them...'); or arbitration ('Let's discuss this with the class teacher, and accept his or her decision...').

The above guidelines are summarized in Box 18.4.

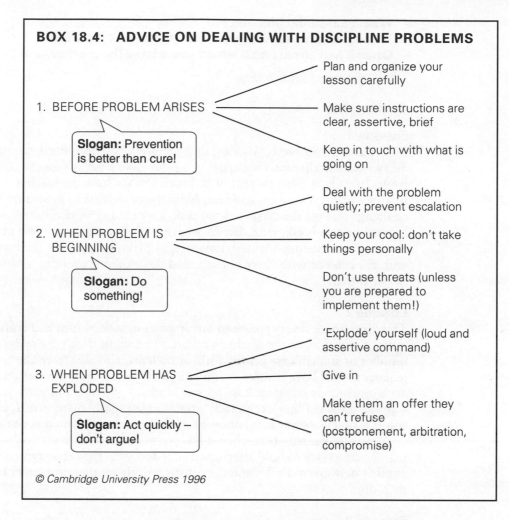

BOX 18.4: ADVICE ON DEALING WITH DISCIPLINE PROBLEMS

1. BEFORE PROBLEM ARISES

Plan and organize your lesson carefully

Make sure instructions are clear, assertive, brief

Keep in touch with what is going on

Slogan: Prevention is better than cure!

2. WHEN PROBLEM IS BEGINNING

Deal with the problem quietly; prevent escalation

Keep your cool: don't take things personally

Don't use threats (unless you are prepared to implement them!)

Slogan: Do something!

3. WHEN PROBLEM HAS EXPLODED

'Explode' yourself (loud and assertive command)

Give in

Make them an offer they can't refuse (postponement, arbitration, compromise)

Slogan: Act quickly – don't argue!

© *Cambridge University Press 1996*

▷ # Unit Five: Discipline problems: episodes

In this unit you are asked to apply your own expertise or knowledge of the subject of classroom discipline to critical analysis of actual classroom incidents. It is, of course, far easier to criticize and recommend when it is someone else's problem, and when you have plenty of time to consider and weigh alternatives than it is to take the right decisions when you yourself are involved in a real-time classroom crisis! Nevertheless, vicarious experience and decision-making like this has its uses for professional thinking, and is an interesting exercise in itself.

Task **Analysing episodes**

Read through the descriptions of episodes shown in Box 18.5. Deal with them in any order that you like and think about or discuss the following questions:

267

> – What caused the problem?
> – What could the teacher have done to prevent it arising?
> – Once it had arisen, what would you advise the teacher to do?

My own comments follow.

Comments

Episode 1

The causes of this were, possibly, that the book is indeed boring, coupled with Terry's wish to disrupt, challenge, or simply take a break from routine. Apart from choosing a different text, it is difficult to see how the teacher could have foreseen or prevented the incident. Now the priority is to neutralize the challenge and get the class back on task. I would say something like: 'Yes, we do have to do this book; we'll discuss whether it's boring later' – and get someone else to go on reading. I would, however, as promised, discuss the book later with the class or with Terry himself, and devote some thought to the selection of the next text.

Episode 2

This situation is a very common one, rooted in lack of firm and consistent rules in the classroom, or the teacher's failure to insist on them: the result is that a number of students are getting little or no learning value from the lesson. The teacher should have insisted on quiet and attention from the start, and stopped each murmur as it began. Possibly she is afraid of losing popularity: her reproaches when they occur, lack 'attack', are rapidly disregarded, and the result is that constant inattention and chat is tacitly accepted as the norm.

To reverse the situation when it has got as far as this is extremely difficult. It may be necessary to hold a serious discussion with the class, agree with them on explicit new ground rules and then insist strictly on their implementation from then on.

Episode 3

Here, the incident was caused by the teacher's over-lengthy explanation, the child's impatience, and the failure of the teacher to pick up and stop the disturbance when it started. Most people's intuitive reaction would be to reprimand John; but probably a more effective response would be to use the silence to instruct the class firmly to start work on the worksheet, promising to deal with any further problems in response to raised hands. Once the class is working, the teacher could go to John, make it clear that his behaviour is unacceptable, but that the incident is now over and he should be working. A further word or two with him after the lesson may make it less likely that he will repeat the behaviour.

Episode 4

The immediate cause of this incident, given the confident and cheeky character of members of the class, was the teacher's mistake in getting into an argument with one boy in the middle of an organizational routine involving all the class – an argument which escalated rapidly into a full-class disturbance. He should have finished distributing and collecting books and dealt with the notebook

---

BOX 18.5:   EPISODES: DISCIPLINE PROBLEMS

Episode 1

The teacher of a mixed class of thirteen-year-olds is working through a class reader in an English lesson. He asks Terry to read out a passage. 'Do we have to do this book?' says Terry. 'It's boring.' Some members of the class smile, one says 'I like it', others are silent awaiting the teacher's reaction.

(from E. C. Wragg, *Class Management and Control*, Macmillan, 1981, p. 12)

Episode 2

The teacher is explaining a story. Many of the students are inattentive, and there is a murmur of quiet talk between them. The teacher disregards the noise and speaks to those who are listening. Finally she reproaches, in a gentle and sympathetic way, one student who is talking particularly noticeably. The student stops talking for a minute or two, then carries on. This happens once or twice more, with different students. The teacher does not get angry, and continues to explain, trying (with only partial success) to draw students' attention through occasional questions.

(adapted from Sarah Reinhorn-Lurie, Unpublished research project on classroom discipline, Oranim School of Education, Haifa, 1992)

Episode 3

The teacher has prepared a worksheet and is explaining how to do it. He has extended his explanation to the point where John, having lost interest in the teacher's words, begins to tap a ruler on his desk. At first the tapping is occasional and not too noticeable, but John begins to tap more frequently and more noisily, building up to a final climax when he hits the table with a very loud bang. The class, startled by the noise, falls silent, and looks at both John and the teacher to see what will happen.

(adapted from E. C. Wragg, *Class Management and Control*, Macmillan, 1981, p. 18)

Episode 4

The teacher begins by giving out classroom books and collecting homework books.

Teacher (to one of the boys): This book's very thin.
Boy 1:   Yeah, 'tis, isn't it.
Teacher: Why?
Boy 1:   I've been drawing in it.
Boy 2:   He's been using it for toilet paper, sir.
(Uproar)

(adapted from E. C. Wragg, (ed.) *Classroom Teaching Skills*, Croom Helm, 1984, p. 32)

Episode 5

The students have been asked to interview each other for homework and write reports. In this lesson they are asked to read aloud their reports. A few students refuse to do so. The teacher tells these students to stand up before the class and be interviewed by them. They stand up, but do not relate to the questions seriously: answer facetiously, or in their mother tongue, or not at all. The teacher eventually sends them back to their places, and goes on to the next planned activity, a textbook exercise.

(adapted from Sarah Reinhorn-Lurie, Unpublished research project on classroom discipline, Oranim School of Education, Haifa, 1992) problem later, privately. Now that there is uproar, he should immediately abandon the individual problem, and devote his efforts to regaining order and finishing the book collection and distribution as quickly as possible. The problem of the mutilated notebook may be taken up again after the lesson with the boy alone.

Episode 5

The cause of this was the lack of authority of the teacher (her inability to demand and get student obedience), and the mistaken tactic of allowing obviously undisciplined students, in a group, to take over centre-stage. What I usually do if students do not want to read aloud something they have written is take it and read it aloud myself: they accept this because I can make it sound much better than they can, and my main objective (displaying students' work to each other) is gained.

Given the very uncomfortable situation of students actually making fun of a teacher-directed learning task, the reaction of stopping it and going on to the next bit of the lesson was the right one, although late. Certainly, however, the teacher should talk to the students later, one at a time, in order to make it clear that this behaviour was unacceptable and to try to prevent a recurrence.

Notes

(1) Defining classroom discipline

A possible definition: Classroom discipline is a state in which both teacher and learners accept and consistently observe a set of rules about behaviour in the classroom whose function is to facilitate smooth and efficient teaching and learning in a lesson.

(2) Distinctions between pairs of concepts

'Control' is imposed from above by an authority who is invested with superior influence; 'discipline' is accepted by participants in the activity of studying as an essential and integral part of that study (compare the use of the term 'discipline' to denote an area of study such as philosophy or science).

'Authoritarian' describes a teacher whose authority derives from some exterior empowering agent, or who is 'bossy'; 'authoritative' describes one who is obeyed because he or she is trusted to know best about the subject of study and how to learn it (hence the phrase 'to be an authority on...').

'Power' is the sheer ability to impose one's will on others, through physical coercion, or other forms of pressure; whereas 'authority' is the demand for cooperation and obedience that is accepted because it is rooted in a law, social order or accepted value system.

(3) Possible characteristics of classroom discipline

My responses would be as follows. Where I have found it difficult to make a clear decision, symbols in brackets indicate possible alternative choices.

1. Learning is taking place. +(?)
2. It is quiet. +
3. The teacher is in control. ++
4. Teacher and students are cooperating smoothly. ++
5. Students are motivated. ?(+)
6. The lesson is proceeding according to plan. +(?)
7. Teacher and students are aiming for the same objective. ?(+)
8. The teacher has natural charismatic 'authority'. ?(+)

My reasons are discussed in the *Comments* section within the unit.

(4) Practical hints for classroom discipline

My chosen 'top ten' would be: 1, 3, 4, 6, 8, 10, 11, 15, 17, 19.

Further reading

Charles, C. M. (1992) *Building Classroom Discipline* (4th edn.), New York: Longman.
   (Practical and readable, written for trainee or practising teachers; a summary of various models of classroom discipline and guidelines for practical application)
Cohen, L. and Manion, L. (1977) *A Guide to Teaching Practice*, London: Macmillan.
   (A valuable practical guide to all aspects of school teaching)
Kounin, J. S. (1970) *Discipline and Group Management in Classrooms*, New York: Holt, Rinehart and Winston.
   (An analysis of various aspects of discipline, some interesting and useful perspectives)
Maclennan, S. (1987) 'Integrating lesson planning and class management', *ELT Journal*, **41**, 3, 193–7.
   (On alternating lively and quiet activities in the lesson process)
Peters, R. S. (1966) *Ethics and Education*, London: George Allen and Unwin.
   (Philosophical analysis of various aspects of education; see particularly Part Three: 'Education and social control')
Underwood, M. (1987) *Effective Classroom Management*, London: Longman.
   (Not just on discipline, but on a variety of aspects of classroom management and lesson planning: practical and comprehensive)
Widdowson, H. G. (1987) 'The roles of teacher and learner', *ELT Journal*, **41**, 2, 83–8.
   (An analysis of the different roles of the teacher as authority, and resulting interaction between teacher and learner)
Wilson, P. S. (1971) *Interest and Discipline in Education*, London: Routledge.
   (A philosophical discussion of the two concepts: see particularly the analysis of discipline versus control, pp. 77–80, quoted in Wragg, 1984)

Wragg, E. C. (ed.) (1984) *Classroom Teaching Skills*, London and Sydney: Croom Helm.
(A collection of research-based articles on various aspects of school classroom teaching; see particularly Chapters 2, 3 and 7)

Wragg, E. C. (1981) *Class Management and Control*, London: Macmillan.
(A slim booklet of highly practical and accessible information, tasks and background reading)

Learner populations differ according to various parameters: whether the learners are beginner, intermediate or advanced; whether they are young children, adolescent or adult; their objectives in learning the language, and how they are motivated; whether their environment outside the classroom is target-language or mother-tongue; how heterogeneous or homogeneous the class is; the size of the group; and many more.

Most of these issues have been touched on incidentally within earlier modules, as they affected the different topics under discussion. Part VI, however, focusses entirely on characteristics of learners, or groups of learners, which seem to me particularly important or problematical: the question of learner motivation; learners of different ages; and heterogeneous classes.

Module 19 looks at different kinds of **learner motivation**, and examines particularly the ways in which the teacher can influence it. The assumption is made here that the teacher has a responsibility not only to provide opportunities for learning, but also actively to 'push' learners to realize their full potential and make maximum progress; and that the enhancement of motivation is probably the most effective way to do this.

The topic of **younger and adult learners** is dealt with in Module 20: differences between the age groups in learning styles, abilities and motivation entail corresponding differences in the selection of materials and methodology and in lesson planning. It is also useful to be aware of the unreliability of various popular myths: for example, that children learn languages better than adults.

Module 21 deals with **heterogeneous classes**, sometimes called 'mixed-ability' classes. The term 'mixed-ability', however, implies that the important difference between members of a mixed class is in their language-learning ability, but this is not necessarily so. Even if the main observed difference between them is in the amount of language they know, this may have its roots in all sorts of other reasons besides ability (previous teaching, motivation, etc.). And there are plenty of other differences between learners that need to be taken into account by a teacher: preferred learning style, personality, interests, cultural background – to name only a few. Thus the term 'heterogeneous' – composed of different kinds of people – is I think more suitable in defining such classes. To some extent, any class is heterogeneous (one definition of the term is 'a class of two'!); but certainly some are more so than others. Very heterogeneous classes can be extremely difficult to teach: hence the importance of studying the main problems and searching for principles and practical ideas that can contribute to effective solutions.

The problem of heterogeneity is, of course, compounded if the class is also large; and in fact many teachers see the 'large heterogeneous class' as a single, generalized problem situation. Hence it seemed logical to treat the two aspects together in a single module.

Module 19: Learner motivation and interest

▷ ## Unit One: Motivation: some background thinking

The abstract term 'motivation' on its own is rather difficult to define. It is easier and more useful to think in terms of the 'motivated' learner: one who is willing or even eager to invest effort in learning activities and to progress. Learner motivation makes teaching and learning immeasurably easier and more pleasant, as well as more productive: hence the importance of the topic for teachers.

This first unit reviews, necessarily briefly, various interesting theoretical aspects of the topic of learner motivation that have been studied and discussed in the literature.

Questions **To stimulate your own thinking in anticipation, try answering the questions in Box 19.1.**

BOX 19.1: ASPECTS OF LEARNER MOTIVATION

1. How important do you think motivation is for success in language learning, compared to, for example, language aptitude?
2. How important is people's past success in language learning for their motivation to learn in the present and future?
3. What characteristics and behaviours do you associate with the image of a motivated learner?
4. Some people are motivated by wanting to integrate into the target-language culture ('integrative motivation'), some by needing the language for their career or other personal advantages ('instrumental motivation'). Which of the two would you imagine to be the stronger motive, on the whole?
5. The urge to engage in learning activity for its own sake (intrinsic motivation) is distinguishable from the urge to learn for the sake of some external reward (extrinsic motivation). Do you think there is any difference between children and adults in the degree of influence of these two kinds of motivation?

© *Cambridge University Press 1995*

The importance of motivation

Various studies have found that motivation is very strongly related to achievement in language learning (e.g. Gardner and Lambert, 1972; Gardner, 1980). The question then needs to be asked: which is the cause and which the result? In other words, does success in language learning breed its own motivation (Burstall *et al.*, 1974; Khan, 1991) or does previous motivation lead to success? Or both? Another question for which there is no conclusive research-based evidence is whether motivation is more, or less, important than a natural aptitude for learning (languages), though at least one well-known study (Naiman *et al.*, 1978) tends towards the claim that motivation is ultimately more important (see below).

The significant message of research in this area for teachers is the sheer importance of the factor of learner motivation in successful language learning. Other questions raised in the above paragraph are arguably academic. The uncertainty as to which comes first, motivation or success, does not entail any particular problems for teaching: it simply means that among other things we do to increase our students' motivation, strategies to increase the likelihood of success in learning activities should have high priority. And as to the question whether motivation is more or less important than language aptitude: motivation is not measurable, and even language aptitude is apparently much more difficult to assess than was once thought, so that the question is probably unanswerable. In any case, perhaps it was not a very helpful one in the first place: our job is to do all we can to encourage the development of ability and enhance motivation, on the understanding that each will contribute to the other.

Characteristics of motivated learners

The authors of a classic study of successful language learning (Naiman *et al.*, 1978) came to the conclusion that the most successful learners are not necessarily those to whom a language comes very easily; they are those who display certain typical characteristics, most of them clearly associated with motivation. Some of these are:

1. **Positive task orientation.** The learner is willing to tackle tasks and challenges, and has confidence in his or her success.
2. **Ego-involvement.** The learner finds it important to succeed in learning in order to maintain and promote his or her own (positive) self-image.
3. **Need for achievement.** The learner has a need to achieve, to overcome difficulties and succeed in what he or she sets out to do.
4. **High aspirations.** The learner is ambitious, goes for demanding challenges, high proficiency, top grades.
5. **Goal orientation.** The learner is very aware of the goals of learning, or of specific learning activities, and directs his or her efforts towards achieving them.
6. **Perseverance.** The learner consistently invests a high level of effort in learning, and is not discouraged by setbacks or apparent lack of progress.
7. **Tolerance of ambiguity.** The learner is not disturbed or frustrated by situations involving a temporary lack of understanding or confusion; he or she can live with these patiently, in the confidence that understanding will come later.

Various other personality traits have been studied, such as field-dependence or independence, empathy, introversion or extraversion, but results have been less conclusive.

Different kinds of motivation

A distinction has been made in the literature between 'integrative' and 'instrumental' motivation: the desire to identify with and integrate into the target-language culture, contrasted with the wish to learn the language for purposes of study or career promotion. Gardner and Lambert (1972) introduced these concepts and claimed that integrative motivation was more influential among learners of French in Canada; but research since has cast doubt on the application of this claim to foreign language learners in general. In any case, at least one other study (Burstall *et al.*, 1974) has indicated that it may be impossible in practice to distinguish between the two.

Another distinction, perhaps more useful for teachers, is that between 'intrinsic' motivation (the urge to engage in the learning activity for its own sake) and 'extrinsic' (motivation that is derived from external incentives). Both of these have an important part to play in classroom motivation, and both are at least partially accessible to teacher influence. Intrinsic motivation is in its turn associated with what has been termed 'cognitive drive' – the urge to learn for its own sake, which is very typical of young children and tends to deteriorate with age.

A third distinction which has been made (Brown, 1987) is that between 'global', 'situational' and 'task' motivation: the first is the overall orientation of the learner towards the learning of the foreign language; the second has to do with the context of learning (classroom, total environment); and the third with the way the learner approaches the specific task in hand. As regards situation: for our purposes, we assume it is the classroom, but the other two may vary and be influenced by teacher action. Global motivation may seem mainly determined by previous education and a multitude of social factors, but it is also affected by the teacher's own attitudes conveyed either unconsciously or through explicit information and persuasion. And the third is probably where most of our effort is invested in practice: in making the task in hand as attractive as possible, and in encouraging our students to engage in it, invest effort and succeed.

▷ ## Unit Two: The teacher's responsibility

In an article written some years ago, Girard (1977) emphasized that it is an important part of the teacher's job to motivate learners. In more recent 'learner-centred' approaches to language teaching, however, the teacher's function is seen mainly as a provider of materials and conditions for learning, while the learner takes responsibility for his or her own motivation and performance.

Which of these approaches is nearer your own? Your answer may depend to some extent on your own teaching situation: classes composed of highly motivated adult immigrants learning the target language for purposes of survival in a new country may only need you as a provider and organizer of learning activities and texts; whereas schoolchildren learning a foreign language may only learn well if you find a way to activate and encourage their desire to invest effort in the learning activity.

One way of studying the question of the contribution of teachers to learner motivation is through the following task.

Task **Reflecting on the characteristics of a good teacher**

Stage 1: Recall

Think back to your own classroom learning, as either child or adult, not necessarily of a foreign language, and try to recall a teacher of yours who was outstandingly good, from whom you really learnt well. (I am deliberately refraining from defining further what I mean by a 'good' teacher – interpret the term as **you** understand it.)

Stage 2: Writing

Write down, possibly in note form, as complete a description as you can of how this teacher functioned, within the classroom and outside it.

Stage 3: Reflection

Reading through what you have written, consider:

1. How much effort this teacher put in to motivating you to learn, whether deliberately or not, and:
2. How far your positive assessment of this teacher is based on the way he or she managed to motivate you.

If you are working in a group, share your accounts of your good teacher with others, and discuss the questions with them.

Results obtained from this task when done by teacher trainees in a group I worked with are described in the Notes.

Results and conclusions

If your results are similar to mine, then you will have found that the learner-centred approach described in the introductory paragraph of this unit does not in fact seem to be implemented very often. Most good teachers seem to accept that it is their responsibility to motivate learners, and invest quite a lot of effort in doing so.

► **Unit Three: Extrinsic motivation**

Extrinsic motivation is that which derives from the influence of some kind of external incentive, as distinct from the wish to learn for its own sake or interest in tasks. Many sources of extrinsic motivation are inaccessible to the influence of the teacher: for example, the desire of students to please some other authority figure such as parents, their wish to succeed in an external exam, or peer-group influences. However, other sources are certainly affected by teacher action. Here are some of them.

Success and its rewards

This is perhaps the single most important feature in raising extrinsic motivation. Learners who have succeeded in past tasks will be more willing to engage with the next one, more confident in their chances of succeeding, and more likely to persevere in their efforts.

It is important to note that 'success' in this context is not necessarily the same as 'getting the answers right' – though sometimes it may be. Further criteria may be the sheer amount of language produced or understood, the investment of effort and care, the degree of progress since a previous performance. All these need to be recognized by the teacher as 'successes' for which the learner can and should take credit.

The teacher's most important function here is simply to make sure that learners are aware of their own success: the message can be conveyed by a nod, a tick, even significant lack of response. But a sense of pride and satisfaction may of course be enhanced by explicit praise or approval, or by its expression in quantitative grades – particularly for young, inexperienced or unconfident learners. The only potential problem with these explicit markers of success is the danger that if over-used learners may become dependent on them: they may lose confidence in their ability to recognize success on their own, and see lack of teacher approval as casting doubt on it, or even as disapproval.

The key, then, is the learners' own awareness of successful performance, however this is attained: the more confident they become and the more able to recognize such success on their own, the less they will need explicit support from someone else.

Failure and its penalties

Failure, too, is not just a matter of wrong answers; learners should be aware that they are failing if they have done significantly less than they could have, if they are making unsatisfactory progress, or not taking care.

Failure in any sense is generally regarded as something to be avoided, just as success is something to be sought. But this should not be taken too far. For one thing, success loses its sweetness if it is too easily attained and if there is no real possibility or experience of failure. For another, it is inevitable that there will be occasional failures in any normal learning experience, and they are nothing to be ashamed of; good learners recognize this, take setbacks in their stride, and look for ways to exploit them in order to succeed next time.

As with success, it is in principle part of the teacher's job to make learners aware of when they are failing. Having said this, however, there is certainly a danger that constant awareness of shortcomings may lower learners' motivation and demoralize them, particularly those whose self-image and confidence are shaky to start with. There may be cases where you may prefer to ignore or play down a failure; and success can be made more likely by judicious selection of tasks, and by setting the (minimum) standard of success at a clearly achievable level.

Authoritative demands

Learners are often motivated by teacher pressure: they may be willing to invest effort in tasks simply because you have told them to, recognizing your authority and right to make this demand, and trusting your judgement. Younger learners on the whole need the exercise of such authority more, adults less: but even adults prefer to be faced with a clear demand such as 'I want you to do this assignment by Friday' than a low-key request like: 'Do what you can, and give it to me whenever you finish.'

Authoritative demands can be, of course, over-used or misused: if learners only do things because they are obeying commands, without any awareness of objectives and results or involvement in decisions, they are unlikely to develop personal responsibility for their own learning or long-term motivation to continue. On the other hand an over-emphasis on learner freedom and autonomy and corresponding lack of authoritative demand by the teacher can lead to noticeable lowering of effort and achievement, and often, paradoxically, to learner dissatisfaction. Teachers have, surely, a duty to use their authority to 'push' their students – particularly the younger ones – beyond what they might be willing to do on their own, towards what Vygotsky (1962: Ch.6) called their 'zone of proximal development' – the next stage in achievement – which can only be attained by a learner with the support and help of a teacher.

Tests

The motivating power of tests appears clear: learners who know they are going to be tested on specific material next week will normally be more motivated to study it carefully than if they had simply been told to learn it. Again, this is a useful incentive, provided there is not too much stress attached, and provided it is not used too often. See Module 3: *Tests*, Unit Two for a discussion of this and related points.

Competition

Learners will often be motivated to give of their best not for the sake of the learning itself but in order to beat their opponents in a competition.

Individual competition can be stressful for people who find losing humiliating, or are not very good at the language and therefore likely consistently to lose in contests based on (linguistic) knowledge; and if over-used, it eventually affects negatively learners' willingness to cooperate and help each other. If, however, the competition is taken not too seriously, and if scores are at least partly a result of chance, so that anyone might win, positive motivational aspects are enhanced and stress lowered. Group contests tend on the whole to get better results than individual ones, in my experience: they are more enjoyable, less tense and equally motivating.

Summary discussion task

A recurring message in the above discussion has been the caution not to rely on any one of the methods too consistently or use it too often, since over-use of any one of them can lead to negative attitudes and harm long-term learning. Do you have any further reservations about any of them, based, perhaps on negative experiences as learner or teacher? Are there others that you have positive experience of and have found particularly useful?

▶ Unit Four: Intrinsic motivation and interest

Global intrinsic motivation – the generalized desire to invest effort in the learning for its own sake – is largely rooted in the previous attitudes of the learners: whether they see the learning as worthwhile, whether they like the language and its cultural, political and ethnic associations. However, you can certainly help to foster these attitudes by making it clear that you share them, or by giving further interesting and attractive information about the language and its background.

Such global motivation is important when the course is beginning, and as general underlying orientation during it; but for real-time classroom learning a more significant factor is whether the task in hand is seen as interesting. It is in the arousing of interest, perhaps, that teachers invest most effort, and get most immediate and noticeable pay-off in terms of learner motivation.

Task   **Finding ways of arousing learner interest**

Stage 1: Brainstorm

How many ways of creating learner interest in doing a task can you think of? Either on your own or with colleagues, make as comprehensive a list as you can.

Stage 2: Extending

Compare your list with mine as shown in Box 19.2. Can you use my list to extend your own, or vice versa?

Note that we may have many of the same ideas perhaps expressed in different words; decide which terms you prefer and stick to them. Also, different ideas may overlap: for example, you may have both 'games' and 'puzzles', where puzzles are arguably one kind of game. This does not matter at all: we are, after all, simply trying to amass as many good ideas for teaching as possible, not attempting a scientific taxonomy of mutually exclusive categories.

Stage 3: Assessing

With your final list before you, think about or discuss: which of the items are used most and which least in a teaching situation you are familiar with? And can you single out those which are, in your opinion, under-exploited and you would like to try to use more yourself?

BOX 19.2: WAYS OF AROUSING INTEREST IN TASKS

1. Clear goals
Learners should be aware of the objectives of the task – both language-learning and content. For example, a guessing-game may have the language-learning goal of practising questions, and the content goal of guessing answers.

2. Varied topics and tasks
Topics and tasks should be selected carefully to be as interesting as possible; but few single types can interest everyone, so there should be a wide range of different ones over time.

3. Visuals
It is important for learners to have something to look at that is eye-catching and relevant to the task in hand (see Wright and Haleem, 1991).

4. Tension and challenge: games
Game-like activities provide pleasurable tension and challenge through the process of attaining some 'fun' goal while limited by rules. The introduction of such rules (an arbitrary time limit, for example) can add spice to almost any goal-oriented task.

5. Entertainment
Entertainment produces enjoyment, which in its turn adds motivation. Entertainment can be teacher-produced (jokes, stories, perhaps songs, dramatic presentations) or recorded (movies, video clips, television documentaries).

6. Play-acting
Role play and simulations that use the imagination and take learners out of themselves can be excellent; though some people are inhibited and may find such activities intimidating at first.

7. Information gap
A particularly interesting type of task is that based on the need to understand or transmit information – finding out what is in a partner's picture, for example. A variation on this is the opinion gap where participants exchange views on a given issue.

8. Personalization
Learners are more likely to be interested in tasks that have to do with them themselves: their own or each other's opinions, tastes, experiences, suggestions.

9. Open-ended cues
A cue which invites a number of possible responses is usually much more stimulating than one with only one right answer: participants' contributions are unpredictable, and are more likely to be interesting, original or humorous.

▷ # Unit Five: Fluctuations in learner interest

The ideas for raising interest suggested in the previous unit are useful as overall guidelines for the design of materials or tasks. This unit looks at how learners' level of attention and interest fluctuates **within** the period of engagement with a task, and what might cause such fluctuations. Some temporary lowering in learner interest can be caused by factors beyond our control – the need of the learner to take a short break, for example, or external distractions – but there are also certain teacher behaviours which can quickly catch or lose learner interest, and it is important to be sensitive to their effect.

Teacher-associated fluctuations in interest are more obvious in classes of younger or less autonomous learners, but can be observed to some extent in all classes.

The following task invites you to study your own data on rises and falls in apparent learner motivation in a lesson; if you are unable to do the necessary observation yourself, then read on to the account of my own observation below.

Observation task

Rises and falls in learner interest

Stage 1: Observation

For this task you will need to observe one lesson. Place yourself somewhere where you have a good view of one or two particular students. Watch them carefully and notice fluctuations in their interest level; at the same time note what was going on in the classroom. I found this easiest to do by noting time, classroom event(s) and then '++' for 'high attention', '– –' for 'very low attention', or appropriate intermediate symbols. Your perception of when interest is rising or falling will be largely intuitive, but look particularly for the direction of the student's gaze, slumping or erect body posture, alert or apathetic facial expression, physical activity that is, or is not, directed at the task in hand.

Stage 2: Summary and conclusions

When you have finished your observation, try to pinpoint some of the apparent causes of rises and falls in attention, and what you might learn from these for your own teaching. If others in your group have also done such an observation, you might find it interesting to compare notes.

I tried this in a class of twelve-year-olds in my school; results are described below.

Fluctuations in learner interest: Observation and reflections

I watched two boys in the front row of a heterogeneous class of twelve-year-olds in my school. They were average, or slightly above-average students, but not outstandingly obedient or self-disciplined. Below are slightly edited notes from the first half of the lesson I observed, followed by some of my reflections.

Time	Classroom events	Student attention
9.03	Teacher says what's planned for lesson, gives instructions: take out books, page 18	++
9.05	Question and answer from book exercise, teacher eliciting answers from volunteers; other students answering; teacher correcting, explaining.	--
9.10	Teacher explains pair work: ask each other questions about picture in book	+
9.11	Pair work under way; my students not doing it, chatting about something else in mother tongue	--
9.12	Teacher notices, brings students back on-task; they are now doing it at full concentration	++
9.13	Instructions for quick dictation-type test; the test given	++
9.15	Papers being collected	-
9.16	Teacher introduces new topic; reads bit from book, while students follow	++
9.17	Individual students reading; others following	+
9.20	Teacher introduces comparison exercises; elicits examples of similarities/differences between two pictures in their textbook, writes on board	+
9.23	Teacher invites students to continue telling each other about similarities and differences in pairs. Most don't do it	--

Some reflections

- On the whole, the teacher addressing the whole class got most people's attention; when she addressed individuals, others sometimes lost interest – particularly if she went into lengthy corrections and explanations of individual error. One possible explanation might be that the teacher's eye contact with individuals raises their attention; extended lack of eye contact lowers it. Hence the importance of constant 'scanning' of the class?
- Blackboard writing on the whole held students' attention, particularly when she was writing something they had said themselves.
- When students had to read or write something down, they concentrated; when they only had to listen, they attended less. Perhaps both this point and the previous one have to do with activation of the visual channel: students who have something to look at attend better?
- Organizational activities (giving out and collecting papers, for example) were usually accompanied by a lowering of attention; such processes therefore need to be managed as quickly and efficiently as possible.
- Pair and group work sometimes produce a very high level of learner concentration and activity, but can also do exactly the opposite. A high degree of teacher sensitivity is needed here, together with very clear instructions, simple and well-structured tasks and careful monitoring.

Notes

Task: Recalling the characteristics of a good teacher

Most of my trainees recalled their good teachers as in some way 'pushing' them to want to give of their best, though there was by no means a consensus on the most common or successful methods.

It is, for example, apparently by no means necessarily true that motivating behaviour on the part of the teacher implies increasing pleasure or enjoyment. People who chose to recall teachers at secondary-school level tended to describe their good teachers as demanding consistently high standards, giving frequent, possibly stressful, tests, punishing slackness and so on. These teachers did, however, in spite of (or because of?) strictness and uncompromising demands, apparently succeed in conveying to their students a faith in their ability to reach the desired standards, and respect for them as individuals and scholars. A typical comment was something like 'I would never have believed I could do it – my teacher showed me I could, and pushed me until I got there.'

Others recalled their teachers as motivating them by gentler and warmer personal support; these are particularly those who chose to recall primary-school teachers. 'I felt she cared about me, and enjoyed teaching me, so I enjoyed learning with her and wanted to do my best.'

Yet another category was those teachers who motivated students by making the tasks and lessons interesting, and thus, eventually, the subject of study as a whole. Interest was aroused not just by careful planning of stimulating topics and tasks, but also by the teacher's own enthusiasm and eagerness: teachers who are excited about their subject or who simply love teaching seem to communicate their own motivation to their students.

Further reading

Brown, H. D. (1987) *Principles of Language Learning and Teaching* (2nd edn.), Englewood Cliffs, N.J.: Prentice Hall.

Burstall, C., Jamieson, M., Cohen, S., and Hargreaves, M. (1974), *Primary French in the Balance*, Windsor: National Foundation for Educational Research Publishing Company.
(An account of an experimental period of teaching French as a foreign language in British primary schools, with some significant conclusions for the functions and causes of motivation to learn)

Csikzsentmihalyi, M. and Nakamura, J. (1989) 'The dynamics of intrinsic motivation', in Ames, C. and Ames, R. (eds.), *Research on Motivation in Education*, Vol. III, London: Academic Press, 152–64.
(Interesting, convincing hypotheses and research on the nature and causes of intrinsic motivation)

Gardner, R. (1980) 'On the validity of affective variables in second language acquisition: conceptual, contextual and statistical considerations', *Language Learning*, 30, 255–70.
(On the relationship between motivation and proficiency)

Gardner, R. and Lambert, W. (1972) *Attitudes and Motivation in Second Language Learning*, Rowley, Mass.: Newbury House.
(A classic study of motivational variables affecting learners of French as a second language in Canada)

Gardner, R. C. and MacIntyre, P. D. (1993) 'A student's contributions to second-language learning. Part II: Affective variables', *Language Teaching*, **26**, 1, 1–11.
(An overview of recent research, relating particularly to attitude, motivation and anxiety)

Girard, D. (1977) 'Motivation: the responsibility of the teacher', *ELT Journal*, **31**, 97–102.
(On the importance of motivation in language learning in general, and the teacher's contribution to it)

Khan, J. (1991) 'Lessons worth remembering from Primary French in Britain' in Kennedy, C. and Jarvis, J. (eds.), *Ideas and Issues in Primary ELT*, London: Nelson.
(A recent reconsideration of the implications of an important foreign language teaching experiment in Britain undertaken by Burstal, C. *et al.*, 1974)

Naiman, N., Froelich, M., Stern, H. H. and Todesco, A. (1978) *The Good Language Learner*, Research in Education Series, No.7, Toronto: Ontario Institute for Studies in Education.
(An interesting and much-quoted study of good language learners and their characteristics)

Stern, H. H. (1983) *Fundamental Concepts of Language Teaching*, Oxford: Oxford University Press, Ch.17.
(This chapter gives a useful overview of various learner characteristics that affect learning, relating particularly to aspects of motivation)

Vygotsky, L. S. (1962) *Thought and Language*, Cambridge, Mass.: MIT.
(On how the child develops the ability to understand and express concepts, and how the (adult) teacher may promote such development; eye-opening)

Wright, A. and Haleem, S. (1991) *Visuals for the Language Classroom*, London: Longman.
(On the creation and use of various kinds of visual materials for use in the language classroom)

Module 20: Younger and older learners

▶ ## Unit One: What difference does age make to language learning?

Many conventional assumptions about differences between children and adults in language learning may turn out, when subjected to careful examination or research to be not quite so obvious or inevitably true as they seem. In Box 20.1 are some statements that represent these assumptions; comments follow.

BOX 20.1: ASSUMPTIONS ABOUT AGE AND LANGUAGE LEARNING

1. Younger children learn languages better than older ones; children learn better than adults.
2. Foreign language learning in school should be started at as early an age as possible.
3. Children and adults learn languages basically the same way.
4. Adults have a longer concentration span than children.
5. It is easier to interest and motivate children than adults.

© *Cambridge University Press 1996*

Task ## Critical assessment

Look at the statements in Box 20.1, and note for each whether you agree or disagree, adding any comments or reservations you might have. Compare your reactions with those of colleagues if possible; then read on.

Comments

1. Young children learn languages better

This is a commonly held view, based on many people's experience seeing (or being) children transplanted to a foreign environment and picking up the local language with apparent ease. The obvious conclusion from this experience would seem to be that children are intrinsically better learners; but this has not been confirmed by research (Singleton, 1989). On the contrary: given the same amount of exposure to a foreign language, there is some evidence that the older the child the more effectively he or she learns (Snow and Hoefnagel-Hoehle, 1978; Ellis, 1994: 484–94); probably teenagers are overall the best learners. (The only apparent exception to this is pronunciation, which is learned more easily by younger children.) The reason for children's apparently speedy learning when immersed in the foreign environment may be the sheer amount of time they are usually exposed to the language, the number of 'teachers' surrounding them, and the dependence on (foreign-language-speaking) people around to supply their needs ('survival' motive).

The truth of the assumption that young children learn better is even more dubious if applied to formal classroom learning: here there is only one teacher to a number of children, exposure time is very limited, and the 'survival' motive does not usually apply. Moreover, young children have not as yet developed the cognitive skills and self-discipline that enable them to make the most of limited teacher-mediated information; they rely more on intuitive acquisition, which in its turn relies on a larger volume of comprehensible input than there is time for in lessons.

2. Foreign language learning in school should start early

Some people have argued for the existence of a 'critical period' in language learning: if you get too old and pass this period you will have significantly more difficulty learning; thus early learning in schools would seem essential. But this theory is not conclusively supported by research evidence: there may not be a critical period at all; or there may be several (Singleton, 1989; Long, 1990). The research-supported hypothesis discussed above – that children may actually become more effective language learners as they get older, particularly in formal teacher-mediated learning situations – means that the investment of lesson time at an early age may not be cost-effective. In other words, if you have a limited number of hours to give to foreign language teaching in school, it will probably be more rewarding in terms of sheer amount of learning to invest these in the older classes. I have heard one authority on the subject, C. Snow (in a lecture 'Using L1 skills for L2 proficiency: Why older L2 learners are better', at the Conference of the English Teachers' Association of Israel, Jerusalem, 1993) claim that twelve is the optimum age for starting a foreign language in school; my own experience is that ten is about right.

Having said this, however, it is also true that an early start to language learning is likely to lead to better long-term results if early learning is maintained and reinforced as the child gets older (Long, 1990). In a situation, therefore, where there are as many teachers and teaching hours as you want, by all means start as early as you can.

3. Children and adults learn languages the same way

In an immersion situation, where people are acquiring language intuitively for daily survival, this may to some extent be true. In the context of formal courses, however, differences become apparent. Adults' capacity for understanding and logical thought is greater, and they are likely to have developed a number of learning skills and strategies which children do not yet have. Moreover, adult classes tend on the whole to be more disciplined and cooperative – as anyone who has moved from teaching children to teaching adults, or vice versa, will have found. This may be partly because people learn as they get older to be patient and put up with temporary frustrations in the hope of long-term rewards, to cooperate with others for joint profit, and various other benefits of self-restraint and disciplined cooperation. Another reason is that most adults are learning voluntarily, have chosen the course themselves, often have a clear purpose in learning (work, travel, etc.) and are therefore likely to feel more committed and motivated; whereas most children have little choice in where, how or even whether they are taught.

4. Adults have a longer concentration span

Teachers commonly notice that they cannot get children to concentrate on certain learning activities as long as they can get adults to do so. However, the problem is not the concentration span itself – children will spend hours absorbed in activities that really interest them – but rather the ability of the individual to persevere with something of no immediate intrinsic interest to them. Here older learners do exhibit noticeable superiority, because they tend to be more self-disciplined. One implication for teaching is the need to devote a lot of thought to the (intrinsic) interest value of learning activities for younger learners (see the next unit and Module 19: *Learner motivation and interest*).

5. It is easier to motivate children

In a sense, this is true: you can raise children's motivation and enthusiasm (by selecting interesting activities, for example) more easily than that of older, more self-reliant and sometimes cynical learners. On the other hand, you can also lose it more easily: monotonous, apparently pointless activities quickly bore and demotivate young learners; older ones are more tolerant of them. Perhaps it would be more accurate to say that younger learners' motivation is more likely to vary and is more susceptible to immediate surrounding influences, including the teacher; that of older learners tends to be more stable.

▷ Unit Two: Teaching children

Note: In this unit 'children' is taken to mean pre-adolescents.

In general, as noted at the end of the last unit, children have a greater immediate need to be motivated by the teacher or the materials in order to learn effectively. Prizes and similar extrinsic rewards can help, but more effective on the whole are elements that contribute towards intrinsic motivation: interest in doing the learning activity itself (for further discussion of intrinsic and extrinsic motivation see Module 19: *Learner motivation and interest*, Units Three and Four). Such elements are most likely to be effective if they are based on an appeal to the senses or activate the children in speech or movement.

Three very important sources of interest for children in the classroom are **pictures**, **stories** and **games**: the first being obviously mainly a visual stimulus; the second both visual and aural; and the third using both visual and aural channels as well as activating language production and sometimes physical movement.

Question   Can you add other important sources of interest for children learning languages besides the three mentioned above? Some suggestions of my own are given in the Notes, (1).

Pictures

Lack of aural stimulus is relatively easy to tolerate: even young learners will work for a while in silence without searching for something to listen to. This, however, is not true of the visual, which is a very dominant channel of input: so much so, that if young learners are not supplied with something to look at that is relevant to the learning task in hand they will find and probably be distracted by something that is not.

The most obvious type of visual material for children is the picture: and the more clearly visible, striking and colourful the better. On the whole, professionally drawn pictures or photographs are used: those in the textbook, or coloured posters, or pictures cut from magazines. But there is also a place for the teacher's own quick sketches on the board (however unprofessional and untidy!); and of course for the children's own drawing. There are, incidentally, books that give advice and help with drawing: have a look, for example, at Wright (1984), *1000 Pictures for Teachers to Copy*.

Application **If you are teaching or going to teach children, and do not already have a collection of pictures of your own, start making one!**

Stories

Young children love having stories told to them (even adults continue to enjoy it!); and older ones begin to read for themselves. Moreover stories – in contrast to pictures or even games – are pure language: telling a story in the foreign language is one of the simplest and richest sources of foreign language input for younger learners.

The most effective combination in teaching is pictures and stories together: and the success of use of picture-books with young learners has been attested by many (see articles in Brumfit *et al.*, 1991 and in Kennedy and Jarvis, 1991).

Application **Can you think of stories or books which you think would be suitable for use in a children's foreign language class? Perhaps pool ideas with other teachers and make a list of recommended material.**

Games

Some years ago I wrote an article which began with the words: 'I am not, in principle, in favour of the use of games in language teaching' (Ur, 1986). This was an obviously provocative statement, but based on a serious argument. Games are essentially recreational 'time out' activities whose main purpose is enjoyment; language study is serious goal-oriented work, whose main purpose is personal learning. Once you call a language-learning activity a 'game' you convey the message that it is just fun, not to be taken too seriously: a message I consider anti-educational and potentially demoralizing. Very occasionally we do play real games in the classroom, (at the end of a course, for example, or as a break from concentrated work); but to call something a game when our goal is in fact serious learning may harm the learning – and/or, indeed, spoil the 'game'! – as well as being dishonest.

Two further dangers are: first, the tendency of some teachers to call activities 'games' for the sake of raising initial motivation, when they are not in fact games at all ('Let's play a game: I'll give you a word, you tell me how it is spelt!'); second, the danger that the obvious activity and enjoyment caused by a game may obscure the fact that its contribution to learning is minimal (see, for example, Scenario 1 in Box 2.2).

However, another definition of 'games' ignores the implication of non-serious recreation and concentrates rather on their quality as organized action that is rule-governed, involves striving towards a clear goal through performance of a challenging task, and provides participants and/or onlookers with a feeling of pleasurable tension. Children in general learn well when they are active; and when action is channelled into an enjoyable game they are often willing to invest considerable time and effort in playing it. If we design our games in such a way that they are productive of language learning they become an excellent, even essential, part of a programme of children's learning activities.

My conclusion would certainly be to include game-based procedures as a substantial component of any children's language course; though I am to this day uncomfortable about using the term 'game', because of the misleading and belittling implication. I would rather think of and present them as (game-like) language-learning activities.

Application   Together with colleagues, describe and list some language-learning games that you know or have used, or seen used, successfully with children. You may find some of the references under *Further reading* helpful; three favourites of my own appear in the Notes, (2).

▷ Unit Three: Teaching adolescents: student preferences

For inexperienced teachers, classes of adolescents are perhaps the most daunting challenge. Their learning potential is greater than that of young children (see Unit One), but they may be considerably more difficult to motivate and manage, and it takes longer to build up trusting relationships.

One source of guidance about how to teach adolescents successfully is books on developmental psychology. Another – arguably no less reliable, and perhaps under-used – is the adolescents themselves.

Inquiry   **Finding out how adolescents like to be taught**

Stage 1: Preparation

Look through the questionnaire shown in Box 20.2, noting down for each item which responses you expect. Optionally, administer it also to an experienced teacher of adolescents, and compare their answers with yours. This will help you to familiarize yourself with the items, and will also raise some interesting speculations to which your later survey may supply answers. Add further items if you wish, or delete any you feel irrelevant.

BOX 20.2: SURVEY OF STUDENT OPINIONS

Put a tick in the appropriate column:

	Very much agree	Agree	Undecided	Disagree	Totally disagree
1. It is important for a teacher to dress nicely and look good.					
2. It is important for a teacher to care a lot about his/her teaching.					
3. A good teacher controls the class firmly.					
4. A good teacher treats his/her students with fairness and respect.					
5. A good teacher is warm and friendly towards students.					
6. A good teacher knows and uses students' names.					
7. A good teacher is interested in each student as a person.					
8. A good teacher will change the lesson plan and do something else if that is what the students want.					
9. A good teacher lets students mark their own tests.					
10. I like it when the students take over and run the lesson.					
11. A good teacher makes sure students have fun in lessons.					
12. A good teacher gets students to work hard.					
13. I prefer working in groups or individually to having a teacher-dominated lesson.					
14. I like it when the teacher asks my opinion in class.					
15. A good teacher always gives interesting lessons.					
16. A good teacher uses corporal punishment occasionally.					
17. If we need help, the good teacher finds time to talk outside the classroom.					

Acknowledgement: Many of the ideas for questions are based on Wragg and Wood, 1984, pp. 220–2.

Stage 2: Interviews

If you are working on your own, find some teenagers learning foreign languages locally who are willing to answer your questions: if possible about fifteen of them, but it is worth doing even with a smaller number. (If you are in a group, each participant may work with two or three respondents, pooling results at the end.)

You may do this as a series of interviews, noting a mark or tick in the appropriate space on your copy of the questionnaire for each answer. Or make multiple copies, and distribute to respondents, collating results later. (I did it by distributing copies in a lesson, letting students fill in answers on their own, but being myself on hand to clarify uncertainties about meanings.)

Stage 3: Summarizing results

Look at your results, or pool them with colleagues. Were there any surprises? If so, how would you account for the difference between your expectations and the respondents' answers?

Stage 4: Drawing conclusions

Assuming that your results are based on honest and fairly representative student opinions, in what way can you use them to guide you in planning your own teaching approach and procedures? Discuss this question with colleagues, or note ideas for yourself in writing.

Some general comments and conclusions of my own, based on a similar survey carried out by teachers in my own school are given in the following section.

Results and comments

The following comments are based on responses from two classes of fifteen-year-olds in the school where I teach, and are not necessarily all true for or applicable to other situations; implications for teaching are therefore expressed as personal conclusions. Nevertheless, you may find some interesting points of similarity between your own results and reflections and mine!

Statement 1
On the whole I found that students in fact care a lot less about their teachers' appearance than the teachers expect. If this is generally true, then relax!

Statement 2
Most agreed. The fact that teachers care about their teaching is apparently clearly, if unconsciously, conveyed; and this appears to be important to adolescent students. I should therefore not be misled by outward displays of indifference or cynicism!

Statement 3
This was strongly agreed with. Most students appear to like to feel that the teacher has authority and is clearly in control.

Statements 4 and 5

These were both predictably agreed with by most adolescents: the interesting point is that the first of the two scored noticeably higher than the second; and this may represent a general truth. In spite of the image of the warm and loving teacher promoted by some romantic fiction, most adolescents may prefer their teachers to value and respect them rather than to be their friends.

Statements 6 and 7

These two questions apparently relate to the same teacher characteristic: but my respondents showed noticeably less enthusiastic agreement with the second than with the first. They certainly want their teachers to identify them as individuals, but do not necessarily want them to be too interested in what may be seen as private territory.

Statements 8–10

Many of my respondents are used to being consulted in classroom affairs, and take quite a lot of responsibility for their own learning. Nevertheless, their responses to statements 8 and 10 were lukewarm, and to 9 outright disagreement. Most students seem to see responsibility for decisions about learning and assessment as part of the teacher's job, and regard you as irresponsible or unprofessional if you 'opt out'. There is something in this. On the other hand, it is clearly desirable to have students participate in decisions on what happens in the classroom, so that they too feel some ownership of and commitment to the learning programme: such participation has also educational value and provides some preparation for adult learning situations. However, collaborative decision-making cannot usually be demanded abruptly or immediately where the students are not used to it, and bringing it about may demand tact and careful planning.

Statements 11 and 12

Here, answers change perceptibly as students get older. The younger adolescents are more in favour of fun, less keen on working; older ones tend to switch priorities. My own conclusion: they judge us, ultimately, by how much they learn from us, not by how much they enjoy our lessons, and as they get older realize that good learning costs effort.

Statement 13

Answers varied, depending on the background of the individuals: whether they were used to doing group or individual work, or were chiefly taught in teacher-fronted lessons. I need to know their preferences, and, if I wish to introduce a change, should be aware that there may be difficulties.

Statement 14

Again, answers here varied very widely, even within one group, since they are closely linked to the individual's personality and learning style: it was difficult here to draw any general conclusions.

Statement 15

Most respondents agreed with this one fairly enthusiastically; they do not stop to consider whether it is reasonable to demand from even a first-rate teacher that all lessons be consistently interesting!

Statement 16

This is another culture-bound proposition. My respondents rejected it strongly; but elsewhere it may well be approved of by students, and seen as making a positive contribution to education.

Statement 17

This was agreed with enthusiastically and almost unanimously; the implications for my own behaviour with students is clear.

▷ Unit Four: Teaching adults: a different relationship

The teaching of foreign languages to adults is arguably less important, world-wide, than the teaching of children: most language teaching takes place in schools, most basic knowledge of and attitudes towards the foreign language are acquired there. However, teaching adults is on the whole easier and less stressful (and better paid!). It is, however, often directed towards special purposes (for business, for academic study and so on), demanding extra areas of expertise on the part of the teacher; and the teacher is often expected to be a native speaker of the target language.

Some of the reasons why it is usually easier to cope with and teach classes of adults than those of children were mentioned in Unit One: you might find it useful at this point to (re)read the *Comments* section in that unit on pages 286–288. However, one aspect which may actually be more problematical is not dealt with there: that of personal relationships.

Discussion Look at Box 20.3, in which are listed definitions of various possible relationships between teacher and class. Which of these do you feel are more, or less, appropriate for adult classes in general? Do the same generalizations apply to a specific class you know or have observed? (You will notice that the dominance shifts from teacher to learners as you go down the list. It looks as if the further down you go the more appropriate the relationship, but this would be an over-simplification.)

You may wish to discuss these questions with colleagues, or note down some personal responses – or simply read on to my comments below.

Comments

Authority – subjects to authority

Even in an adult class, the teacher's status as an authority is usually maintained. This, however, is based more on the teacher's being 'an authority on ...' (the language and how to learn it) than on their being a legally appointed superior: a

---

BOX 20.3: RELATIONSHIPS BETWEEN TEACHER AND ADULT STUDENTS

authority – subjects to authority
assessor – assessed
transmitter – receivers
motivator – people to be motivated
activator – people to be activated
counsellor – clients
seller of services – buyers of services
resource – users

© Cambridge University Press 1996

---

distinction expressed in the French terms *enseignant* and *professeur* respectively (see Widdowson, 1987). In any case, there is a certain deference on the part of the learners: the teacher is expected to give instructions, the learners are expected to respect and obey them. However, there is also the important factor of **accountability**: in return for conceding authority to the teacher in the classroom, adult learners demand ultimate returns in terms of their own benefit in learning outcomes.

Assessor – assessed

The moment one person is placed in the position of having the right to criticize the performance of another, the relationship becomes asymmetrical, dominance being attributed to the assessor. Even if someone else actually checks a final exam and passes or fails course participants, the teacher will be seen as assessor in the daily classroom process; and this contributes to their role as authority, already discussed above. In this aspect, there is little difference between young and adult classes.

Transmitter – receivers

This relationship can occur in adult classrooms just as it can in others; it is a function of the methodology the teacher has chosen to employ rather than of the age of the learner. Because of the less formal authority of the teacher with most adult classes (as described in the paragraph 'Authority – subjects to authority' above), adults are perhaps in a better position to assert their right to question, criticize and generally participate actively; on the other hand, they do tend to be more disciplined and conform more to teacher demands than younger learners. The two factors probably offset one another, and it is difficult to draw any firm conclusions about the 'typical' adult class in this respect.

Motivator – motivated

As a generalization, adults take **responsibility** in society: for their own **actions** and for their consequences. In the classroom also, adults take more responsibility for the learning process, and rely less on the teacher's initiative in making activities attractive or providing incentives. They are also usually more motivated in the first place (partly because most of them are learning voluntarily, while most children are given no choice!), and this motivation, as noted in Unit One, tends to be relatively stable: it does not, for example, rise or fall so much in immediate response to more interesting or more boring teaching.

Thus although the raising and maintaining of learner motivation is an essential and basic component of teaching activity with all age groups, it usually demands perhaps less investment of effort and time on the part of teachers working with adults.

Activator – activated

As with 'transmitter – receivers' this is a relationship that depends more on the teacher's chosen methodology than on the age of the learners, and can be true for any class.

Counsellor – clients

This relationship entails a view of the teacher as an accepting, supportive professional, whose function is to supply the expressed needs of the learner rather than to impose a predetermined programme. It involves a perceptible shift of responsibility and initiative in the classroom process from the teacher to the learners themselves. It is a typically adult relationship, and is unlikely to occur in classes of children; even in adult classes it is rare to find it consistently used: perhaps only where the methodology known as Community Language Learning is used (a brief summary of this is given in the Notes, (3); for further detail see Richards and Rodgers, 1986). But occasional exchanges and some general 'feel' of the counsellor–client relationship may enrich the interaction in many otherwise conventional adult classes.

Seller – buyers

This is an essentially business relationship: the teacher has a commodity – knowledge of the language – which the learner is willing to pay money to acquire. The implication is a relative lowering of the prestige of the teacher, and greater rights of the learner to demand appropriate results (value for money), and even to dismiss the teacher if the results are not forthcoming. This relationship may underlie quite a high proportion of adult learning situations, and the juxtaposition of the traditional authoritative role of the teacher with their role as employee or seller may be an uneasy one.

Resource – users

Here the implication is that the teacher is a mere source of knowledge to be tapped by learners, and is virtually passive in classroom interaction: it is the learner who tells the teacher what to do. Total and consistent implementation of such a teaching–learning relationship is difficult to envisage, but many adult classes may implement it partially, particularly where the students are experienced learners who know what they want and how to get it, and/or where the teacher knows the language but has no knowledge or experience of how to teach it.

Notes

(1) Other sources of interest for children

Some other ideas are: physical movement (dancing, gymnastics, aerobics); drama (mime, role play, putting on plays); projects (exploring a topic and making booklets or displays on it); doing decorative writing or other graphic design.

(2) Language-learning games for children

Here are three game-like activities I have used successfully with younger classes.

1. Association dominoes

You need a collection of small pictures – about three times as many as there are students in the class. Give each student two. Stick up one from the pool of remaining pictures on the board. Students may suggest adding one of their pictures either side of the original one if they can think of a convincing link or association between the two: for example, a camel may be put by a table because they both have four legs. The aim is to make as long a line of pictures as possible, or to make the line reach the sides of the board; students who run out of pictures may take more from your pool.

(The original 'dominoes' rule, that the winner is the one who gets rid of their pictures first I discarded, because this shortens the activity – lessening participation and language production – and also makes the whole atmosphere less pleasant: competitive rather than cooperative.)

2. Doodles

Draw an abstract 'doodle' on the board and invite students to say what they think it represents. The idea you think most interesting or original 'wins' and its producer gets to draw the next doodle and judge the resulting suggestions.

3. Decide on names

Each student is given a copy of the picture shown below. The students are divided into pairs, and are given the task of allotting names to the people in the picture, taking turns to choose and name a character. The condition is that they may not look at their partner's picture: they may mark in the names on their own picture, but the identification of the character to be named has to be done entirely through talking. After a certain time, stop them. They lay their pictures on their desks and check that they have in fact given the same names to the same people.

Note that just as good children's literature can be enjoyed by all ages, so can good children's games: I have used all three of the above with adult classes, with good results.

(3) Community Language Learning

In this methodology the aim is for learners to learn the language, promote their own personal development as individuals and together form a warm supportive community (hence its name). The teacher acts as a non-judgemental counsellor who helps to achieve these aims.

A basic initial procedure is for learners to sit in a circle, with the teacher (called a 'knower') outside. A learner who wishes to say something whispers it to the 'knower' who translates into the target language. Another learner who wishes to reply goes through the same procedure. The individual contributions are recorded, and the recording represents a full conversation. This conversation may then be transcribed, studied and used as the basis for further language development.

Other procedures include group discussions on the feelings and reactions of participants, teacher monologues re-presenting learner-initiated language, free conversation.

For a more detailed description of the method and some criticism, see Richards and Rodgers (1986).

Further reading

AGE DIFFERENCES

Burstall, C., Jamieson, M., Cohen, S., and Hargreaves, M. (1974), *Primary French in the Balance*, Windsor: National Foundation for Educational Research Publishing Company.
(An account of an experimental period of teaching French as a foreign language in British primary schools; the results overall were disappointing, and the teaching was discontinued: see Khan, 1991)

Ellis, R. (1994) *The Study of Second Language Acquisition*, Oxford: Oxford University Press: 484–94.
(A survey of research on the influence of age in second language learning: concludes, roughly, that older learners learn faster, but that given extensive and consistent exposure learners who started young eventually learn better)

Khan, J. (1991) 'Lessons worth remembering from Primary French in Britain' in Kennedy, C. and Jarvis, J. (eds.), *Ideas and Issues in Primary ELT*, London: Nelson.
(A recent reconsideration of the implications of an important foreign language teaching experiment in Britain (Burstall *et al.*, 1974))

Long, M. H. (1990) 'Maturational constraints on language development', *Studies in Second Language Acquisition*, **12**, 217–85.
(Research-based article on the age factor in language learning: conclusions similar to these of Ellis, above)

Singleton, D. (1989) *Language Acquisition: The Age Factor*, Clevedon, Philadelphia: Multilingual Matters.
(A thorough overview of the research, with useful summaries at the end of each chapter: few 'easy answers')

Snow, C. and Hoefnagel-Hoehle, M. (1978) 'Age differences in second language acquisition' in Hatch, E. (ed.), *Second Language Acquisition*, Rowley, Mass.: Newbury House.
(Research on English speakers of various ages learning Dutch in Holland; older learners on the whole progressed faster)

TEACHING CHILDREN

Argardizzo, C. (1993) *Children in Action*, Hemel Hempstead: Prentice Hall International.
(Clearly laid-out activities for children, accompanied by interesting suggestions for reflection by the teacher)

Brewster, J., Ellis, G. and Girard, D. (1992) *The Primary English Teacher's Guide*, Harmondsworth: Penguin.
(A systematic and sensible guide to the teaching of English as a foreign language to younger children, with a rich, well-organized selection of teaching ideas, and suggestions for teacher development)

Brumfit, C. J., Moon, J. and Tongue, R. (1991) *Teaching English to Children*, London: Collins.
(A collection of articles on the teaching of English as a foreign language, divided into two sections: the first and longer one devoted to practical classroom ideas, the second to background theory; to be read selectively)

Kennedy, C. and Jarvis, J. (eds.) (1991) *Ideas and Issues in Primary ELT*, London: Nelson.
(Another collection of articles on teaching English as a foreign language, mainly on aspects of practical research and experience; also for selective reading; cautious, sensible conclusions at the end)

Phillips, S. (1993) *Young Learners*, Oxford: Oxford University Press.
(A collection of suggested activities for young learners, sensibly classified under listening, speaking, grammar, etc.)

Scott, W. A. and Ytreberg, L. H. (1990) *Teaching English to Children*, London: Longman.
(A relatively short, readable and practical guide to teaching language skills to children, obviously based on the authors' classroom experience)

Ur, P. (1984) 'Getting younger learners to talk 1, 2, 3', *Practical English Teaching*, 4, 4, 23–4; 5, 1, 16–18; 5, 2, 15–16.
(Various guidelines on fluency practice for children, and a number of practical suggestions)

Vale, D. and Feunteun, A. (1995) *Teaching Children English*, Cambridge: Cambridge University Press.
(A course for teachers, including information, training tasks, and a rich collection of ideas for activating young learners)

PICTURES

Gerngross, G. and Puchta, H. (1992) *Pictures in Action*, Hemel Hempstead: Prentice Hall International.
(Practical ideas for using pictures in the classroom)

Wright, A. (1984) *1000 Pictures for Teachers to Copy*, London: Collins.
(Gives clear, easy guidance on how to draw simple figures, animals, objects, with plenty of models to copy)

Wright, A. and Haleem, S. (1991) *Visuals for the Language Classroom*, London: Longman.
(Guidelines on how to create and use various kinds of visual materials)

STORIES

Ellis, G. and Brewster, J. (eds.) (1991) *The Storytelling Handbook for Primary Teachers*, Harmondsworth: Penguin.
(On using children's picture-stories for foreign-language teaching; relates particularly to certain English storybooks, but the ideas are generalizable; clear, basic, practical)

GAMES

Hadfield, J. (1984) *Elementary Communication Games*, London: Nelson.
(Ideas for communication games for younger learners, with plenty of accompanying visual material; note that there is also an *Advanced Communication Games* by the same author)

Rixon, S. (1991) 'The role of fun and games activities in teaching young

learners' in Brumfit, C. J., Moon, J. and Tongue, R. (eds.), *Teaching English to Children*, London: Collins, pp. 33–48.
(General guidelines on game construction and use, with examples and recipes)

Rixon, S. (1992) 'English and other languages for younger children: practice and theory in a rapidly changing world', *Language Teaching*, 25, 2, 73–94.
(An overview of research, theory, training schemes and developments in methodology and materials; followed by a comprehensive bibliography)

Ur, P. (1986) 'How is a game like a GLALL?', *Practical English Teaching*, 6, 3, 15–16.
(On the nature and place of games in language teaching)

Wright, A., Betteridge, M. and Buckby, M. (1984) *Games for Language Learning*, Cambridge: Cambridge University Press.
(A collection of games and fun activities for language learning at all ages)

TEACHING ADOLESCENTS

Puchta, H. and Schratz, M. (1993) *Teaching Teenagers*, London: Longman.
(Suggestions for fluency activities with teenagers, based on humanistic self-expression; accompanied by interesting accounts of how similar activities worked when tried with German teenagers)

Wragg, E. C. and Wood, E. K. (1984) 'Pupil appraisals of teaching' in Wragg, E. C. (ed.), *Classroom Teaching Skills*, London and Sydney: Croom Helm, pp. 79–96, 220–2.
(Reports a piece of research done on pupils' opinions on the characteristics of the good teacher)

TEACHING ADULTS

Richards, J. C. and Rodgers, T. S. (1986) Ch. 8: 'Community Language Learning' in *Approaches and Methods in Language Teaching*, Cambridge: Cambridge University Press.
(A critical account of the principles and procedures of a counselling-based language teaching methodology)

Widdowson, H. G. (1987) 'The roles of teacher and learner', *ELT Journal*, 41, 2, 83–8.
(An analysis of the different roles of the teacher as authority, and types of interaction between teacher and learner)

Wright, T. (1987) *Roles of Teachers and Learners*, Oxford: Oxford University Press.
(A more detailed and thorough exploration of the topics discussed in Unit Four, presented mainly through tasks for the reader)

Module 21: Large heterogeneous classes

Note: At first sight, it might seem that the topics of 'large' and 'heterogeneous' classes are separate ones: why treat them together? One reason is that the two features coincide more often than not: large classes are almost invariably heterogeneous, heterogeneous classes are most problematical when they are also large. Many practitioners perceive the encounter with large, heterogeneous classes as in practice a single, and common, teaching problem, demanding study and guidance.

Unit One: Defining terms

Large classes

Large is of course a relative term, and what a 'large class' is will vary from place to place. In some private language schools a group of twenty students may be considered large; in my own teaching situation, 40–45; in some places numbers go up to the hundreds. A study done by the team of the Lancaster–Leeds *Language Learning in Large Classes Research Project* (*Project Report No. 4* of Coleman *et al.*, 1989) indicates that an average perception of the large class may be around 50 students.

Probably, however, the exact number does not really matter: what matters is how you, the teacher see the class size in your own specific situation. Most of what will be said in the following pages will be found relevant to any class perceived as large, regardless of the actual number of learners in it.

Question   In your own situation: how big is a 'large' class?

Heterogeneous classes

A 'heterogeneous' class is one that has different kinds of learners in it, as opposed to a 'homogeneous' class, where the learners are similar.

This definition cannot, however, be directly applied to the real world: there is in fact no such thing as a 'homogeneous' class, since no two learners are really similar; and therefore all classes of more than one learner are in fact heterogeneous. Thus for our purposes the term may be better defined as 'classes whose members are particularly, or unusually, heterogeneous', and which therefore present special problems for both learners and teacher.

Another definition sometimes applied to such classes is 'mixed-ability'. This term is, I think, misleading. What most teachers understand by it in practice is

302

classes of learners among whom there are marked differences in level of performance in the foreign language. However, the implications of the term 'ability' include not just the immediate observable 'ability to perform' of the learners, but also their 'potential learning ability'; and the former is not likely to be a simple one-to-one result of the latter. Learners' present proficiency may have been influenced by various other factors such as different previous opportunities for learning, better or worse previous teaching, higher or lower motivation. Even if we rephrase the term 'mixed-ability' and say 'mixed proficiency', this still does not cover all aspects of heterogeneity as applied to a class of language learners. Learners are different from one another in all sorts of other ways that affect how they learn and need to be taught.

Question How many ways can you think of in which learners differ from one another in a heterogeneous class, and which are likely to affect the way you teach them? Try making a list, then compare it with that shown in Box 21.1 on page 304.

▶ Unit Two: Problems and advantages

The fact that learners vary in the ways indicated in Box 21.1 within large classes produces various teaching problems. Some of these are listed in Box 21.2 in the form of teacher statements.

Discussion task **Problems**

Looking at the set of problems described in Box 21.2, which seem to you to be the most significant in classes of this type that you know?

BOX 21.2: TEACHING PROBLEMS IN LARGE HETEROGENEOUS CLASSES

1. **Discipline.** 'I have discipline problems in these classes; I find them difficult to control.'
2. **Correcting written assignments.** 'I can't keep up with the marking load.'
3. **Interest.** 'They get bored: I can't find topics and activities that keep them all interested.'
4. **Effective learning for all.** 'I can't make sure they're all learning effectively; the tasks I provide are either too difficult or too easy for many of them.'
5. **Materials.** 'I can't find suitable material: the textbooks are 'homogeneous' – rigidly aimed at one kind of learner, with no options or flexibility.
6. **Individual awareness.** 'I can't get to know and follow the progress of all the individuals in my class: there are too many of them, and they're all so different.'
7. **Participation.** 'I can't activate them all: only a few students – the more proficient and confident ones – seem to respond actively to my questions.'

© *Cambridge University Press 1996*

Try categorizing them into three groups:

1. Crucial: These are problems which worry you and which you definitely need to solve.
2. Fairly important: You would like to be able to deal with these problems, but they are not top priority.
3. Not important, or not relevant to your teaching situation.

You may find there are problems you have come across which are not mentioned here: if so, add and decide how to categorize them.

If you are working in a group, try to come to a consensus; if not, classify the problems for yourself in writing. You may find it interesting to compare your ideas with mine as described below.

Comments on Box 21.2: Problems

In my own situation, the most crucial problems are, in order of importance as I experience them:

4. Effective learning for all
5. Materials
7. Participation
3. Interest
1. Discipline

Important, but slightly less so are the following:

6. Individual awareness
2. Correcting written assignments

The last two I find less problematical in that they are potentially soluble simply by the investment of extra work: in the first case by meeting or corresponding with students outside lessons, in the second by taking more time to go over written work (or by asking the students themselves to help correct each other's work). The 'crucial' problems listed previously seem to me more difficult; and even my best efforts and most careful thought and planning may not result in totally satisfactory solutions.

BOX 21.1: SOME DIFFERENCES BETWEEN LEARNERS IN HETEROGENEOUS CLASSES

language-learning ability	age or maturity
language knowledge	gender
cultural background	personality
learning style	confidence
attitude to the language	motivation
mother tongue	interests
intelligence	independence
world knowledge	self-discipline
learning experience	educational level
knowledge of other languages	

© Cambridge University Press 1996

Advantages

Large heterogeneous classes are seen mostly as problematical; but they have their advantages as well, and some of these can be used to help solve the problems.

Question   What positive aspects of large heterogeneous classes can you think of that might aid teaching? Make a quick list (if you are working with other teachers, pool ideas with them). Then look at my suggestions as shown in Box 21.3; can you add more?

Task   **Matching solutions to problems**

In Box 21.4 are some generalized suggestions for teaching that may go some way towards providing solutions to some of the problems. More specific and practical aspects of some of these suggestions will be explored in following units.

For each of the problems outlined in Box 21.2 try to find one or more ideas in Box 21.4 that might help to solve it. Perhaps note, as you are doing this, which of the advantages of large, heterogeneous classes described in Box 21.3 are exploited. When you have finished: are there any problems left without even partial solutions? If so, can you suggest some solutions of your own?

My own responses to this task follow.

BOX 21.3: ADVANTAGES OF LARGE HETEROGENEOUS CLASSES

1. Such classes provide a much richer pool of human resources than do smaller or less mixed classes. The individuals have between them far more life experience and knowledge, more varied opinions, more interests and ideas – all of which can be used in classroom interaction.
2. There is educational value in the actual contact between very different kinds of people: co-students get to know each other's values, personalities and perhaps cultures, and thereby increase their own knowledge and awareness of others, as well as tolerance and understanding.
3. The fact that the teacher is very much less able to attend to every individual in the class means that in order for the class to function well the students themselves must help by teaching each other and working together: peer-teaching and collaboration are likely to be fairly common, fostering an atmosphere of cooperation.
4. These classes can be seen as very much more challenging and interesting to teach, and provide greater opportunity for creativity, innovation and general professional development.

© Cambridge University Press 1996

Matching solutions to problems: Some possibilities

By each numbered item I have written the letters of the suggested solutions I think are relevant, with a following note of explanation.

BOX 21.4: LARGE HETEROGENEOUS CLASSES: SOME TEACHING SOLUTIONS

a) **Vary your topics, methods, texts:** thus, if one day the material is not of the right level for, ordoes not interest certain members of the class, maybe the next day it will (be).

b) **Make activities interesting:** so that even if the language is not challenging for some of the learners, the content will hold interest and keep everyone participating. (Some ideas on the provision of interest can be found in Module 19: *Learner motivation and interest*, Unit Four.)

c) **Encourage collaboration:** get learners to work cooperatively and peer-teach, so as to maintain engagement with the language material even when you cannot directly interact with every individual yourself.

d) **Individualize:** allow learners choice in what tasks or materials they use and how. (Various ideas on how to do this can be found in Module 16: *Classroom interaction*, Unit Four.)

e) **Personalize:** whenever possible design or adapt tasks in order to allow for different individual responses, based on learners' own experience, opinions or imagination.

f) **Use compulsory plus optional instructions:** tell the class that everyone has to do a certain minimal part of the task, the rest is optional – that is, available to those who understand / can do it / have time / wish to do more. (See Unit Three.)

g) **Use open-ended cues:** invite the class to respond to stimulus tasks or questions that have a range of possible acceptable answers rather than a single right solution. (See Unit Four.)

© Cambridge University Press 1996

---

1. **Discipline:** (a) and (b). Discipline problems are largely caused by boredom and lack of challenge; these can be mitigated by varying tasks and materials and making activities interesting.

2. **Correcting written assignments:** (c). One way of lessening your work load is to enlist the help of the students themselves in correcting and improving each other's work. For some further comment on this see the last section of Module 11: *Teaching writing*, Unit Five.

3. **Interest:** (a), (b), (e) and (g). Obviously relevant suggestions are to make activities interesting and to provide variety; but involving students' own ideas and experiences can also add interest, as can the use of open-ended tasks (see Unit Four).

4. **Effective learning for all:** (d), (f) and (g). In individualized activities students learn at their own pace and sometimes choose their own tasks and materials. The strategy of compulsory plus optional tasks allows learners to decide for themselves what quantity of content and level of challenge to aim for; and open-ended cues also allow a degree of personal choice. All these help to make procedures more flexible and enable the learner to adapt materials and tasks in order to make them maximally effective and useful for him or her.

5. **Materials:** all. Textbook materials very often need to be adapted and supplemented for heterogeneous classes in order to add variation and interest, in order to get more collaboration and participation, and in order to introduce elements of choice and individualization.

6. **Individual awareness:** (c), (d) and (e). While students are engaged in collaborative activity – pair work on a textbook task, for example – you have an opportunity to go from pair to pair listening in and getting to know them; or even to take one or two aside for a brief talk. Periods of individual reading or writing tasks also allow you time for personal interaction. Personalization of student contributions, even within full-class discussion, gives you the chance to hear different students' ideas and to get to know individual personalities.

7. **Participation:** (b), (c), (d) and (g). Interesting stimuli will raise students' motivation to engage in the task. The use of collaborative and individual work drastically increases the number of students who can be actively participating at any one time; this is particularly noticeable in contrast to teacher-led verbal interaction in the full class, where only one student at a time (if any) can make a spoken contribution. Finally, even within teacher-led full-class interaction, learner participation can be raised, relative to teacher talk, by the use of open-ended cues rather than closed-ended ones: each teacher question then stimulates a number of responses.

▶ ## Unit Three: Teaching strategies (1): compulsory + optional

What it is

The 'compulsory + optional' strategy means that the class is given material or a task and told that a certain minimal component of it has to be learned or done by everyone, the rest only by some. The basic attainment requested should be accessible to all, including the slowest; but provision should be made for more, or more advanced, work by those for whom it is appropriate. Thus, everyone should be able to succeed; but the amount actually done to achieve this success will vary from individual to individual. Typically, instructions that introduce 'compulsory + optional' work include phrases like 'do at least', 'if you have time', 'do as much as you can of …'.

This strategy can be applied to the syllabus, practice activities and tests.

Syllabus

The syllabus of a heterogeneous class should define what material every learner is expected to master, and what further items are suggested for learning for the more advanced. In vocabulary lists, for example, compulsory items will be carefully presented, practised and tested, while the optional ones will be taught more casually and checked only in the optional sections of the tests (see below).

Practice activities

In an exercise consisting of, say, ten questions, learners may be told: 'Do at least six; do all ten if you can or have time'. Similarly in a reading activity: 'Read at least half of this passage'; or 'Read as much of the passage as you can in half an hour'; or in writing: 'Write one paragraph (or more) about …' or 'Spend at least forty minutes writing me an account of ...'. As these examples illustrate, different amounts of work may be demanded from different learners simply by defining the time they are to spend on it rather than the number of items, pages or books they are to get through.

Tests

Instead of making all sections of a test compulsory, two or three of the (more difficult) sections may be made optional. Alternatively, the entire test may be made up of sections of gradually increasing difficulty, with the overall instruction: 'Do as much as you can in the time'. Learners who tackle the more difficult optional sections may then be rewarded by bonus marks; or, if you know your students well, they may be told in advance who is expected to do what in order to pass or get full marks.

Problem

The main problem that teachers usually bring up here is: 'How do I get students to work according to their full potential? Given the choice, surely they will opt for the easier 'compulsory' work?'.

The short answer is: no, in my experience they do not. On the contrary: if I have a problem, it is rather that the less advanced students given a 'compulsory + optional' task try to do too much. I am not sure why this is: perhaps partly because they prefer challenge and interest to easiness and boredom; partly from considerations of self-image ('I wish to see myself as the kind of student who does more advanced work'); in any case, usually these motives apparently weigh more heavily than the wish to take easy options.

The most effective way to study this problem and its answer is to try out some form of the compulsory plus optional strategy in class. One such experiment is suggested below; or you may prefer to devise your own.

Experience **Classroom or peer-teaching**

Preliminary note

This may be tried either with a class of students or with a group of colleagues. If the latter, divide them into three groups, each role-playing a different learner level: Group 1 will be of fairly low proficiency, Group 2 intermediate, Group 3 advanced. Tell them each to respond to the listening task according to their allotted roles.

Stage 1

Choose a situation or institution you know quite a lot about, or an experience you remember vividly, and be ready to describe it to the class. Make sure that you will be using some quite easy language and some fairly advanced.

Stage 2

Inform the class that they are going to do a listening comprehension activity: they will hear something from you (tell them roughly what it is about) and are asked to find out and write down in note form at least three facts they have found out about the topic. Those who can should note down more than three – as many as they can.

Stage 3

Deliver your description at normal speaking speed.

Stage 4

Check results. Have all the students succeeded in getting at least three facts? Did the more advanced ones accept the challenge and write more?

▶ Unit Four: Teaching strategies (2): open-ending

'Open-ending' means the provision of cues or learning tasks which do not have single predetermined 'right' answers, but a potentially unlimited number of acceptable responses. See Box 21.5 for illustrations of a closed-ended versus open-ended exercise on the present simple tense.

BOX 21.5: CLOSED- AND OPEN-ENDED EXERCISES

Closed-ended

Choose the most acceptable alternative:

A good teacher _____ to class on time.

a) come b) is coming c) comes d) came

Acceptable learner response: A good teacher comes to class on time.

Open-ended

A good teacher comes to class on time. Can you suggest other things a good teacher does?

Acceptable learner responses: A good teacher makes the lessons interesting, a good teacher smiles, a good teacher explains well, etc.

© *Cambridge University Press 1996*

Closed-ended cues are by their very nature homogeneous. They address, and provide valuable learning for, a limited range of learners: those who have just about mastered the relevant language, can rehearse it successfully given a cue like this, and for whom such rehearsal gives useful practice. Learners who are at a lower level and have not yet mastered the language will either not respond at all, or are quite likely to get the answer wrong; the result may be to clarify what they need to work on in the future, but they will have got no useful practice as such. The more advanced learners are also neglected: the item is easy and boring, provides them with no opportunity to show what they can do or engage with language of an appropriate level.

Open-ended cues, on the other hand, provide opportunities for response at various levels. The more advanced learners can make up more sophisticated and longer answers (as in the first example in Box 21.5), the less advanced can listen to other learners' responses and use them as models before volunteering simpler ideas of their own (such as 'A good teacher smiles'). Moreover, even a basic exercise like this allows for expression of personal experience and opinion. Finally, the increase in number of learner responses to any one teacher cue means an increase in the amount of learner talk relative to teacher talk. This means there will be a significant rise in the proportion of learners in a large class who can make active contributions to the lesson.

Task ### 'Open-ending' closed-ended exercises

In Box 21.6 is a set of conventional textbook exercises, obviously intended to be 'closed-ended'. They can, however, be adapted during classroom work in order to transform them into 'open-ended' ones. Note down your own ideas on how to do this, and/or exchange ideas with colleagues, before reading on to the *Suggestions* section following.

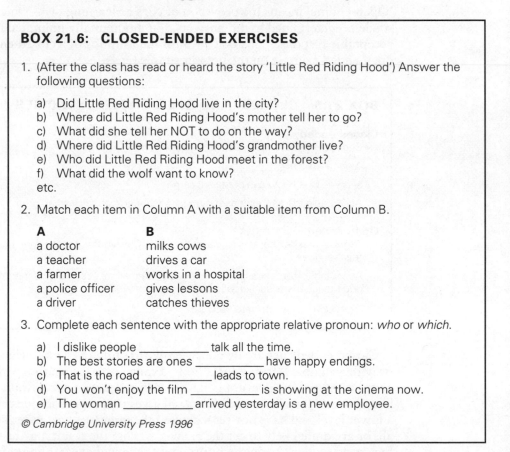

BOX 21.6: CLOSED-ENDED EXERCISES

1. (After the class has read or heard the story 'Little Red Riding Hood') Answer the following questions:

   a) Did Little Red Riding Hood live in the city?
   b) Where did Little Red Riding Hood's mother tell her to go?
   c) What did she tell her NOT to do on the way?
   d) Where did Little Red Riding Hood's grandmother live?
   e) Who did Little Red Riding Hood meet in the forest?
   f) What did the wolf want to know?
   etc.

2. Match each item in Column A with a suitable item from Column B.

A	B
a doctor	milks cows
a teacher	drives a car
a farmer	works in a hospital
a police officer	gives lessons
a driver	catches thieves

3. Complete each sentence with the appropriate relative pronoun: *who* or *which*.

   a) I dislike people _____ talk all the time.
   b) The best stories are ones _____ have happy endings.
   c) That is the road _____ leads to town.
   d) You won't enjoy the film _____ is showing at the cinema now.
   e) The woman _____ arrived yesterday is a new employee.

   © Cambridge University Press 1996

Suggestions

1. Questions

This is a set of conventional comprehension questions on a reading or listening text, which are usually presented within an 'IRF' classroom interaction pattern (teacher Initiative, learner Response, teacher Feedback; see Module 16: *Classroom interaction*).

A very simple way to make this activity more heterogeneous without actually changing the text of the questions is to invite students to choose which they want to answer first, instead of using the conventional 1, 2, 3 … order. In this way individual students can immediately select questions which they are sure they know the answers to, or consider more interesting. This can be done, of course, with any exercise based on a list of questions, and has the immediate effect of speeding up and increasing participation.

Other strategies: invite students to delete questions they do not think interesting, to add further ones they can think of, or to suggest totally 'way-out' answers and thereby rewrite the original story.

2. Matching

Students may be told that they may combine any item from Column A with any item from Column B provided they can justify it. The original obvious combinations are still available for less confident or slower students, but there is also the possibility of suggesting that, for example, a farmer listens to lectures (in order to learn more about farming), or a police officer gives lessons (on road safety or the functions of the police force). A useful side-benefit of this way of doing the exercise, in this particular example, is the breaking of the stereotypes implicit in the original!

Another useful option is to delete either Column A or Column B and ask students to suggest their own matching subjects or predicates.

3. Slot-filling

Delete, or tell students to ignore, the entire second part of each sentence and invite them to suggest a variety of possible endings. You may wish to direct them explicitly to use the target items in doing so; otherwise answers may include sentences like 'You won't enjoy the film because it's boring'.

The same strategy – partial deletion of individual items – works well with many types of textbook exercises, and results in a more interesting, as well as more heterogeneous, activity.

It is certainly not recommended here that activities done with large heterogeneous classes should always be open-ended; but certainly the introduction of such procedures can increase learning and interest. Note, however, that the exercises in textbooks you use are likely to be based mainly on closed-ended items.

Follow-up task Look at a textbook commonly used in your own teaching context. Is the statement at the end of the previous paragraph true of it? If so, select two or three closed-ended exercises and see if you can suggest ways of 'open-ending' them. Look also for other ideas for rendering them more appropriate and productive for use in large heterogeneous classes (you may find it helpful to refer to the suggestions in Box 21.4).

▷ # Unit Five: Designing your own activities

The two previous units dealt mainly with the adaptation of conventional materials for use in large heterogeneous classes. This one suggests a set of teacher-initiated activities that may be used to supplement published materials. These are fairly clearly based on principles that have already been discussed in previous units, but the emphasis here is on the implementation of these principles in practical techniques.

Five 'families' of techniques are presented here: *Brainstorm, Recall and share, Doing your own thing, Fluid pairs, Passing it round*. As you read, consider which of the activities might work well in a class you teach. They are summarized in a 'mind map' in Box 21.7.

Brainstorm

This activity consists of simple pooling of ideas: as many contributions are made as quickly as possible by as many participants as possible; ideas may or may not be written down. No time is spent on critical discussion of contributions; transitions from one to the next are swift.

The brisk pace of brainstorms ensures maximum participation in the time available; and the open nature of the task means that contributions of vastly differing level and content will be acceptable.

Example 1: Say things about a picture
Students are invited to say anything they like about a publicly displayed picture: they may be asked to aim for a total of twenty/thirty/forty utterances; or every student may have to supply at least one idea; or they may be given a time limit. The same can then be done in groups, which drastically raises the number of students who can participate. (See Box 9.4, Activity 1.)

Example 2: How many things can you think of that are ...?
Again this may be done in full-class or in small groups. The students are given a definition such as 'made of wood', 'square', 'sweet', 'worked by electricity', and have to find (through discussion in groups, or through individual writing, or by a combination of the two) as many things as they can that fit it.

Recall and share

The class is exposed to some kind of material, written, spoken or graphic – for example, a set of words or phrases. The material is then withdrawn, and students are asked to write down as much as they can remember of it. Subsequently they come together in twos or threes to share results. Finally, the teacher may re-present the original material or initiate a pooling of results.

Collaboration is seen as worthwhile if a group can get better results than an individual: and here this is obviously true. However advanced (or not) the individual members of a group are, their pooled recalling is almost inevitably going to be superior to that of any single one of them. This is a good opportunity for cooperation and peer-teaching: a review of material for all, using learner interaction rather than teacher direction.

Example 1: Spelling

The teacher writes ten or fifteen words on the board that have been recently learnt or are difficult to spell. After a minute or so the words are erased, and students challenged to recall and write them down correctly. They then come together to add to and correct each other's answers; the result is presented as a group achievement.

Example 2: What have people said?

In order to practise forms of indirect speech, students are invited to write down all the utterances they can remember that have been said since the beginning of the lesson. In pairs or small groups they then pool their utterances and rephrase them in indirect speech.

Doing your own thing

In these activities each student writes or says a totally individual response to a stimulus. They may share responses with each other later for the sake of interest or to get to know each other's ideas, but there is no attempt to reach a common result or consensus. Responses may be simple or sophisticated, in elementary or advanced language: the main objective is to get individuals to express their own ideas in their own way, without feeling the need to conform to a general norm.

Example 1: Five-minute writing storms

A topic is given to the class ('A good friend', 'A surprise I had', 'A film worth seeing') and the students are given five minutes to write down a paragraph or two about it. They may then, if they are willing, read out their texts to each other, or have the teacher read them out. Later, the texts may be rewritten as formal essays, or used as a basis for discussion.

Example 2: Metaphors

The class is given a set of metaphors for a familiar experience or function, and each student is asked to select the one that seems to them most appropriate. For example, they might be given the subject 'home' and the metaphors: a pillar, a bed, a springboard, a garden, a bank account, a chain. They then explain to each other why they chose what they did, perhaps find others who chose the same and compare reasons. (For another example, see Box 15.1.)

Fluid pairs

This is another way to activate the members of a large class simultaneously. They are given a task which involves short exchanges with as many other members of the class as they can find: a survey of opinions, for example. The students move around the class, finding out the desired information from one peer before moving on to another.

Example 1: Finding twins

Students fill in forms answering certain questions about themselves: for example, their favourite colour, singer, television programme, leisure-time activity. They then try to find as many other students as they can who have the same answers as they do to each question, and note names. At the end the class discusses conclusions that can be drawn about the most popular colours etc.

Example 2: Marketplace
Each student gets three slips of paper; on each of these they write a sentence expressing their opinion on a given topic (possibly a locally controversial one), and their name. They then find a partner, and present their opinions. If the partner identifies with the opinion, they may 'buy' it: sign their name to it, and take it. If not, it remains with its original owner. When the pair have decided what to buy, or not, of each other's 'wares' they part and each finds someone else with whom to repeat the process. The more popular opinions change hands rapidly and amass signatures; the minority ones move more slowly. (*Acknowledgement*: I learned this activity from Tessa Woodward.)

Passing it round

This is also a collaborative activity, but it involves reading and writing and is done quietly. Each student (or pair of students) writes something on a large piece of paper and passes it on to their neighbour(s) who adds a further word or sentence, and so on. The game 'Consequences', if you know it, is one well-known entertaining example; but on the whole I prefer versions that leave the paper open all the time so that each participant has plenty to read as well as a contribution to write.

Example 1: Collaborative composition
A topic is given, and each student writes a brief sentence or phrase at the top of their paper about it: the first ideas or associations that occur to them. They then pass it on; the next student reads what is written, responds to it or continues it on a new line, and passes it on. And so on, until there are about ten contributions on each page. Some of the results may be read out by volunteers, or displayed on the wall.

Example 2: Passive possibilities
Each pair of students is given a large piece of paper with a subject at the centre: 'a baby', for example, or 'money', 'paper', 'a pencil'. Around this subject they write all the things they can think of that *are done* with it: 'a baby', for example, *is washed*, *is played with*, *is loved*. After not more than a minute, at a signal from the teacher, the paper is passed on, and the next pair have a minute to read what is written and try to add further ideas.

Application   Choose one or two of the activities described above, and try them out, either with other teachers or, if possible, in a large heterogeneous class of language learners. Afterwards consider and/or discuss with colleagues the following questions:

- How easy was the activity to prepare and administer?
- How far were learners engaging with the language at a level appropriate to them, and learning well?
- How far did the procedure succeed in activating all or most of the learners in language use?

314

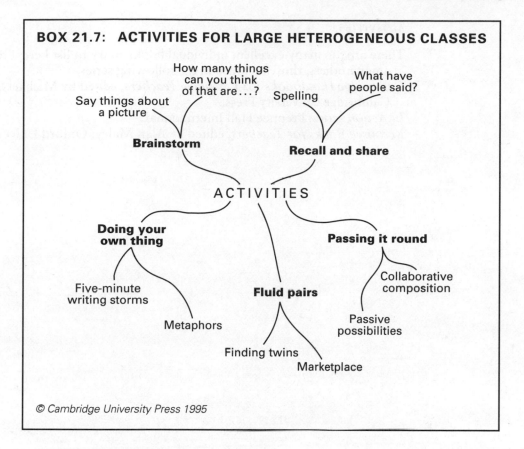

BOX 21.7: ACTIVITIES FOR LARGE HETEROGENEOUS CLASSES

How many things can you think of that are...?

Say things about a picture

Spelling

What have people said?

Brainstorm

Recall and share

A C T I V I T I E S

Doing your own thing

Passing it round

Five-minute writing storms

Collaborative composition

Metaphors

Fluid pairs

Passive possibilities

Finding twins

Marketplace

© *Cambridge University Press 1995*

– How interested or motivated did the participants seem?
– Were there any problems of organization or control?

There is a large number of excellent teacher's handbooks on the market containing descriptions of activities many of which are suitable for large heterogeneous classes. Some series you might look at are noted at the end of *Further reading* below.

Further reading

BACKGROUND AND TEACHER'S HANDBOOKS

Coleman, H. *et al.* (1989) *Language Learning in Large Classes Research Project*, Leeds: Leeds and Lancaster Universities.
(A series of booklets, all project reports on various aspects of learning and teaching languages in large classes)
Hadfield, J. (1992) *Classroom Dynamics*, Oxford: Oxford University Press.
(Ideas for mixed-skills activity to foster good relationships, awareness of others, group solidarity)
Prodromou, L. (1992b) *Mixed Ability Classes*, London: Macmillan.
(Thought-provoking and readable; practically-oriented with suggestions for activities and tasks to stimulate teacher thinking and learning)

ACTIVITIES

There are too many excellent individual books to try to list here: I recommend, among others, those included in the following series.

Cambridge Handbooks for Language Teachers, edited by Michael Swan: Cambridge University Press.

In Action series: Prentice Hall International.

Resource Books for Teachers, edited by Alan Maley: Oxford University Press.

It has been said that teachers who have been teaching for twenty years may be divided into two categories: those with twenty years' experience and those with one year's experience repeated twenty times.

In other words, sheer time on the job does not ensure fruitful experience and professional progress. Successful teachers are those who continue to develop throughout their professional lives: the completion of a pre-service course and initial qualification are only the beginning. A pre-service course should not only enable you to start teaching with competence and confidence: it should also give you the tools and understanding for further development.

Part VII of this book, which consists of only one module, addresses teachers at any stage of their career. It looks at various aspects of continuing professional development, and suggests practical ways in which you may further your own.

Module 22: And beyond

▷ ## Unit One: Teacher development: practice, reflection, sharing

This unit discusses the nature and importance of teacher development and then looks at ways you can progress professionally in the course of a full teaching schedule: through private reflection and interaction with colleagues.

Development for survival and progress

A teacher can and should advance in professional expertise and knowledge throughout his or her career, and such advances do not depend on formal courses or external input. You have within your own teaching routine the main tools for personal progress: your own experience and your reflections on it, interaction with other teachers in your institution. Teacher development takes place when teachers, working as individuals or in a group, consciously take advantage of such resources to forward their own professional learning.

Ongoing teacher development is important not only for your own sense of progress and professional advancement; in some situations it may even make a crucial difference between survival and dropping out.

The first year of teaching, for example, can be very stressful. This is true particularly, though not only, of those teaching large heterogeneous classes of children or adolescents in schools. Difficult first years cause some new teachers to leave the profession; and even many of those who remain find their original confidence and optimism significantly, if temporarily, undermined. (My own experience of this is described in the Notes.)

There is also a problem of professional survival in later years of one's career, caused by the phenomenon known as 'burn-out'. This is not so much a feeling of failure as one of disillusionment, boredom, loss of momentum. Burn-out usually comes on gradually, although it may be accelerated by personal crises such as family or financial problems. Sometimes burn-out may be ended only by retirement or a change of profession, but it may also be prevented or cured by deliberate action on the part of the teacher.

Constant teacher development and progress can forestall or solve problems caused by both first-year stress and later burn-out. More positively, it is a necessary contributor to your success and satisfaction in professional work today, and to your career in the future as teacher and/or in other allied professions: materials writer, trainer, author, researcher.

318

Personal reflection

The first and most important basis for professional progress is simply your own reflection on daily classroom events. Very often this reflection is quite spontaneous and informal, and happens without any conscious intention on your part. Travelling to and from the institution where you teach, or at other odd moments when you have nothing particular to occupy your mind, things that happened in the classroom come to mind and you start puzzling about what to do about a problem, work out why something was successful, rethink a plan in the light of the last lesson. This sort of spontaneous reflection is the necessary basis and jump-off point for further development: it is the hallmark of the conscientious professional.

Such reflection, however, can help you only up to a certain point, for two main reasons.

1. It is not organized

Your thinking in situations like those described above is basically undisciplined. This is to some extent an advantage, as it allows you to give full rein to your imagination and creativity and to use all your personal knowledge, but sooner or later the disadvantages become apparent. You find your thoughts are easily diverted into less productive channels (irritation at an uncooperative student or colleague, for example); you may not have available all the information you need to draw valid conclusions; and later, when you wish to do so, you may not remember what the original reflections were!

In order to get over these problems you will find it necessary at some stage to write something down. This may be in the form of a brief note on a piece of paper, a reminder to yourself when you come to prepare the next lesson. For many teachers, systematic journal-writing is even more productive: entries are made in a separate notebook at regular intervals, recording things that have happened or that are planned and that you wish to remember, noting thoughts or ideas. Such journals can be reread later to contribute to further reflection and learning.

One advantage of writing is that putting things into words forces you to work out exactly what you mean, whereas abstract thinking does not. Many people – myself included – only discover what they really think when they have to express it in writing. In a sense, writing *is* thinking: but thinking that must be disciplined and productive.

Application If you have not done it before, try writing down your thoughts about lessons you have taught or will teach, say twice or three times a week. This can be in a rough scrawl – it does not matter if it is illegible to anyone else! You can use a separate notebook (journal), or make brief notes at the bottom of your lesson plans. After a while, reread your notes. Do you find them interesting? Useful as reminders? Thought-provoking?

2. It is solitary

Personal reflection enables you to draw on your own experience only. The latter is indeed the basic and primary source of professional learning, but there comes a point when it is not enough. Even the most brilliant and creative of us can learn from others things we could not learn on our own. There are, for example, some problems which we can puzzle at for hours without finding a solution, but which could be solved in a moment by the experience or different thinking of a colleague. Also, when we find interesting solutions or have flashes of insight or inspiration of our own, it is natural to wish to share them with a fellow-teacher: why keep them to ourselves?

This brings me on to the next section.

Sharing with a colleague

Informal discussions with a colleague with whom you feel at ease can contribute a lot to your own development, as well as boosting morale. What you wish to share may be negative or positive: on the one hand you may wish to find a solution to a problem, confide a failure, get an idea as to how to teach something; on the other, you may wish to tell someone about an original solution you have found to an old problem, share your delight at a success, discuss a new teaching idea you have had.

1. Sharing problems

There is, unfortunately, a sense of shame or inhibition, a fear of losing face, that sometimes prevents some teachers from admitting the existence of teaching problems to others; but once this is overcome, the results are usually rewarding. Colleagues are unlikely to exploit your frank description of problems or failures in order to reproach or 'crow'. They are far more likely to be sympathetic, try to stop you worrying so much, recall similar incidents from their own experience, suggest solutions. The awareness that other people have the same problems is perhaps the major comfort here, and has the effect of encouraging you to look for your own solutions. At the same time you may very well find that you are providing a similar service to your colleague: problem-sharing can contribute to encouragement and progress all round, it is not a uni-directional process.

2. Successes

There are difficulties about sharing successes as well!

In some institutions there is a feeling of rivalry between teachers which stops them revealing professional 'secrets' to one another for fear of being 'overtaken' in some kind of professional race. Where this exists it will sooner or later be to the detriment of the entire staff: everyone can gain by learning from everyone else; and everyone loses if they cannot do so.

A more delicate personal problem here is the natural reluctance some people feel about 'boasting': if I tell my friend about something really good I did, won't they feel I'm conceited and showing off? No, they will not, if your goal in telling them is frankly stated, and they are given the choice whether to listen or not: 'I had a marvellous experience today, I've got to tell someone about it, have you got time to listen?'; or 'You remember that problem we were talking about the other day? I think I have an idea about how to solve it – can we find time to talk?'.

Meetings with a colleague may take the form of spontaneous, informal chats; or you may find it helpful to structure your interaction consciously: have a look at Edge (1991) and Lansley (1994) for some possible guidelines.

Question   Can you recall informally sharing problems with a colleague? What was it like, and what were its results?

In-house staff meetings

Meetings of groups of teachers in the same institution can also provide a forum for sharing reflections, problems and successes. In this case, the meeting may need to be more formally structured, to make sure everyone participates and benefits. Some possible formats are the following.

1. Decision-making

A problem is brought to the meeting that may demand some specific action, innovation or change in policy. For example, teachers may feel assessment procedures are inadequate, or there may be a proposal to buy new materials. Participants discuss the problem in order to achieve consensus on the solution. The explicit objective here, of course, is functional rather than for the sake of participants' learning; nevertheless, the discussion must involve issues that have to do with professional knowledge and action, and therefore is likely to contribute indirectly to teacher development.

2. Individual presentation

One of the members of staff begins the meeting by making a presentation: this may be a problem they have had, a new teaching idea, a thought-provoking experience, something they have read. The presenter should prepare the session in advance, including making enough copies of any necessary materials. The presentation is followed by open discussion.

3. May we recommend...?

In turn, each teacher suggests a teaching idea they have used recently and describes how it went. Contributions have to be kept fairly short in order to enable everyone to participate. Discussion of each idea is therefore limited; but if one particular idea is seen as deserving further discussion, it might be used as a basis for a later 'Individual presentation' session as described above.

4. Teacher training or development sessions

The staff decide together on a topic connected with teaching which they would like to study. One of the members of staff initiates a session on this topic based on a teacher-training or teacher-development activity: one of the units in this book, for example. There is no 'trainer', though the initiating participant may be responsible for making copies of necessary handouts and act as discussion leader.

   Such sessions work best if there is a set time-slot set aside for them during the week, and if members of staff take turns preparing the activity which will function as their basis. Further ideas for teacher development activities may be found in Parrott (1993) and Woodward (1992).

Questions   Does your institution hold regular staff meetings? If so, how are they organized: are they only for decision-making, or do they also include any of the other kinds of sessions suggested above?

▷ # Unit Two: Teacher appraisal

Few institutions have systematic teacher-appraisal systems; and where these do exist, they are very often for hiring-and-firing purposes rather than to assist professional improvement and learning. The effect may therefore be stressful and demoralizing rather than helpful.

However, for your own benefit it is important to carry out some periodic appraisal of your teaching, on the principle that you cannot move ahead without having a fairly clear idea of where you are now. Obvious sources of feedback on your teaching are colleagues, your own students – and yourself.

Feedback from colleagues

Asking a colleague to come in and observe a lesson of yours and give you feedback may present difficulties: most of us feel a little uncomfortable about being observed teaching, and cannot function naturally when we know an observer is in the room; and it takes some courage deliberately to expose yourself to criticism in this way. Moreover, you may feel reluctant to impose on (probably hardworking) fellow teachers. One possibility is to make a mutual arrangement with a like-minded colleague: 'I'll observe your lesson, you observe mine, and we'll share feedback.'

The observer should make notes during the lesson: and it may help if they have an observation sheet to fill in. This may be fairly open: for example, the sheet shown in Box 22.1.1 (which is the one I myself usually use) simply asks for the events, their timing and any comments or questions that occur to the observer as the lesson goes on. A more detailed sheet may relate to particular aspects of the lesson, the learners, the language, your own behaviour. See, for example, the sheet shown in Box 22.1.2 which relates to learner activity. For many other suggestions for observation tasks, see Wajnryb (1992).

BOX 22.1.1: OBSERVATION SHEET 1

Time	Events	Comments/Questions

© Cambridge University Press 1995

OBSERVATION SHEET 2

What learners do	What this involves	Teacher's purpose	Comment

(Based on Ruth Wajnryb, *Classroom Observation Tasks*, Cambridge University Press, 1992, p. 35)

© *Cambridge University Press 1995*

Student feedback

It is relatively unusual for teachers to ask their students for feedback on their teaching; perhaps because of a fear of undermining their (the teachers') authority or of losing face. This is a pity. Students are an excellent source of feedback on your teaching: arguably the best. Their information is based on a whole series of lessons rather than on isolated examples, and they usually have a fairly clear idea of how well they are learning and why. Moreover, they appreciate being consulted, usually make serious efforts to give helpful feedback; and my experience is that the process tends to enhance rather than damage teacher–student relationships. (A useful spin-off is the interesting and communicative language use!)

Applications to students should be phrased so as to direct their appraisal towards themselves as well as to you, and towards positive suggestions rather than negative criticisms. A structured questionnaire is one possibility (see an example in Box 22.2): this way you can be sure that students will respond to the questions you are interested in. Another less structured method, which I use with more advanced or older classes, is to write the students a letter, giving your own feedback to them and your opinion about how the course is going, and asking for their responses and suggestions in the form of an answering letter.

Either way, the results are not always clearcut on all issues, as there may be disagreement due to differing student personalities and needs, and some responses may be confusing or unhelpful. Nevertheless, I have found when trying this myself that there is usually enough consensus on major items to provide useful and constructive feedback that I can use immediately to inform and improve my teaching.

Self-appraisal

Personal self-appraisal should also be done in writing. Unrecorded reflection, as noted in the previous unit, allows you to digress, or to indulge disproportionately

---

BOX 22.2: STUDENT FEEDBACK SHEET ON TEACHING

Name _____ Class _____

1. On the whole I feel I am learning very well / fairly well / don't know / not very well / badly

2. I find the lessons interesting / moderately interesting / boring

3. Things I would like to do MORE in our course:
   pronunciation practice / vocabulary / grammar / listening / speaking / reading / writing / literature / homework / group or pair work / individual work
   Other (say what):

4. Things I would like to do LESS in our course:
   pronunciation practice / vocabulary / grammar / listening / speaking / reading / writing / literature / homework / group or pair work / individual work
   Other (say what):

5. In order to get the most out of the course, I need to try to . . .

6. In order to make the course better, my suggestions to my teacher are . . .

7. Anything else:

© Cambridge University Press 1996

---

in whatever is currently occupying your mind, whereas writing forces you to stick to the topic in hand, and to be concise and reasonably ordered and balanced in your thinking. One simple system is to divide a page into two columns, headed 'problems' and 'successes', to fill in appropriate items as completely and honestly as you can, and then go on to consider conclusions.

Application   If you are currently teaching, try out at least two of the three methods of appraisal suggested above. Did you find the results helpful?

▷ Unit Three: Advancing further (1): intake

The first two units dealt with some ideas for professional progress and development within the routine of a full teaching schedule. These, however, can advance you only up to a point: sooner or later you will be looking for ways to learn more, to broaden your professional knowledge and thinking outside the immediate resources of your own institution. What are the possibilities?

Reading

If your circumstances do not allow you to attend formal courses of study, this does not mean that you cannot advance your own learning beyond that afforded by interaction with people within your own institution. The main source of such further learning is simply reading.

Most institutions have a basic library of professional literature and this is where you will probably start. When choosing what to read, it is a good idea first to ask colleagues what books they have found interesting and useful. Another source of recommendations is this book: suggestions for reading on specific topics are appended to each module; and some suggestions for reading on language teaching and learning in general can be found at the end of this one. A third source of ideas is simply a 'browse' through the relevant sections of a library or bookshop until you find a book or journal that attracts you.

Journals are an excellent and convenient source of reading material: their articles are relatively short and easier to cope with than a full book, and recent issues will have up-to-date news and ideas; also, the book reviews and the bibliographies that are attached to most articles will give you ideas for further reading.

Reading is also a necessary accompaniment to formal study, and hopefully continues after it. It may be, for some, a substitute for courses and conferences – but the converse is not true: courses and conferences are no substitute for reading.

Task   Ask some colleagues what book(s) have had most influence on their professional thinking, or proved most useful for their teaching. (They might find it interesting to hear your own answers to the same question.)

University study

If you have the opportunity, it is of course very worthwhile taking further courses of study. This usually means a degree: an academic course at a university in foreign language teaching or one of the associated subjects: pure or applied linguistics, the various branches of education, psychology or sociology. The attraction of such studies is not only the satisfaction of the learning itself and its contribution to your professional expertise, but also the usually internationally recognized qualification, with its associated prestige and aid to promotion.

An academic course provides a valuable opportunity to take a step back from the demands of everyday practice, reflect quietly on what you do, and rethink your own principles and practice in the light of other people's theories and research. But such rethinking works both ways: you will find that you need to approach academic theories and research cautiously and critically, checking the ideas you are learning against your own experience and if possible applying and testing them in practice.

You may, however, find that you wish to abandon 'practical' considerations, and engage in reading, research and theorizing mainly for the sake of the sheer intellectual satisfaction of it. This is, of course, a legitimate and worthwhile pursuit, but it needs to be distinguished from the 'here-and-now' orientation of the professional. If you find research- and theory-oriented learning attractive, you may wish eventually to leave teaching and move over to academic work full-time!

Conferences and in-service courses

More exciting in many ways than formal courses are the conferences that are being organized with increasing frequency for foreign language (particularly English) teachers in many countries. These, though sometimes expensive to attend, offer a rich selection of lectures, workshops, seminars, panel discussions and so on from which you may be able to update yourself on the latest research and controversies, learn new techniques and methods, become acquainted with the latest published materials in your field and meet other professionals.

The strength of conferences – the sheer wealth and variety of sessions and materials available to participants – is also, however, their weakness. Usually the schedule is based on a number of parallel sessions held at any one time, so you can attend only a small proportion of them; and they vary widely in level and effectiveness as well as in topic and orientation. What you select from the 'menu' of sessions may or may not satisfy you; it is unlikely that you will find everything worthwhile; in fact, if each day you feel that one or two of the events you attended were of real value to you, you are doing well!

Conferences cannot supply the systematic coverage of topics that is provided by formal courses, but among the large number of semi-random encounters at conferences you may well come across new publications or ideas which, immediately or eventually, 'spark off' inspirations or innovations of your own. Their other major advantage, of course, is the opportunities they provide for meeting practitioners from other places, exchanging ideas and learning about each other's problems and solutions. Arguably at least as much interesting learning takes place between sessions as during them!

Short in-service courses are in a sense 'mini-conferences', also offering useful learning and contact with other teachers. They can very often be more relevant to your own needs, as they are organized locally – in your country, district or even institution.

Application   **Find out what national or international organizations there are for the teaching of your target language, which holds conferences in your country or not too far away! For teachers of English in Europe, for example, IATEFL (the International Association of Teachers of English as a Foreign Language) holds big annual conferences as well as smaller meetings for Special Interest Groups.**

Question   **Have you attended at least one professional conference or in-service course? If so, how much do you feel the experience contributed to you as a professional, and how? If feasible, compare your experiences with those of a colleague.**

▷ Unit Four: Advancing further (2): output

Units One and Two discussed professional development through reflection, discussion and learning. This unit takes the concept of 'teacher development' one step further, and suggests ways in which you yourself can make a contribution to the field through sharing your own ideas, innovations or research with others.

Techniques and methods

Very often the first step in this direction for practising teachers is the sharing of a practical classroom innovation: a technique, a bit of material, an idea that worked. You describe it to a colleague and he or she is enthusiastic: why not let other teachers benefit as well? Organizers of conferences – particularly of national rather than international ones – are always on the lookout for practising teachers with new ideas and will welcome your contribution. Moreover, participants often prefer this type of session to the more prestigious lectures given by international 'names'. Usually such sessions are most effective if built round a workshop format: a clear explanation backed up by visual materials, followed by an experiential component (such as trying out an example of whatever it is) and plenty of opportunity for the audience to participate and discuss.

The same innovation can reach a wider audience if written out as an article. If your country or area has its own foreign language teaching journals, start with these; or you may try ones with a more international circulation. Keep your article short, and make sure ideas are clearly expressed in straightforward 'lay' language and illustrated by practical examples. It is a good idea to ask colleagues to read through your article and make comments before finalizing it and sending it off: often other people find errors or obscurities which you may not have noticed.

Do not be discouraged if your first article is not accepted: take note of any constructive criticisms, and keep trying.

Materials writing

Another way of contributing to the profession is by writing foreign language teaching/learning materials. This often means coursebooks, but not always. Today there is a need – and a market – for a wide range of supplementary materials: books devoted to one aspect of language learning, such as listening, or reading, or grammar; theme-based 'enrichment' booklets; simplified readers; computer software; visual materials; audio cassettes; videos; teacher's handbooks suggesting ideas for classroom techniques. The best materials are undoubtedly those written by authors who are themselves practising teachers, or have had extensive teaching experience.

The way in to this kind of writing is, again, producing and publishing material for a local market: your own institution, your own region or country. Publishers are constantly looking for new authors with teaching experience and interesting and original ideas, but they do demand also, obviously, a high standard of good, clear and organized writing. Do not be discouraged if your first submission is sent back. If there are constructive criticisms, implement them; if not, ask colleagues for comments, rewrite and try again!

Classroom research

The term 'research' sounds a bit intimidating, but it need not necessarily be so. The term may be defined, after Stenhouse, as 'systematic, self-critical enquiry' (in Rudduck and Hopkins, 1985: 8); as such, it does not have to be based on complicated statistics or lengthy, detailed observation or experiment; nor do its results necessarily have to claim wide application. It does, however, have to be disciplined and rigorous, applying objective, though not necessarily quantitative, criteria; and it has to state clearly its own limitations of context. Some simple small-scale research projects are often an integral part of pre- or in-service training: there are plenty of examples (usually labelled 'Inquiry' or 'Experiment') in the present book.

Research on foreign language teaching and learning does not need to be the monopoly of the academic establishment; as in medicine, any practitioner has the right – perhaps even duty – to embark on research in his or her field. However, few practitioners have the know-how, the time or the money to embark on the more ambitious research enterprises that academics can: we are usually limited to more small-scale projects, based on classrooms and resources readily available to us. Our research is therefore nearly always context-specific and of limited generalizability. Nevertheless, provided this is frankly stated, our results can be of interest and real value both to fellow-professionals working in other contexts and to professional researchers. A bit of research on your classroom may spark off an examination of similar topics in mine or someone else's, stimulate new thinking, lead to significant innovation or further research.

One model that has been suggested as feasible for practising teachers is that known as 'action research': research carried out by teachers on phenomena in their own classrooms.

Action research

According to one convention, action research is meant primarily to improve the teacher-researcher's own teaching. It is based on a cycle of investigation, action and re-investigation, as shown in Box 22.3, and is usually done by two or more collaborating teachers.

For example, a teacher may be wondering whether it is worth dividing a class into groups for oral work in spite of the noise and widespread use of the mother tongue. A colleague might be asked to observe the activity of two or three specific students in group work and in class discussion, and note how many foreign language utterances were produced and attended to in each case for a similar period of time. As a result the teacher might decide to cut down or increase the use of group work. If the latter, then the next problem would be how to minimize mother-tongue use.

The main weakness of this version of action research, in my opinion, is that it does not include publication. Stenhouse (in Rudduck and Hopkins, 1985: 56–9) insists that publication is essential, in order that the results of teacher research may benefit other teachers. It is necessary also in order to submit the resulting

> **BOX 22.3: THE ACTION RESEARCH CYCLE**
>
> 1. A problem is identified.
> 2. Relevant data are gathered and recorded.
> 3. Practical action is suggested that might solve the problem.
> 4. A plan of action is designed.
> 5. The plan is implemented.
> 6. Results are monitored and recorded.
> 7. If the original problem has been solved, the researchers may begin work on another; if not, the original problem is redefined and the cycle is repeated.
>
> © *Cambridge University Press 1996*

hypotheses to criticism: public discussion, or testing through further research. The appropriate forum for publication may be simply an informal presentation to colleagues in the same institution or area, or a talk at a conference or an article in a professional journal.

Another weakness is that this version of action research is based almost exclusively on observation of one's own classes as the source of data. Other classes, surveys, interviews and so on can also provide interesting and relevant information, although these may involve a greater investment of time and work, as will background reading of the relevant literature.

How much effort you can afford to put into your research will depend of course on your own circumstances and time or money resources. But the point I am trying to make here is that classroom research can and should be done by teachers: the results are valuable not only for your own learning and development but also because they can contribute to the advancement of professional knowledge as a whole.

For more information on different types of research see under *Further reading*: in particular Cohen and Manion (1980) for an overview of educational research, and Edge and Richards (1993) for recent developments in foreign language classroom research.

Application   Plan and carry out a limited research project of your own. Most of the modules in this book include at least one inquiry-oriented task: leaf through for some ideas or devise your own. When you have finished, share your results with colleagues.

Notes

First year

My recollections of my first year of teaching English as a foreign language are on the whole negative. There were, it is true, some positive aspects: an end-of-term play, for example, that children and parents enjoyed; the awareness that the children were progressing. But my main memories are of investing an enormous amount of work in preparing lessons and materials, much of which was in the event wasted; horrific discipline problems; feelings of disappointment and humiliation.

The outstanding event which helped me was at the end of my first year, when I went to the 'homeroom' teacher of one of the classes I had been teaching and told him I thought I was unsuited to be a teacher and wished to leave. He told me to think less about my own feelings and to look at the students: to try to assess as objectively as I could what **they** had acquired from my teaching: mainly how much English they had learned, but also whether they had progressed in learning skills, and whether their motivation and attitude to the language had been enhanced. He said that if I honestly thought they had not learned, I should leave. I stayed.

Further reading

FOREIGN LANGUAGE TEACHING IN GENERAL

Ashworth, M. (1985) *Beyond Methodology*, Cambridge: Cambridge University Press.
(On influences and resources outside the classroom: the community, educational policies and programmes, sources of information)

Brown, H. D. (1987) *Principles of Language Learning and Teaching* (2nd edn.), Hemel Hempstead: Prentice Hall International.
(Basic information derived from research and study: topics such as first and second language learning, individual and social learning variables, assessment)

Brown, H. D. (1994) *Teaching by Principles: An Interactive Approach to Language Pedagogy*, Englewood Cliffs, N.J.: Prentice Hall Regents.
(A readable guide to language teaching, covering a wide selection of topics and including discussion questions and suggestions for further reading)

Ellis, R. (1990) *Instructed Second Language Acquisition*, Oxford: Blackwell.
(A comprehensive summary of research and thinking on subjects such as classroom versus 'naturalistic' learning, classroom interaction, the nature of instruction)

Ellis, R. (1994) *The Study of Second Language Acquisition*, Oxford: Oxford University Press.
(A very comprehensive survey of research on second language acquisition, clearly written but rather long: for selective reading and reference rather than cover-to-cover reading)

Stern, H. H. (1983) *Fundamental Concepts of Language Teaching*, Oxford: Oxford University Press.

Stern, H. H. (1992) *Issues and Options in Language Teaching*, Oxford: Oxford University Press.
(The second of these two volumes is a supplement to the first: together they give comprehensive coverage of the major theoretical issues. A lot of reading, but well-written and accessible)

Harmer, J. (1991) *The Practice of English Language Teaching* (2nd edn.), London: Longman.
(A coursebook in foreign language teaching; refers particularly to English, but largely relevant to other languages: practical and readable)

Legutke, M. and Thomas, H. (1991) *Process and Experience in the Language Classroom*, London: Longman.
(Discussion of classroom events and phenomena; oriented towards communicative, learner-centred teaching)
Littlewood, W. (1984) *Foreign and Second Language Learning*, Cambridge: Cambridge University Press.
(A fairly brief and accessible summary of the main topics)
McLaughlin, B. (1987) *Theories of Second-Language Learning*, London: Edward Arnold.
(A critical, scholarly study of some of the main language-learning theories and corresponding teaching methodologies)
Richards, J. C. and Rodgers, T. S. (1986) *Approaches and Methods in Language Teaching*, Cambridge: Cambridge University Press.
(A summary of the main features of some accepted language teaching methodologies)

CLASSROOM RESEARCH

Allwright, R. and Bailey, K. M. (1991) *Focus on the Language Classroom: An Introduction to Classroom Research for Language Teachers*, Cambridge: Cambridge University Press.
(Guidance to the teacher on doing research: models, methods, problems; plus an overview of actual research projects on some aspects of classroom action)
Brumfit, C. J. and Mitchell, R. (1989) *Research in the Language Classroom*, London: British Council with Modern English Publications; Macmillan.
(A collection of articles on various kinds of research, with examples; see particularly the opening article by the editors, and van Lier on ethnography)
Chaudron, C. (1988) *Second Language Classrooms: Research on Teaching and Learning*, Cambridge: Cambridge University Press.
(A scholarly overview of research; thorough and dense, not for light reading)
Cohen, L. and Manion, L. (1980) *Research Methods in Education*, London and Sydney: Croom Helm.
(Clearly-written and comprehensive guide to research on learning, teaching, education in general)
Larsen-Freeman, D. and Long, M. (1991) *An Introduction to Second Language Acquisition Research*, London: Longman.
(A comprehensive overview of research on language learning)
Lightbown, P. and Spada, N. (1993) *How Languages are Learned*, Oxford: Oxford University Press.
(A not-too-long, readable summary of theories and research on first and second language learning)
McDonough, S. (1991) 'Survey review: approaches to research in second language teaching and learning', *ELT Journal*, 45,3, 260–6.
(A useful brief critical survey of various books on foreign language teaching research)
Noffke, S. E. (1992) 'The work and workplace of teachers in action research', *Teaching and Teacher Education*, 8, 1, 15–29.
(On action research, its history and development, and use for and by teachers)

Nunan, D. (1990) 'Action research in the language classroom' in Richards and
Nunan (eds.), *Second Language Teacher Education*, pp. 62–81
(What action research is; with examples and illustrations from actual research
projects carried out by teachers)

Nunan, D. (1992) *Research Methods in Language Learning*, Cambridge:
Cambridge University Press.
(A clear, critical overview of various types of research, with examples; useful
conclusions and tasks at the end of each chapter)

Richards, K. and Edge, J. (eds.) (1993) *Teachers Develop Teachers Research*,
London: Heinemann.
(A collection of conference papers: discussion of the concept of teacher
research, and descriptions of particular projects)

Rudduck, J. and Hopkins, D. (1985) *Research as a Basis for Teaching: Readings
from the Works of Lawrence Stenhouse*, London: Heinemann Educational
Books.
(Short extracts from Stenhouse's writing and lectures: on the role and
function of the teacher as practitioner and researcher)

TEACHER DEVELOPMENT

Edge, J. (1991) *Cooperative Development: Professional Self-development
through Cooperation with Colleagues*, London: Longman.
(Teacher development through interaction between colleagues involving
understanding of and non-judgemental response to each other's problems and
ideas)

Lansley, C. (1994) '"Collaborative Development": an alternative to phatic
discourse and the art of Co-operative Development', *ELT Journal*, 48, 1,
50–6.
(A criticism of and important supplement to Edge's ideas; suggests that
colleagues should not just empathize with one another, but provide some
input of personal opinion and judgement)

Parrott, M. (1993) *Tasks for Language Teachers*, Cambridge: Cambridge
University Press.
(A wide selection of interesting teacher-training or development tasks, with
notes that include possible answers and comments)

Wajnryb, R. (1992) *Classroom Observation Tasks*, Cambridge: Cambridge
University Press.
(A very useful resource book of focussed observation tasks, with worksheets
and comments)

Wallace, M. (1993) *Training Foreign Language Teachers: A Reflective
Approach*, Cambridge: Cambridge University Press.
(A rationale of the reflective approach to teacher training and development)

Woodward, T. (1992) *Ways of Training*, London: Longman.
(A collection of imaginative and stimulating activities for teacher training and
development)

Module 1: Presentations and explanations

Note that the concept of 'presentation' as discussed here is rather broader than the first component of the conventional 'presentation–practice–production' model you may be familiar with. It refers here to any teaching act that is designed to mediate new material or activity in order to make it accessible to learners; thus it may be applied to both fluency- and accuracy-oriented language use, and to any size of unit, from single phoneme to full discourse.

▶ Unit One: Effective presentation
(About an hour and 20 minutes)

The question may be used as a basis for the sharing of anecdotal experiences; this will enable you to check if the concept of presentation has been thoroughly understood, and provide further personal illustrations.

Note the instruction at the end of the group task to look for 'what was effective about it'; try to discourage negative criticism and focus the participants on what was good about each other's performance. This helps them to define the positive characteristics of effective presentation in general; also, as this activity is likely to occur at an early stage in the course, it contributes to the formation of a comfortable atmosphere and supportive relationships in the group.

I have, incidentally, found this peer-teaching idea to be an excellent introductory activity for a teacher-training course as a whole, even if not specifically associated with the topic of presentation. It puts the participants quickly into the teaching role in a relatively relaxed situation, teaching something they are confident they know. The presentations are usually interesting and enjoyable, and provide a basis for productive initial discussion of various aspects of teaching.

▷ Unit Two: Examples of presentation procedures
(45 minutes to an hour)

The discussion here is similar to the one at the end of the previous unit – analysing different presentations – with two important differences: first, these examples are specifically to do with language teaching; and second, since the presenters are not members of the group, teachers can express freely any negative criticisms. However, the two units are sufficiently similar in their objectives to make it feasible, if time is short, to opt for only one of them: whichever you feel is more suitable for your group.

A practical suggestion for the administration of this task: divide the class into small groups, and ask each to work on a different extract. Groups who finish quickly may go on to another of their choice. This allows you to limit time in advance (I find twenty minutes is enough), and ensures that at least one group will have studied each extract. They can then share reactions in a full-class exchange of ideas and drawing of conclusions.

▶ Unit Three: Explanations and instructions
(If the instructions are tried out in class, then an hour or a little more; if only the discussion, then 20-40 minutes)

I find that the giving of clear explanations and instructions is something inexperienced teachers very often do badly, partly simply because they are unaware quite how difficult it is! Hence the careful examination of the topic in this unit.

The structure of the task is the reverse of that used in Unit One: here the experience comes first and the guidelines are considered and applied later.

The guidelines are thus immediately illustrated and applied in retrospect as they are read; they will then function as a means to raise awareness of what has been done, and, hopefully, polish future performance.

Module 2: Practice activities

▶ Unit One: The function of practice
(About 40 minutes)

The purpose of this unit is to define what practice is, what it does for the learner, and how important it is. It may be given as a brief lecture (using the two questions for intermittent brief pair or group discussions), or as reading. It is important to stress that the definition of 'practice' here includes not only 'drills' but any activity whose purpose is to reinforce knowledge or skills: thus it includes reading, writing essays, communication activities, etc.

The question at the end of the unit is a key one, and worth discussing with the full group. Whether or not you and/or your trainees agree with my statement, it is certainly important for them to define how important they see the teacher activity that is concerned with the provision of practice, as distinct from that which has to do with presenting new material, explaining, instructing, testing or metalinguistic discussion. And if they do come to the conclusion that providing practice is one, at least, of the most important functions of a teacher, then there are clear implications for the amount of time and effort that should be spent on it during a lesson.

▶ Unit Two: Characteristics of a good practice activity
(About an hour)

The main purpose of the introductory task is to get participants to engage with the key issue in advance, in order to heighten their appreciation and understanding of the list of characteristics of good practice suggested later. A further purpose is to contribute further ideas and extend the range of the analysis. It is, however, quite difficult for beginner trainees to define on their own

characteristics of good practice in terms of theoretical generalizations, which is why only two such suggestions are asked of them.

The task may be omitted if you are short of time or feel it is too difficult, and the 'characteristics' presented as a lecture-demonstration. In either case, it is important to illustrate the ideas at every stage with examples of classroom practice techniques, which may be suggested by participants.

For further discussion of the last item, the creation of interest, you may find it helpful to refer to Module 19: *Learner motivation and interest*, Unit Four.

▶ Unit Three: Practice techniques
(About an hour)

Many classroom procedures and textbook exercises that are intended to provide practice do not in fact do so very effectively. Their ineffectiveness may not be obvious, and can only be discovered by fairly rigorous analysis of how the participants (teacher and learners) are actually investing their time and energy. This unit is designed to sharpen teachers' critical awareness of some potential shortcomings of such procedures.

One particular point that perhaps should be emphasized is that enjoyment and motivation on the part of participants is no guarantee that valuable learning is taking place, as exemplified in the first scenario.

My own comments refer occasionally to the characteristics discussed in the previous unit; if you did not do the latter with your teachers then some of these concepts may need clarifying (though most are fairly self-explanatory in context).

You may wish to add – or substitute – actual classroom observation or descriptions of other scenarios as a basis for this task.

▷ Unit Four: Sequence and progression in practice
(45 minutes to an hour)

Assessing the relative difficulty of activities can be quite hard for inexperienced trainees. It might be helpful to start off with a full-class trainer-supported discussion of what each activity in Box 2.3 is in fact practising and – even more important!

– what it is not; and only afterwards ask participants to try the ordering task.

You may find the discussion throws up all sorts of interesting ideas other than relative difficulty (suitability for different age groups, practical administration, or whatever); and you may, of course, decide to encourage the development of whatever topics the class finds interesting instead of doing the task originally suggested. (One of the things that is very likely to happen, particularly in tasks based on a set of different scenarios or activities, is that these can 'take off' in all sorts of directions and produce fruitful learning in unpredicted – and unpredictable – areas!)

An alternative way of doing this task with more experienced teachers is to ignore my sample activities completely, and start by pooling ideas drawn from the participants' own experience or creative thinking. These ideas can then be sorted into a logical chronological order: the sorting process itself will provoke critical assessment of the individual activities and of what is or is not covered by the series as a whole. If you adopt this suggestion, then there is of course no particular reason for using numbers as the basic target language topic; perhaps use a topic suggested by participants.

Once the ideas have been collected and discussed it may be a good idea for the group to write out their suggested activities, in the order on which they have decided, and publish them as a class booklet. The writing itself is a useful learning activity, and participants may find the resulting material of real practical value.

Module 3: Tests

Note: In a training course it may be most effective to do Unit Two first (as I usually do): it faces participants with the raw experience of being tested – an excellent entry-point for building discussion and understanding. I have put it second in this book because for readers it is more logical to start with a basic treatment of the place of testing in teaching.

▶ Unit One: What are tests for?
(About 45 minutes; it is assumed that the brief interviews with experienced teachers and learners on reasons for testing will be done outside class

time. Note, however, that if you intend to go on to the test experience as suggested in the following unit, you may wish to spend a few minutes at the end of this one teaching or reviewing the concepts to be tested)

There is a vast literature on the subject of language testing, in which the topic is often treated as something that can be isolated and discussed separately from the teaching process as a whole. Very often, as mentioned at the beginning of the unit, it is assumed to be integrally bound up with formal assessment. Here, the emphasis is different: testing is treated, like presentation and practice, as a part of the teaching process, and the aim of the unit is to elicit and define some reasons for testing that have to do with enabling or enhancing learning.

As regards the definition of 'test' given at the beginning: it may be better first to try to elicit a definition from the participants and discuss critically their suggestions in order to sharpen their awareness of what is, or is not, essential to the concept.

The distinction between practice and testing techniques is a significant one that many teachers and textbook writers do not seem to be sufficiently aware of. Overleaf is a table showing the differences systematically; you may find it helpful if you wish to discuss the topic more in depth.

The Inquiry stage, of asking about reasons for testing, makes available to participants richer sources of ideas and approaches than those they possess on their own. However, it is time-consuming: simply brainstorming ideas within the group will of course be much quicker.

The main purpose of the final discussion in Stage 4 is not so much the ostensible one of summarizing reasons for testing (or not testing) as to refine the teachers' own general conceptions of the place of testing in teaching. Some people approach the subject with rather unthinking blanket assumptions such as: 'You have to test students regularly' or 'Testing is a bad thing'. This discussion is intended to 'destabilize' such assumptions and get participants to rethink them, creating more carefully defined personal theories.

▶ Unit Two: Basic concepts; the test experience
(About an hour, out of which 20 minutes should be allowed for doing the test itself; it is

	Practice	*Test*
Aims	learning	feedback on learning
Content	process-oriented	product-oriented
	cues most effective if open-ended	cues most effective if closed-ended
Learner activity	plenty of 'volume' and repetition	not much 'volume' or repetition
	learners know the material	learners do not necessarily know the material
	task is success-oriented	task may be success- or failure-oriented
	there may be peer-teaching	no peer-teaching
Teacher activity	gives task and helps performance	gives task, does not help performance
	monitors, reinforces	assesses
Classroom climate	intrinsic motivation (based on interest, or desire to learn)	extrinsic motivation (based on desire to get good grade)
	(relatively) relaxed	(relatively) tense
	cooperative	individual or competitive

assumed that the concepts will have been learned as a home assignment or in a previous session)

This unit aims to kill two birds with one stone: to get participants to learn some basic theoretical concepts connected with the topic, as well as to refresh their memories of what it feels like to be tested as a basis for later reflective discussion.

The source information can be given, as suggested, by asking participants to read the literature; or delivered in lecture form within a previous session. You may, of course, wish to add further information beyond the set of concepts given here (for example, 'progress' may be added to 'achievement' and 'proficiency' tests).

With my own group of trainees I pretend that this is a serious test, in order to get as authentic reactions as possible. I tell them the week before that they are to be tested on some given material, and will be given a percentage grade on the results. The trainees are only told that it is a simulation after they have finished (they usually hear the news with a smile; some sigh with relief or disappointment, others tell me they guessed because they felt the task did not suit my training style: there had to be a catch somewhere!). We then go through the answers together, and finally discuss their reactions and feelings, based on the given questions.

Other topics that sometimes arise during the

discussion are: the question of competition between testees; how easy people found it to concentrate; how much effort they put into doing the test; cheating.

An important result of this discussion is often the discovery of how differently people react to tests – and hence appreciation of how inappropriate it is to make 'black-and-white' pronouncements on their positive or negative effects on learners.

▶ Unit Three: Types of test elicitation techniques

(About an hour and a half; but only 45 minutes or so if the trainees have studied and commented on Box 3.3 as a previous home assignment)

The short paragraph on formal and informal testing aims to raise teachers' awareness of how often they in fact do test: tests, if you accept the definition given at the beginning of the module, are not always explicitly labelled as such.

I suggest you check through Box 3.3 to see if I have omitted some techniques which you think important: you will need to remedy this by bringing your own examples. Equally, of course, you may wish to omit some of the given list.

It can be quite tedious to present and discuss the elicitation techniques one by one in discussion.

Alternative methods are: ask participants to choose two or three items each to analyse, perhaps as a pre-session assignment, then to present in the session; or select for analysis only a few of the items (those most commonly used locally; or those which are most interesting and productive to discuss).

If you choose to omit Unit Four (which asks participants to write their own tests) you may find it interesting and useful to apply some of the points suggested in Box 3.4 within the present discussion.

▷ Unit Four: Designing a test
(The test-writing itself and possibly trying-out will be done elsewhere; the discussion may take about 45 minutes)

This is a useful 'hands-on' experience, but there is a problem of time: both the test-writing assignment itself and the provision of feedback are very time-consuming. A shorter, easier alternative is to take a ready-made test they know and discuss it in the light of the *Guidelines* in Box 3.4 (those that are appropriate) together with the four questions asked under the heading *Analysing elicitation techniques* in the previous unit.

If the participants do write their own tests, then probably the most helpful feedback to them is that which you yourself give, combined – if practicable – with the results of the actual administration of the test to learners.

▷ Unit Five: Test administration
(45 minutes to an hour)

In the selection and formulation of the questions and my own answers the emphasis is clearly on the test as a tool for teaching: a way to enhance learning, to encourage, to help learners make and feel progress; the 'judging' aspect is played down. Note that my suggested answers are inevitably specific to my own situation, and to be used (if at all) only as an illustration of one possible approach, or as a basis for criticism and further discussion.

Module 4: Teaching pronunciation

▶ Unit One: What does teaching pronunciation involve?
(About an hour)

This may be presented as an input session, using the 'To check understanding' tasks for brief group or full-class discussion interaction. Note that you will need dictionaries with phonetic transcriptions for the tasks.

▷ Unit Two: Listening to accents
(The preliminary home assignment of recording accents takes about half an hour; class discussion, if there are several recordings studied first in small groups, about an hour and a half in all)

You may prefer to use one previously prepared recording for the entire group to study. In this case you will have less varied samples, and participants will lose the experience of preparing and recording and may feel less interested in the analysis; on the other hand the whole process will go much faster and the whole-group discussion is simpler and easier to organize.

If you do ask your trainees to prepare recordings as described in the unit, it is a good idea to take in at least a selection of the recorded cassettes between Stages 2 and 3, and fill in a worksheet for yourself for each one. This is additional work: but it does help you to make the information-sharing process of Stage 3 more effective, by drawing trainees' attention to errors they may not have heard, and by defining those that they may have heard but find difficult to describe. Your participation will also make it easier to exploit the use of phonetic, stress and intonation symbols for the definition of errors.

▶ Unit Three: Improving learners' pronunciation
(An hour to an hour and a half)

This unit can be presented as an 'interrupted lecture', the questions being used as stimuli for short 'buzz' sessions between pairs or small groups of participants. The second and third questions may be usefully followed by application: participants try out their tests or explanations on learners as a home assignment, and report back in the following full session.

The task at the end of the unit is probably best done as pair or group work, followed by general pooling.

▷ Unit Four: Further topics for discussion
(About 45 minutes)

If you wish your trainees to do some reading on these topics (see the *Further reading* section), it may be better to get them to do it after the discussion rather than before. If they read before, they tend to come to the discussion with borrowed, ready-made ideas and lose the challenge of thinking things out for themselves, whereas if they go to the literature after seriously considering the topics on their own, they are likely to find the reading interesting, and will be more informed and selective about what they learn from it.

A thorough study of some or all of the questions can be ensured by adopting a three-stage process: group discussion → reading → summarizing answers in writing.

The section *Some possible answers* will probably be superfluous if you have had a full-class discussion; though perhaps participants will be interested in reading it as a follow-up and comparing my ideas with theirs.

▶ Unit Five: Pronunciation and spelling
(About 45 minutes)

This unit will be useful for those teaching English, or other languages whose spelling is difficult; it may be unnecessary for those teaching languages whose spelling is more or less phonetic.

The topic of spelling is treated as associated with pronunciation rather than as part of writing, since its teaching usually emphasizes the learning of accurate discrete items, rather than fluent use as a part of written communication.

The questions are aimed mainly at raising teachers' linguistic awareness of the problems

associated with the pronunciation–spelling correspondences, whereas Box 4.6 and the attached task deal with practical teaching ideas. The main part of the task may be done by you and the class together, pooling ideas for appropriate texts.

Module 5: Teaching vocabulary

▶ Unit One: What is vocabulary and what needs to be taught?
(An hour to an hour and a half)

This unit may be presented as input (from you), using the questions as stimuli for brief clarifying discussions.

For examining aspects of meaning: in class, I would use a dictionary sparingly; it is more interesting and produces better learning to rely on your and your trainees' own intuitions. The dictionary may then be used as a retrospective check.

If your target language is not English, you will need to substitute different examples for some of the questions.

▶ Unit Two: Presenting new vocabulary
(About 45 minutes)

This task contextualizes in practice many of the concepts introduced in Unit One, and can be used as a follow-up to it.

At Stage 4, it is worth devoting a few minutes to a discussion of the role of translation, which is particularly controversial. My own feeling is that translation, if the teacher speaks the mother tongue of the learners, is often a quick and convenient way to convey meaning, particularly if the concept is one that it is difficult to explain in the target language. But it may sometimes be inaccurate and misleading and appears to invite learners to think in their own language rather than in the target one. It can be used, perhaps, to facilitate first understanding, to be followed by techniques that emphasize use of the item in target-language contexts.

▷ Unit Three: Remembering vocabulary
(About an hour)

This looks a little long and tedious to do, but it is in my experience quite enjoyable, and effective in terms of learning outcomes: graduates of my courses often quote it as one of the sessions whose process and conclusions they remember best.

The group experiment is most easily and efficiently done if you yourself lead the proceedings with clear instructions and strict timekeeping. If the sheet shown in Box 5.4 is copied onto a transparency and projected on the OHP then results can be displayed as soon as they are counted at the end of each round; this enables participants to keep track of the results as they develop and adds momentum and interest.

Other aspects of vocabulary learning can also be examined, making the experiment more complex: for example, you might ask half the teachers each time not to teach each other, but to study the lists silently, as individuals; and then check whether the cooperative teaching–learning did in fact produce on average better results (in my experience it does). Or you might add lists of nonsense-syllables, and look at how well they are learned, and what strategies are used.

▶ Unit Four: Ideas for vocabulary work in the classroom
(An hour to an hour and a half, assuming participants have prepared their ideas in advance; more than that becomes tedious)

This unit's main aim is simply to give participants more ideas for vocabulary-practice procedures that they can use in the classroom; and critical discussion of each helps to increase awareness of what exactly they are doing and why.

You should also contribute an activity, perhaps to start the session or to end it.

It is a good idea to ask participants to write out descriptions of their activities after the session. This affords them an opportunity to reflect on and refine their ideas; it also makes it possible to copy and distribute a useful set of vocabulary-teaching activities to all members of the group.

▷ Unit Five: Testing vocabulary
(About half an hour to study the examples, which can be done at home; an hour for discussion)

The set of examples provided here does not, of course, represent a comprehensive taxonomy of test types: if you wish to go into the topic in depth you may wish to refer teachers to the books suggested under *Further reading* in Module 3: *Tests*. The main teaching point here is not testing as such, but awareness of what aspects of knowledge of lexis are in fact elicited through the different techniques.

Module 6: Teaching grammar

▶ Unit One: What is grammar?
(About 45 minutes)

An alternative to the preliminary process suggested here is to start by asking participants 'What is grammar?', eliciting ideas, and working towards an acceptable definition by 'Socratic' critical questioning of their suggestions. One important point is to make them aware that 'grammar' is not necessarily about complete sentences or complete words.

The exercise given in the second question is intended to clarify, through examples, the meaning of a 'structure'; it may be sufficient to elicit examples in one language.

The third section is worth spending time on, for the sake of awareness-raising.

▷ Unit Two: The place of grammar teaching
(If preliminary study is done at home, the discussion session will take about half an hour)

This is a fairly demanding and academic task, so perhaps more suitable for relatively knowledgeable or advanced trainees. Probably the most effective use of class time is to ask participants to read and prepare their comments at home, then discuss in class.

Your interpretations and criticisms of the readings may of course be different from mine. The main aim is to get the participants to engage with the problem of the usefulness, or uselessness, of grammar teaching as a component of foreign language teaching, and to arrive at some kind of conclusion: 'This is what I/we think.' You might wish to challenge them by suggesting different teaching contexts: would you say the same if you were teaching adults in a language school? Primary-school children in a less developed country? Adolescents in a large heterogeneous class?

▷ Unit Three: Grammatical terms

(Up to two hours, depending on participants' previous knowledge)

If you feel your trainees need some kind of explanation of grammatical terms, then this is probably best done as a kind of lecture, eliciting the examples from them as you go along. If, however, they are already fairly well informed on the topic, the definitions may be elicited from them themselves in order to refresh and consolidate knowledge. A third possibility is to give them the terms and ask them as a home assignment to find out, or check, their meanings, using reference books; then go over results in class.

As noted, this section is necessarily based on English, but much of it may be found relevant and helpful for grammar descriptions of other languages. The tasks given in the questions may of course be done on the basis of non-English texts.

▶ Unit Four: Presenting and explaining grammar

(About an hour if based on peer-teaching; about 30 minutes if the actual teaching is done elsewhere)

If your trainees have access to classes of 'real' foreign language learners, then the experimental presentations should be done there. If not, and they have to be done as peer-teaching, there will probably not be time for more than four or five volunteers to present; the others should, however, prepare and write down how they would have presented.

In Stage 1 I have made the consultation of grammar books optional, because I feel it is quite a helpful exercise for teachers to explore their own intuitions about the language and try to put them into words, using the grammar book later (in Stage

2) to supplement and improve their ideas. It is, however, obviously quicker to consult the books first, and you may wish to do it this way round. Similarly, the guidelines suggested by the questions in Box 6.2 may be studied before the actual presentations rather than after.

Make sure that Stage 3 is done very soon after the presentation, so that the events are still clear in participants' minds.

The task can end at Stage 3. If you continue, Stage 4 may provide the basis for a class discussion, while Stage 5 could be used as a follow-up home assignment.

Stage 6 is most relevant for people who are regularly teaching classes of foreign language learners.

▶ Unit Five: Grammar practice activities

(About 45 minutes)

The aim of this is mainly to make participants aware of the wide variety of activity-types available, and of the importance of not confining themselves to conventional form-focussed grammar exercises. They should be encouraged to invent their own activities as well as recalling or reading about them.

If participants look at coursebooks, as suggested at the end of the unit, and find results similar to those I suggest, then the obvious conclusion would be that the teacher should make up the deficit by supplementing them with activities of his or her own. You might select one such coursebook unit and discuss what sorts of grammar-practice activities might be introduced as supplements.

▷ Unit Six: Grammatical mistakes

(About 45 minutes to an hour, not including the preliminary gathering of data)

If you feel that you need a section on practical grammar testing as such, it is possible to take the last section of Module 5: *Teaching vocabulary* and redesign the items, or ask your trainees to do so, as grammar tests.

A list of 'important' mistakes could be based only on an introspective brainstorm on the part of the participants and yourself; this is of course much less time-consuming. However, I feel it is in principle preferable to go to the primary source of information, the learners themselves, rather than relying on subjective judgement, which may not always be reliable. Hence the Inquiry task.

With regard to the section *Using the information*: teachers tend to think of errors only as bases for correction, and it is important to draw their attention to the more positive teaching activities which knowledge of probable errors can contribute to: initial presentation and remedial practice.

Module 7: Topics, situations, notions, functions

▶ Unit One: Topics and situations
(About an hour)

Practical ideas for introducing new topics or situations may be brainstormed by the class before they look at Box 7.1; the box material may then simply be used to supplement or confirm ideas.

In the task I recommend having all the groups work on the same suggestion: this then highlights the variety of procedures that may be used for a single topic or situation. The actual peer-teaching may be time-consuming, particularly if the preparation is done in class. It is therefore preferable to give this preparation as an out-of-class assignment: the participants then have time to search for or make up texts or dialogues, use a thesaurus to find appropriate vocabulary items, and so on.

▶ Unit Two: What ARE notions and functions?
(About half an hour)

As noted, there are in fact different definitions of these terms; but the one given here seems to me to be a fairly useful and widely accepted one. It is based on that used by Van Ek (1990).

Functions are usually defined by gerund verb forms (*informing*, *greeting*, etc.) and notions by nouns (*time*, *difference*, etc.). The forms used in Box 7.2 are base verb or noun forms throughout, in order not to 'give away' the solutions.

▶ Unit Three: Teaching chunks of language: from text to task
(About an hour)

The issue of learning by heart as a contribution to meaningful learning is an interesting one that you might like to discuss with participants. Ask them, perhaps, to recall their own experiences of learning by heart in school, and whether in retrospect these were helpful or 'deadening'. If both positive and negative outcomes are recalled, perhaps they can pinpoint some of the factors which contributed to the difference? Such a discussion should help participants to realize that learning by heart is not in itself a 'bad' thing, but can contribute to overall learning and 'ownership' of knowledge and ideas provided that it is combined with thoughtful reflection and discussion of content.

The dialogue task demands fairly creative, divergent thinking: participants will probably find a good many more, and better, ideas than those suggested! As a follow-up, you may wish to repeat the task using a dialogue from a local textbook.

With regard to the final task: note that many coursebooks provide situational dialogues or texts, but then proceed only to 'milk' them for factual reading comprehension, vocabulary and grammar, without doing anything to explore further the basic topics, situations, notions and functions through more meaning-oriented tasks. These are the kinds of tasks the teachers should be looking for, and perhaps suggesting ideas to supplement.

▷ Unit Four: Teaching chunks of language: from task to text
(About an hour)

The technique of starting from a communicative task and eliciting from the results the language to be taught has been recommended by some methodologists: its main advantage is, as mentioned in the unit, that it does focus learners' and teacher's attention unequivocally on the communicative use of the language rather than on form and possibly replicates 'natural' or 'immersion' learning.

It is not, however, in fact very widely implemented in the classroom. The question is whether this is due to conservatism on the part of teachers, or whether it is because the technique is in fact less effective or a difficult one to implement. The role-play experiment suggested here is one way to try to explore this question; it also gives teachers first-hand experience of a method which they may not have had other opportunities to see.

▷ Unit Five: Combining different kinds of language segments
(About an hour)

This unit moves away from practical classroom technique, and back into language study: it is an attempt to pull together this set of four modules and clarify participants' thinking on the relationship between the 'communicative' language categories of notion, function, etc. and the 'non-communicative' ones of grammar, vocabulary and pronunciation.

If the examples given in the body of the unit are understood and the question is successfully tackled, you may find that the final task, which is fairly time-consuming, may be skipped. Another possibility is to do (part of) the task fairly briskly on the board through full-class discussion, rather than individually or in groups.

Module 8: Teaching listening

▶ Unit One: What does real-life listening involve?
(About an hour)

The first stage of the task is fairly easy: perhaps let the trainees write down ideas first for a moment or two, and then 'pool' them on the board. The second is considerably more difficult: they will need more time for preliminary thinking and writing, and you may need to hint, encourage and add further ideas in order to facilitate the pooling stage. It may help to provide them with a copy of a transcript of a typical listening situation – as in Box 11.1, for example.

Alternatively, the second stage can be omitted, and the content given as a mini-lecture. This would lead immediately to the question about applying the guidelines in Unit Two.

The application task is intended to illustrate and

clarify the preceding rather theoretical ideas by applying them to a particular situation fresh in the participants' memory. The ongoing session can in itself provide an example.

▶ Unit Two: Real-life listening in the classroom
(About an hour)

One way of doing this is to have the 'real-life characteristics' listed briefly in a left-hand column on the board or OHP, and invite trainees to suggest implications for teaching to fill in appropriate spaces in the right-hand column. Invite them to start at whichever item they like.

As guidelines for teaching are suggested, encourage trainees to think critically: to suggest possible disadvantages or problems, as well as extra (pedagogical) advantages.

▷ Unit Three: Learner problems
(45 minutes' discussion, assuming that interviews with learners have been done outside the classroom)

If you have trainees who are not native speakers of the target language in the class and who learnt the language through formal courses not too long ago, they might be able to function as 'interviewees' (Stage 2 of the Inquiry), supplying the learner insights through recalling their own experience.

In the discussion (Stage 3), keep participants steadily focussed on the main objective: to think about what we, the teachers, can do to help learners with these problems.

▶ Unit Four: Types of activities
(About 45 minutes, assuming you demonstrate briefly some of the types of activities)

This is straight input, and difficult to absorb in the concentrated form in which it is given here. One of the purposes of the following task – to look at a coursebook and see if these types of listening tasks appear – is simply to get participants to re-process the categories through having to apply them themselves, and thus to absorb the ideas better. This may, of course, be done as a home assignment.

If you are giving the list of categories as lecture-type input, then provide some short illustrations for some of the items; this will make the ideas clearer and easier to absorb, as well as more interesting.

▷ Unit Five: Adapting activities
(About an hour to an hour and a half, including trying out)

Encourage participants to adopt the suggestion in the task to try out the activities in small groups before criticizing them; this can be surprisingly revealing. Where 'recordings' are needed, the texts can be read aloud by one of the participants.

If you have done previous units, this can be related to as a summing-up activity: recall with the participants previously discussed criteria for the design of effective listening activities (does the activity take into account real-life aspects, pedagogical considerations, learner problems?), and encourage them to apply them here.

The activities can be discussed in small groups and suggestions then shared in a full-class summary.

Module 9: Teaching speaking

▶ Unit One: Successful oral fluency practice
(About 45 minutes)

After noting the importance of fluent speech in the foreign language, and agreeing on how you would describe a successful speaking activity, you might invite participants to brainstorm problems they have had, or anticipate, with getting students to talk in the classroom. Then use my and/or your own ideas to refine or extend the list in Box 9.2.

The practical conclusions at the end of the unit may provide a starting-point for a collection of 'tips' suggested by you and the class together.

▶ Unit Two: The functions of topic and task
(About 45 minutes; allot about three to five minutes each for trying out the two activities in Box 9.3)

This is usually an enjoyable and profitable session, clarifying the contribution of 'task' to a fluency activity. You are likely to get the same results as I do (see *Which is better?*) unless you are working with a fairly sophisticated population familiar with debate-type open discussion.

It is preferable not to reveal in advance the basic topic/task distinction between the two activities: tell the class only that they are going to do two different kinds of discussions, and you want them to note how well each works; hopefully they will arrive at the distinction(s) through their own following analytic discussion.

▶ Unit Three: Discussion activities
(Timing depends on how many of the activities you look at, and whether you try them out during the session: allow not more than ten minutes for trying out each, and up to fifteen minutes for the following discussion)

If you wish at this point to give your trainees some practical advice on the organization of group discussions, see Module 16: *Classroom interaction*, Unit Three.

Either different groups of participants within the session can try different activities, then give feedback; or individuals go away and try them out with 'real' classes, reporting back later. The latter will get 'truer' and more interesting results, but is more time-consuming.

If you are short of time, you may prefer simply to use the activities as a basis for critical discussion without the trying-out stage. Ones they like should be noted by participants for future use in the classroom; you might direct them to some of the references in the *Further reading* section for additional ideas.

▷ Unit Four: Other kinds of spoken interaction
(About 45 minutes)

Some of the reading here is quite heavy, perhaps too difficult for some less advanced groups of trainees; my (non-native-speaker) trainees, however, cope with it satisfactorily. I sometimes ask them to read the entire first chapter from Brown and Yule (1983) from which Extract 2 is taken: the topics of long/short turns and

343

transactional and interactional speech are discussed there in more detail, as well as several other interesting and important issues.

The final section is of course suitable for full-class discussion. The main point is that the participants should reach decisions about what they think about these aspects of spoken language, and how (or if) they plan to teach or give practice in them.

▷ Unit Five: Role play and related techniques
(About 45 minutes)

If your trainees have no experience of simulation or role play, it may be worth trying out an activity with them as an introduction to this unit; you might use one of the examples given within the text of the unit, or take an idea from Porter-Ladousse (1987).

Teachers' attitudes to role play vary according to their personalities and backgrounds: some are enthusiastic, others cautious or even reluctant to try it. The main objective here is not to 'advertise' role play, but simply to familiarize teachers with the various options, clarify what they can contribute to oral fluency and suggest some practical ideas.

▷ Unit Six: Oral testing
(About 45 minutes)

I have supplied a ready-made summary of some of the advantages and disadvantages of oral testing in Box 9.6, but it might be better, particularly if you are working with experienced teachers, to elicit ideas in a preliminary brainstorm.

This is a good context for reading background literature: either a selection of articles, as the two suggested here, or others that you recommend. If you do the debating task, then the reading may be done before it, so that participants come to the discussion with some background knowledge; or after it, in which case contributions to the debate will be less informed, but the reading itself may be more interesting, since participants will already have explored the issues and their own approach to them.

A follow-up task might be to listen to a recording of learner speech and invite your trainees to try to assess it using the scale shown in the Notes; if possible use a video rather than just an audio recording. Then ask them to compare and justify their assessments.

Module 10: Teaching reading

▶ Unit One: How do we read?
(About half an hour)

This unit is a practical introduction to the idea that understanding meanings takes precedence over decoding of letters in successful reading.

One effective way of displaying the various texts in the boxes is to use an overhead projector, with strips of card to hide and reveal the texts. Thus the 'knight' text in Box 10.4 can be displayed very briefly in order to encourage fast reading.

The implications of each little experiment are best elicited through class discussion. The reformulation of the original statements in Box 10.1 may also be elicited through discussion, though you may wish to add further ideas.

Most important here is the idea of reading as 'constructing' (rather than 'gathering') meanings through a combination of top–down strategies, involving the activation of schemata, and bottom–up ones that are text-dependent. If they have not met it before, participants may find it difficult to let go of the idea of reading as a passive reception of a unidirectional flow of ideas, and will appreciate the opportunity to hear about and discuss the concept of interactive reading and the role of the reader as constructor of meanings.

▷ Unit Two: Beginning reading
(About 45 minutes)

Many textbooks – particularly those teaching languages based on the Roman alphabet – take it for granted that the learners' mother tongue has the same alphabet as that of the target language, and do not teach the new one systematically. If the teachers you are training need to teach a new alphabet, they may have to compose supplementary materials for the purpose, and will therefore find it useful to discuss the issues treated here.

The questions in Box 10.5 can be used for open discussion; if this is thorough and productive, then my own suggested guidelines may be unnecessary. The practical reading/writing tasks shown in the Notes can be criticized, changed or added to. If any of your class are currently teaching beginners, they may be able to try out some of the resulting ideas.

▶ Unit Three: Types of reading activities

(An hour to an hour and a half; most of the time should be spent on discussing alternative reading tasks)

For the second and third tasks I have shown rather short, made-up activities because of space constraints; it is preferable, if you can, to make copies of and use similar, full-length activities that actually appear in locally-used textbooks (for Task 3, simply separate the comprehension questions from the text, and distribute them first).

It is important for participants actually to experience doing the three sample activities, not just look at them. When they do so, the difference between the second two in terms of interest and motivation is quite startling, and provokes lively discussion.

The task on thinking of alternative reading activities can be prepared as a home assignment, and ideas pooled in the following session.

▶ Unit Four: Improving reading skills

(About 45 minutes; the application to teaching materials may take another hour, but can be done at home)

The 'implications for teaching' items asked for in the task can be prepared by participants in small-group discussions or as a home assignment, but it is a good idea to refine and summarize them in a discussion with the whole class together. The use of these conclusions to evaluate and criticize actual teaching materials, as suggested, is time-consuming, but may help trainees to learn the ideas more thoroughly and apply them better in teaching.

▷ Unit Five: Advanced reading

(About an hour)

The criteria for designing and assessing advanced reading materials presented here are based on the

assumption that the language is being taught for general communicative purposes. If your trainees are concerned with teaching the foreign language for academic study, or for special professional purposes then criteria will of course need to be adapted accordingly. The main point is that participants should approach the materials applying consistent criteria which they understand and accept, so that they can give reasoned and coherent rationales when suggesting alterations or additions.

For the practical work on texts and tasks you may prefer (as I do) to have participants work on materials taken from local textbooks rather than the ones provided here; or you may let them choose their own. They can work on each item individually before comparing their ideas with each other's and yours.

Module 11: Teaching writing

▷ Unit One: Written versus spoken text

(About half an hour)

Participants can be asked to produce their own written and spoken texts: invite them to improvise instructions, a description or a story into a cassette recorder, and then write out a careful account of the same thing. Then their own texts can be used as the basis of the comparison. This is obviously much more time-consuming, but makes the exercise more personal, and the results more memorable.

The comparison itself I usually do as an open class brainstorm, writing up suggestions, clarifying connections between the different ideas as they are given, and supplementing myself where necessary.

The question at the end is optional: it may be used as a basis for follow-up discussion.

▶ Unit Two: Teaching procedures

(About an hour)

Writing as a means or an end

You may prefer to use instances of writing activities from books familiar to your trainees

345

rather than the ones given in Box 11.2.

People are likely to disagree about where exactly to place the activities on the scale given; and my own answer in the Notes is not the only possible 'right' one. This does not matter: the main purpose of this task is not to get a 'right' answer but to come to grips with the issue: to attempt to evaluate the real objective of given procedures through thinking and discussion.

Writing for content or form

This is, I think, a less important issue than the previous one, and could be omitted if you are short of time. It is again a 'diagnostic' task, attempting to define what a specific procedure is in fact trying to do. The 'form versus content' issue in giving feedback is dealt with in more depth in Unit Five.

▶ Unit Three: Tasks that stimulate writing
(About an hour)

You may wish to change the criteria suggested in Box 11.3 in order to make them more relevant to your class; or you may decide to select only part of the rather long list of writing activities given in Box 11.4.

▷ Unit Four: The process of composition
(About an hour if writing is done in the session)

Participants can be asked to do the writing at home in advance, which saves class time; but I usually prefer to do it in class, so that the discussion takes place when the writing process is still fresh in everyone's mind. About twenty minutes, or a little more, should then be allowed for the writing, and about 30–40 minutes for the discussion.

Usually, people find it quite easy to concentrate and do good writing in class. Various things can help: for example, if you make it clear in advance that they are likely to spend much of the time on apparently non-productive thinking rather than writing, and that that is normal; if you tell them that you do not expect them to produce a finished version; if you insist on absolute silence; if you write yourself at the same time as the class.

You may wish to suggest different writing topics. In principle, any topic will serve as a basis

for the writing; but on the whole, people find it easier to write effectively in this sort of situation where the topic is a problem to which they have to suggest a solution, and about which they know something from their own experience or study.

A point-by-point consideration of the questions raised in Box 11.6 can serve as a good basis for the discussion; and implications for teaching can be suggested in the course of this discussion, rather than waiting until after it.

▶ Unit Five: Giving feedback on writing
(About 45 minutes)

You may prefer to elicit 'Advice' from the class in response to the problems, or suggest your own, rather than asking them to evaluate the 'Advice' given here. In any case, an important objective is to encourage participants to evaluate any advice in the light of their own experience and knowledge, not to accept it uncritically.

Module 12: Syllabus

▶ Unit One: What is a syllabus?
(About 20 minutes; an hour if you do the Application task)

The definition of a syllabus suggested in this unit is not, of course, limited to language syllabuses; you may find it edifying and interesting to bring in syllabuses from other subjects, and invite participants to apply to them the criteria suggested here.

If you base the study of this unit, as suggested, on application to a specific syllabus, make sure participants acquire copies in advance: preferably all should work on the same one, to facilitate interchange of ideas and discussion.

An alternative with more experienced teachers who know what a syllabus is and have used one, is briefly to run through the 'characteristics of a syllabus' without immediate application to an example: the aim being simply to systematize and 'surface' the information. For these teachers, it may be appropriate to spend more time on the critical discussion suggested in the Application task.

▶ Unit Two: Different types of language syllabus
(About 45 minutes)

This unit as it stands aims only to get participants to appreciate the different possibilities of syllabus design, and how these may be mapped onto, or contribute to, their own conceptions. However, the discussion suggested in the task at the end of the unit is likely to lead to a more critical evaluative debate about the advantages and disadvantages of the different kinds of syllabus, and how appropriate each is to teaching situations participants know about.

▶ Unit Three: Using the syllabus
(About 45 minutes)

You may find it useful to point out the main variables that influence teachers' decisions as to how to use the syllabus: the affluence or poverty of the institution; the amount of leeway allowed the teacher by his or her immediate superiors; the knowledge and personality of the teacher.

The basic issue is one of freedom versus structure, or flexibility versus rigidity – though it would be an over-simplification, even misleading, to present these as mutually exclusive oppositions. Many teachers – myself among them – find it far easier to be creative and flexible on the basis of a clear and structured syllabus than when left to themselves with the invitation 'do whatever you like'.

The questions based on Box 12.2 will, it is hoped, lead to a discussion about how best to use the syllabus in teaching situations that participants know about; and also to a sympathetic consideration of different ones, and an understanding of the considerations that lead to decisions which may at first sight appear unacceptable.

Module 13: Materials

▶ Unit One: How necessary is a coursebook?
(About 45 minutes)

The first question may be discussed by the full group; or participants may note down their responses individually. In any case, it is a good idea to record answers in writing: partly because the actual writing process forces participants to define their stance more clearly; and partly so that answers can be easily referred back to when discussing the second question later.

Another interesting way to engage with the ideas in this unit is to have a debate. Regardless of their actual preferences, participants are divided into two groups, one of which is to argue for and one against adopting a coursebook. Each group prepares its arguments, then elects two main speakers, who present its case. After the four opening speakers have finished, the discussion is opened for free participation. At some point you may change the rules, and invite people to express their own, genuine points of view.

A conventional debate ends with a vote for and against: you may or may not feel this appropriate here. If you do, participants should cast their votes according to their own views, not according to their group's; and make it clear to them that the result will reflect only the distribution of opinions within this group, not any kind of generally accepted 'right' answer.

If you decide to do the debate, I suggest you use the list of arguments given in Boxes 13.1.1–2 as follow-up reading: to give it earlier may deprive participants of initiative and challenge in preparing their case.

▶ Unit Two: Coursebook assessment
(An hour to an hour and a half)

One important underlying message of this unit is that there **are** such things as 'good' or 'bad' coursebooks! – they are not just appropriate or inappropriate to a particular context. An enormous number of foreign language coursebooks (particularly for the teaching of English) are available on the market; it is important for participants to be aware that some of these are rather poor, and to know how to distinguish which are worth buying and using, and why.

You may prefer to elicit from participants their own criteria for assessing coursebooks, rather than using the list given in Box 13.2. In either case, the essential processes in this unit are: first, some kind of decision-making as to which criteria are important and which are relatively trivial; and, second, the application of the criteria to locally-used materials.

▶ Unit Three: Using a coursebook
(Half an hour in class, followed by home assignment)

I usually present the first part of this unit as an 'interrupted lecture', or lecture-discussion, in the course of which the 'questions' and 'implications' may be altered or added to. The Application activity is then given as a home assignment. The resulting notes are taken in to be read and commented on; alternatively they may be discussed in class, or exchanged and discussed in small groups. Participants may all work on the same unit, or on different ones.

It is important to discuss at some stage how far the participants in their 'home' context will actually be allowed to deviate from and/or supplement their coursebook: what are the local constraints?

You will probably have noticed that the first three units of this module are gradually narrowing their focus from the 'macro' to more 'micro' aspects of a coursebook. A further narrowing may be provided to complete the process: ask participants to select, or give them, specific exercises or texts-with-tasks and ask them to define what prior knowledge these assume on the part of the learner and what their objective is.

▷ Unit Four: Supplementary materials
(About 40 minutes)

This unit is suitable for teachers who are working, or likely to work, in relatively well-resourced and well-equipped institutions.

The objective of the Simulation task is first to raise participants' awareness of the different kinds of materials available; and second to induce them to think carefully about the relative usefulness of the various types in their own teaching situation, and about some of the factors affecting the materials' contribution to learning and user-friendliness for teacher and learners.

The decisions about what to buy on a limited budget are ones which many teachers may indeed need to be involved with in the course of their careers, so this simulation may provide a useful preparation for real situations.

▷ Unit Five: Teacher-made worksheets and workcards
(Up to an hour and a half)

This is a very practical workshop, valuable for inexperienced teachers or trainees, who very often underestimate the difficulties of making their own materials and can benefit from guidance.

I find it helpful to demonstrate the classroom use of workcards with the group in a previous session. A set of cards with questions on topics we have recently learned in our course are prepared, and laid out on a central table in the room: participants take a card, answer in writing, and then compare their answers with sample acceptable ones supplied in an open file on my desk. They then take a new card, and repeat the process. This not only gives participants the 'feel' of the workcard process; it also provides an opportunity for useful review of course content.

Module 14: Topic content

▶ Unit One: Different kinds of content
(About an hour)

This is a very context-bound topic, which you will need to relate closely to your trainees' own situations. You may, for example, need to replace or supplement the examples illustrating the items in Box 14.1 with more relevant ones. It may be a useful exercise to elicit such examples from them.

The order of the session might be: a preliminary discussion, clarifying some advantages or disadvantages of the different kinds of content, followed by the writing of personal summaries similar to the one I have done for my own context in the Notes at the end of the module.

▶ Unit Two: Underlying messages
(An hour to an hour and a half)

Participants should be introduced to this topic through brief input from you, or independent reading (see *Further reading*); but the main part of the session will be based on critical examination of materials.

Note that it is not suggested here that all underlying messages are necessarily bad! The point is simply that teachers should know of their existence and nature, in order not to find themselves in the position of blindly passing on someone else's attitudes. Awareness of what the messages are empowers teachers to take their own decisions as to whether to adopt, make explicit or try to counteract them.

The task is a very interesting one to do, and may produce some surprising results. Participants may work in small groups on different books or on different tasks, sharing their results towards the end of the session.

▷ Unit Three: Literature (1): should it be included in the course?
(About 45 minutes)

This can be run as a 'for and against' debate, with or without the support of the ideas in the boxes. The main objective of this unit is not the drawing of a final conclusion – which, of course, depends to a large extent on the kind of courses your trainees are or will be involved with – but rather a thorough exploration of the arguments, and thoughtful weighing of their importance in teaching.

If you have chosen to do the literature units at all this probably means that the teaching of literature is at least a feasible option in your trainees' situations. So the direction the discussion is likely to take will be a basic consensus that yes, literature should be included in the foreign language course, followed by serious consideration of the very real problems involved and some attempt to suggest solutions.

▶ Unit Four: Literature (2): teaching ideas
(An hour to an hour and a half)

This unit necessarily provides only a small sample of the huge range of classroom procedures which can be used for literature teaching. You may wish to add extra blank space to Box 14.4 in order to elicit or suggest more ideas, and/or refer your teachers to the books listed under *Further reading*.

Specific types of technique used in literature teaching which you might find it interesting to discuss with teachers are:

– learning texts by heart
– preparing recitation or reading aloud
– using role play or simulation
– putting on plays
– creative writing inspired by the literature
– written criticism.

▷ Unit Five: Literature (3): teaching a specific text
(About an hour)

You may choose a text and ask all your trainees to prepare the same one for teaching; or each participant may prepare a different text of their own choosing. On the face of it, the second is the more attractive option; but I have found that more interesting and useful learning actually results from the first, since it reveals the surprising variety of ways a single text can be taught; and participants can learn from one another's interpretations and ideas, or talk through differences of opinion in order to arrive at thoughtful conclusions.

Module 15: Lesson planning

▶ Unit One: What does a lesson involve?
(About 40 minutes)

This unit studies the lesson in the abstract, as a phenomenon of social organization. The metaphors activity is an enjoyable introduction to the topic, whose aim is to raise awareness of some perspectives that participants may not have thought of.

Note that it is important at the first stage for participants to choose their own metaphors individually, uninfluenced by their friends' opinions. In subsequent sharing, there should be no implication that one choice is in any way better than another; the main aim should be to open participants' eyes to new approaches and interpretations.

The article by Prabhu (1992) referred to provides some interesting background reading which you may find it useful to ask your trainees to study before or after this activity.

A shorter alternative is to omit the metaphors activity and simply discuss the section *Aspects of the lesson* as it stands.

▷ Unit Two: Lesson preparation
(About 40 minutes; more if the interviewing is done in class)

The interviewing will normally be done as a home assignment.

Another possibility is to interview selected teachers yourself in advance, and then hand out copies of their answers to the group for analysis and discussion. If the participants do the interviewing, then you yourself should perhaps be one of the interviewees.

Comments on some of the questions:

1. Most experienced teachers actually prepare lessons twice: they have ready in advance a general syllabus of what activities, texts, etc. they want to get through during a certain period of the course; and then they plan the actual sequence of components for a specific lesson and prepare supplementary materials a day or two before.
2. All good professionals I know write lesson notes; though some are very brief and sketchy.
5. Trainees are usually exhorted to write down their objectives; research, however, indicates that experienced teachers rarely if ever do so, though they are capable of defining them retrospectively (Calderhead, 1987).
7. Many teachers keep notes until the volume becomes unwieldy and then throw them away! There are, however, valuable 'nuggets' in lesson plans that are worth keeping: activities that we may want to use again, or something about our own teaching that we have learned. It is a pity, in my opinion, that more teachers do not find the time to go through their lesson notes afterwards,

reflecting and picking out for further reference things they have learned.

At the Conclusions stage it is advisable to discuss and clarify ideas as a whole group, with your own active participation. This may be followed by individual writing of conclusions.

▶ Unit Three: Varying lesson components
(About an hour)

The gathering of ideas on variation of activities within a lesson is probably best done as a general class brainstorm; participants usually have plenty of ideas if challenged to suggest them, though they do not always demonstrate the same awareness in practice! The discussion and follow-up observation tasks at the end are designed to encourage this kind of transfer of awareness.

▷ Unit Four: Evaluating lesson effectiveness
(About 45 minutes)

As with many tasks in this book, the process is probably more important than the result. The hard thinking that has to be invested into a prioritizing exercise like this forces participants to clarify and articulate their ideas: why should one criterion be more important than another, and what are the implications for my teaching? The task should lead to the destabilizing of conventional or over-facile assumptions and stimulate interesting and productive discussion.

Nevertheless, I do not wish to underestimate the importance of personal decisions on what is important and what is not. The task should be pursued to its end; though the final decision on ranking the different items may perhaps be left to the individual rather than made as a group consensus.

If your trainees do the Follow-up task suggested at the end of the unit by evaluating one of their own lessons, it will be difficult to give them any useful feedback on the results unless you yourself have seen the lesson. It may be useful, however, to have people share their reflections and evaluations with each other in a later session. If they use the lesson report given in Box 15.5, you may find my comments in the Notes useful as a basis for discussion.

▶ Unit Five: Practical lesson management
(About 45 minutes)

This final unit consists of very practical advice, balancing the rather theoretical orientation of Unit One.

The key problem is that expressed in the *Postscript*: hints like this – however true and useful they appear – rarely result in real learning (that transfers to practice) when they are given, as here, detached from experience. The aim of the suggested interaction between experienced and inexperienced teachers in the follow-up Discussion task is to supply a link, albeit vicarious, with experience: the experienced teachers' personal anecdotes and opinions can help to make the advice more real and personal for the inexperienced, while clarifying their own thinking in the process. If your group is composed only of trainees, they may have to do this part of the unit as a home assignment; alternatively, you may like to invite an experienced teacher in to discuss the 'Hints' with the class.

You may feel you need to add some more 'Hints' yourself!

Reference

Calderhead, J. (1987) *Exploring Teacher Thinking*, London: Cassell Education.

Module 16: Classroom interaction

▶ Unit One: Patterns of classroom interaction
(About half an hour, not including the observation task)

As the opening sentence indicates, the 'IRF' interaction pattern is dominant, not always justifiably, in most classrooms; this unit draws attention to other possible types of interaction, and to their value in activating students.

Note that I have introduced a perhaps unfamiliar distinction between 'collaborative work' and 'group work': in the former, the basic interaction is between student and learning task and the function of the collaboration is merely to

facilitate or improve performance; whereas in the latter the basic interaction is between participants. It may be worth making sure that participants are clear about the difference before embarking on the task.

▶ Unit Two: Questioning
(About 45 minutes)

Much has been written on the topic of questioning: you might like to ask participants to read, for example, the article by Brown and Edmondson (1984) or an extract from Sinclair and Coulthard (1975).

The topic is an extremely broad and complex one: I have necessarily had to select one aspect of it, the one which I consider most useful for language teachers. Other aspects you may like to discuss with teachers are: techniques of nominating responders; pace and waiting (for answers) time; the justification for 'display' versus 'reference' (genuine) questions (see Brock, 1986).

The decision to focus on these particular criteria (especially 'availability' and 'extension') was based on my observation that most teachers tend to overuse closed-ended 'test' questions, and that therefore it is worth raising awareness of the importance of using open-ended ones that stimulate multiple and longer answers.

An alternative procedure is to invite participants to identify their own criteria (for effective questioning), perhaps within specific contexts, and justify them.

▶ Unit Three: Group work
(About 45 minutes)

It may be appropriate here to refer to a recent group-work activity you have actually done in your own (training) sessions, and ask your trainees to think about how far the guidelines in Box 16.5 applied to this. Which was/were used? Which are perhaps not suitable within a teacher-training context, but would be in a language class?

▶ Unit Four: Individualization
(45 minutes to an hour)

If you have a currently functioning self-access centre in your institution, it is certainly worth taking participants to visit it and see it in action.

However, on the assumption that many teachers do not have this facility, the objective of this unit is to give ideas for and encourage individualized procedures within the conventional classroom. (Some learners, incidentally, actually dislike self-access work and prefer direct teacher-fronted lessons: it may be worth discussing why.)

The grid in Box 16.7 may be drawn on the board and filled in fairly quickly through group discussion. The conclusions suggested – that usually, but not inevitably, more individualization means more teacher preparation – are perhaps worth investigating further in the light of participants' own experience.

▷ Unit Five: The selection of appropriate activation techniques
(About 45 minutes)

One thing about this task that is a little disquieting is that it implies the existence of teacher thinking that is in fact rare: objectives are not usually defined in the way imagined here, even by experienced practitioners. Many teachers will, for example, go through a reading passage and then do the textbook comprehension questions through 'IRF' as a matter of course, without asking themselves why. Thus a secondary – perhaps, ultimately, most important! – aim of this task is to get participants to become more aware of objectives in the use of texts or materials – and the implications of these for the planning of interaction patterns.

Module 17: Giving feedback

▶ Unit One: Different approaches to the nature and function of feedback
(About 45 minutes)

You might start by eliciting participants' own definition of 'feedback' in teaching, and get them to define their own approaches to the usefulness of assessment and correction before presenting the various theories.

I usually present the various theoretical approaches via my own input, encouraging critical comments throughout rather than waiting to the end. In this way, by the time we reach the end most of the participants have more or less crystallized their own views and reactions.

▷ Unit Two: Assessment
(About 45 minutes)

Summative evaluation is an interesting and complex topic which could in itself provide the content of a full course. It is, however, questionable whether the amount of time and effort needed to master this topic fully is a good investment, relative to its importance in practice. I have contented myself here with a brief unit that raises awareness of the nature and complexity of summative evaluation in general, and some of the less conventional options available to the evaluator.

Your trainees may, however, be in a situation where this topic is of particular importance, and you will therefore wish to go into the topic more fully. One possibility is to invite them to do some background reading on the various topics, using the references given under *Further reading*, before discussing or writing answers to the questions.

▶ Unit Three: Correcting mistakes in oral work
(About 30 to 45 minutes, assuming the interviews and observation are done elsewhere)

A discussion of the question is an essential preliminary to study of how to correct; it is a specific aspect of the general topic of the place of correction which was discussed in Unit One. The following inquiry project presupposes that the participants have defined under what circumstances they would correct in the first place, and explores how best to do it.

The summary discussion should result in some redefining of theories in the light of the evidence: in particular, the declared preferences of learners. It might be useful after the end of the discussion for participants actually to write down what they see as their own (future) policy with regard to oral correction. But, as noted at the end of the section *How the correction is expressed*, teachers should be cautious and sensitive about applying such policy in practice: it is useful – even essential – to have some general principles, provided you are aware that they do not necessarily apply in every specific case.

The final Observation and inquiry task might also throw up some thought-provoking discrepancies between both the perceptions of different observers, and between the perceptions of observer and observed. Such discrepancies need to be talked through and an attempt made to decide which perception was probably nearer the truth; this is not a place where you can smooth away conflicts by saying it is 'a matter of opinion'.

▶ Unit Four: Written feedback
(An hour to an hour and a half)

I usually ask trainees to do their marking of the different assignments at home, and bring them to class the next day. Comparing differences in pairs or threes gives rise to some useful thinking, which can be followed by a general discussion of the points raised in Box 17.4.

One practical problem which is not raised in this unit due to lack of space is that of the amount of time and work necessary for correcting written assignments, particularly in large classes. You might wish to discuss this with participants, and explore different ways of easing the load: taking in only part of the class's assignments each time; peer-correction; self-correction; and so on.

▷ Unit Five: Clarifying personal attitudes
(About 45 minutes)

The most convenient way to do this unit is to have participants fill in their answers in Box 17.5 individually and then share and discuss in groups or in a full-class forum. Do not let them look at my opinions as expressed in the Notes while writing their own, in case these influence them – though they (my ideas) may be useful later in the discussion as a basis for deeper probing.

You may wish to fill in further statements to agree or disagree with yourself, before presenting the task to your trainees; or, of course, elicit these from them.

I find that my trainees tend to go for over-facile, obvious answers (for example, that of course positive feedback is 'good' and negative is 'bad'); the objective of the discussion should be to

examine such assumptions carefully in order to work out what seems really true and valid in the light of the participants' own experience and critical thinking.

Module 18: Classroom discipline

▶ Unit One: What is discipline?
(30 to 45 minutes)

It is possible to try to elicit a definition of 'classroom discipline' directly, instead of doing so in the roundabout way I suggest; but in my experience this tends to result in a set of very widely differing definitions, each focussing on a different aspect of what is, after all, a very complex concept, and I usually end up by doing what is here suggested in the first place: pooling key concepts, and eliciting a final definition based on them. If you do it this way, check my list of concepts in Box 18.1 to make sure there is nothing missing there that you consider important.

The optional follow-up activity of distinguishing between pairs of concepts helps to clarify thinking, and is best based on reading.

You may find it appropriate here to discuss the different norms and behaviours associated with classroom discipline that are acceptable in different cultures.

▶ Unit Two: What does a disciplined classroom look like?
(30 to 45 minutes)

This unit aims to 'destabilize' conventional assumptions through first 'surfacing' them (putting plus or minus signs by the statements in Box 18.2), then re-examining them in the light of the following critical Comments, and finally restating. The re-examination and restatement may be done through class discussion, item by item; and of course the final 'verdict' does not need to be expressed only through participants' reconsidered decisions on which symbol to put by each item: you may find it more appropriate actually to reword or expand the statements in order to express conclusions more precisely.

▷ Unit Three: What teacher action is conducive to a disciplined classroom?
(About 45 minutes)

There is a common mistaken assumption that classroom discipline is achieved by the teacher's wielding of authority and/or skilled use of classroom management strategies. In fact there are several other important factors at work, and the first part of this unit suggests what they are: the question elicits illustrations of ways the theoretical concepts are represented in practice, and also familiarizes participants with the list of practical hints in Box 18.3 in preparation for the prioritizing task.

The task is best done in small groups. The number of ten items is arbitrary; you may wish to ask for a different number. Inevitably some groups finish earlier than others: they can be asked to put the individual items in their 'top ten' in order of priority. Other groups never manage to find as many as ten at all: this is fine, and often indicates that these groups are engaged in very careful and rigorous examination of the issues. The summary discussion may be based on a pooling of however many items each group has chosen.

I usually organize this pooling stage by writing up a list of numbers (1–22) on the board, and asking a representative of each group to put a tick by the numbers it chose. A picture is then available to the class of which items were most popular, and interesting discussion may ensue based on arguments for or against the more controversial items. It is important, I think, for you to share with participants your own priorities, and participate freely and actively in the discussion.

▶ Unit Four: Dealing with discipline problems
(About 30 minutes)

The advice in Box 18.4 is, as you see, presented informally and semi-humorously; and the session in which it is presented I also run in a fairly light-hearted tone. One reason for this is that the underlying topic of the session is a problem which can lead to extremely stressful, intimidating and distressing situations for the teacher, and which is a major source of apprehension for many new entrants to the profession. A 'light' treatment can help to demystify and lower the profile of the topic, and facilitate a practical and more confident approach.

I usually make an OHP transparency out of the box, and talk my trainees through it, peppering the input with personal illustrative anecdotes (my own or theirs).

It would be thoroughly unrealistic to hope that the advice will be either remembered in detail or implemented in practice from the next day by new teachers in training! The ideas recommended here need to be thoroughly acquired and 'owned' by teachers before they are any use, and this can only be brought about by experience and reflection. However, the explicit discussion of the different ideas is likely to raise awareness, and provide participants with potential schemata: ready 'frames' in their minds which will enable them to perceive and appreciate the significance of different classroom incidents and their own reactions as they happen, and hence ultimately facilitate and accelerate their learning from experience.

Experienced teachers react differently: some of the suggestions they recognize, and greet with a pleased or rueful smile; others represent half-felt, intuitive impressions that they are glad to have put into words in order to make them accessible for critical discussion or application.

▷ Unit Five: Discipline problems: episodes
(About an hour)

This is usually an interesting and enjoyable session: participants work in groups noting their responses to the three stimulus questions for each episode. Obviously not all groups work at the same speed, so you will need to stop the discussions as soon as the first group finishes, and share ideas and conclusions.

You may wish to use incidents from your trainees' experience as a basis for this activity instead of the ones given here. If so, these should be written out, so that participants can refer back to the text to check details.

(Incidentally, this task can also be used as a classroom exercise with learners: they have their own ideas on classroom discipline which are worth hearing, and a lot of talk is generated!)

Module 19: Learner motivation and interest

Note: Learner motivation as an aspect of cognitive psychology or psycholinguistics has been fairly extensively researched; but the topic of teaching for motivation has been relatively neglected in modern books on language teaching methodology. In my opinion the subject is crucial and well worth the investment of thought and study.

▷ Unit One: Motivation: some background thinking
(About 45 minutes)

The unit represents, of course, only the tip of the iceberg: there is an immense amount of literature and research on learner motivation. You may wish to expand on my summary, or select certain topics to dwell on.

The text may be simply read by trainees; or delivered orally in lecture form, by you or by (prepared) participants; or they may be asked to read some of the background literature themselves. In any case, it is useful to relate each of the theoretical points (as I have tried to do) to classroom practice: emphasizing how awareness of them might affect teaching behaviour or attitudes to learners.

▷ Unit Two: The teacher's responsibility
(About 45 minutes)

Recalling good teachers and then trying to analyse what made them good is a useful training activity in itself, even if not related specifically, as here, to motivation. It does tend to cast doubt on the popular illusion that good teachers are usually loving and gentle! – and sets participants delving rather deeper for 'good teacher' qualities such as respect for their students and belief in their ability, the ability to explain clearly, enthusiasm, love of teaching, sheer hard work . . .

In any case, every time I have done this activity it has revealed the typical teacher characteristic of the fostering of student motivation – which is why it is particularly useful for awareness-raising here.

Another possibility at this point is to watch films or read books about teachers – preferably ones based on true stories! – and analyse how the teacher motivated the students. The film *Stand and Deliver* is one interesting example: it recounts in fictionalized form the true story of the success of a mathematics teacher working with previously low-achieving Hispanic American students in California.

▶ Unit Three: Extrinsic motivation
(30 to 45 minutes)

There is quite a lot which you may find controversial here: whether or not you agree with my ideas, they are probably worth discussing with trainees, along the lines suggested under the Summary discussion task. Note that I have stressed, in the task, the use of experience as a basis for critical comment as well as intuition and general attitude: if there is a conflict between the two it needs to be brought into the open and resolved. For example: participants may find the idea of motivating through the threat of a test repugnant in principle, but know from their own experience that it appears to work; can they define a viable, acceptable personal approach to the use of tests to motivate, taking into account both aspects?

▶ Unit Four: Intrinsic motivation and interest
(About 45 minutes)

A useful preliminary to this unit is a discussion in which participants share their perceptions of how motivated they think their students are, on the whole, to study the foreign language for its own sake, and why: for example, is it because the language is seen as high-prestige, or connected in their minds with various positive images? The discussion can then move on smoothly to a consideration of how this initial motivation can be enhanced and encouraged by teachers in classroom practice.

The discussion of factors that arouse interest I usually run as a full-class brainstorm, not using the box, except for my own reference, and supplementing participants' contributions with further suggestions of my own if necessary. It is important not to leave the results of the brainstorm as a mass of raw ideas, but to go on to some kind of critical awareness-raising process, as suggested in the final stage of the task.

▷ Unit Five: Fluctuations in learner interest

(The observation is done elsewhere; follow-up discussion takes 30 to 45 minutes)

I have in the past used this observation process as the basis for a trainee classroom research project, written up in a term paper. The main positive result was a rise in the trainee's awareness of her students' level of interest and attention, and of what she herself could do to affect it.

An optional summarizing activity might be the drawing up of a list of 'dos' and 'don'ts' for the teacher, based on what people have found out through their observation. For example: 'Don't carry on one kind of activity too long: if you detect signs of restlessness, make a change.'

Module 20: Younger and older learners

▶ Unit One: What difference does age make to language learning?

(About 45 minutes)

This unit aims to re-examine popular assumptions about the way different age groups learn, in the light of experience and research.

The first two statements in Box 20.1, to do with the popular belief that younger children are better at learning languages, are at least dubious, if not actually false, as indicated by the research literature referred to and further confirmed by the thinking of many experienced practitioners (myself, incidentally, included). They are, however, firmly believed by many people and you may find your trainees unwilling to forgo them! The aim should be at least to introduce some doubt, and make them more cautious about making over-generalized assumptions that may be used as a basis for policy decisions.

The next three statements are less controversial,

and discussed in the light of experience rather than research; you may find a pooling of participants' own experience as learners very helpful and relevant here.

▷ Unit Two: Teaching children

(45 minutes to an hour)

This may be run as a short input session, followed by some examining of relevant material and ideas. I would suggest if possible providing a display of materials: posters, magazine pictures, books and booklets, ideas for games. Such a display may be set up by the participants themselves, or drawn from materials available at your institution.

The final Application activity can lead to a pooling of ideas for children's language-learning games which can be written out and collated into a booklet of practical suggestions made available to all participants.

▷ Unit Three: Teaching adolescents: student preferences

(About 20 minutes' class preparation of the survey and about 40 minutes' discussion after)

It is worth going through the questionnaire in class and inviting participants to express their own opinions: this process familiarizes them with the items and clarifies any obscurities, as well as raising speculations and expectations that will be re-examined in the light of student responses later.

Each participant then goes off to interview one or two adolescent acquaintances and in the next session the results are pooled and discussed.

My own trainees find this project interesting and learning-rich: there are inevitably discrepancies between their own preconceptions and what most respondents tell them, which result in thoughtful and fruitful discussion and re-evaluation of theories.

▷ Unit Four: Teaching adults: a different relationship

(About 45 minutes)

This unit defines and invites participants to think about different kinds of relationships between teachers and adult classes. The *Comments* simply explore the implications of each relationship and their relevance to the teaching of adults, with little implied judgement or preferences. A frank group discussion may, however, lead to interesting and valuable exchanges of ideas on participants' own beliefs and priorities.

Module 21: Large heterogeneous classes

▶ Unit One: Defining terms
(About half an hour)

A critical examination of what in fact the terms 'large' and 'heterogeneous' mean is a necessary preliminary to any study of practical problems. The second term is discussed more in depth. Participants are asked to think about three connected propositions: first, that any class is to some degree heterogeneous; second, that the term 'mixed-ability' is unsatisfactory as a synonym for heterogeneous classes, and why; and third, that heterogeneity involves a lot more than mere differences in proficiency.

For the third topic an effective procedure is to have participants brainstorm ideas, which are pooled on the board and may be added to by you or by reference to Box 21.1. Having done this, it may be appropriate to point out to participants that the brainstorming technique they have just performed is itself an excellent 'heterogeneous' activity, inviting contributions that may be of different levels, express different ideas and interests and which result from differences in experience and personality.

▶ Unit Two: Problems and advantages
(About half an hour)

Some of the problems vary, of course, from place to place: those teaching highly motivated adult groups may find that they have no problem of discipline or boredom; for teachers of schoolchildren these may be major issues. However, the items to do with materials, effective learning for all and participation are likely to be of high priority for all teachers.

The aim of the categorization task is to get participants to think carefully about the meanings and implications of the different problems, and their overall importance in effective teaching. The discussion can be 'sharpened' still further, if you demand an actual order of priority of the items, one by one, instead of three rough groupings.

The final (matching) task has a similar objective. It is rather easy to say: 'Oh yes, that' (the use of collaborative work, for example) 'is a nice idea', without actually defining specifically what its contribution is and what problems it is likely to help to solve. This task forces participants to think about links between problems and solutions, thereby making it more likely that the same links may occur to them and be exploited in classroom teaching.

▶ Unit Three: Teaching strategies (1): compulsory + optional
(If the experiment is done in class as peer-teaching, then the session will take about 45 minutes)

The principle of 'compulsory + optional' is a very helpful and effective one: I am always surprised how little it is exploited in learning materials. It might be worth looking at local courses to see if and where it is used in them.

The experiment at the end of the unit can be very easily done on the spot, with you role-playing the teacher and group participants the learners, in three proficiency groups as suggested in the Preliminary Note. The results are usually fairly clear; but it is useful, if there is time, to have teachers try out the same thing again in 'real' classes and report back.

▶ Unit Four: Teaching strategies (2): open-ending
(45 minutes to an hour)

Again this is an extremely useful type of stimulus for interaction in the classroom, and again sadly under-used, both by textbook writers and by teachers. Both teachers and many learners often say they prefer closed-ended questions, saying they are easier (not true: difficulty depends on whether the learners understand the question and whether they have the knowledge needed to answer it, not on the number of possible answers). This preference may perhaps be based on the feeling of false security that closed-ended questions give both sides: the comforting assumption that there *is* only one possible right solution, there is one straight road to tread. But this is no more true of language than it is of life in general: an illusion that we, as educators, should surely not encourage.

Box 21.6 I present as a worksheet or display using an overhead projector; I then invite participants to suggest ways of open-ending the exercises and add my own ideas if necessary.

It is probably worth spending most time and effort in this session on the work on local textbooks suggested in the task at the end of the unit: either invite participants to choose their own material, or choose and make copies of appropriate varied samples yourself. Discussion should not be limited to suggesting open-ended variations of the material as illustrated in this unit, but should include any creative ideas participants can suggest that will make it appropriate for large heterogeneous classes. They should, however, be asked in every case to define **why** their suggestion will have such an effect: the fact that it is a pleasing or original idea is not enough.

▷ Unit Five: Designing your own activities
(About an hour)

This can be very enjoyable if run as a practical workshop session, trying out as many of the activities as possible and gradually filling in a 'mind map' on the board as appropriate. There is not, of course, usually time for all of the activities: some will simply be explained.

Instead of doing the Application task at the end of the unit you can use it immediately after each activity.

You might like to continue this session into further creative work by inviting participants to take the 'mind map' and draw in more lines and ideas: ideas for additional 'families' of activities suitable for large heterogeneous classes; or other activities based on the 'families' given; or further variations on the activities already described.

Module 22: And beyond

Note: All the units in this module are optional: choose those which are appropriate for your trainees. No time estimates are given, since the tasks here are based on personal reflection and action rather than structured group activity, and will therefore vary a great deal according to individual situation and need.

These units may be used in the final stages of a pre-service programme, if trainees are regularly teaching, or for in-service courses or teacher development. They are less appropriate for those who are not engaged in at least part-time professional practice.

The underlying message is of encouragement to new teachers to look beyond their daily routine: that professional activity is not just lesson-giving, but also constant personal and professional progress: learning, changing and producing.

▷ Unit One: Teacher development: practice, reflection, sharing

If you are using this unit at the end of a pre-service course, then this is an appropriate time to discuss the problems of new teachers in their first year or two of professional practice. It is important to get across the message that 'first-year stress' is an entirely normal phenomenon (my anecdote in the Notes may help), and to suggest some ways of dealing with it.

The reservations that participants usually express about the suggestions made in this and the next unit is that they are time-consuming and need a lot of initiative: both commodities being hard to come by when you are engaged in a full teaching schedule! Again, this is something that needs discussing: both time and initiative can be found if teachers feel the objectives are important enough. Meanwhile, they can be asked to try out some of the ideas as part of the present course.

▷ Unit Two: Teacher appraisal

If your trainees are at the end of a pre-service course, they are probably used to having their classroom performance assessed (by you). Here, the objective is to get them to start taking responsibility for their own self-assessment.

My own experience is that of the three sources of appraisal suggested here by far the most useful and productive is the students themselves. However, in some situations cultural and social norms may make it difficult if not impossible to ask students to criticize their teachers; if this is true of your trainees' teaching context you may wish to omit this section.

▷ Unit Three: Advancing further (1): intake

This is an informative and awareness-raising unit, mainly aimed at getting participants to think about the various possibilities for learning available to them, and the advantages and disadvantages of each mode.

▷ Unit Four: Advancing further (2): output

A useful bit of experience here can be supplied by organizing your own in-house conference, where participants can share their ideas with each other in semi-formal sessions, and get a first taste of what it feels like to talk to a professional audience. Similarly, a journal can be published, either within your institution or together with nearby 'sister' institutions: in this way novices can gain some experience of writing, editing and publishing professional material.

As regards the research: if the participants have been following the course laid out in this book, they will have already had some experience of carrying out and documenting inquiry based on observation, interview and questionnaires. They have probably not, however, tried to initiate their own: hence the importance of the Application task at the end of the unit.

This is something I do regularly with my own trainees: it is the major assignment of their course. Each chooses a topic that they are particularly interested in or worried about and formulates a question or hypothesis they wish to examine. I provide individual guidance in planning the research method, suggest appropriate background reading, and make extensive comments on the first draft of the resulting paper before it is finalized. The papers are then presented in an 'in-house' conference as suggested above. All this is extremely time-consuming, but results in excellent learning and some very interesting research.

Bibliography

Alderson, J. C. and Urquhart, A. H. (eds.) (1984) *Reading in a Foreign Language*, London: Longman.

Alderson, C., Clapham, C. and Wall, D. (1995) *Language Test Construction and Evaluation*, Cambridge: Cambridge University Press.

Allan, M. (1988) *Teaching English with Video*, London: Longman.

Allen, V. F. (1983) *Techniques in Teaching Vocabulary*, New York: Oxford University Press.

Allwright, R. L. (1981) 'What do we want the teaching materials for?', *ELT Journal*, **36**,1, 5–18.

Allwright, R. and Bailey, K. M. (1991) *Focus on the Language Classroom: An Introduction to Classroom Research for Language Teachers*, Cambridge: Cambridge University Press.

Alptekin, C. (1993) 'Target-language culture in EFL materials', *ELT Journal*, **47**, 2, 136–43.

Anderson, A. and Lynch, T. (1988) *Listening*, Oxford: Oxford University Press.

Anderson, J. R. (1985) *Cognitive Psychology and its Implications*, New York: Freeman.

Argardizzo, C. (1993) *Children in Action*, Hemel Hempstead: Prentice Hall International.

Argyris, C. and Schön, D. A. (1974) *Theory in Practice: Increasing Professional Effectiveness*, San Francisco: Jossey Bass.

Ashton-Warner, S. (1980) *Teacher*, London: Virago.

Ashworth, M. (1985) *Beyond Methodology*, Cambridge: Cambridge University Press.

Bartram, M. and Walton, R. (1991) *Correction: Mistake Management – A Positive Approach for Language Teachers*, Hove: Language Teaching Publications.

Bassnett, S. and Grundy, P. (1993) *Language through Literature*, London: Longman.

Bejarano, Y. (1987) 'A cooperative small-group methodology in the language classroom', *TESOL Quarterly*, **21**, 3, 483–501.

Bloom, B. S. (1956) *Taxonomy of Educational Objectives*, Vol. I, New York: McKay.

Bolitho, R. (1988) 'Teaching, teacher training and applied linguistics', *The Teacher Trainer*, **2**, 3, 4–7.

Bowen, B. M. (1982) *Look Here!: Visual Aids in Language Teaching*, London: Macmillan.

Bowen, T. and Marks, J. (1992) *The Pronunciation Book*, London: Pilgrims-Longman.

Brazil, D., Coulthard, M. and Johns, C. (1980) *Discourse Intonation and Language Teaching*, London: Longman.

Brewster, J., Ellis, G. and Girard, D. (1992) *The Primary English Teacher's Guide*, Harmondsworth: Penguin.

Brindley, G. (1989) *Assessing Achievement in the Learner-Centred Curriculum*, Macquarie University, Sydney: National Centre for English Language Teaching and Research.

Brock, C. A. (1986) 'The effects of referential questions on ESL classroom discourse', *TESOL Quarterly*, **20**, 1, 47–59.

Brown, G. (1977) *Listening to Spoken English*, London: Longman.

Brown, G. and Yule, G. (1983) *Teaching the Spoken Language*, Cambridge: Cambridge University Press.

Brown, G.A. and Armstrong, S. (1984) 'Explanations and explaining' in Wragg, E. C. (ed.) *Classroom Teaching Skills*, London and Sydney: Croom Helm.

Brown, G. A. and Edmondson, R. (1984) 'Asking questions', in Wragg, E. C. (ed.), *Classroom Teaching Skills*, London and Sydney: Croom Helm.

Brown, H. D. (1987) *Principles of Language Learning and Teaching (*2nd edn.*)*, Englewood Cliffs, N. J.: Prentice Hall.

Brown, H. D. (1994) *Teaching by Principles*, Englewood Cliffs, N. J.: Prentice Hall Regents.

Brumfit, C. J. (1984a) *Communicative Methodology in Language Teaching: The Roles of Fluency and Accuracy*, Cambridge: Cambridge University Press.

Brumfit, C. J. (ed.) (1984) *General English Syllabus Design (ELT Documents 118)*, Oxford: Pergamon Press.

Brumfit, C. J. and Carter, R. (eds.) (1986) *Literature and Language Teaching*, Oxford: Oxford University Press.

Brumfit, C. J. and Mitchell, R. (1989) *Research in the Language Classroom*, London: British Council with Modern English Publications; Macmillan.

Brumfit, C. J., Moon, J. and Tongue, R. (eds.) (1991) *Teaching English to Children*, London: Collins.

Burstall, C., Jamieson, M., Cohen, S., and Hargreaves, M. (1974) *Primary French in the Balance*, Windsor: National Foundation for Educational Research Publishing Company.

Bygate, M., Tonkyn, A. and Williams, E. (eds.) (1994) *Grammar and the Language Teacher*, Hemel Hempstead: Prentice Hall International.

Byrne, D. (1986) *Teaching Oral English* (2nd edn.), London: Longman.

Byrne, D. (1987) *Techniques for Classroom Interaction*, London: Longman.

Byrne, D. (1988) *Teaching Writing Skills* (2nd edn.), London: Longman.

Calderhead, J. (1987) *Exploring Teacher Thinking*, London: Cassell Education.

Cambridge International Dictionary of English (1995) Cambridge: Cambridge University Press.

Candlin, C.N. (1984) 'Syllabus design as a critical process' in Brumfit, C. J. (ed.) (1984) *General English Syllabus Design (ELT Documents 118)*, Oxford: Pergamon Press.

Carrell, P. L., Devine, J. and Eskey, D. E. (eds.) (1988) *Interactive Approaches to Second Language Reading*, Cambridge: Cambridge University Press.

Carter, R. and Long, M. N. (1991) *Teaching Literature*, London: Longman.

Carter, R. and McCarthy, M. (1988) *Vocabulary and Language Teaching*, London: Longman.

Celce-Murcia, M. and Larsen-Freeman, D. (1983) *The Grammar Book*, Rowley, Mass.: Newbury House.

Celce-Murcia, M. and Hilles, S. L. (1988) *Techniques and Resources in Teaching Grammar*, New York: Oxford University Press.

Charles, C. M. (1992) *Building Classroom Discipline* (4th edn.), New York: Longman.

Chaudron, C. (1988) *Second Language Classrooms: Research on Teaching and Learning*, Cambridge: Cambridge University Press.

Clarke, D. F. (1991) 'The negotiated syllabus: what is it and how is it likely to work?', *Applied Linguistics*, **12**, 1, 13–28.

Clarke, J. and Clarke, M. (1990) 'Stereotyping in TESOL materials', in Harrison, B. (ed.), *Culture and the Language Classroom*, Hong Kong: Modern English Publications and the British Council.

Close, R. A. (1992) *A Teachers' Grammar: The Central Problems of English*, Hove: Language Teaching Publications.

Cohen, L. and Manion, L. (1977) *A Guide to Teaching Practice*, London: Macmillan.

Cohen, L. and Manion, L. (1980) *Research Methods in Education*, London and Sydney: Croom Helm.

Coleman, H. *et al.* (1989) *Language Learning in Large Classes Research Project*, Leeds: Leeds and Lancaster Universities.

Collie, J. and Slater, S. (1987) *Literature in the Language Classroom*, Cambridge: Cambridge University Press.

Cook, V. J. (1983) 'What should language teaching be about?', *ELT Journal*, **37**, 3, 229–34.

Cooper, R., Lavery, M. and Rinvolucri, M. (1991) *Video*, Oxford: Oxford University Press.

Coulavin, A. (1983) 'Excuses, excuses' in *Practical English Teaching*, 4, 2, 31.

Csikzsentmihalyi, M. and Nakamura, J. (1989) 'The dynamics of intrinsic motivation', in Ames, C. and Ames, R. (eds.), *Research on Motivation in Education*, Vol. III, London: Academic Press.

Cunningsworth, A. (1984) *Evaluating and Selecting EFL Teaching Materials*, London: Heinemann.

Davis, E. and Whitney, N., Pike-Blakey, M, and Bass, L. (1990) *Task Reading*, Cambridge: Cambridge University Press.

Davis, P. and Rinvolucri, M. (1988) *Dictation: New Methods, New Possibilities*, Cambridge: Cambridge University Press.

Dickinson, L. (1987) *Self-Instruction in Language Learning*, Cambridge: Cambridge University Press.

Doff, A. (1988) *Teach English: A Training Course for Teachers* (Teacher's Workbook and Trainer's Handbook), Cambridge: Cambridge University Press.

Dörnyei, Z. (1986) 'Exploiting textbook dialogues dynamically' in *Practical English Teaching*, 6, 4, 15–16.

Dörnyei, Z. and Thurrell, S. (1992) *Conversation*

and Dialogues in Action, Hemel Hempstead: Prentice Hall International.

Dubin, F. and Olshtain, E. (1986) *Course Design*, Cambridge: Cambridge University Press.

Duff, A. and Maley, A. (1992) *Literature*, Oxford: Oxford University Press.

Edge, J. (1989) *Mistakes and Correction*, London: Longman.

Edge, J. (1991) *Cooperative Development: Professional Self-development through Cooperation with Colleagues*, London: Longman.

Ellis, G. and Brewster, J. (eds.) (1991) *The Storytelling Handbook for Primary Teachers*, Harmondsworth: Penguin.

Ellis, G. and McRae, J. (1991) *The Extensive Reading Handbook for Secondary Teachers*, Harmondsworth: Penguin.

Ellis, R. (1990) *Instructed Second Language Acquisition*, Oxford: Blackwell.

Ellis, R. (1994) *The Study of Second Language Acquisition*, Oxford: Oxford University Press.

Flanders, N. A. (1970) *Analyzing Teaching Behavior*, Reading, Mass.: Addison-Wesley.

Fortescue, S. and Jones, C. (1987) *Using Computers in the Language Classroom*, London: Longman.

Freedman, A., Pringle, I. and Yalden, J. (eds.) (1983) *Learning to Write: First Language/Second Language*, London: Longman.

Gairns, R. and Redman, S. (1986) *Working with Words*, Cambridge: Cambridge University Press.

Gardner, R. (1980) 'On the validity of affective variables in second language acquisition: conceptual, contextual and statistical considerations', *Language Learning*, 30, 255–70.

Gardner, R. and Lambert, W. (1972) *Attitudes and Motivation in Second Language Learning*, Rowley, Mass.: Newbury House.

Gardner, R. C. and MacIntyre, P. D. (1993) 'A student's contributions to second-language learning. Part II: Affective variables', *Language Teaching*, 26, 1, 1–11.

Gatbonton, E. and Segalowitz, N. (1988) 'Creative automization: principles for promoting fluency within a communicative framework', *TESOL Quarterly*, 22, 3, 473–92.

Geddes, M. and Sturtridge, G. (eds.) (1982) *Individualization*, Oxford: Modern English Publications.

Gerngross, G. and Puchta, H. (1992) *Pictures in Action*, Englewood Cliffs: Prentice Hall.

Gimson, A. C. (1978) *A Practical Course of English Pronunciation*, London: Edward Arnold.

Girard, D. (1977) 'Motivation: the responsibility of the teacher', *ELT Journal*, 31, 97–102.

Graham, C. (1978) *Jazz Chants*, New York: Oxford University Press.

Greenall, S. and Swan, M. (1986) *Effective Reading: Skills for Advanced Students*, Cambridge: Cambridge University Press.

Greenwood, J. (1988) *Class Readers*, Oxford: Oxford University Press.

Grellet, F. (1981) *Developing Reading Skills*, Cambridge: Cambridge University Press.

Hadfield, J. (1984) *Elementary Communication Games*, London: Nelson.

Hadfield, J. (1992) *Classroom Dynamics*, Oxford: Oxford University Press.

Harmer, J. (1984) 'How to give your students feedback', *Practical English Teaching*, 5, 2, 39–40.

Harmer, J. (1989) *Teaching and Learning Grammar*, London: Longman.

Harmer, J. (1991) *The Practice of English Language Teaching (2nd edn.)*, London: Longman.

Harrison, B. (ed.) (1990) *Culture and the Language Classroom*, Hong Kong: Modern English Publications and the British Council.

Hawkins, E. (1984) *Awareness of Language: An Introduction*, Cambridge: Cambridge University Press.

Haycraft, B. (1971) *The Teaching of Pronunciation: A Classroom Guide*, London: Longman.

Hayward, T. (1983) 'Testing spoken English – an introduction', *Practical English Teaching*, 4, 2, 37–9.

Heaton, J. B. (1990) *Classroom Testing*, London: Longman.

Hedge, T. (1988) *Writing*, Oxford: Oxford University Press.

Hewings, M. (1993) *Pronunciation Tasks*, Cambridge: Cambridge University Press.

Hill, J. (1986) *Using Literature in Language Teaching*, London: Macmillan.

Hughes, A. (1989) *Testing for Language Teachers*, Cambridge: Cambridge University Press.

Hurford, J. R. (1983) *Semantics: A Coursebook*, Cambridge: Cambridge University Press.

Hyland, K. (1990) 'Purpose and strategy: teaching extensive reading skills', *English Teaching Forum*, 28, 2, 14–17.

Hyland, K. (1991) 'Developing oral presentation skills', *English Teaching Forum*, **29**, 2, 35–7.

Johnson, K. (1988) 'Mistake correction', *ELT Journal*, **42**, 2, 89–96.

Johnson, K. (1995) *Language Teaching and Skill Learning*, Oxford: Basil Blackwell.

Kennedy, C. and Jarvis, J. (eds.) (1991) *Ideas and Issues in Primary ELT*, London: Nelson.

Kenning, M. J. and Kenning, M.-M. (1983) *An Introduction to Computer Assisted Language Teaching*, Oxford: Oxford University Press.

Kenworthy, J. (1987) *Teaching English Pronunciation*, London: Longman.

Khan, J. (1991) 'Lessons worth remembering from Primary French in Britain' in Kennedy, C. and Jarvis, J. (eds.) *Ideas and Issues in Primary ELT*, London: Nelson.

Klippel, F. (1984) *Keep Talking*, Cambridge: Cambridge University Press.

Kolb, D. A. (1984) *Experiential Learning: Experience as the Source of Learning and Development*, Englewood Cliffs, New Jersey: Prentice Hall.

Kounin, J. S. (1970) *Discipline and Group Management in Classrooms*, New York: Holt, Rinehart and Winston.

Kramsch, C. (1993) *Context and Culture in Language Teaching*, Oxford: Oxford University Press.

Krashen, S. D. (1982) *Principles and Practice in Second Language Acquisition*, Oxford: Pergamon Press.

Kroll, B. (ed.) (1990) *Second Language Writing*, Cambridge: Cambridge University Press.

Lansley, C. (1994) '"Collaborative Development": an alternative to phatic discourse and the art of Co-operative Development', *ELT Journal*, **48**, 1, 50–6.

Larsen-Freeman, D. and Long, M. (1991) *An Introduction to Second Language Acquisition Research*, London: Longman.

Lazar, G. (1993) *Literature and Language Teaching*, Cambridge: Cambridge University Press.

Leech, G. (1974) *Semantics*, Harmondsworth: Penguin.

Leech, G., Deuchar, M. and Hoogenraad, R. (1983) *English Grammar for Today*, London: Macmillan.

Leech, G. and Candlin, C. (1986) *Computers in English Language Teaching and Research*, London: Longman.

Legutke, M. and Thomas, H. (1991) *Process and Experience in the Language Classroom*, London: Longman.

Leki, I. (1991) 'Teaching second language writing; where we seem to be', *English Teaching Forum*, **29**, 2, 8–11, 26.

Leki, I. (1991) 'The preferences of ESL students for error correction in college-level writing classes', *Foreign Language Annals* (New York), **24**, 3, 203–18.

Lightbown, P. and Spada, N. (1993) *How Languages are Learned*, Oxford: Oxford University Press.

Littlewood, W. (1984) *Foreign and Second Language Learning*, Cambridge: Cambridge University Press.

Lombardo, L. (1984) 'Oral testing: getting a sample of real language', *English Teaching Forum*, **22**, 1, 2–6.

Long, M. H. (1990) 'Maturational constraints on language development', *Studies in Second Language Acquisition*, **12**, 217–85.

Long, M . H. and Crookes, G. (1992) 'Three approaches to task-based syllabus design', *TESOL Quarterly*, **26**, 1, 27–56.

Long, M. H. and Porter, P. A. (1985) 'Group work, interlanguage talk and second language acquisition', *TESOL Quarterly*, **19**, 2, 207–28.

Long, M.H. and Sato, C. J. (1983) 'Classroom foreigner talk discourse: forms and functions of teachers' questions', in Seliger, H. W. and Long, M. H. (eds.) *Classroom Oriented Research in Second Language Acquisition*, Rowley, Mass.: Newbury House.

Longman Dictionary of Contemporary English (1995) London: Longman.

Looking at Language Classrooms (1996) Cambridge: Cambridge University Press.

Maclennan, S. (1987) 'Integrating lesson planning and class management', *ELT Journal*, **41**, 3, 193–7.

Madsen, H. and Bourn, J. D. (1978) *Adaptation in Language Teaching*, Rowley, Mass.: Newbury House.

Malamah-Thomas, A. (1987) *Classroom Interaction*, Oxford: Oxford University Press.

Maley, A. and Duff, A. (1978) *Variations on a Theme*, Cambridge: Cambridge University Press.

McCall, J. (1992) *Self-access: Setting up a Centre*, Manchester: The British Council.

McCarthy, M. (1990) *Vocabulary*, Oxford: Oxford University Press.

McDonough, S. (1991) 'Survey review: approaches to research in second language teaching and learning', *ELT Journal*, **45**, 3, 260–6.

McLaughlin, B. (1987) *Theories of Second-Language Learning*, London: Edward Arnold.

Morgan, J. and Rinvolucri, M. (1986) *Vocabulary*, Oxford: Oxford University Press.

Murphy, R. (1985) *English Grammar in Use*, Cambridge: Cambridge University Press.

Naiman, N., Froelich, M., Stern, H. H. and Todesco, A. (1978) *The Good Language Learner*, Research in Education Series, No. 7, Toronto: Ontario Institute for Studies in Education.

Nation, I. S. P. (1990) *Teaching and Learning Vocabulary*, New York: Newbury House.

Newmark, L. (1979) 'How not to interfere with language learning' in Brumfit, C. J. and Johnson, K. (eds.), *The Communicative Approach to Language Teaching*, Oxford: Oxford University Press.

Noffke, S. E. (1992) 'The work and workplace of teachers in action research', *Teaching and Teacher Education*, 8, 1, 15–29.

Nolasco, R. and Arthur, L. (1987) *Conversation*, Oxford: Oxford University Press.

Norrish, J. (1983) *Language Learners and their Errors*, London: Macmillan.

Nunan, D. (1988) *Syllabus Design*, Oxford: Oxford University Press.

Nunan, D. (1990) 'Action research in the language classroom' in Richards, J. and Nunan, D. (eds.), *Second Language Teacher Education*, Cambridge: Cambridge University Press.

Nunan, D. (1992) *Research Methods in Language Learning*, Cambridge: Cambridge University Press.

Nuttall, C. (1983) *Teaching Reading Skills in a Foreign Language*, London: Heinemann.

O'Malley, J. M. and Chamot, A. U. (1990) *Learning Strategies in Second Language Acquisition*, Cambridge: Cambridge University Press.

O'Neill, R. (1982) 'Why use textbooks?', *ELT Journal*, **36**, 2, 104–11.

Paran, A. (1993) *Points of Departure*, Israel: Eric Cohen Books.

Parrott, M. (1993) *Tasks for Language Teachers*, Cambridge: Cambridge University Press.

Pattison, P. (1987) *Developing Communication Skills*, Cambridge: Cambridge University Press.

Peters, R. S. (1966) *Ethics and Education*, London: George Allen and Unwin.

Phillips, S. (1993) *Young Learners*, Oxford: Oxford University Press.

Phillipson, R. (1992) *Linguistic Imperialism*, Oxford: Oxford University Press.

Porter-Ladousse, G. (1987) *Role Play*, Oxford, Oxford University Press.

Porter-Ladousse, G. and Noble, T. (1991) 'Oral presentations: Group activity or one-man show?', *English Teaching Forum*, **29**, 2, 31–2.

Prabhu, N. S. (1987) *Second Language Pedagogy*, Oxford: Oxford University Press.

Prabhu, N. S. (1992) 'The dynamics of the language lesson', *TESOL Quarterly*, **26**, 2, 225–41.

Prodromou, L. (1992a) 'What culture? Which culture? Cross-cultural factors in language learning', *ELT Journal*, **46**, 1, 39–50.

Prodromou, L. (1992b) *Mixed Ability Classes*, London: Macmillan.

Puchta, H. and Schratz, M. (1993) *Teaching Teenagers*, London: Longman.

Quirk, R. and Greenbaum, S. (1973) *A University Grammar of English*, London: Longman.

Raimes, A. (1983) *Techniques in Teaching Writing*, Oxford: Oxford University Press.

Raz, H. (1992) 'The crucial role of feedback and evaluation in language classes', *The Teacher Trainer*, **6**, 1, 15–17.

Reinhorn-Lurie, S. (1992) Unpublished research project on classroom discipline, Haifa: Oranim School of Education.

Richards, J. C. (1976) 'The role of vocabulary teaching', *TESOL Quarterly*, **10**, 1, 77–89.

Richards, J. C. and Schmidt, R. W. (eds.) (1983) *Language and Communication*, London: Longman.

Richards, J. C. and Rodgers, T. S. (1986) *Approaches and Methods in Language Teaching*, Cambridge: Cambridge University Press.

Richards, J. C. (1990) *The Language Teaching Matrix*, Cambridge: Cambridge University Press.

Richards, J. and Nunan, D. (eds.) (1990) *Second Language Teacher Education*, Cambridge: Cambridge University Press.

Richards, K. and Edge, J. (eds.) (1993) *Teachers Develop Teachers Research*, London: Heinemann.

Rixon, S. (1991) 'The role of fun and games activities in teaching young learners' in Brumfit, C. J., Moon, J. and Tongue, R. (eds.), *Teaching English to Children*, London: Collins.

Rixon, S. (1992) 'English and other languages for younger children: practice and theory in a rapidly changing world', *Language Teaching*, **25**, 2, 73–94.

Roach, P. (1991) *English Phonetics and Phonology: A Practical Course* (2nd edn.) Cambridge: Cambridge University Press.

Rost, M. (1990) *Listening in Language Learning*, London: Longman.

Rost, M. (1991) *Listening in Action: Activities for Developing Listening in Language Education*, Hemel Hempstead: Prentice Hall International.

Rudduck, J. and Hopkins, D. (1985) *Research as a Basis for Teaching: Readings from the Works of Lawrence Stenhouse*, London: Heinemann Educational Books.

Schmidt, R. W. (1990) 'The role of consciousness in second language learning', *Applied Linguistics*, **11**, 2, 129–58.

Schön, D. A. (1983) *The Reflective Practitioner: How Professionals Think in Action*, New York: Basic Books.

Scott, W. A. and Ytreberg, L. H. (1990) *Teaching English to Children*, London: Longman.

Seliger, H. W. and Long, M. H. (eds.) (1983) *Classroom Oriented Research in Second Language Acquisition*, Rowley, Mass.: Newbury House.

Selinker, L. (1972) 'Interlanguage', *IRAL*, 10, 219–31.

Selinker, L. (1992) *Rediscovering Interlanguage*, London: Longman.

Sheerin, S. (1989) *Self–access*, Oxford: Oxford University Press.

Sinclair, J. (1992) *Collins COBUILD English Usage*, Birmingham University with London: HarperCollins.

Sinclair, J. and Coulthard, R. M. (1975) *Towards an Analysis of Discourse*, Oxford: Oxford University Press.

Singleton, D. (1989) *Language Acquisition: The Age Factor*, Clevedon, Philadelphia: Multilingual Matters.

Smith, F. (1978) *Reading*, Cambridge: Cambridge University Press.

Smith, F. (1982) *Writing and the Writer*, London: Heinemann.

Snow, C. and Hoefnagel-Hoehle, M. (1978) 'Age differences in second language acquisition' in Hatch, E. (ed.) *Second Language Acquisition*, Rowley, Mass.: Newbury House.

Sotto, A. (1986) Letter in *The English Teachers' Journal* (Israel) 33.

Stern, H. H. (1983) *Fundamental Concepts of Language Teaching*, Oxford: Oxford University Press.

Stern, H. H. (1992) *Issues and Options in Language Teaching*, Oxford: Oxford University Press.

Stevick, E. (1976) *Memory, Meaning, Method*, Rowley, Mass.: Newbury House.

Sturtridge, G. (1992) *Self-access: Preparation and Training*, Manchester: The British Council.

Sunderland, J. (ed.) (1994) *Exploring Gender: Questions and Implications for English Language Education*, Hemel Hempstead: Prentice Hall International.

Swan, M. (ed.) (1979) *Kaleidoscope*, Cambridge: Cambridge University Press.

Swan, M. (1980) *Practical English Usage*, Oxford: Oxford University Press.

Swan, M. and Smith, B. (1987) *Learner English*, Cambridge: Cambridge University Press.

Tannen, D. (1982) 'Oral and literate strategies in spoken and written narrative', *Language*, 58, 1, 1–21.

Tomalin, B. and Stempleski, S. (1993) *Cultural Awareness*, Oxford: Oxford University Press.

Underhill, N. (1987) *Testing Spoken Language*, Cambridge: Cambridge University Press.

Underwood, M. (1987) *Effective Classroom Management*, London: Longman.

Underwood, M. (1989) *Teaching Listening*, London: Longman.

Ur, P. (1981) *Discussions that Work*, Cambridge: Cambridge University Press.

Ur, P. (1984) *Teaching Listening Comprehension*, Cambridge: Cambridge University Press.

Ur, P. (1984) 'Getting younger learners to talk 1, 2, 3', *Practical English Teaching*, 4, 4, 23–4; 5, 1, 16–18; 5, 2, 15–16.

Ur, P. (1986) 'How is a game like a GLALL?', *Practical English Teaching*, 6, 3, 15–16.

Ur, P. (1988) *Grammar Practice Activities*, Cambridge: Cambridge University Press.

Ur, P. and Wright, A. (1992) *Five-Minute Activities*, Cambridge: Cambridge University Press.

Vale, D. and Feunteun, A. (1995) *Teaching Children English*, Cambridge: Cambridge University Press.

Van Ek, J. A. (1990) *The Threshold Level in a European Unit-Credit System for Modern Language Learning by Adults*, Strasbourg: Council of Europe.

Vygotsky, L. S. (1962) *Thought and Language*, Cambridge, Mass.: MIT.

Wajnryb, R. (1992) *Classroom Observation Tasks*, Cambridge: Cambridge University Press.

Wallace, C. (1992) *Reading*, Oxford: Oxford University Press.

Wallace, M. (1993) *Training Foreign Language Teachers: A Reflective Approach*, Cambridge: Cambridge University Press.

Weir, C. (1990) *Communicative Language Testing*, Hemel Hempstead: Prentice Hall International.

Weir, C. (1993) *Understanding and Developing Language Tests*, Hemel Hempstead: Prentice Hall International.

White, R. V. (1980) *Teaching Written English*, London: Heinemann Educational Books.

White, R. V. (1988) *The ELT Curriculum: Design, Innovation and Management*, Oxford: Basil Blackwell.

White, R. V. and Arndt, V. (1992) *Process Writing*, London: Longman.

Widdowson, H. G. (1979) 'Directions in the teaching of discourse' in Brumfit, C. J. and Johnson, K. (eds.) *The Communicative Approach to Language Teaching*, Oxford: Oxford University Press.

Widdowson, H. G. (1987) 'The roles of teacher and learner', *ELT Journal*, **41**, 2, 83–8.

Widdowson, H. G. (1989) 'Knowledge of language and ability for use', *Applied Linguistics*, **10**, 2, 128–37.

Wilkins, D. A. (1976) *Notional Syllabuses*, Oxford: Oxford University Press.

Williams, E. (1984) *Reading in the Language Classroom*, London: Macmillan.

Williams, R. (1986) '"Top ten" principles for teaching reading', *ELT Journal*, **40**, 1, 42–5.

Willis, D. (1990) *The Lexical Syllabus*, London: Collins.

Wilson, P. S. (1971) *Interest and Discipline in Education*, London: Routledge.

Woodward, T. (1992) *Ways of Training*, London: Longman.

Wragg, E. C. (1981) *Class Management and Control*, London: Macmillan.

Wragg, E. C. (ed.) (1984) *Classroom Teaching Skills*, London and Sydney: Croom Helm.

Wragg, E. C. and Wood, E. K. (1984) 'Pupil appraisals of teaching' in Wragg, E. C. (ed.), *Classroom Teaching Skills*, London and Sydney: Croom Helm.

Wright, A. (1984) *1000 Pictures for Teachers to Copy*, London: Collins.

Wright, A., Betteridge, M. and Buckby, M. (1984) *Games for Language Learning*, Cambridge: Cambridge University Press.

Wright, A. and Haleem, S. (1991) *Visuals for the Language Classroom*, London: Longman.

Wright, T. (1987) *Roles of Teachers and Learners*, Oxford: Oxford University Press.

Yalden, J. (1987) *Principles of Course Design for Language Teaching*, Cambridge: Cambridge University Press.

Zamel, V. (1985) 'Responding to student writing', *TESOL Quarterly*, **19**, 1, 79–101.

Index